Socioeconomic Change and Individual Adaptation: Comparing East and West

MONOGRAPHS IN ORGANIZATIONAL BEHAVIOR AND INDUSTRIAL RELATIONS, VOLUME 18

Editor: Samuel B. Bachrach, *Department of Organizational Behavior, New York State School of Industrial and Labor Relations, Cornell University*

MONOGRAPHS IN ORGANIZATIONAL BEHAVIOR AND INDUSTRIAL RELATIONS

Edited by
Samuel B. Bacharach
Department of Organizational Behavior
New York State School of Industrial and Labor Relations
Cornell University

Socioeconomic Change and Individual Adaptation: Comparing East and West

Editors: AVI GOTTLIEB
EPHRAIM YUCHTMAN-YAAR
*Department of Sociology
and Anthropology
Tel Aviv University*

BURKHARD STRÜMPEL
*Department of Economics
Freie Universität Berlin*
(deceased)

 JAI PRESS INC.

Greenwich, Connecticut   London, England

Library of Congress Cataloging-in-Publication Data

Socioeconomic change and individual adaptation / editors, Avi
  Gottlieb, E. Yuchtman-Yaar, B. Strümpel.
    p. cm. — (Monographs in organizational behavior and
  industrial relations ; v, 18)
    Includes bibliographical references (p.   ) and index.
    ISBN 1-55938-913-3
    1. Europe, Eastern—Economic conditions—1989- 2. Europe,
  Eastern—Economic policy—1989- 3. Europe—Economic
  conditions—1945- 4. Europe—Economic policy. I. Gottlieb, Avi.
  II. Yuchtman-Yaar, Emphraim. III. Strümpel, Burkhard. IV. Series.
HC244. S5915 1994
  330.94—dc20   94-44280
                                           CIP

CONTENTS

FOREWORD

In mid-1989, Professor Burkhard Strümpel succeeded in bringing together political and social scientists from Eastern and Western Europe for an international seminar at the Free University of Berlin, where the participants discussed the public's experiences with and reactions to recent changes in economic and labor-market conditions. Out of that meeting grew a comparative research project that crystallized into two additional conferences, one in Poznań, Poland (May 1990), the other in Ladenburg, Germany (April 1991). Comprising contributions by social scientists from the Soviet Union, Poland, Hungary, Czechoslovakia, the former German Democratic Republic, Israel, Sweden, Italy, the Federal Republic of Germany, Great Britain, and Canada, this book recapitulates the findings of the project.

The aims of this project closely correspond to the principal scientific concerns of the Research Institute for the Socioeconomics of Labor (FSA) at the Free University of Berlin, which was founded by Burkhard Strümpel and Michael Bolle in 1978. Grounded in the tradition established by George Katona and Günther Schmölders, the research conducted by members of the institute is focused on questions related to individual behavior in an economic context: How do people experience work and economic processes? What are their personal and collective aspirations, preferences, and desires? What material and nonmaterial efforts are they willing to exert to realize these preferences?

The many projects Burkhard Strümpel initiated during his 12 years as director of the FSA have substantively contributed to the study of economic and work-related behavior. In particular, his work emphasized the need to complement work productivity and humanitarian concerns about the quality of life and the welfare of the public as tax payers, employees, consumers, and citizen. Throughout his career, and to the unceasing fascination and astonishment of his colleagues and coworkers, Burkhard repeatedly demonstrated an uncanny talent for anticipating themes and problems that subsequently became issues of pivotal social and political concern. His work on the crisis of affluence, on changing work values, and on the contradictions between the economy and ecology pointed to critical social dilemmas before their existence had even been discerned in the "mainstream" of the discipline. Such was also the case with respect to the structural transformation in eastern Europe, to which he already began to address himself in 1987.

Embracing both market-oriented and socialist economies, the original theme of the comparative project on which this book is based pertained to the mismatch between structural opportunities for work and income on the one hand and public expectations on the other. But as the dramatic events of 1989 suddenly overturned the prevailing, relatively static conditions, and as eastern European societies went through the most rapid political and economic transformation in modern history, the international research team opted to modify the focus of this study accordingly.

Burkhard Strümpel witnessed these events until his untimely death in July 1990, eight months after the fall of the Berlin Wall. This research, like his other work, instills in us, his colleagues, the recognition that human factors are crucial in the quest for an understanding and explanation of economic processes.

This project could not have been completed without the initiative and involvement of Burkhard's associates. In particular, we wish to underscore the dedication of his long-time friend and colleague Ephraim Yuchtman-Yaar and of Professor Avi Gottlieb (both of the Department of Sociology, Tel Aviv University), who accepted the scientific responsibility for the work after Burkhard's death and who spared no effort in bringing it to its successful conclusion.

We also wish to thank the Department of Economics at the Free University of Berlin, which has furnished the FSA with the infrastructure needed to complete this research, and Professor Meinolf Dierkes of the Wissenschafts-zentrum Berlin für Sozialforschung, who was generous in his support and advice as a social scientist with extensive experience in managing and conducting international research projects.

This study could not have succeeded without the generous financial support and the organizational assistance contributed by the Gottlieb-Daimler and Karl Benz Foundation, which included the project in its research program "Innovation and Perpetuation in Labor Policy." The efficient and nonbureaucratic assistance of the foundation's business office, especially of its director Dr. Horst Nienstädt, helped remove many of the obstacles of international project management. The second international conference, held in Poznań, Poland, was sponsored by Professor Marek Ziółkowski of the Department of Sociology, Poznań University. Petra Jung and Bärbel Mack of the Daimler-Benz Foundation were in administrative charge of the third meeting, which took place at the Karl Benz House in Ladenburg. Their hospitality and professional organization of that event were greatly appreciated.

The European Coordination Centre for Research and Documentation in Social Sciences (the Vienna Centre) has notably contributed to the international coordination of this project. The center, established to promote the cooperation between eastern and western European social scientists engaged in cross-national research, greatly facilitated the initial contacts and the subsequent communication and collaboration with our eastern European colleagues—and this during an era when such links were still anything but routine. Moreover, through its WORK program (comparative studies of work and technology, the international division of labor, and changes at the workplace) and its RECO program (research on the economic and environmental reconstruction of eastern Europe), the Vienna Centre contributed to the substantive debates in the course of this project.

Last but not least, our linguistic editor, David Antal, spared neither time nor effort to transform our sometimes deficient style and language into an intelligible manuscript.

The international research project *Socioeconomic Change and Individual Adaptation: Comparing East and West,* which culminates in this publication, corresponds to the major aims of the Vienna Centre's WORK and RECO programs and addresses the main themes of interest to the FSA. One of the more attractive aspects of the project was that its comparative framework encompassed central and eastern European countries that were still socialist when the project commenced, as well as western European, market-oriented economies.

By utilizing a common conceptual model, the chapters of this book collectively clarify the relation between macroeconomic and societal change and the dynamics of microsocial processes: The socioeconomic and political attitudes of the public, its views about work and the workplace, and its capability to cope with scarce jobs, income, and consumer goods. The authors' inferences and conclusions are well supported by empirical measures of macroeconomic and social change, and by survey data on the attitudes and coping behaviors of individuals and households.

No doubt, however, the most significant, albeit unexpected, contribution of this comparative research project derives from its concurrence with the fundamental political and economic changes in the socialist world, which affected all the nations represented herein. In most countries of the socialist world, this transformation climaxed approximately one year after this study had begun. Fortunately, the focus, conceptual model, and empirical methods were well suited to the close examination of these processes.

This book not only constitutes an important contribution to comparative social research but also provides many first-hand insights into the processes of transformation in central and eastern Europe. It may well serve as a significant resource for understanding these changes and the planning for the reconstruction of these countries' national economies. We are confident that this book succeeds in reflecting and clarifying both the original issues and the subsequent foci of this study: (a) the theoretical and empirical correspondence between structural economic conditions and the public's subjective responses and coping behaviors as seen from a comparative perspective and (b) a portrayal and analysis of the new economic and social realities in Eastern Europe following the demise of "real socialism."

Peter Pawlowsky
George Muskens

INTRODUCTION:
ECONOMIC CITIZENS, ECONOMIC PERSONS, AND
ECONOMIC UNCERTAINTY

Avi Gottlieb

In recent years, work and income opportunities in many industrialized nations have diminished considerably. This decline may largely be attributed to the growing discrepancy between supply and demand on the labor market: Both the volume and the variety of available employment are increasingly failing to meet the demands and the expectations of the work force.

The mismatch between the aspirations of the labor force and labor-market opportunities first became evident in the mid-1970s, and its salience has increased ever since. Its principal origins may be found in the ongoing "second industrial revolution": Due to rapid technological progress and development, industrial rationalization has accelerated to the extent that massive gains in productivity and productive efficiency have been accomplished without increasing manpower requirements, and at times even while reducing the need for labor (Strümpel, 1989; Strümpel & Schramm, 1989; Schramm, in this volume).

This transformation has restricted the availability and accessibility of suitable jobs in entire industrial sectors. The most visible manifestation of the consequent contraction of the labor market is the persistent and even growing rate of unemployment, which has plagued most industrialized nations in the past two decades. Yet, while the common cyclical surges in unemployment have usually been ascribed to the transitory vicissitudes typical of the capitalist

1

marketplace (e.g., Schumpeter, 1950), the current labor-market crisis—precipitated, as it is, by a consistent reduction in the demand for labor—is inherently structural in nature, and may well be more enduring.

The consequent loss of employment and income opportunities has occurred in the aftermath of a prolonged era of rapid economic growth, intense industrialization, and expanding welfare services during the 1960s and the early 1970s. This period of economic expansion was also marked by rising demands and public expectations regarding income and consumption levels, and by mounting entitlements (e.g., Thurow, 1981; Bell, 1975). Needless to say, these and similar material aspirations are increasingly frustrated by the escalating labor-market mismatch.

The predicaments of an unstable and shrinking labor market are aggravated further by the increasingly adverse subjective experience of work itself, and by the growing divergence between actual and desired working conditions (e.g., von Klipstein & Strümpel, 1984). Sizable segments of the labor force report difficulties in coping with their increasingly complex and technological work environments (e.g., Ackerman, 1981; Yuchtman-Yaar & Gottlieb, 1985). Others are dissatisfied with the quality of their workplace, or with the organization of work time.

These voices of discontent not only indicate a prevalence of occupational strain, undesirable work environments and objectionable working conditions, but also articulate a rather encompassing transformation of social value orientations. This shift, away from materialistic concerns and toward a growing emphasis on self-actualization and postmaterialist values (Inglehart, 1977; 1989), has contributed further to the widespread decline in work motivation and commitment evident among western labor forces.

The economic and social policies which have been employed to contend with these challenges vary widely, even among those industrialized countries which share a similar socioeconomic ideology, and which confront comparable structural and labor-market problems (e.g., Gershuny; Gottlieb & Ziółkowski; Schramm; van den Berg & Szulkin, in this volume).

Some segments of the public have reduced their demands and expectations in response to the current economic and labor-market problems; others have reacted in a more ambivalent and even antagonistic manner by evincing apathy, resentment and alienation. At the same time, many workers have sought to cope with the combined threats of unemployment, the loss of income opportunities and adverse working conditions by adopting diverse and at times unorthodox behavioral strategies, ranging from secondary labor-market participation and moonlighting to self-provisioning and self-help. Different practices may be more or less prevalent depending on specific local conditions and national socioeconomic policies.

It is the study of these individual sentiments, attitudes and coping behaviors, and of their correspondence to changing economic, employment and working conditions which constitutes the principal objective of the present study. Differences in individual adaptations and coping behaviors are analyzed from a comparative perspective, and examined in the context of diverse socioeconomic ideologies, labor-market conditions and corrective policy measures.

In other words, the purpose of this study is to analyze the manner in which the public, as "economic persons" and "economic citizens" (see below), adapts and subjectively responds to variations and changes in structural or objective economic and labor-market conditions. Relevant variations in these attitudes and behaviors are underscored by contrasting the attitudes and coping behaviors of publics in both the East and the West—that is, in societies that were still governed by two antithetical political and economic systems when this study commenced.

When this study was initiated in 1988, eastern and central Europe still seemed to be firmly under socialist rule. For the perfunctory observer, the differences between the planned economies of the East and the market-economic systems of the West could not have been more apparent. However, the labor-market dilemmas that plagued the socialist economies differed from those typical of the industrialized West only in appearance; their specific consequences were quite similar.

Ostensibly, the government-controlled labor markets of eastern Europe, which prided themselves in their ability to sustain full employment, were not threatened by the loss of jobs due to technological progress and industrial rationalization. However, due to erroneous decision-making and investments, and following years of mismanagement, the labor-market status quo was nonetheless seriously compromised. The aging industrial infrastructure and the deficient technological base severely impaired productivity, the competitiveness of eastern Europe's economies, and therefore also the prospects of full employment.[1]

However, the perennially low productivity of eastern Europe's industrial sectors was handicapped by more than just an inadequate infrastructure. Low motivation, insufficient commitment to work, and the declining loyalty to the workplace contributed significantly to the continuous regression of work performance in eastern Europe. Workers' substandard performance, in turn, was primarily due to the insufficient income opportunities and work incentives available in socialist economies, and to the consequent stagnation in the labor force's standard of living.[2]

In short, while unemployment—at least overt unemployment—was not yet an issue in eastern Europe when this research project commenced, and while unemployment did not evolve into a manifest concern until after the 1989 overthrow of its socialist regimes, insufficient work and income opportunities have had an extended tradition as critical problems in both East and West. Moreover, the public increasingly rejected the economic institutions and policies and the prevailing labor-market status quo in both systems. Thus, both these prototypical economic orders had to contend with comparable dilemmas: increasingly scarce work and income opportunities, adverse working experiences, and a growing discrepancy between public expectations and actual labor-market conditions.

As in the West, the labor forces of central and eastern Europe had developed cognitive and behavioral strategies to cope with this curtailment of work and income opportunities. Here, the engagement in secondary work activities to compensate for the inadequate rewards from the primary labor market was perhaps the most visible outcome of the loss opportunities.

When the socialist regimes of eastern Europe began to collapse in 1989, we were no less surprised than most of our colleagues. With the defeat of "real socialism," some of the original concerns of this study became less salient; others had to be modified; and our attention shifted to additional aspects of socioeconomic change and to more contemporary social conflicts.

However, our interest in the analysis of individual adaptations to socioeconomic and labor-market change was hardly invalidated by this rapid and unexpected transformation. On the contrary, following the dramatic developments in the East, the theoretical concerns that had provided the original impetus for this research project perhaps even gained in relevance. Reality itself had furnished the ideal background for the analysis of subjective reactions to structural change: A major political and socioeconomic metamorphosis, albeit unexpectedly sudden, radical, and swift.

If the events of 1989-1990 nonetheless dictated a departure from the original research paradigm, it pertained to a shift in emphases rather than a revision of theoretical objectives. Thus, our interest in the mismatch between opportunities and expectations in socialist societies became more peripheral, and was replaced by a growing concern with the ongoing struggle to reform the obsolete state-controlled economies, with the difficulties faced by eastern Europe's incipient market economies, and with the public's ability to cope with these new adversities and uncertainties.

Needless to say, all eastern European contributions reflect both these themes: The crisis of the now defunct socialist system, and the dilemmas of its contemporary transformation. The analysis of changes in work and income opportunities in the industrialized nations of the West, on the other hand, proceeded as originally planned. Western market economies are also used as prototypes for examining the current social and economic changes in central and eastern Europe (e.g., Gottlieb & Ziółkowski, in this volume).

The team of participating social scientists from 11 countries[3] conducted its first coordinating research meeting in May 1988 in Berlin. In this meeting, a general heuristic model was formulated, which was to provide a common conceptual framework for all country-specific analyses, and thus to facilitate the comparative perspective adopted in this study. Two additional research conferences—in Poznań, Poland in September 1989, and in Ladenburg, Germany in April 1990—were devoted to a collective assessment of the variables selected for each of the secondary analyses, and to the review and preliminary revision of all chapter drafts.

The conceptual framework, which is to be considered as the normative paradigm for all the analyses presented in this book, is shown in Figure 1. The figure depicts the research group's general working hypotheses regarding the correspondence between structural and objective economic conditions and subjective responses and coping behaviors, as mediated by the individual's personal experiences with changes in economic and labor-market conditions.

Relevant objective economic processes may include, for example, changes in employment and income opportunities, rising unemployment rates, a decline in the standard of living, a shortage of capital or of consumer goods, a reduction of welfare allocations, or variations in the political control of the economy and the labor market.

These macroeconomic transformations may either affect or be stimulated by changes in *"economic culture"*—economic ideologies, value orientations and goal priorities such as individualism versus collectivism, capitalist versus socialist orientations toward processes of production and redistribution, materialism versus postmaterialism, and so forth. These value systems are held by individuals occupying broadly similar locations in the social structure, and may be associated with their personality or with deeper cultural premises, such as distributive justice (e.g., Gershuny, in this volume). Economic culture may change over time, as the economic environment changes (Figure 1), or as new cultural attributes emerge, new technologies develop, new (e.g., ecological) knowledge accumulates, and so forth.

Economic culture[4] expresses itself in two domains of subjective experience (Yuchtman-Yaar, 1989). The term *"economic person"* refers to the individual's attitudes toward work and the workplace, such as job satisfaction and commitment, alienation from work, a sense of inequity, unsatisfied entitlements, and so forth. It also includes those behaviors aimed at coping with changing work and income opportunities—such as participation in the secondary labor market, self-provisioning, self-help, networking, moonlighting, and so forth.

Complementary to these attitudes and behaviors at the individual level are the *"economic citizen's"* responses and orientations toward macroeconomic processes and "the economic system": Views on economic growth, technological progress, labor-market conditions, and socioeconomic and welfare policies; positions on economic developments, policies and institutions; the attribution of blame and responsibility for current economic problems; and so forth.

The point of departure of most chapters in this volume is the economic crisis of the early 1980s—prompted by the late 1970s recession in the West, and

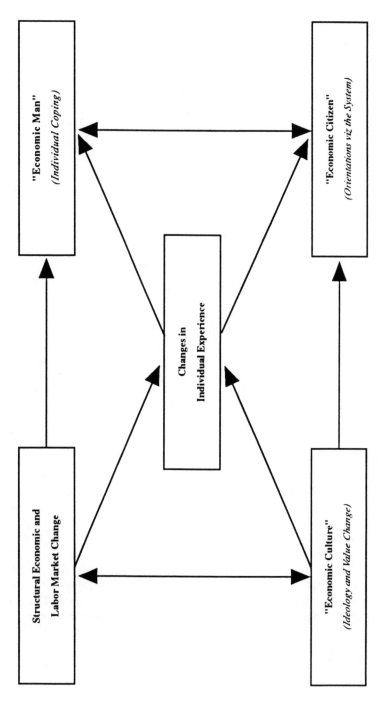

Figure 1. Adapting to Socloeconomic Change: A Conceptual Model

produced by the protracted and misguided economic policies of the socialist regimes in the East. The ensuing economic malaise was rather severe and prolonged. In western industrialized nations, it entailed beyond the typical manifestations of stagnating growth and rising budget deficits, inflation and unemployment rates, also a growing labor-market mismatch, and a consequent decline in job opportunities and job security.[5] In the East, where these predicaments were concealed and kept latent, declining productivity was the most evident symptom of the crisis.

In both cases, the labor force was compelled to compensate for its insufficient income from the primary labor market by expanding its participation in the second economy. Moreover, the work ethic declined, and engagement in illegal activities (the black market, bribery, tax evasion, etc.) burgeoned.

Similarities can also be observed with respect to attitude and value change. The publics of both the East and the West grew more skeptical about their social, economic and political systems, lost confidence in their government and its policies, became increasingly concerned and about their countries' and their own economic prospects, and more dissatisfied with work and working conditions. In eastern European countries, the tendency to escape from the public and work domains to the private sphere of family and community was also especially evident.

The "economic citizen's" reactions varied considerably as a function of the specific policies espoused by different administrations to cope with their countries' economic predicaments. Both the Italian and the Israeli publics have continued to support their governments' interventionist policies, the latter even condoning the incongruity between the political rhetoric about market reforms and the government's persistently interventionist policies (see Masi; Yuchtman-Yaar & Gottlieb, in this volume).

Until recently, Swedes have also evinced little change in their economic attitudes, even though the Swedish government had reversed its attempt to sustain its comprehensive welfare system and its emphasis on full employment after the massive subsidization of failing industries had rendered the budget deficit and the tax burden intolerable (van den Berg & Szulkin, in this volume).

Public reactions to Thatcher's neoclassical economic policies in Britain have been more differentiated: While a majority have come to endorse privatization and deregulation, the cutbacks in welfare spending and the revocation of redistribution policies meet considerable opposition (Gershuny, in this volume).

Such differences were more attenuated in eastern Europe. Despite the growing rejection of the socialist ideology, the public evinced little opposition to the political and economic order until its very collapse (Ziółkowski, in this volume). Moreover, much of this population continues to be characterized by political indifference—perhaps because the introduction of market-economic policies has, at least for the time being, caused more personal hardship than it has alleviated.

Current material and labor-market problems[6] may also help to clarify the backlash identified by all eastern European authors: The diminishing acceptance of market-economic policies and the renewed support for state ownership and control in Poland (Ziółkowski, in this volume), the nostalgia for the presumed achievements of socialism in the former German Democratic Republic (Hahn & Zierke, in this volume), and the renewed desire for "strong-handed leadership" in the former Soviet Union (Radaev, in this volume).

The concluding essay (Gottlieb & Ziółkowski) endeavors to extrapolate from the considerations and analyses presented in the individual chapters. Three specific aspects are examined in some detail: The antecedents and reasons of the collapse of "real socialism"; the future prospects of eastern Europe's incipient market economies, and the relevance of the economic paradigms of the industrialized West to these developments; and the extent to which the perseverance and continued legitimation of eastern Europe's post-socialist regimes depends on the attainment of tangible economic progress and individual affluence.

Does this volume indeed constitute a comparative study? Of the numerous definitions of comparative research proffered in the literature (e.g., Alapuro et al., 1985; Etzioni, 1970; Niessen, Peshar, & Kurilsky, 1984; Nowak, 1989; Przeworski, 1970; Ragin, 1987; 1989; Rokkan, 1978; Szlazai & Petrella, 1977; Smelser, 1976; Teune, 1990), it is perhaps Kohn's (1989) fourfold distinction of types of comparative research which best captures the intent of this endeavor.

Kohn's (1989) taxonomy is based on a classification of research objectives. Countries may either be the *object* of the study—in which case the researcher's interest lies primarily in their own intrinsic characteristics, or its *context*—if we are principally concerned with the cross-national generality of observed social phenomena. If we wish to consider the systematic relationship between national or cultural characteristics and social processes, countries constitute the *unit of analysis*. Finally, if we are treating nations as part of the larger international system, we are engaged in *transnational research.*[7]

The current study concentrates on the universality of individual responses to socioeconomic change across national contexts. Thus, it essentially corresponds to Kohn's second cluster, which employs countries as the context of the study. Nonetheless, other perspectives, such as Kohn's category of countries as the unit of analysis, have been adopted in some of the chapters, and most certainly in the concluding essay (Gottlieb & Ziółkowski, in this volume).

Beyond the typical and often consciously ignored challenges of cross-national research (Øyen, 1990),[8] the unique context of this study also produced a number of unique methodological problems, pertaining primarily to the availability, reliability and validity of (especially subjective and behavioral) data from socialist countries, and to the obstacles created by rapid pace of change in central and eastern Europe.

These difficulties may have imposed certain compromises beyond those common in comparative research (e.g., Rokkan, 1978). Nonetheless, our adherence to a common conceptual model, and our commitment to the empirical test of hypotheses derived from it, enabled us to observe those very principles which are fundamental to any social research, whether comparative or not: The construction of concepts and abstractions, the establishment of a correspondence between theory and data, the use of theory-based inferences (e.g., Galtung, 1990; Nowak, 1989).

NOTES

1. As delineated by Gottlieb & Ziółkowski (in this volume), it is precisely this failure to sustain economic growth and an acceptable standard of living which contributed not only to the dislodging the entrenched socialist economic policies, but ultimately to the very collapse of the socialist regimes.

2. There were also incipient signs of those changes in value orientations and in attitudes toward work which had begun to gather force in the industrialized West.

3. The countries represented included Poland, the former Soviet Union, the former CSSR (Czechia and Slovakia), Hungary, the former German Democratic Republic, Israel, Sweden, Italy, the former Federal Republic of Germany (West-Germany), Canada, and Britain. The Hungarian contribution was ultimately omitted from this book.

4. The terms "economic culture," "economic citizen," and "economic person" have been adopted from Strümpel & Yuchtman-Yaar (1986). The nonsexist term "economic person" is used here instead of the originally used term "economic man."

5. The mismatch between labor volume and productivity, and that between the labor force's occupational skills and labor-market demand are explicated in Schramm (the former Federal Republic of Germany) and Schmucker (Canada) in this volume.

6. The German monetary union of 1990, analyzed in the chapter by Schlese, Pawlowsky, Schramm, and Zierke, clearly illustrates the consequences of a rapid transition from an economy based on the scarcity of goods to one based on budgetary constraints. In the German case, this transformation involved the almost immediate collapse of the industrial sector, and the consequent skyrocketing of unemployment rates. Another chapter about eastern Germany (Pawlowsky, Schlese, & Schramm) explores how some of the most dire ramification of this transformation, at both the macro- and the microeconomic levels, may be prevented by implementing less conventional industrial policies.

7. Ragin's (1989) two-dimensional matrix of comparative research offers a substantively similar classification. Beyond the number of countries compared, Ragin suggests a distinction based on the type of explanation sought: it may involve intrinsic characteristics of the countries studied, strive for generalizations across countries, or favor features of larger units of which these countries form a part. Again, it is the second category which is most pertinent here. As Ragin notes, the fact that "...characteristics of macrosocial units appear in [all these] explanatory statements..." (1989, pp. 65-68) is a unifying feature of all types of comparative research.

8. Such as the possible nonequivalence of concepts, the interaction of unknown variables in unknown contexts, and so forth.

REFERENCES

Ackerman, W. (1981). Cultural values and social choice of technology. *International Social Science Journal, 23*, 447-465.

Alapuro, R. M., Alestalo, M., Haavio-Mannila, E., & Vayrynen, R. (Eds.). (1985). *Small states in comparative perspective.* Oslo: Norwegian University Press.

Bell, D. (1975, April). The revolution of rising entitlements. *Fortune,* pp. 98-103.

Etzioni, A. (Ed.) 1970. *Comparative perspectives: Theories and methods.* Boston: Little, Brown.

Galtung, J. (1990). Theory formation in social research: A plea for pluralism. In E. Øyen (Ed.), *Comparative methodology: Theory and practice in international social research* (pp. 96-112). London: Sage.

Inglehart, R. (1989). *Culture shift in advanced industrial society.* Princeton: Princeton University Press.

_____. (1977). *The silent revolution: Changing political styles among western publics.* Princeton: Princeton University Press.

Klipstein, M. v., & Strümpel, B. (1984). *Der Überdruss am Überfluss. Die Deutschen nach dem Wirtschaftswunder* [Great wealth, great weariness: The Germans after the economic miracle]. Munich: Günter Olzog.

Kohn, M. (Ed.). (1989). *Cross-national research in sociology.* Newbury Park: Sage.

Niessen, M., Peshar, J., & Kurilsky, C. (Eds.). (1984). *International vergleichende Sozialforschung.* Frankfurt: Campus Verlag.

Nowak, S. (1989). Comparative studies and social theory. In M. Kohn (Ed.), *Cross-national research in sociology* (pp. 32-67). Newbury Park: Sage.

Øyen, E. (1990). The imperfections of comparisons. In E. Øyen (Ed.), *Comparative methodology: Theory and practice in international social research* (pp. 1-18). London: Sage.

Przeworski, A. (1970). *The logic of comparative social inquiry.* New York: Wiley.

Ragin, C. (1989). New directions in comparative research. In M. Kohn (Ed.), *Cross-national research in sociology* (pp. 128-174). Newbury Park: Sage.

_____. (1987). *The comparative method: Moving beyond qualitative and quantitative strategies.* Berkeley: University of California Press.

Rokkan, S. (1978). A quarter century of international social science: Papers and reports on developments, 1952-1977. *Publications of the International Social Science Council, 19*, 3-15.

Schumpeter, J. (1950). *Capitalism, socialism, and democracy* (3rd Ed.). New York: Harper & Row.

Smelser, N. (1976). *Comparative methods in the social sciences.* Englewood Cliffs, N.J.: Prentice Hall.

Strümpel, B. (1989). Popular bases of conflict and solidarity: A review of the evidence from a decade of *èconomie problèmatique.* In B. Strümpel (Ed.), *Industrial societies after the stagnation of the 1970s* (pp. 185-208). Berlin: de Gruyter.

Strümpel, B., & Schramm, F. (1989). *Arbeitslosigkeit und Arbeitsumverteilung in der Bundesrepublik Deutschland: Betroffenheit, Konflikt, Reformpotential* [Unemployment and redistribution of work in the Federal Republic of Germany: Impact, conflict, and reform potential]. Advisory paper prepared for the Office of the Federal Chancellor. Berlin: Free University of Berlin.

Strümpel, B. & Yuchtman-Yaar, E. (1986, July). *Germany and Israel: Contrasting cases in popular culture.* Paper presented at the 6th Annual Meeting of the International Society of Political Psychology, St. Catherine's College, Oxford, England.

Szlazai, A., & Petrella, R. (Eds). (1977). *Cross-national comparative survey research.* Oxford: Pergamon Press.

Teune, H. (1990). Comparing countries: Lessons learned. In E. Øyen (Ed.), Comparative methodology: Theory and practice in international social research (pp. 38-62). London: Sage.

Thurow, L. C. (1981). *The zero-sum society: Distribution and the possibilities for economic change.* Middlesex, England: Penguin.

Yuchtman-Yaar, E. (1989). Economic culture in post-industrial society: Orientations toward growth, technology and work. In B. Strümpel (Ed.), *Industrial societies after the stagnation of the 1970s* (pp. 159-184). Berlin: de Gruyter.

Yuchtman-Yaar, E., & Gottlieb, A. (1985). Technological development and the meaning of work. *Human Relations, 35,* 603-621.

INDIVIDUAL ADAPTATION TO A SYSTEM IN TRANSITION:

THE CRISIS OF "REAL SOCIALISM" IN POLAND

Marek Ziółkowski

Like most eastern European societies, Polish society is going through a period of transition. Although recent political developments have been the most conspicuous manifestation of the country's new course, changes have also occurred at a deeper level. The whole socioeconomic edifice of "real socialism," that is, socialism as it is actually practiced in everyday life, is disintegrating, and a new type of society is in the making. This process is visible in the mechanisms of the system and in the modes of individual adaptation to the systemic changes.

I begin by presenting a general picture of the socioeconomic order of the *ancien régime* in both objective and subjective aspects. I then describe the effects of the crisis of the system in 1980s and, lastly, attempt a tentative description of recent emerging processes that are giving birth to a new social order.

THE POINT OF DEPARTURE: THE SOCIAL ORDER OF "REAL SOCIALISM" IN POLAND

The essential features of the socioeconomic order of "real socialism" conceived of as an ideal type are presented in the concluding chapter of this book (see also Ziółkowski, 1990). I refer here only to those aspects of the *ancien régime* that serve as a point of reference for the analysis of the more recent periods.

13

The nature of the socialist order seems to have consisted of the attempt to subordinate all the different spheres of social life to one center. This was also the case with the economy. The principle of economic rationality (e.g., profitability) was subordinated and sometimes even suppressed by different social considerations, and the main social objective of production was "the maximization of the volume of the material means under the global disposition of the apparatus of power" (Feher, Heller, & Markus, 1983, p. 65).

Drawing upon Markus's ideas, one can say that the socioeconomic order, in particular the patterns of the resulting income distribution under "real socialism" conceived of as an ideal-type model, consisted of three basic features. The first was etatistic homogenization, that is, an attempt to ensure that everybody was employed or economically controlled directly by the state. The vast majority of Poles were employees in the state sector, and the state salary constituted an essential source of personal income. As illustrated by mandatory deliveries of grain by private farmers, state control was exerted also over those who, from the formal, legal point of view, were the private owners of their property.

Second, the basic structural dichotomous antagonism was between the corporate ruling group composed of party ideologue, policeman, manager, and bureaucrat (Lane, 1982, p. 142; Wright, 1985, p. 83)—a group that may be called *praetorians* of the *ancien régime*—and all direct producers as a whole. The dominant role of the ruling group in the control and management of the economy was accompanied by a system of privileges. There was a detailed, consistent system for the remuneration of praetorians, who were adequately rewarded for their services.

The third basic feature of the old socioeconomic order in Poland was that the existence of the basic dichotomy did not mean that the two antagonistic groups were homogeneous. The ruling group was not only hierarchically differentiated, but also split into different factions with different particular interests. The main differences within the working population originated within the state sector of the economy and, by the same token, were to a large degree deliberately shaped and controlled by state policy. The differences within the working population stemmed from the "sector principle" (Wesołowski, 1989, pp. 4-5), according to which the political power and resulting special position attributed to the production sector (especially heavy industry) in the national economy secured much bigger salaries for the employees in that sector than the salaries earned by equally qualified employees in the same occupation but working in the nonproduction sector.

Apart from the undeserved privileges for the *nomenklatura,* however, the economic social differences were not very accentuated in comparison with capitalist societies. These social differences were further reduced by the so-called decomposition of the factors of social position, that is, a relative independence of income, access to power, prestige, and way of life

(Wesołowski, 1979). In addition, social differences were not highly visible. Individual wealth tended to be hidden; conspicuous consumption was not socially accepted. Objective leveling down as an aspect of etatistic homogenization was therefore accompanied by a general egalitarian system of values.

This general description of the social order of "real socialism" is largely consistent with the subjective perception of the social structure, which was rather stable over the years. For example, according to a 1984 survey of the workers of our large industrial plants (see Ziółkowski, 1988) policemen, professional military officers, and party activists were clearly perceived as the upper, privileged, and satisfied class. All of them were the members of "the state," the state praetorians, pillars of state authority. These three groups were also seen as emotionally distant. Another group perceived by the workers as relatively privileged, prosperous, satisfied, and emotionally rather distant were private entrepreneurs. The distance to the group of private entrepreneurs was much smaller and did not have a political aspect. It was connected only with economic differences.

All other social groups, although a bit differentiated, formed in fact one unprivileged and dissatisfied lower class. The structure of society was thus clearly perceived as a dichotomy, one expressed through the popular distinction between "us" and "them," and based on the observed link between political power and economic privilege.

Although politically oppressive and economically not very efficient, the system of real socialism developed a certain logic of functioning, a well-defined social structure based on clear (which does not mean just) principles of remuneration and income distribution, a system of state protection at a minimum level, and a largely viable socioeconomic ideology. It formed habits of adaptation and did enjoy some level of popular support, or at least grudging acceptance.

THE CRISIS OF THE SYSTEM IN THE 1980S AND NEW TENDENCIES IN THE ADAPTIVE BEHAVIOR OF THE INDIVIDUAL

Objective Economic Change

The deep, all-embracing crisis started in the late 1970s. Whereas the decade of the 1960s was a period of stagnation, the early 1970s—largely thanks to Western loans—constituted a time of relatively rapid growth and a considerable rise in income and consumption. The growth continued until 1978, but the regression in living conditions had already become apparent by then.

Despite growing sales of consumer goods, the supply of many articles was much smaller than demand because of production difficulties and a considerable rise in the consumption aspirations of all social strata. For many years, both the objective level of need satisfaction achieved in the mid-1970s and, especially, the raised aspirations constituted the point of comparative reference in assessing the decreasing living standards, and became an important source of a wide-spread sense of deprivation.

The growth rate gradually slowed, and the economic slump started in 1979. The economic crisis was caused by a combination of exogenous and endogenous factors. The effects of general mismanagement, unchecked over-accumulation, an excessive number of investment projects with lengthening gestation periods and "frozen" resources were exacerbated by growing external debt, the oil crisis, world recession, and unfavorable terms of trade (see Nuti, 1982). A decrease in real income soon followed. While the level of real income per capita rose in 1980 to 175.9% of the 1970 figure, real income in 1986 was only 93.3% of the 1980 figure. In 1988, it was only 106.4% thereof (see Table 1).

The most important element of the Polish situation in the 1980s was an acute economic crisis. The crisis of the socialist economy was primarily the crisis of the state sector. It did not work, and it became less and less clear whether it could work at all. There was a growing sense that the economy of real socialism was unworkable not only in terms of achieving technological development, economic progress, and efficiency, but also in terms of securing decent wages and maintaining the standard of living.

Economic reform and radical change in this sector was treated as a necessity. Some partial and gradual attempts to implement a few elements of this long-sought economic change were made but were in vain. In addition, one of the main problems was that the very concept of a viable social sector as a normative model of reform could not be precisely formulated, and was mostly only a vision, murky and incoherent, looming somewhere on the horizon and untrusted by the growing majority. By the same token, the economic crisis became a severe ideological crisis.

Table 1.   Development of Real Income in Poland (preceding year = 100)

1981	1982	1983	1984	1985	1986	1987	1988
103.3	82.0	100.4	101.8	106.0	101.7	100.8	113.2

Source: Adapted from *Rocznik statystyczny* [Statistical Yearbook] (1990).
Warsaw: Główny Urząd Statystyczny.

The Political Dimension of the Crisis: Political Values and the Modes
of the Individual's Adaptation to the System in the Political Sphere

From the very beginning, one of the main aspects of the Polish situation was
that the degree of support for the political order of real socialism differed from
the degree of support enjoyed by the economic order. The vast majority of
Poles tended to oppose the country's political system while accepting, until
very recently, the main elements of the economic order.

The crisis that erupted in the late 1970s led first to the open political conflict
of 1980-1981. Very critical attitudes toward the system, openly expressed and
communicated on a mass scale, constituted premises for collective action within
the Solidarity movement. After the imposition of martial law, although conflict
became latent, the political opinions of the population remained generally the
same. The general attitude of Poles to the system was, however, more complex,
and may best be described by the concept of individual adaptation to the system
(see Merton, 1957, pp. 139-157).

The individual adaptation to the social system in both political and everyday
economic spheres can be defined as a combination of (1) value ideals (visions
of an ideal social order), (2) attitudes toward existing reality, and (3) behavioral
strategies that are considered effective in the present situation. The last element
consists of (a) practical, everyday economic activities that may satisfy various
individual needs and have only indirect, unintentional, rather long-term impact
on the state of the system, and (b) politically oriented activities that are an
attempt to strengthen, maintain, change, or destroy the system directly. Let
me single out two forms, or rather aspects, of the politically oriented activities:
instrumental and symbolic. The latter does not influence the system, but serves
only as an attempt to express one's own political values and attitudes in order
to bear witness, to remain faithful to oneself. It can be argued that these
symbolic political activities used to constitute one of the most characteristic
features of the Polish situation.

In Poland, the range of politically oriented activities was very extensive, and
its limits were rather blurred. When the tendency was for the state to control
and dominate social life, even a group conflict over wages (e.g., miners versus
teachers) was regarded as a conflict, with the state having an obvious political
aspect. Somewhat paradoxically, however, too much control could eventually
increase political vulnerability, for the central power was held responsible for
almost everything.

On the other hand, this phenomenon was strengthened from below. The lack
of genuine political institutions that could have expressed different political
interests brought about the tendency to express political attitudes through
normally neutral political institutions and events such as university elections,
quotations in a scientific paper, or audience reactions to a classic play in a
theater. This practice was especially evident in periods of open conflict. Polish

social life under real socialism was saturated with the political, but more in symbols than in politically instrumental behavior.

The very idea of combining the different aspects is inherent in the typology by Merton (1957), who discerned conformity, innovation, ritualism, retreatism, and rebellion. Similar elements are discussed by Balandier (1984). Goffman (1969), in describing the adaptation techniques of inmates in total institutions (e.g., prisons and asylums), cited retreat, rebellion, colonization, conversion, and finally cool calculation. Koralewicz-Zębik's (1983) conception singled out five possible strategies that can appear under conditions of external constraint: conformity, opportunism, controlled courage, retreatism, and activism. The global individual adaptation to the social system can also be discussed in terms of legitimation, especially if one takes into account different levels of legitimation of the system (ideological, political, and economic), and considers various manifest and latent forms of legitimation (see Habermas, 1976).

As an illustration of the modes of the political adaptation to the system in the mid-1980s, the results of a 1984 survey of the working class in Poland are presented in Table 2. Fully-fledged, ideologically based support for the existing system was clearly very meager. Of the one quarter of the population that behaviorally supported the system, the vast majority did so only for pragmatic or opportunistic reasons. The remaining three-quarters of the population declared their support for democratic values and their negative assessment of the existing political system. But only some of those people tried to fight the system or express their critical attitude at least symbolically. Fatigue, disillusionment, and the feeling of helplessness led most people to choose passive contestation (resistance), and abstain from all open political activities.

The general pattern of political adaptation to the social system in Poland remained virtually the same until 1989, but some changes must be noted. Support for democratic values became even larger than before. In the 1988 national sample, 91% of the respondents declared that freedom to form independent organizations was an indispensable feature of a good social system; 96% declared the same for the freedom of speech (see Koralewicz & Ziółkowski, 1990).

In the late 1980s, the changes in the political system began. Despite temporary setbacks, rollbacks, and hesitations, a general tendency to diminish the domain directly controlled by the state could be detected. Some concessions were necessitated or fought out; some spheres were given up by the state. This opening up occurred first in the realm of information, freedom of expression, and public discourse. Many taboos were eliminated, the official version of Polish history was changed, some of the blank spots were officially filled in. New proposals for the organization of economic, political, and cultural life, some of them unthinkable only a couple of years earlier, were freely discussed. At the beginning these ideas were mostly words, symbols without any tangible,

Table 2. Modes of Political Adaptation
to Real Socialism Among Poles in the 1980s

Mode of Adaptation	Values	Attitudes	Behavioral Strategies	Percentage of Respondents
Active acceptance	$+$ [a]	$+$	$+$	4.4
Realistic pragmatism	$-$ [b]	$+$	$+$	13.1
Opportunism	$-$	$-$	$+$	7.3
Passive approval	$+$	$+$	$=$ [c]	11.6
Ambiguous retreatism	$=$	$=$	$=$	11.5
Passive contestation	$-$	$-$	$=$	25.8
Qualified rejection	$-$	$=$	$-$	5.1
Total opposition	$-$	$-$	$-$	19.4

Notes: [a] Acceptance of values officially adopted and propagated by the system, positive evaluation of the present actual state of the system, and behavioral support for the system (actual or symbolic).

[b] Rejection of values propagated by the system and their substitution for other ones, negative evaluation, and behavioral rejection of the system (actual fighting of the system or symbolic expressions of one's critical attitudes).

[c] Mixed values, ambiguous evaluation, and abstention from behavior openly supporting or rejecting the system.

Source: Adapted from Robotnicy '84-'85. Swiadomość pracowników czterech wielkichzakładów przemysłowych [Workers '84-'85: Consciousness of employees of four large industrial plants], by M. Ziółkowski, 1990, Wrocław: Ossolineum; and Individuals and the social system: Values, perceptions and behavioral strategies, by M. Ziółkowski, 1988, *Social Research, 55,* (1-2), p. 174.

instrumental consequences. The possibilities of real change in the sphere of power were opened with the breakdown of the communist party's monopoly on power and the reappearance of the Polish trade union, Solidarity, which led to the Round Table talks and the country's first semifree election in June 1989. The results of this election seem to have confirmed the configuration of the political opinions in 1984. Those who supported the ruling coalition of the *ancien régime* constituted less than 10% of the entire population. The opposition linked with Solidarity, on the other hand, received the votes of about 40% of the Polish electorate, which meant that the opponents were joined by a large faction of former retreaters, especially those who had so far chosen passive contestation. It must be added, however, that more than one third of the Polish population cast no ballots at all, abiding by its retreating attitude.

To sum up Polish developments in the political sphere until 1989, one can say that (a) the political value ideals of the population were still the same, with democratic values gradually becoming even more accentuated than before; (b) the attitudes toward the existing political order, which was clearly at variance with these values, were very critical; (c) the retreating strategy dominated for many years, although new opportunities for symbolic expression of different political values and critical attitudes were gradually created; and (d) the new possibilities for bringing about tangible, instrumental political changes in the core of the political system changed the political behavior of some of the former retreaters.

The Coping of "Economic Man": The Changing Patterns
of the Individual Adaptation to The Economic Crisis in the 1980s

Although the political order of real socialism was clearly rejected in Poland,
the model of an ideal socioeconomic order has always been rather complex
and not completely consistent. Until quite recently, the acceptance of the
socialist principles of economic organization has been much higher than the
acceptance of socialism as such, which was linked with the rigid political
system and general inefficiency of the regime. Research in 1984 revealed that
56.9% of the respondents still treated the social ownership of the means of
production as a necessary feature of a good economic system; 57.1% of the
respondents reacted the same way about the planned economy. By contrast,
11.0% opted for private ownership, and 40.0% chose free competition in
economic life. Socialist principles were espoused despite the fact that the
belief in the effectiveness of the socialist economy had gradually been eroded.
Even though Poland's recent history can be seen as a series of crises and
unsuccessful reforms aimed at correcting the flaws in the basic mechanism
of the system, the system was accepted because it was linked with other
values: job security, the protective role of the state, egalitarian distribution
of the economic product, a minimum standard of living and minimum
satisfaction of basic economic needs, a significant place for nonmonetary
factors (e.g., education, cultural contributions, life style) as determinants of
job status and individual prestige, social insurance, and peace and quiet. The
need for protection by the state had been stressed even more since 1980
because of an acute economic crisis. The values of a clearly defensive and
protective character had gradually replaced more ambitious ideals of
economic development.

Eventually, however, the economic crisis, unsuccessful attempts at economic
reforms, spontaneous economic processes, and, most of all, new patterns of
individual adaptive behavior not only led to a change in the economic values
of society, but also undermined the very identity of the economic system, and
became the most important causal factor in the recent change of the whole
social order.

The overall effect of the generally poor performance of the state sector was
that salaries in state institutions and enterprises were usually very low, rather
undifferentiated, and ever less central to the total income of the average Polish
family. One's standard of living decreased and became increasingly difficult
to maintain by working only in the state sector. The abrupt rise in the prices
of consumer goods and services, which led to a considerable decline in real
incomes and acute shortages on the market, made new types of adaptive
economic behavior necessary.

In the context of the crisis of the state sector, the second most important
element of economic changes in Poland in the 1980s was the continuous rise

of the sector not controlled by the state. A steadily growing part of the population opted to leave the state sector and take advantage of the new money-making opportunities provided by second full-time or part-time jobs, the private sector, opportunities to work abroad, and private foreign trade. In effect, all these new opportunities created a growing second economy and second society parallel to the official state economy and first society (see Hankiss, 1988). Drawing upon Hankiss, I would like to adopt the broadest possible concept of the second economy: all those economic activities that—contrary to the main tendency of real socialism—do not come under the control of the state and that therefore undermine the very logic of the state's economic, political, and social functioning. Accordingly, the second economy includes "all of the non-regulated (legal and illegal) aspects of economic activities in state and cooperative organizations, plus all unreported activities, plus forms of private (legal, semilegal and illegal) economic activity" (M. Marrese, quoted in Sampson, 1987, p. 124).

The main adaptive reactions to the economic crisis during the 1980s can be enumerated as follows (see Beskid, 1989; Milic-Czerniak, 1989; Misiak, 1988; Sikorska, 1989).

1.   A substantial, although gradually decreasing, part of Polish urban society was still willing to live within the state sector under the peculiar socialist social contract of the previous 40 years—a contract based on mutually low expectations on the part of the government and the workers. Under this arrangement, the workers traded off the prospects of high wages for predictability, job security, and a guarantee of at least minimum social welfare benefits. Beginning in the early 1980s, however, even this social contract was subject to considerable strain, because workers' real wages had shrunk and shortages and price increases had undermined the workers' willingness to continue accepting the terms. This phenomenon was also reflected in the diminishing importance of one's main job in the system of values (Milic-Czerniak, 1989).

2.   Because work in the state sector could neither secure need satisfaction nor maintain previous living standards, labor resources went outside this sector. The share of total household income accounted for by the main job declined from 86% in 1974 to only 72% in 1983.

3.   Working time in the state sector shrank by approximately 50 minutes from 1976 to 1984. Time free from work in the state sector was used for such activities as work at home, and the category of *prosuments* (those who produce for their own consumption) was quickly expanded. In 1984, the time sacrificed to household activities was the same as the time spent working at one's main job. The trend toward home private activity in the sphere of production and services was strengthened by the general underdevelopment of the service sector and the fact that the prices of services went up more quickly than the prices

of goods, materials, and tools. From 1975 to 1982, the share of home private activity increased from 39% to 70% in the case of apartment renovations, from 26% to 39% for sewing, and from 10% to 24% for hairdressing (Pałaszewska-Reindl, Strzelecka, & Tylec Durand, 1983, p. 79).

4. The crisis in the first economy and the rise of the second changed the structure of employment in many ways. The basic official salary became less and less important to people employed in the state sector, while additional sources of income gradually became more important. However, people with the same official professional position (e.g., shop assistant) and the same basic official salary may or may not have had access to these secondary sources of income. (In this regard a furniture shop assistant was a much better position than a colleague selling basic food products.) This mechanism of income differentiation differed from the above-described sector principle in one important respect: It was not determined from above, but was a result of spontaneous economic activities.

In the Polish occupational structure of the late 1980s, one could in fact discern three types of occupations in the state sector. The first type consisted of work such as that done by gas station attendants, plumbers, and English teachers, whose jobs nearly always created opportunities for perks and additional income. These opportunities gradually became one of the main incentives for taking such positions. The second type of occupation opened these possibilities to only a few people—those who were better qualified, more privileged, or, sometimes, merely luckier (e.g., scientists working in the West). The third type of occupation in Poland's state structure of the late 1980s made it very difficult to supplement the official salary. This type especially included workers in steel and ship-building, which were domains of the economy hitherto privileged by the sector principle and which offered few opportunities for extra work on the side. It is no accident that both the core of the Solidarity movement and the strikes of May and August 1988 developed in such work environments. One can say that two modes of adaptation were possible: (a) the individual reaction of "economic man," who sought opportunities, especially gaps, in the existing system without any direct attempt to alter its basic mechanisms, but who had an obviously corrosive impact on the system, and (b) the collective reaction of the "economic citizen," who aimed at a deeper change in the mechanisms of the system's functioning.

5. An important element of the rise of the broadly conceived second economy was the growth of the legal private sector. The participants in this private sector gave up their job security and many of their social welfare benefits for the promise of high incomes and freedom from at least most of the direct state control of their work and their lives. Such a choice, however, involves a willingness to take great risk and to live in a world much less certain and predictable than one shielded by the state. This option, while still limited, had been growing rapidly over the years, and had increasingly been accepted as

a desirable and prestigious alternative to employment in the state sector. The number of private enterprises outside agriculture rose from 255,000 in 1976 to 500,000 in 1986. The percentage of the work force in the official private sector increased from 3.5% of all employees in 1980 to 5.8% in 1986, 6.1% in 1987, and 7.0% in 1988.

    6. The "dollarization" of the Polish economy, visible already in the 1970s, gained momentum. Convertible currency in Poland was always drastically overvalued. For many years the average wage in the state sector was equivalent to a sum ranging between $25 and $35 at black market rates. Working abroad, which was made relatively easy thanks to a fairly liberal travel policy, thus became a main source of high income. In addition, even slight economic assistance from relatives living abroad acquired enormous value. In the late 1980s, $1.4 billion were brought into Poland every year, which, at black market rates, constituted more than 40% of all wages in the country. Convertible currencies, treated as the best protection against inflation, also became a main form of savings. In 1983 the convertible currency accounts in official Polish banks alone constituted 15% of Poland's entire savings; in 1988 that figure was already 60% (Kozłowski, 1988). Travel abroad had multiple forms, ranging from brief "tourist trade" expeditions and short-term holiday work to official, long-term employment contracts and permanent emigration. Within the five years from 1983 through 1987, 58,500 people (including 5,000 specialists with the benefit of higher education) left Poland officially, and 117,000 (including 16,500 specialists) illegally prolonged their stay abroad (Misiak, 1988, p. 46). In 1987, 87% of Poland's elementary school students declared a willingness to go abroad (an increase from 60% compared to previous years), with 42.7% of the respondents thinking of it in terms of economic opportunity. This opening to the West also had profound psychological effects. The affluent countries of Western Europe became an obvious comparative reference point for the Polish population, an orientation that only strengthened the feeling of relative deprivation. The impact of Western consumption patterns—a clear case of cultural diffusion—considerably changed the needs and aspirations of Polish society.

    7. The economic crisis and the Polish population's spontaneous adaptation to it gradually brought the old logic of remuneration into question. With increasing differences in the distribution of income and wealth, the ways in which various parts of Polish society tried to cope simultaneously diverged more and more. The major beneficiaries were the private entrepreneurs; the major losers were pensioners and state employees in the public service sector (e.g., teachers, health workers, and clerks). Key industrial workers, miners, and especially military officers and the police had at least kept pace with the rate of inflation.

    8. It became ever more difficult to maintain the previously achieved standards of consumption. Consumers had either to find new sources of income

(active adaptation) or revise the hierarchy of their needs and reduce and limit their expenses for, say, culture, sport, recreation, and social life (passive, defensive adaptation). Milic-Czerniak (1989), drawing upon ideas in Merton (1957, pp. 139-157), presented a six-fold typology of adaptive consumption among the 1982 representative national sample of 3,000 people. In the basic dichotomy by Milic-Czerniak, people still trying to attain new important consumption goals in view of the drastic average decrease of real income (all A types: 55%) had been differentiated from people willing only to defend the former standard of consumption (all B types: 45%). Milic-Czerniak (1989) then further diversified that distinction according to the means that people used to satisfy their current needs: (A_1 and B_1) no new means, or only former sources of income, treated as satisfactory; (A_2 and B_2) new active solutions, or taking up additional job or credits; and (A_3 and B_3) new passive solutions, or accepting relatives' assistance and church charity and using up accumulated savings.

The final typology looked as follows:

Type I (A_1) Consumption	10.6%
Type II (A_2) Innovation	22.9%
Type III (A_3) Consumption "under the protective umbrella"	22.5%
Type IV (B_1) Consumption abjection	11.7%
Type V (B_2) Ritualism	11.7%
Type VI (B_3) Helpless discontent	14.6%

More often than not, young people and those with higher education adopted the innovation strategy (A_2). Advanced age and a lower level of education tended to be linked with routine or passive strategies (B_2 and B_3). Especially from 1982 to 1984, many people benefited from various forms of help and assistance provided by families and friends abroad, the church, and charitable institutions.

9. The new forms of coping were connected with growing inflation. People hoarded all possible kinds of goods (including alcohol), bought convertible currency, took officially granted loans with fixed interest much lower than the actual rate of inflation, bought apartments that they had thus far rented because their price, unadjusted for inflation, became ridiculously low at a certain point.

10. The paralegal and illegal ways of coping became more and more frequent. They included paying bribes or tips in order to be able to buy something in a store, selling scarce or rationed goods taken from state enterprises, paying for a good room or even a bed in a hospital, pilfering, working privately while on one's official job, using tools and materials from one's official job, and appropriating state resources for private ends. The spread of these practices was linked with growing moral relativism, the acceptance of pathology as a justified, even natural, taken for granted necessity. "New speak" emerged: "organizing" was substituted for "stealing" and "rewarding someone's efforts" became the expression for "bribing."

Types of Mentality as a Legacy of "Real Socialism"

The individual experience of and adaptation to the political, economic, and social system of "real socialism" also shaped human mentality, defining popular tendencies to perceive, evaluate, and act in the social reality of Poland. As an illustration, I outline three empirically derived types of mentality exhibited by Poles in 1988, that is, during the ultimate decline of the *ancien régime* (see Koralewicz & Ziółkowski, 1990).

The first type of mentality can be called "passive-productive-antiindividualistic." It depicts a person believing that the most important thing is to work hard for the sake of society in a responsible and obedient way. The honest completion of duties amounts mainly to tested, routine behavior and subordination to discipline, and is associated at the same time with the rejection of political autonomy and individualistic strivings. Every individual should be but a cog-wheel in the social machine of production. This type of mentality is an embodiment of the long-propagated model of a "hero of socialist work," a politically passive, obedient, and hard-working member of a work collective. Such has been the positive human ideal of socialism. As a nurtured, cherished, and propagated product of the system, the person is functional to the aims of the system.

The second type of mentality may be described as "defensive-conservative-solicitive." A person of this type has a tendency to avoid unnecessary effort and to look for perks and additional privileges. It is linked to a "gimme-syndrome," a strong "solicitive" orientation toward both the state and one's parents and family. It is connected to a model of child-rearing that teaches children to fight for their interests and to defend themselves against the external dangers created by hostile reality and egoistic people who are bad by nature. At the same time, the child is expected to hold to all tested methods of doing things and avoid risks. In this mentality, a pessimistic vision of the world is adopted and individual autonomy is rejected.

This type, like the one above, is also a product of the system. It is based upon a peculiar social contract that obligates the state to provide a minimum of social benefits virtually regardless of the work performed. This type of mentality is, however, an unwanted and, in effect, disfunctional product of the socialist system. An able-bodied person with this mentality can be called a "real, though unwanted, socialist man." Such a person is also characterized by what has been aptly called a "thieving-begging" attitude represented by the groups "that gladly steal from the weaker and beg from the stronger" (Tischner, 1985, p. 135). People of this mentality do not reject the system, but neither do they represent the tendency for active participation in its development. This mentality is, rather, a specific individual attempt at coping with and adjusting to the system, at exploiting its gaps and weaknesses as well as using its benefits.

The third and last type of mentality is the "autonomous-enterprising" type. It is based on the emphasis of the necessity for individual autonomy at all levels, from the autonomous attitude toward authorities all the way to the vision of a democratic partnership within the family. This type of mentality is associated with the spirit of enterprise. It clearly corresponds to a model of an ideal member of "civil society." For many years this type of mentality occurred only on the periphery of the system, which was continuously trying to eradicate it. In the 1980s, when certain efforts were made to reform the system, economic enterprise began to be officially propagated, but political autonomy remained anathema.

Analyzing the social distribution of these types of mentality, one can discern three basic constellations of the occupational groups. Blue-white collars (*fizyczno-umysłowi*), unskilled workers, and farmers tend to represent types I and II, much less often type III. Among specialists with higher education, white-collar workers, and artisans, the pattern is exactly reversed. Top bureaucrats and military personnel occupy the intermediate position. As with the specialists, employees, and craftsmen, they represent type III rather than type II. By contrast, however, top bureaucrats and military personnel tend to show the prosystem type-I mentality. The least clear seems to be the mentality of the skilled workers. On the average, they represent all types of mentality, showing only slightly more enterprise and autonomy and slightly more of the "gimme syndrome" than of the type-I mentality.

THE EFFECTS OF THE ECONOMIC CRISIS AND POPULAR ADAPTIVE BEHAVIOR ON THE ULTIMATE "IDENTITY CRISIS" OF REAL SOCIALISM

The objective economic change and adaptive behavior at the individual level gradually shook the very identity of the system. One can say that in the late 1980s economic survival, the need to make ends meet, and, especially, economic success could be secured not in the core of the socialist economy, that is, in the state sector and as a result of its normal functioning, but rather in its gaps and as a result of its shortcomings—or outside the state sector, in the private sector and other forms of the second economy. The attempts to improve one's situation by reforming the mechanism of the system gave way to endeavors to satisfy one's needs outside the system. The next logical step that was soon taken was to change the whole system completely.

One of the most significant changes in Poland in those years was the general decrease in direct economic dependence on the state as the sole source of employment, income, and security, both in the objective sense and in the subjective sense of the reduced psychological feeling of dependence on the state. This change also had obvious political consequences. It was important, however, that decreased dependence on the state came to be even more evident among the social elite, who enjoyed economic and political privileges guaranteed by the state.

Of the four sources of the highest incomes in Poland, only one was fully and directly controlled by the state in the late 1980s, namely, the wages and other privileges of the ruling group—the highest paid functionaries of the Party, military, police, government, and public enterprise management. The growing inefficiency of the system made even this source of income much less secure. The other three sources of high income were much more difficult for the state to control: the legal private sector, the semilegal and illegal activities of both public officials and private entrepreneurs, and private foreign trade and work abroad. Although the state could attempt to regulate, tax, restrict, or harass people engaging in such activities, it could neither provide nor cut off the opportunities for such income. According to the data collected by Mieszczankowski (Ziółkowski, 1990, p. 298), Poland's economic elite in 1987, defined as that 10% of the population having 30% of the general income, consisted of those engaged in the state sector (21%), private work abroad (15%), "trade tourism" (15%), farming on an individual basis (14%), the illegal part of the second economy (12%), the legal private sector beyond agriculture (10%), the liberal professions (7%), or official work abroad (4%), and people who were retired, including those drawing pensions from abroad (2%).

As a consequence, there was a tendency for top incomes in the private sector to outstrip those of all but perhaps a handful of top Party and state officials. This circumstance, in turn, led to both frustration on the part of the official elite and the need to provide commensurate rewards for the most deserving of the Party and state elites. One of the solutions was a peculiar fusion of the power elite of the *ancien régime* and the private economy. Some members of this elite started to enter private enterprises or form various cooperatives, using their channels and influence to protect and develop their economic activities. One can say that this tendency toward the "affranchisement of the nomenklatura" was one of the most important factors contributing to and perpetuating the systemic changes in Poland. It must be borne in mind, however, that such an option was open only to some members of the state apparatus. Moreover, it required special psychological characteristics (i.e., spirit of initiative) that were neither needed nor pervasive in the state bureaucracy. Many other observers would have much preferred the old economic regime of traditional state socialism.

The economic ideals of the members of the opposition and the silent majority of the retreaters also became somewhat diversified. Both in the society and among the praetorians of the old system—party and state apparatus, military officers, police—enormous differences appeared not only in the objective economic situation but also in economic interests, values, attitudes, and behavioral strategies. Although there existed considerable support for the economic reforms and changes in society and the apparatus of power, on both sides there was also powerful opposition to them. It can be said that the differences between the economic interests and economic values and attitudes have become largely independent of the political cleavages. This phenomenon could also be observed during the Round Table talks. The communist party was deeply divided; the activists of the official trade unions represented the party's left, more populist wing. Solidarity, on the other hand, faced the problem of how to represent the workers' interests in big state enterprises while championing privatization and the free market.

All these emerging tendencies not only changed the old logic of income distribution, but also posed the previously mentioned questions about "real socialism." First, etatistic homogenization decreased, objective and subjective independence from the state increased, and the role of the second economy grew. Second, both the economic privileges associated with the apparatus of power and the decision-making role of that apparatus shrank drastically in relative terms. Third, new mechanisms of income differentiation developed within the working population. The role of the division of labor in the state sector of the economy together with its differentiating mechanisms (e.g., the sector principle) diminished somewhat, whereas the access to secondary sources of income for employees in the state sector and of income in the private sector became more important and more economically differentiating.

The growing subjective rejection of these three organizing principles of the *ancien régime* can be also seen in a significant change in the value ideals of the economic order. In the 1988 national survey quoted earlier (Koralewicz & Ziółkowski, 1990), 86.3% of the respondents considered free competition in economic life as the feature necessary for a good social system, as compared to only 31.6% who expressed support for the centrally coordinated command economy. In a more recent 1989 survey of the Warsaw sample (Guzek & Ziółkowski, 1989), the reintroduction of private property, a free market, and competition was selected by 92% of respondents as the most basic prerequisite for overcoming the present Polish crisis. This figure was far greater than that for all the other listed requirements, including far-reaching democratic changes.

Economic consciousness in Poland has, therefore, rapidly altered. In the economic domain, socialism has been generally rejected as the system of production, but for lack of other, better experience, it is still accepted as the system of distribution and social protection.

By the end of the 1980s, Poland, along with other eastern European countries, found herself in a unique historical situation. Intended and unintended objective economic processes, individual ways of coping with the economic situation, and new elements of social consciousness brought about the system's loss of social, economic, and ideological unity, even an evident crisis in the system's basic identity.

SOCIAL ORDER IN TRANSITION: INTERESTS, ADAPTIVE BEHAVIOR, AND HUMAN MENTALITY IN THE PERIOD OF TRANSFORMATION

Political developments in Poland, Round Table talks, and the election and formation of the Solidarity-led government ushered in the formulation and, since January 1990, the implementation of a radically new economic policy. This policy changed the economic environment and created new types of adaptive behavior. A new economic order seems to be in the making. The general orientation is to a market economy or a "social market economy." Accepting the new economic rationality, Poland has dismantled communism and broken away from the bondage of ideology. The details of this new, desired order are still far from clear, however.

The main elements of the new economic apparatus designed by the government have been (a) a nearly balanced budget, (b) the abolition of most subsidies (a move that resulted, among other things, in a high increase in energy costs), (c) the freeing of almost all prices, (d) strict monetary policy with high interest rates adjusted monthly to the rate of inflation, (e) wage rises held below inflation by punitive tax regulations, (f) adjustments to devalue the Polish currency to a sustainable rate and to make it internally convertible, and (g) the beginning of the privatization of the state sector.

The effects have been profound. The budget deficit has been reduced, inflation has been slowed, and in the first half of 1990 even a trade surplus was achieved. The market has been stabilized, and for the first time since World War II consumer power has almost replaced the tyranny of perpetual shortages. Factories short of money started selling assets for cash and created competition for inefficient distribution and retail monopolies by selling directly to consumers and private middlemen. The strongest competition was created, however, by the private import of Western goods made affordable by the change in currency rates. Many streets have become bazaars, goods have been sold from sidewalk stalls and the back of trucks—a form of trade that has accounted for approximately 30% of retail sales. Some elements of the government program have thus been largely successful.

It was all accompanied, however, by a deep recession, falling real wages, a general collapse of living standards, and growing unemployment. The scale and meaning of these events has been an object of continuing dispute. Production declined by about 25% within one year, although two thirds of this slump is attributed to the breakdown of trade with the former Soviet Union and the former German Democratic Republic (GDR). On the other hand, one can say that if factories were subsequently producing fewer uncomfortable shoes or unusable machines, so much the better. Real incomes shrank by one-third, and families commonly had to spend 60% of their budget on food. Income differentiation has been growing. On the other hand, Polish housewives no longer had to spend two hours a day in lines. Unemployment rose to 1,400,000 people at the end of May 1991—8% of the work force. It must be added, however, that about one-third of the population currently unemployed were previously in fact jobless (e.g., housewives) but have only now registered to collect newly available unemployment benefits.

The main problem with the program is that it has failed so far to stimulate production growth, especially in the still-dominant state sector of the economy. It is said to be successful in creating the new macroeconomic environment, but largely unsuccessful in influencing the way enterprises function at a microlevel. The most dangerous aspect of this program seems to be the new patterns of adaptation, a clear conflict between the original symbolic acceptance of the program and the lack of real behavioral support for its implementation.

On the one hand, there has been enormous patience, acceptance of sacrifice, and tolerance for the drastic decrease in the standard of living. For many months the Solidarity-led government enjoyed the support and trust of the vast majority of the population at a symbolic level. It has been clear that no other government could have imposed such austerity and gotten away with it for such a long time. There was also more docility on the job and much higher reluctance to take sick-leave in view of the perceived lack of job security. Absenteeism dropped considerably, and there were suddenly takers for previously unwanted jobs. This passive acquiescence—social, industrial, and political peace—was crucial in keeping the whole experiment running for many months.

On the other hand, the economic transformation no longer has a viable social base. The Polish economy remains regulated by two opposite mechanisms: the still dominant old one of state command, protection, and distribution, and the new one of the market. The immediate short-term interests of the most numerous social groups such as industrial workers, peasants, and members of the intelligentsia are still clearly linked with the old mechanism. Market reform is supported because of "theoretical interest," but it has failed so far to produce the desired economic reactions among private producers and, especially, among the management and the employees in the state sector.

For many months there was a common expectation that the whole situation would sooner or later somehow improve almost automatically as a result of the new mechanism and as a natural reward for the present sacrifices, but virtually without one's own personal initiative and commitment. People are accustomed to and still expect state presence, protection, and control. They want to see great changes but on the condition that these changes do not affect their individual work and living conditions too much. The most common policy pursued by the factory management facing financial restrictions has been simply to reduce production by sending people first on a forced paid holiday, then on unpaid temporary leave. The final resort has been to reduce employment. This practice has been aimed at gaining time, at waiting for the government to loosen strict monetary controls. The old habit of waiting for the central power to define the rules of the game still lingers. Thus far there have been almost no attempts to play an active role in restructuring production, changing its profile, and adapting it to the new market conditions.

The private sector has grown enormously. Its output (excluding farming) grew by approximately 50% in one year, accounting for 18% of national income in 1990 (up from 11% in 1989). The number of people employed in this sector has risen considerably as well. The figures are imprecise because much of Poland's private industry goes unrecorded, for private traders, plumbers, and carpenters still underreport their income in order to avoid high taxes. High interest rates, however, choked investment in the private sector, discouraging private entrepreneurs from expanding production and prompting them to concentrate mainly on trade (particularly the import of consumption goods), where little investment is required and where the circulation of capital is the fastest. This tack, in turn, has created excessive competition for Polish products and has been rather detrimental for the trade balance. Also, farmers have complained that the high cost of machinery and fertilizers, together with foreign competition, have made food production unprofitable and have asked for state protection, higher import taxes, and even the suspension of the market mechanism.

On the eve of the transformation processes, most of the people in Poland supported both democracy and the market economy as a set of distant ideals, as an omnipotent remedy for all social problems. These stereotypes, however, encountered the harsh realities of life, and their implementation has proved to be much more costly than expected. In the political domain, two kinds of expectations of new democratic power have been formulated. Some social groups link democracy with an increase in individual chances, and define it as a democracy of equal opportunity that helps people take their own lots into their own hands. Other, and seemingly more numerous groups connect democracy with the growth of social security and protection, and treat it as a democracy of equal conditions and equal results. In the former case, democracy means the increase of individual activity; in the latter, the growth of individual and group claims and solicitive attitudes.

The situation is even more complicated in the economic sphere. One could say that there is some disillusionment with the market economy, especially with that of the neoliberal type, which was adopted in Poland. There were high expectations, but they were based more on the assessment of economic results and consumption standards in the West than on the perception of the means and costs of achieving them. The main problem facing Poland and the whole of eastern Europe is how to combine more economic freedom and a substantial increase in economic efficiency without a sharp, even though temporary, decrease in the standard of living and a considerable increase in inequalities (Wnuk-Lipiński, 1991).

In the public discussion both neoliberal and social-democratic measures are advocated. The popular economic consciousness is very complex and hesitant. The results of the May 1991 survey (Jerschina, 1991) showed, for example, that although most Poles were for a free-market economy, they were also of the opinion that the employees in the private economy were more exploited, that capitalist society usually suffered from a high unemployment rate, and that it did not provide adequate safeguards for weaker members of society. The majority wanted to maintain state property in heavy industry and in general services such as health care, railways, and schools. Only a minority (48.3%) held that virtually all businesses in Poland should be privately owned, whereas 51.7% think that the government should continue to run most businesses. Even more significant, only 37% of the employees in the state sector supported the idea of privatizing the firm they worked for. Popular support for privatization reached its peak about 1989, when the implementation of changes was only an abstract promise. That support began to dwindle when the social cost of the reforms became evident. The main problem for both the experts and the general public is to single out the necessary elements (especially the social costs) of a well-functioning market system, to identify the consequences of its poor implementation, and to sort out the simple mistakes that have been made and that should be eliminated.

There seem to be two main conditions for success with the transformation toward a market economy in Poland. The first condition, the sociopsychological one, is to coax people out of the spell cast by an omnipresent and omnipotent state and to create suitable conditions for individual activities, initiative, and enterprise. This persuasion, however, must provide people with incentives to act for their own benefit and for that of the new system. It particularly concerns people with the "enterprising-autonomous" mentality. The old patterns of functioning in the second economy within the economic environment of the shortage economy in the socialist state sector are often clearly inadequate in the new situation. Such a change in attitude also requires changes in the "passive-productive-antiindividualistic" mentality. Its ethos of hard, productive, albeit routine, work should be accompanied by more political and social autonomy of the employees. The most important thing is to confine the "defensive-conservative-solicitive" mentality mainly to those groups that genuinely require the help and care of the state and of other people because of helplessness due to age, disease, accidents, or other circumstances. To achieve all that, the first step should be to change the political and economic systems so that they would cease being perceived as unfriendly, unwanted, imposed, and designed for the more or less cynical exploitation or passive solicitation of benefits. The existence of the solicitive attitudes seems to be based largely on the "us-them" dichotomy. To change them, one must eliminate the objective and subjective conditions for this dichotomy.

The second condition for success with the transformation toward a market economy in Poland, the socioeconomic condition, requires the formation of an economically efficient market system without a considerable decrease in living standards and a simultaneous increase in inequalities. More specifically, it requires the creation of a real social base for the transformation—that is, large social groups having both short-term and long-term interest in the development of a market economy—before social patience and symbolic support grow thin or disappear altogether.

REFERENCES

Balandier, G. (1984). Łod tradycyjny i kontestacja [Traditional order and contestation]. In J. Kurczewska, & J. Szacki (Eds.), *Tradycja i nowoczesność* (pp. 179-211). Warsaw: Czytelník.

Beskid, L. (Ed.). (1989). *Warunki i sposób życia—zachowania przystosowawcze w kryzysie* [Conditions and way of life—Adaptive behavior in crisis]. Warsaw: IFIS PAN.

Feher, F., Heller, A., & Markus, G. (1983). *Dictatorship over needs.* Oxford: Basil Blackwell.

Goffman, E. (1969). The characteristics of the total institutions. In A. Etzioni (Ed.), *A sociological reader of complex organizations* (pp. 312-338). New York: Holt, Reinhard and Winston.

Guzek, M., & Ziółkowski, M. (1989). *Research report on the social perception of the private economy.* Unpublished manuscript in Polish. Warsaw.

Habermas, J. (1976). *Legitimation crisis.* London: Heineman.

Hankiss, E. (1988). The "second society": Is there an alternative social model emerging in contemporary Hungary? *Social Research, 55,* Nos. 1-2, pp. 13-42.

Jerschina, J., & Górniak, J. (1991). *Western businessman as Hamlet: To invest or not to invest in Poland.* Unpublished manuscript.

Koralewicz-Zębik, J. (1983). Postawy wobec zewnętrznego przymusu [Attitudes toward external coercion]. In A. Siciński (Ed.), *Styl życia, obyczaje, ethos w Polsce lat osiemdziesiątych* (pp. 19-35). Warszaw: IFIS PAN.

Koralewicz, J., & Ziółkowski, M. (1990). *Mentalność Polakow. Sposoby myúlenia o polityce, gospodarce i życiu społecznym w końcu lat osiemdziesiątych* [Mentality of Poles: Ways of thinking about politics, economy, and social life in the late 1980s]. Poznań: Nakom.

Kozłowski, M. (1988). Złotówki i pieniądze [Polish zlotys and money]. *Tygodnik Powszechny,* No. 33.

Lane, D. (1982). *The end of social inequality? Class, status and power under state socialism.* London: George Allen and Unwin.

Merton, R. (1957). *Social theory and social structure.* Glencoe: Free Press.

Milic-Czerniak, R. (1989). Adaptacja konsumentów do warunków kryzysu ekonomiczno-spoecznego w pierwszej połowie lat osiemdziesiątych [Consumers' adaptation to the conditions of the socioeconomic crisis]. In L. Beskid (Ed.), *Warunki i sposob życia—żachowania przystosowawcze w kryzysie* (pp. 93-155). Warsaw: IFIS PAN.

Misiak, W. (1988). *Nowe formy zaradności młodzieży* [Youth's new forms of coping]. Toruń: Universytet Mikołaja Kopernika.

Nuti, D. M. (1982). The Polish crisis: Economic factors and constraints. In J. Drewnowski (Ed.), *Crisis in the East European economy* (pp. 18-64). New York: St. Martin's Press.

Pałaszewska-Reindl, T., Strzelecka, J., & Tylec Durand, B. (1983). *Gospodarstwa domowe. Funkcja i rola na rynku* [Household economy: Its function and role on the market]. Warsaw: IRWIK.

Sampson, S. (1987). The second economy of the Soviet Union and eastern Europe. *Annals of the American Academy, PSS, 493,* 120-136.

Sikorska, J. (1989). Społeczne zróżnicowanie wzorów konsumpcji w warunkach polskiego wzrostu i kryzysu [Social differentiation of the consumption patterns in the conditions of Polish growth and crisis]. In L. Beskid (Ed.), *Warunki i sposób życia-żachowania przystosowawcze w kryzysie* (pp. 157-193). Warsaw: IFIS PAN.

Tischner, J. (1985). Widnokrąg pracy ojczystej [The horizon of the homeland's work]. *Colloquia Communia,* No. 1.

Wesołowski, W. (1989). *Does socialist stratification exist?* Essex, The Fifth Fuller Bequest Lecture. Unpublished Manuscript.

———— (1979). *Classes, strata and power.* London: Routledge and Kegan Paul.

Wnuk-Lipiński, E. (1992). Wolnosc czy Rownosc: Stray dylemat w nowym kontekscie [Freedom or equality: An old dilemma in the new context]. In E. Wnuk-Lipiński (Ed.), *Rozpad polowiczny: Szkice z socjologii transformacji ustrojowei* (pp. 105-117). Warsaw: Instytut Studiow Politycznych.

Wright, E. (1985). *Classes.* London: Verso.

Ziółkowski, M. (1990). Social structure, interests and consciousness: The crisis and transformation of the system of "real socialism" in Poland. *Acta Sociologica, 33,* 289-302.

———— (1988). Individuals and the social system: Values, perceptions and behavioural strategies. *Social Research, 55,* Nos. 1-2, 139-177.

ADAPTATION TO SOCIOECONOMIC REFORMS IN THE FORMER SOVIET UNION

Vadim Radaev

What are the current changes in the socioeconomic and, partially, political relationship in the Soviet Union? How do these changes influence the economic consciousness and behavior of people? To answer these questions, I turned primarily to statistical reviews and sociological data published in the Soviet mass media from 1989 through the beginning of 1991. The main accent is on the secondary analysis of the results of Public Opinion polls conducted on the basis of All-Union samples by the All-Union Center for Study of Public Opinion (VTZIOM); the Center for Sociological Research, Academy of Social Sciences (CSR ASS); the Bureau of Sociological Research, State Committee on Statistics (BSR SCS); and other institutions. The analysis presented here, which was completed in early 1991, obviously contains a number of important limitations. Sociological data taken in some cases is not detailed, and points of research methodology are not adequately enlightened.

There is still a dearth of valid information sources surveying the current trends in the Soviet Union, and it is difficult to obtain sufficient empirical substantiation. Moreover, one should treat all these figures cautiously and use them rather as illustrations in the general context presented in my analytical position. The empirical results selected are, I think, the most reliable ones.

Lack of space precludes discussion of differences in the positions, attitudes, and behaviors of various social strata and ethnicities, and of people from different regions, though such differentiation is particularly important. But despite all these inevitable limitations, this sort of analysis has a certain explanatory power and seems to be useful for understanding socioeconomic shifts in the Soviet-type system.

FACING THE DEEPENING CRISIS

In the late 1980s, after long-term stagnation, the Soviet economy faced real economic crisis. Since mid-1989, growing financial instability and inflation have been followed by the curtailment of production affecting 64 out of 144 basic production items despite government plans to increase economic output (Gaydar, 1990a, p. 27). In 1990 Soviet national income declined by 4% (according to the officially accepted version). In the first three months of 1991, production declined from 1990 figures by 10% in terms of GNP and 14% in terms of national income (Grigoriev, 1991).

The deterioration of the financial system became evident in 1989, when the state debt reached 120 billion rubles and state foreign indebtedness came to 54 billion dollars (according to the IMF; see Voprosy ekonomiki, 1990a, p. 11). Subsidies maintaining the low state-fixed prices absorbed 21% of the entire state budget. The two-fold increase in the issue of Soviet currency was used as a solution.

The situation had turned into one of stagflation. In 1989 the annual inflation rate rose to 7.5% (in the officially accepted version) and to 14% (according to Research Institute of Banks version; see Bazhan, 1990, p. 5). The population's entire savings was reported to range between 300 and 350 billion rubles (75%-80% of 1989 retail turnover). Western experts estimated the amount of "excess money" possessed by enterprises and the population at 250 billion rubles in 1990 (Voprosy ekonomiki, 1990a, pp. 11, 13). "Escape from the ruble" grew monthly. Barter exchange between producers was flourishing.

In 1991 the Soviet economy found itself on the brink of hyperinflation, which until then had remained mostly in its hidden form. But the officially adopted two-fold increase in wholesale prices and then in retail prices (April 1991), accompanied by partial monetary compensations; step-by-step increases of 50% or more in wages, salaries, and pensions; a 40% indexation of personal savings (40%); and other measures had created the ground for transforming inflation into its open form. The monetary reform undertaken in January 1991 was not very helpful because in basic economic areas the policy of monetary restrictions was still avoided.

Until at least 1991, under conditions of fixed prices, inflation had progressed mainly in the form of increasing scarcity of goods and services. According to data from the All-Union Research Institute of Conjuncture and Demand (VNIKS), fewer than 60 out of 1,000 consumer goods considered were in constant supply in 1989 (Kolesnikova, 1990, p. 6). At the beginning of 1991, only 20 items out of 1,100 consumer goods were available (Gurtovoy, 1991, p. 10).

Rationing of goods had an obvious tendency to widen. A survey made in 146 Soviet cities showed that, by the end of 1989, meat and poultry were being distributed by ration cards in 33 cities; butter, in 20; and tea and vodka, in 16. Washing detergent was being rationed in 78 of the cities surveyed; sugar, in all of them (Gaydar, 1990a, p. 28). At the beginning of 1991, rationing covered 90% of all commodity groups (Gurtovoy, 1991, p. 10). The new practice of protectionism (the sale of goods only to residents registered in a given region) spread in some capital cities. It was supplemented by the departmental distribution of scarce goods through enterprises and other institutions.

Both inflation and the dramatic situation on the consumer market have led to a decrease in real income for broad strata of Soviet society. The existence of poverty has been admitted in the Soviet Union at least. According to official statements, 41 million people (14.5% of the population) were living below the poverty line (considered to be less than 78 rubles per capita a month) in 1989. (The data was taken from a survey of 90,000 family budgets; see Argumenty i fakty, 1989; Rytov, 1989, p. 12.) But if one takes the figures of a minimum consumer budget presented by the group headed by the academician S. Shatalin (138.2 rubles per capita a month), up to 55% of the entire population are living below the poverty line (Arkhangel'skoe, 1990,p. 211). Even official data show that 60% of the population in Tadzhikistan, 50% in Uzbek, and 33% in the republics of Azerbaijan, Kirgizia, and Turkmenistan earn less than the minimum wage (Rimashevskaya, 1990, p. 36). Soon after the last price reform (April 1991), no less than a half the population found themselves below the poverty line automatically.

The structure of family expenses is another important characteristic of mass poverty in the USSR (see Table 1). The disproportion in spending was enormous. Moreover, subjective feelings of Soviet citizens were much different from the version presented by state authorities. Of the people interviewed by VTZIOM, 22% said that they spent almost all their income on food; 38%, more than half their income; 25%, about half; and only 10%, less than half (Ogonyok, 1990, p. 1).

In the half century after 1930, the phenomenon of mass unemployment had been acknowledged again. IMF experts noted the 1.5% rate of unemployment in the USSR in 1990 (Voprosy ekonomiki, 1990a, p. 12). In the Central Asian republics alone, two million people were out of work in 1989, amounting to as much as 13% of all labor resources in those republics (Morozova, 1989, p. 74). Meanwhile, the problem of unemployment was obviously underestimated by authorities. By 1991 there were still no efficient institutions dealing with the country's unemployment problems.

Table 1. Average Family Budget in the USSR in 1988 (in percentages)

Item	Workers & employees (state sector)	Collective farmers
Goods & services	76.4	74.3
Food	32.2	35.4
Cultural & communal services	10.1	5.5

Source: "Narodnoye Khozyaistvo SSSR v 1988 godu" [USSR National Economy in 1988]. 1989. *Finansy i statistika*, pp. *90*, 92.

The high rate of wear and tear on fixed assets in the economy (the average period of service being 27 years) makes for the gradual deterioration of working conditions. Fully 90% of all new equipment produced by industrial enterprises and examined by the trade-union commission did not meet safety requirements. It is one reason for the fact that 14,000 Soviet workers are killed in accidents annually (Izvestiya, 1989, p. 10). Fifty million work places involving hard manual labor (mostly of the preindustrial type) are still in operation (Telyukov, 1989, p. 11).

During the years of reform, the range of work and income opportunities has been widened by the development of a second economy and new forms of organization permitted by the official authorities in the state-run sector. Before 1985 this permitted second economy was mostly a rather sizable, illegal, "shadow" phenomenon. In 1989 it accounted for about 12% of the entire national income and involved almost 30 million workers (Koryagina, 1990, p. 116; Koryagina, 1989, p. 12), though the reliability of this data was difficult to check.

Since 1988 there has been an expansion of cooperative enterprises relatively independent from the bureaucracy of the party and state. In quantitative terms coop production (amounting to only about 40 billion rubles in 1990) has not yet become a very significant part of the Soviet economy. But it has been growing at a surprising speed. The number of people engaged in cooperatives nearly tripled in 1989 (from 1.4 to 4.1 million) and rose to 5.2 million by the end of 1990. At a monthly wage level more than 33% higher than that in the economy as a whole, coop activities are considerably better paid than other forms of work in the USSR (Voprosy ekonomiki, 1990, p. 37; Tikhonov, 1990a, p. 8).

Thousands of lease-holding and "collective" (paid-off) enterprises, joint-stock companies, and joint ventures resulted from several campaigns. In agriculture, the system of independent farming is recovering, though very slowly. By September 1990 more than 30,000 peasant (private) farms had been founded. Another 150,000 farms are supposed to start by the end of 1991 (Shatalin, 1990, p. 2). Four million workers, self-employed on their personal plots, and 333,000 of those engaged in individual labor were added by the beginning of 1990.

Nevertheless, it is very important not to overestimate the independence of new economic forms. To a considerable extent these forms of enterprises resulted from a very formal transfer of state-run institutions, keeping almost everything unchanged, sometimes as the simplest way to avoid state-imposed restrictions on the increase in the wage fund. However, all these new economic phenomena can be considered small steps on the way to gradual decentralization and privatization of ownership.

By the end of 1990, cooperative production still accounted for most of the new informal economic activities (at least on the surface of events). At the outset, more-or-less independent cooperative enterprises found themselves under heavy administrative and political pressure. There were several attempts to thwart them with the help of direct restrictions, higher prices (3 to 8 times the standard rate) on their raw materials and equipment, price limitations on their finished products, tax discrimination, and other such handicaps. In the first quarter of 1990, one of the last political campaigns against cooperative activities in different regions succeeded in curtailing coop production almost 20% in comparison to that of 1989. The number of trade-and-purchase cooperatives declined by almost 35%; public catering, 31%; and agricultural cooperatives, 19.5% (Tikhonov, 1990b). Moreover, at the beginning of 1991 security forces (KGB and the Ministry of Home Affairs) were given authorization to check all accounts of commercial enterprises. Of course, simultaneously proclaiming the transition to the market economy and closing coop enterprises that carry out intermediate functions was a rather controversial policy, to say the least.

Step-by-step democratization in the political sphere created the room for multidirectional decentralization of power accompanied by decreased efficiency of ruling authorities. The Communist Party of the Soviet Union (CPSU), which has played a kind of integrative role as the ruling party, is about to split and lose its social support. Communists have already lost power in a number of republics (the Baltic region and Georgia). Meanwhile, the new-born political parties (such as the Social Democrats, Liberal Democrats, and the Democratic Union) still lack mass support.

The increasing role of newly re-elected and much more democratic Soviets of People's Deputies has become a remarkable feature of the contemporary political scene. But their endless debate over their lack of real power contributes largely to discrediting the efficiency of democratic bodies under the conditions of the Soviet crisis.

The most influential new political forces have emerged as an outcome of the Union republics' movement for political and economic independence and the formation of mass, primarily ethnic, Popular Fronts. Sovereignty or independence was proclaimed by all 15 Union republics. They were joined in their demands by the autonomous republics inside the Russian Federation (Tatarstan, Udmurtia, and Sasha, for example) and even autonomous regions.

Perhaps the most significant blow, however, came from the Program for the Sovereignty of Russia initiated by the new Russian President, Boris Jeltzin. The Soviet Union has been brought to the crossroads of either splitting up or renewing the Union Treaty.

The political ambitions of local authorities to shake off imperial domination and the policy of local protectionism damaged economic ties between different regions and worsened the whole situation. The most striking events were connected with the numerous interethnic clashes and bloody riots in the Caucasus and Central Asia. Central authorities failed to prevent local civil wars in Nagorny Karabakh and South Ossetia. The Soviet authorities made their first attempt to solve the Baltic problem through military invasion in January 1991.

In 1989 another powerful force appeared on the political scene—a worker's strike movement opposing the Communist authorities. In the first quarter of 1990, there were 130,000 persons on strike daily (Gaydar, 1990b). During the first eight months of 1990, 10 million working days were lost because of strikes, twice as many as in the same period of 1989 (Rytov, 1990, p. 3). The most influential movement was inspired by the workers of basic industries, who made both economic and political demands. In the month of March 1991, 220,000 miners were registered as being on strike.

To summarize, the causes of the deterioration of the Soviet economy in the late 1980s were—

1. the intentionally misleading character of official Soviet statistics (in fact, the deterioration had started before perestroika),
2. the cumulative effect of long-term economic distortions (structural imbalance and the stagnation of science and technology),
3. the financial destabilization caused by shifts on the world market (especially falling oil prices), and
4. partial democratization at the end of 1980s, which kindled additional issues such as (a) inconsistences between mechanisms of mandatory planning and those of a market economy when the former had been partially destroyed but the latter not yet established and (b) the destructive influence of interethnic tensions that had been frozen for decades by the Communist regime.

An equally important cause of the deterioration of the Soviet economy in that period was the inefficient activities of the ruling party and Communist government. Failure to deal effectively with the problems confronting the country stemmed from tacit ideological boundaries, pressure of influential political lobbies and social groups (such as defence industries, the agrarian sector, and miners), the inadequate professional skills of persons in charge, and the resulting absence of a reform program, or even a consistent strategic concept, for economic transformation (the liberalization program known as the "500 days" had been rejected). All in all, these circumstances built up a situation from which there seemed to be no escape.

FROM MATERIALISM TO MATERIALISM

The dramatic events of sociopolitical and economic crisis are leading to the gradual erosion of the so-called socialist values. The entire society has been divided into two groups holding opposite views on the same basic questions. Apart from the considerable number of people who are still consistently indifferent, these two groups are regarded today as being approximately equal. Of 1,848 respondents interviewed by VTZIOM in 17 regions of the country, 31% agreed with the statement that the October Revolution in 1917 expressed the will of the people, but 36% disagreed (with 25% stating that it was difficult to say); 45% had positive feelings about the effects of the October coup on the lives of citizens, and 37% expressed negative attitudes (with 18% stating that it was hard to say; see Levada, 1990b, p. 8).

Only 10% of the respondents were regarded by VTZIOM experts as orthodox socialists. An additional 20% of the respondents followed the populist slogans, concealing, implicitly or explicitly, a rather pervasive form of "socialist" values. By contrast, 14% of the respondents took a sharp stand against socialism, and an additional 20% supported the radical changes in the society; 35% still possessed no distinct views (Golov et al., 1990, p. 3).

The principal diversity of views has thus become evident. As I will try to show in a later section, however, the rejection of socialist terminology frequently does not mean rejection of socialist modes of production and distribution. Nor does it mean that the eroded "socialist values" are replaced by neoliberal views on economic development. Despite all claims to self-reliance and freedom of activity, people are still very paternalistically oriented. As a result, Soviet society is experiencing a kind of ideological crisis.

A broad variety of ideas and priorities were expressed by Soviet citizens at the end of 1989 (VTZIOM survey). The question was: "What is the most important thing to do for the country today?" The responses were as follows:

1. To provide for the material well-being for the people (38%)
2. To establish fair distribution without privileges (29%)
3. To restore villages with a traditional way of life (24%)
4. To build a free, democratic society (19%)
5. To give every ethnic community the right of sovereignty (17%)
6. To restore moral values (12%)
7. To regenerate national culture (12%)
8. To return to building real socialism (9%)

9.   To abolish limitations on entrepreneurial activity (7%)
10. To recover the country's leading position in the world (5%)

These data reflect the materialistic orientations of people under the present conditions. In fact, 55% of the respondents were sure that the lack of material well-being was the most important problem for Soviet citizens today (Zorkaya, 1990, p. 2).

The current situation can thus be characterized as the transition from materialism to even more materialistic values and orientations. This statement is supported also by the higher rank given to material preferences that are considered most acute and vital (see also the following section of this chapter). What makes it more controversial is that these materialistic values are developing in a traditional rather than a rational economic sense, to speak in Weberian terms. The basic orientation is still to secure the means of subsistence in a period of economic crisis, not to raise capital by entrepreneurial activities.

Traditional values were expressed in the priority accorded to the egalitarian feelings of people who are becoming anxious about their material position. In autumn 1989 only 2% of the VTZIOM respondents considered the current distribution of income fair; 53% believed it was unfair; and 45%, not too fair. The majority (63%) thought the gap between higher-income and lower-income families had increased. Only 5% considered it to have decreased. In the opinion of 18%, it had stayed unchanged, with 14% stating that it was difficult to say (Voprosy ekonomiki, 1990b, p. 139). As for egalitarian feelings, the important point was to diminish the privileges acquired by top officials. (These claims were often of purely populist, redistributive character.) Zaslavskaya (1989, p. 94) noted that from 25% to 42% of the respondents demanded that all chiefs be deprived of all privileges regardless of the amount and efficiency of their work. The elimination of privileges of top functionaries has always been among the vital social and economic tasks. Another target of people's concern was the relatively high income of coop and people dealing on the shadow market.

Rising material demands were accompanied by the instrumental approach to the role of work in the lives of people. Attitudes to the importance of work were expressed in the following way in 1989 (VTZIOM survey):

1.   Work is crucial in life (14.9%)
2.   Work is not so important (53.9%)
3.   I work for pay (25.6%)
4.   I would not work if I could (6.4%) (Ogonyok, 1989c, p. 1)

Another remarkable feature having to do with the restoration of cultural heritage and self-identity was an emphasis on ethnicity. It was often manifested as rising nationalism characterized by a rather low degree of tolerance toward other cultural values. Widespread populist movements have created fertile ground for wholesale criticism and rejection while allowing alternative value orientations.

Thus, here and there a certain ideological vacuum is filled by a cynical kind of pragmatism on the one hand and nationalistic egocentrism on the other, a combination that is extremely dangerous for overall social stability.

WHAT TROUBLES THE INDIVIDUAL

The dominance of materialistic values is sustained by the everyday individual economic experience that people are finding it ever more difficult to subsist. As a result, there are shifts in attitudes about what people think the main cause of their troubles is.

If, by the end of 1988, the acquisition of proper housing was acknowledged as the most vital and widespread problem (ordinary residents have waited for 10 to 12 years to receive adequate dwellings), by the end of 1989 it had been partially replaced in people's responses by two other key problems: "low income—high prices" and the shortage of goods. It is rather characteristic that the poor quality of education, the upbringing of young people, and insufficient care of the elderly ranked last as answers to the question of what the most widespread and acute problems were (Sogomonov & Tolstykh, 1989, pp. 74-76).

The range of problems mentioned by people in their interviews was closely connected with their feelings about the material position of their families. Only 23.8% of all respondents believed that their family living standards had been improved during the previous 2 to 3 years; 23.5% of the respondents expressed the opposite opinion. More than half of all respondents (52.7%) thought it had not changed. The feeling of material insecurity was also reflected in reported survey results (see Table 2).

The perception of material insecurity stems from uneasiness about food consumption. Over 73% of the respondents considered that they experienced a lack of food constantly or rather often, including the lack of meat, fish, and poultry (76.8%) and vegetables, fruits, and berries (63.6%) (Ogonyok, 1990, p. 1). These data have been fully corroborated by results of the All-Union survey made by the State Committee on Statistics, in which 30,000 people were interviewed (Shashnov, 1990b). They are also borne out by a CSR ASS survey, according to which 70% of consumers faced difficulty in procuring food and 82% in acquiring industrial necessities (Boikov, 1990, p. 9). A similar situation continues to exist where other consumer goods are concerned. At the end of the 1980s, about half the people experienced difficulties in obtaining cloth, and only 16% of them had no trouble acquiring durables (Pokrovskaya, 1990, p. 50).

The characteristic trends in job satisfaction during the period of economic reform are reflected by the data presented by Gimpelson and Magun (1990),

Table 2.   Distribution of Answers to the Question "What
Can You Say about Your Family Income?" (in percentages)

Response	VTZIOM Survey[a]	CSS ASS Survey[b]
Live under the poverty line	2.6	8.0
Hardly make both ends meet	31.1	16.0
Live more or less properly, economizing	52.7	65.0
Have no material difficulties	10.1	11.0
Hard to say	3.5	...

Notes: [a] All-Union Center for Public Opinion.
   [b] Center for Sociological Research, Academy of Social Sciences.
Sources: Za i protiv [Pro and contra]. (1989b, December). *Ogonyok, 48*, p. 3; "Chelovek na poroge rynka: trevogi i nadezhdy" [Man on the Edge of Market: Anxieties and Hopes] by V. Boikov. (1990, September). *Ekonomika i zhizn', 39*, 9.

a survey in which 415 manual laborers of two enterprises in Moscow (one state-run and the other a cooperative) were interviewed in 1988. On 17 basic work parameters, more than half the respondents at the state-run enterprise expressed the opinion that no changes had occurred. The only exception was growing work pressure, mostly as a result of additional working hours (cited by 62% of the men and 72% of the women). The situation at the coop enterprise was slightly more optimistic, though the majority of workers still considered the work conditions unchanged: 62% of the male and 70% of the female coop workers mentioned that their income had increased, but 91% of both the men and the women said that the increase had entailed additional work pressure (Gimpelson & Magun, 1990, p. 6).

According to the 1988 VTZIOM survey (see Ogonyok, 1989c, p. 1), the most frequent answers to the question: "What does not attract you in your job?" were as follows:

1. Low pay (27.4%)
2. Overall job conditions (17.9%)
3. Organization of work (17.7%)
4. Bad organization or absence of departmental (closed) food "distribution" and sales (15.2%)
5. No opportunity to acquire housing (13.1%)
6. Other features (less than 10%)

Important issues in people's attitudes and expectations have been reflected in the All-Union surveys organized by CSR ASS among 18,000 respondents from 1986 to 1990. The workers noted the gradual decline in correlation between their work efforts and their pay (see Table 3).

The absence of close and steady correspondence between pay and work efforts is a negative stimulus. Moreover, there is a noticeable rate of indifference

Table 3. Percentage of Soviet Workers Seeing
a Correlation between Work and Payment

"If I worked harder"	1986	1988	1989	1990
My pay would be reduced	40	34	12	6
I would get the same reward	7	9	18	46

Source: "Chelovek na poroge rynka: trevogi i nadezhdy" [Man on the edge of market: Anxieties and hopes]
by V. Boikov. (1990, September). *Ekonomika i zhizn', 39,* 9.

even to material incentives. One-third of the workers thought they would not improve their labor activity even if "fair payment" were instituted (Kommunist, 1989a, p. 31).

To make matters worse, respondents did not expect much of their future from the economic reform that was proclaimed. Half of them worried that price increases would probably follow the marketization of the economy in June 1990, and 40% indicated anxiety that privatization would inevitably increase unemployment. Only 23% of the respondents felt prepared for activities under market conditions. Large shares of population felt barely prepared for (48%) or undecided (29%) about the economic reforms (Boikov, 1990, p. 9). The USSR State Committee on Statistics reported that 6 out of 10 respondents saw the danger of rising unemployment and that one-third of them acknowledged the real possibility of losing their jobs (Shashnov, 1990b).

The first years of reform brought no fundamental changes and inspired little confidence in people. In February 1989, after four years of perestroika, 90% of the respondents considered the improvement in the mass media to be the only clearly positive consequence (Gudkov, 1990, p. 6). Every year has seemed to be harder than the previous one, a view expressed in 1988 by 80% of all VTZIOM respondents; in 1989, by 83%; and in 1990, by 91% (Golov et al., 1991). It has influenced expectations as well (see Table 4). I can hardly agree with Golov et al. (1990) that these figures indicate increasing hope. They seem to express failing confidence instead.

As pointed out by Pischulin (1990), the 3,800 people interviewed by CSR ASS characterized the situation at the end of 1989 as "nearly a crisis" (37%), "a crisis" (31%), or "controversial" (26%). Nor is that all. Golov et al. (1991) cites a 1990 VTZIOM survey showing that many respondents regarded various disasters as possible: (a) economic catastrophe (54%), (b) mass unemployment (49%), (c) ecological crisis (48%), (d) famine (42%), (e) civil war (42%), (f) military dictatorship (23%), and (g) mass repression (17%).

Dramatic situations elicit dramatic feelings, and the time that has passed since those surveys were conducted has brought nothing but more tension.

Table 4.   Distribution of Responses to the Question
"Do You Think the Next Year Will be Better for
You Than the Current One?" (in percentages)

Statement	1989	1990
Definitely, yes	34	4
Hope very much it will be	5	40
Do not think it will be worse	35	13
Unlikely that anything will change	13	22
No, will be worse	6	14

Source: "1990 god: Nashi nadezhdy" [The year of 1990: Our hopes]. by A. Golov,
A. Grazhdankin, L. Gudkov, N. Zorkaya, Yu. Levada, & L. Sedov. (1990,
April). *Ogonyok, 15,* 1.

ANY PLACE IS BETTER THAN YOUR OWN

The necessity of coping with financial difficulties and shortages encouraged
individuals to work out different socioeconomic strategies, which, in turn, can
be divided into production strategies and consumption strategies. The most
obvious course in terms of a producer's behavior is to increase additional
income through a secondary job or another kind of occupation. The strict
administrative restrictions on secondary employment existed long before 1985.
Only 1% to 2% of the total work force was involved in it. Through
moonlighting, the practice of being mostly illegal or half-legal became
widespread.

Some of those restrictions have meanwhile been lifted. According to a 1988
VTZIOM public opinion poll, 13.5% of the respondents had an additional job;
14.9% were about to take one, and 15.4% were undecided. The vast majority
(83.8%) backed the idea of lifting of all restrictions on secondary-job contracts.
The reasons that people sought an additional job revealed rather distinctly the
material character of their preferences: (a) need to increase family income
(56.7%), (b) desire to apply one's knowledge and skills (10.6%), (c) desire to
become the head of your own business (7.4 %), (d) desire to utilize one's working
time more actively (6.8%), (e) the felt need for some other kinds of activity
(5.3%), and (f) other reasons (1%) (Ogonyok, 1989b, p. 1).

Many workers searched for a new kind of job, though their number is not
as large as it might be. Some 36% of them wanted to work at coop enterprises—
only 7% on a full-time basis, 29% on secondary terms (Voprosy ekonomiki,
1990, p. 130). According to BSR SCS data based on a sample of 100,000
respondents, only 17% of those interviewed expressed their readiness to start
coop activities or work on their own (Shashnov, 1990a).

Table 5, based on documentation of 11,800 Moscow cooperatives, presents
some of the preferences in the forms of activity. These estimations were

Table 5.   The Structure of Employment in
the Soviet Coop Sector, 1990 (in percentages)

Full-time Workers	Part-time Workers
55.0	44.0
Full-fledged Members	Hired Hands
44.1	55.9

Source: "Kooperativnaya forma truda ili chastnopredprinimatel's-
kaya?" [Cooperative form of labor of private entrepreneurial
activity?] by A. Glaushetsky. (1990, April). *Ekonomika i
zhizn', 17,* 19.

challenged by Tikhonov (1990a), who stated that the employees hired at the
All-Union level comprised not more than one third of all workers.

People's attitudes to different forms of economic opportunities were
recorded in a survey by VTZIOM and the USSR State Committee on Labor.
As cited in Kommunist (1989b, p. 29), respondents would in future like to work
in a (a) joint venture (29%), (b) state-run, self-accounting enterprise (21%), (c)
lease-holding enterprise (13%), or (d) cooperative enterprise (10%). Others were
indifferent (10%) or would like to open a cafe or shop of their own (9%), lease
a cafe or store (4%), or not work at all (15%).

People are losing confidence in the Soviet ruble. They are trying to find jobs
paid, at least partially, in hard currency. This attitude explains the popularity
of joint ventures. The relatively small number of people seeking entrepreneurial
activities is another characteristic feature. No more than 10% of the workers
are eager to start an independent farm in agriculture, which has deteriorated
(Pravda, 1990, p. 3; Pushkar, 1990, p. 3).

There are two main features characterizing the workers' behavior at their
primary working places. The first is restrictionism, such as intentional
restriction of labor productivity. In different surveys no fewer than two thirds
of the workers have admitted that they work at a slower pace than they could
(Kozlov, 1990, pp. 51-55). Economizing of work efforts is a common practice
under conditions of distorted material stimuli at state-run enterprises. The
second feature is the increasing demands for higher pay and improved working
and living standards (irrespective of productivity level), demands encouraged
by political democratization.

Another VTZIOM public opinion poll can be considered a kind of a
summary of the projects and strategies of the people. The question was "What
would you do if the material standards of your family fell?" Answers were as
follows:

1. Try to find a job with higher pay (37%)
2. Most likely not be able to take any steps (23%)

3. Find a secondary job (22%)
4. Start individual labor activity (9%)
5. Try to get a job in a coop enterprise (8%)
6. Move to the countryside (4%)
7. Move to a region where life is cheaper (2%)
8. Cut the consumption of higher-priced goods (1%)

It is very significant and to some extent even puzzling that no one is eager to earn more money at his own working place (Rutgaizer, Kinsburgsky, & Kirichenko, 1990, p. 91). These observations were corroborated by Sokolov (1990, p. 75), who pointed out that the worker would bargain with the superintendent, continue to moonlight, change his profession, or simply make an attempt to increase his official qualification standing but that the possibility of increasing one's own productivity hardly occurred to the worker as a proper version of activity.

Consumption strategies under conditions of shortage have their common and rather pervasive features. According to Gurtovoy (1991) and Kogai and Uspenskaya (1990), ever more people are trying to gain security by piling up commodities and making home stocks of goods: 25% (1988), 90% (1989), and 100% (1990). VNIIKS has reported that 80% of all consumers buy durable goods for which they have no urgent need (Protzenko, 1989, p. 2). The more prosperous strata of Soviet society have been forced to purchase luxuries, particularly jewelry (Voronov, 1990, p. 29). Up to 40% of the people hoard expensive hi-tech durables to save their money (Kogai & Uspenskaya, 1990).

Consumers do their best to cope with shortages in various ways. Some people prefer to spend their spare time, and even some of their work time, on shopping. According to one VTZIOM survey, 60% of the respondents spend a great deal of time looking for and lining up for food, and 16% must travel to other cities and regions to buy it (Voprosy ekonomiki, 1990b p. 76). Other consumers may have to pay higher market prices. Some 80% of the consumers faced difficulties obtaining necessities and had to pay up to twice the state prices for goods and services (Boikov, 1990, p. 9). Around 3% of all city residents who were surveyed regularly (once a week or more) bought coop products, whose prices were 1.7 times higher than state prices on the average; 44% of them purchased goods from coop dealers at least once a month (Voprosy ekonomiki, 1989, p. 129).

Frequently, high prices keep consumers from buying things. One third of the consumers, for instance, were forced to reject the idea of acquiring industrial goods often (Shashnov, 1990b). Another way to obtain scarce goods and services is to extend the system of departmental rationing or to obtain them via the enterprises and other social institutions mentioned in the first part of this chapter. According to the VTZIOM survey, almost 60% of the respondents used various forms of "closed" ration food distribution; almost 30% of all the respondents used them at their enterprises (Ogonyok, 1990, p. 1).

Table 6.   Increase in Economic Crime in
the Soviet Union 1989-1990 (in percentages)

Type of Crime	Ministry of the Interior version (9 months)	Unofficial version (6 months)
Large-scale theft of state property	25.0	42.0
Corruption	10.8	22.2

Sources: "Kriminogenny defitzit" [Crime-provoking scarcity] by N. Sobol. (1990). *Ekonomika i zhizn',* 50, 7. "Novye metamorfozy, kriminal'noi nazhivy" [The new metamorphoses of criminal greed] by G. Sinolov & S. Golovnin. (1990). *Ekonomika i zhizn',* 40, 17.

Increasing masses of people have been involved in illegal activities. Boikov (1990, p. 9) reported that 62% of the respondents admitted that they happened to give "gifts" for services; 42%, ordinary bribes in cash. Educated guesses that 20% of the nation's food and 50% of the industrial consumer goods are purchased through "shadow" dealers no longer seem an exaggeration, as they did a year ago (Pravitel'stvenny vestnik, 1990). There are also certain activities lying beyond the alternative of production and consumption strategies as such. Because of the distorted consumer market, economic crime is flourishing. Over the last decade, economic losses due to criminal factors increased 57.3%. The process is accelerating dangerously (see Table 6).

A good opportunity to raise one's living standard or find a more interesting job is to go abroad. In 1990 2.5 million Soviet citizens went abroad for private reasons (20 times more than the number in 1986). Emigration from the Soviet Union is obviously increasing (2.2 times more people left the country in the first seven months of 1990 than in the same period in 1989). The number of emigrants is expected to reach 7 or 8 million in the first year after restrictions on emigration are eased (Kuznetzov, 1990, p. 6). Compounding the problem of mass migration, the tense interethnic relations in some Union republics have forced residents there to leave their houses. Some 600,000 refugees have now been registered by the authorities.

In short, the great variety of behavioral strategies for coping with the extraordinary situation in the Soviet Union in recent years were born of, or developed by, the crisis and partial democratization of interactions characterized as a search for material improvement without additional work efforts.

BASIC SHIFTS IN THE SYSTEM: DIFFERING ATTITUDES

In this section the focus changes from individual experiences and strategies to the attitudes toward the macrolevel changes discussed thus far, attitudes that reflect the formation of different social forces in the society. First, there is a certain indifference to the problems of growth rates and scientific and technological progress since the failure of the policy of accelerated socioeconomic development in 1987-88. The greatest amount of attention has been attracted by the issues of property rights and marketization in the economy and by the political problems of the "central region."

According to VTZIOM data, half the respondents in 1990 claimed that they supported the marketization of Soviet economy, and 61% of them backed the idea of private ownership of land (Augumenty i fakty, 1990, p. 3). In general, more than half of the Soviet population supported development of the private economy in the Soviet Union (Golov et al., 1990, p. 2). About two thirds of the people welcomed the transition to the market (Zhelnorova, 1990, p. 2). Admittedly, however, most of the Soviet people have a rather vague idea of such concepts as competition and the market. A common implicit notion of "market" seems to be merely that there are plenty of goods in the stores. Otherwise, those responses could not be so "liberal-minded." For example, only one respondent in 10 supported the idea of free price- setting, whereas seven in ten opposed it. Nearly half of the people interviewed by BSR SCS advocated state-fixed prices on all commodities, and about 30% of the respondents approved of such price-setting for a certain range of goods (Shashnov, 1990b).

The possibility of unemployment is another challenge to marketization programs. Well over half (58%) of the respondents considered unemployment in the USSR to be unacceptable in principle; 17% accepted it as a temporary phenomenon limited in scale (Zaslavskaya, 1989, p. 94).

People's attitudes toward private enterprise was reflected indirectly in the long debate about coop activities. These activities were welcomed by 45% of the VTZIOM respondents, whereas 30% rejected them (10% were indifferent, and 15% answered that it was hard to say) (Ogonyok, 1989a, p. 5). No fewer than half of the respondents judged cooperatives in public catering, health service, trade, and education as unnecessary, whereas only 9% to 10% went against coop institutions in the construction and utilization of wastes. Moreover, repeated surveys disclosed that attitudes towards cooperatives had been worsening (Antonosenkov, Degtyaryov, & Katul'sky, 1988, p. 8). According to more than 90% of the responses, the main reason for the negative attitude lay in higher prices of goods and services (Voprosy ekonomiki, 1989, p. 129).

Thus, even though entertaining a general idea of marketization, people still preserve some socialist beliefs (such as the absence of both exploitation and unemployment and the maintenance of stable prices). The obstacles to far-reaching reform have therefore come not only from the conservative wings of the bureaucratic apparatus but also from broad social strata, mostly semiskilled and low-skilled workers in all branches of economy.

Political attitudes are characterized by the falling confidence in the action taken by the government and the ruling party. According to VTZIOM data, confidence in the CPSU fell from 27% to 7% during 1990 (Golov et al., 1991).

About two-thirds of the respondents believed the authority and influence of the CPSU to have declined. Only 17% of the respondents in towns believed that the leaders had a thoroughly considered economic program; 39%, that they had a general idea of such a program; 19%, that decision-making was influenced mainly by present-day circumstances without any program; and 25%, that it was hard to say (Voprosy ekonomiki, 1990c, p. 137). Two-thirds of the VTZIOM respondents had no hope that the Ryzhkov government was capable of extricating the country from the economic crisis. The country's leadership was not trusted at all by 45% of the people (Levada, 1990a). The Party and the state bureaucracy were regularly blamed for the dramatic situation in the country.

Meanwhile, the newly emerging public organizations and political parties usually had no clear-cut economic programs and could not reflect distinct economic interests. An exception was the Popular Fronts built on nationalistic platforms and vague ideas of "regional self-accounting." There has been a rising wave of "green" movements. Yanitsky (1989, p. 33) reported that 8% of the adult population in the USSR was participating in the activities of various ecological groups (1% on a constant basis).

All social forces have been roughly differentiated into five groups on the basis of a VTZIOM analysis of the 1989 electoral campaign for the Soviet Parliament:

1. Supporters of radical reform more or less according to western patterns (10%)
2. Supporters of moderate reform following the guidelines set by the authorities (10%)
3. People rallied by critical populist slogans with no program (20%)
4. Conservatives, frequently with an imperial mentality (20%)
   5. People showing no distinct interest in political life (40%) (Kommunist, 1989, p. 29)

A more sophisticated scheme was presented in another survey, which divided 900 Moscow residents into the following social groups:

1. Supporters of Western-type changes (15%)
2. Left-wing populists (critics from the standpoint of "socialist humanitarianism") (17%)
3. Right-wing populists (critics of bureaucracy on the basis of the class approach) (25%)
4. Statists (Gosudarstvenniki, or advocates of preserving a strong state influence) (27%)
5. National patriots (people who place priority on ethnic interests) (5%) (see Byzov & Gurevitch, 1990, p. 6).

VTZIOM surveys have also revealed the diversity of opinions on the character of such activities as strikes. Nearly half of the respondents (47%) occupied the "centrist" position, viewing strikes as a possible, but an extreme, measure; 13% of the respondents regarded strikes as a normal way to solve the country's urgent problems. For 16% of the actors, strikes represented the only way to achieve their requirements; 5% of the people interviewed recognized no use in that kind of activity, and 13% considered it inappropriate in the Soviet Union (Voprosy ekonomiki, 1990d, p. 97).

Nevertheless, despite gradual politization of the broad masses of the population, the majority is still indifferent. They are alienated from any real decision-making. Their participation in public life consists of periodic eruptions, adding to social instability rather than contributing to the process of democratization in Soviet society.

IS THERE ROOM FOR PREDICTIONS?

The answer on the question as to whether predictions can be ventured should obviously be negative. The reason is not that the economy is changing rapidly but rather that the economic structure of the Soviet Union is characterized by considerable inertia. The reason is mainly the country's overall political instability, which is capable of changing the entire scene radically in relatively short period of time. Nevertheless, it is possible to elaborate some scenarios of potential development, which, of course, should be treated rather cautiously, like all comparisons with the other countries in Eastern Europe, Southwest Asia, or Latin America.

It is evident to both Soviet and Western experts that the economic crisis in the Soviet Union will inevitably deepen. Soviet experts guess that it will result in a decline of national income of up to 15% in 1991. Inconsistencies in the government's economic policy will no doubt lead to further distortions in the financial system and monetary circulation, the consumer market, and interregional economic supplies. Another 33% decline in living standards is expected in 1991 (Bogomolov, 1990). Even state authorities expect the rate of unemployment in 1991 to rise to 4% of the total work force, or 6 million workers (Voprosy ekonomiki, 1990a, p. 17).

Chances for peaceful and democratic solutions to interethnic problems will diminish. The formal results of the "All-Union" referendum held in March 1991 will trick no one. Only 7% of VTZIOM respondents believed at the end of 1990 that the Soviet Union would preserve its integrity until 2000 (Golov et al., 1991).

There is evidence that people are disappointed with democratic authorities and perestroika as a whole. Of the people interviewed by VTZIOM at the end of 1990, 33% would not have supported perestroika if they had known its consequences beforehand; 33% would have supported it, and 34% remained undecided (Levada, 1991). Disappointment in the work of parliamentary democratic bodies came very soon. Immediately after the First USSR Congress of People's Deputies in July 1989, 70% of Moscow's residents claimed that their expectations had not been met (Betanely & Lapayeva, 1990, p. 26).

Thus, there is a swing in mass expectations toward the "strong-hand" policy. Of the managers in the largest Soviet association of state-owned enterprises, 91% claimed that "extraordinary economic order" was necessary (Pischulin & Alferov, 1990). The expectations that the Army and the KGB will exert direct influence are strengthening. In September 1990 only 8% of VTZIOM respondents expressed positive feelings about an establishment of military rule in the country. By December 1990 that share had increased to 22% (Levada, 1991). In January 1991, 49% of VTZIOM respondents supported the idea of KGB involvement in combatting "economic sabotage" (Argumenty i fakty, 1991, p. 3).

Taking all this into account, one can currently venture at least three general versions of future development in the Soviet Union. The first scenario is one of progressive paralysis in the form of a continuation of present trends and attempts to find semidemocratic solutions in a situation where stable democratic political institutions are absent. This scenario is a picture of the spontaneous political and economic disruption of the Soviet Union; latent denationalization of state-run property; painful losses; and increasing tensions between different regions and ethnicities, masses of people, and authorities. It is a description of the potential, complete deterioration of economic interaction and the risk of social catastrophe and the chaos.

Such conditions will force a choice between various types of authoritarian rule, which has even become desirable. Thus, the second scenario is the establishment of authoritarian rule of neocommunist type (or communist in its methods) with a strong leader who finds support from the military and security forces and who imposes strict order and discipline. This type of authority would be legitimated with the help of populist programs of "democratic socialism," "fair distribution," camouflaged imperial claims, and a battle against bureaucracy and a "new bourgeoisie" of coop and "shadow" dealers. This turn of events would inevitably bring about an antiliberal reaction in all spheres (economy, polity, and ideology), throwing the country back into the past.

The third and final scenario is the establishment of authoritarian rule, but of a different type—one using strict executive power and the ideas of national revitalization for the gradual liberalization of the economy. This scenario contains the retirement of Communist government, renewal of the Soviet Union Treaty, and thereby also an agreement on the new mutual rights and obligations of the center and the Union republics, making it possible for the republics to carry out their own diverse programs. In this version of the future, that kind of authoritarian rule is exercised both on the All-Union level (for the transitional period) and the republican level and is used to ensure compliance with adopted laws and to prepare the step-by- step liberalization of society. This scenario also leaves room for great varieties of social, economic, and political regimes on the territory of the Soviet Union. Basic activities would be the installation of tough budget constraints and a strict policy of financial stabilization, consistent and gradual privatization of a large share of state-run property on market terms, a battle against any monopolistic and corporate-like economic and political institutions, and the elaboration of a program for thorough economic restructuring.

In summary, the third scenario looks preferable to the first two. But given the rise of "right-wing" (antiliberal) sentiment, which has become obvious in both economy and political life, the second view of the Soviet Union's future is admittedly the most realistic one.

REFERENCES

Antonosenkov, E., Degtyaryov, G., & Katul'sky, E. (1988). Obschestvennoye mneniye o kooperatzii [Public opinion on cooperation]. *Sotziologicheskiye issledovaniya, 6,* 3-11.
Argumenty i fakty. (1991, February, vol. 7). Interfax (p.3.)
————— . (1990, August, vol. 34). Sotziologichesky opros [Sociological survey] (p. 3).
————— . (1989, August, vol. 32). Goskomstat soobschayet [State committee on Statistics informs] (p. 3).
Arkhangel 'skoe (Moscow). (1990, August). *Perekhod k rynku. Kontzeptziya i programma* [Transition to the market: Concept and program].
Bazhan, A. (1990, March). Soizmerit' tzel' i sredstva [To bring into correlation goals and means]. *Ekonomika i zhizn', 11,* 5.
Betanely, N., & Lapayeva, V. (1990). Sotziologicheskaya sluzhba Pervogo S'ezda Narodnykh deputatov SSSR: pervy opyt [Sociological Service of the First Congress of USSR People's Deputies: The first experience]. *Sotziologicheskiye Issledovaniya, 4,* 25-35.
Bogomolov, O. (1990, December). Vrozdennye bolezni sotzializma [The inborn diseases of socialism]. *Argumenty i fakty, 49,* 5-6.
Boikov, V. (1990, September). Chelovek na poroge rynka: trevogi i nadezhdy [Man on the edge of market: Anxieties and hopes]. *Ekonomika i zhizn', 39,* 9.
Byzov, L. & Gurevitch, G. (1990, February). Peremeny v politicheskom soznanii [Changes in political consciousness]. *Argumenty i fakty, 7,* 6.
Chk'ya ty, zemlya? [To whom does the land belong?]. (1990, February 16). *Pravda* (Moscow), N 47, p. 3.
Ekonomika SSSR: Vyvody i rekomendatzii [USSR economy: Conclusions and recommendations]. (1990). *Voprosy ekonomiki, 3,* 6-72.
Finansy i Statistika. (1989). *Narodnoe khoziaistvo SSSR v 1988 godu* [USSR national economy in 1988]. Moscow: Finansy i statistika.
Gaydar, E. (1990a). Trudny vybor. Ekonomicheskoye obozreniye po itogam 1989 goda [The difficult choice: Economic review of 1989]. *Kommunist, 2,* 23-34.
————— . (1990b, April 29). Chto novogo v ekonomike? [What is new in the economy?]. *Pravda* (Moscow) N 119, p. 3.

Gimpelson, V., & Magun, V. (1990). V ozhidanii peremen (rabochiye o situatzii na promyshlennom predpriyatii) [Waiting for the changes: Workers' opinion on the situation of the industrial enterprise]. *Sotziologicheskiye issledovaniya, 1,* 4-20.

Glushetsky, A. (1990, April). Kooperativnaya forma truda ili chastnopredprinimatel'skaya deyatel'nost'? [Cooperative form of labor or private entrepreneurial activity?]. *Ekonomika i zhizn', 17,* 19.

Golov, A., Grazhdankin, A., Gudkov, L., Dubin, B., Zorkaya, N., Levada, Yu., & Sedov, L. (1990, April). 1990 god: nashi nadezhdy [The year of 1990: Our hopes]. *Ogonyok, 15,* 1-3.

Golov, A., Grazhdankin, A., Gudkov, L., Dubin, B., Levada, Yu., Levinson, A., Sedov, L., & Shinkarev, V. (1991, March 12). S kazhdym godom vsyo huzhe [Each year is going from bad to worse]. *Nezavisimaya,* N 31, p. 5.

Goskomstat soobschayet [State Committee on Statistics informs]. (1989, August). *Argumenty i fakty, 32, 3.*

Grigoriev, L. [*1991, April 14*]. Do upadu [*Until the drop*]. *Moskovskiye novosty, 15,* 7.

Gudkov, L. (1990, May). Krepostnaya pechat [Serf press]. *Ogonyok, 19,* 6-7.

Gurtovoy, M (1991, March 24). Rekviem po gostorgovle [Requiem to the state-run trade]. *Moskovskiye novosty, 12,* 10.

Interfax. (1991, February). *Argumenty i fakty, 7, 3.*

Izvestiya (Moscow). (1989), December 17). Vtoroi s'ezd narodnykh deputatov SSSR [The Second Congress of the USSR People's Deputies] (pp. 2-15).

Kogai, R., & Uspenskaya, O. (1990, March). Defitzit rozhdayet defitzit [Scarcity brings scarcity]. *Ekonomika i zhizn', 10,* 16.

Kolesnikova, E. (1990, February). Vyezdnaya torgovlya [Out-of- doors trade]. *Pravitel'stvenny vestnik, 6,* 6-7.

Kommunist. (1989a, vol. 12). Obschestvenny vybor: peremeny v sotzial 'noi psikhologii v zerkale obschestvenno-politicheskikh diskussy 1989 goda [The public choice: Changes in social psychology morrored by socio-political disputes in 1989] (pp. 28-35).

————. (1989b, vol. 18). Umneye zhizni byt' nel 'zya [One cannot be more clever than life itself] (pp. 28-39).

Koryagina, T. (1990). Tenevaya ekonomika v SSSR (analiz, otzenki, prognozy) [The shadow economy in the USSR (analysis, estimations, forecasting)]. *Voprosy ekonomiki, 3,* 110-120.

————. (1989, December 13). Trillion na melkiye raskhody [Trillion in pocket money]. *Literaturnaya gazeta,* N 50, p. 12.

Kozlov, V. (1990). Pochemu rabochiye ogranichivayut vyrabotku [Why workers restrict productivity]. *Sotziologicheskiye issledovaniya, 2,* 50-56.

Kuznetzov, R. (1990, September 26). Ne popast' v ruki mafii [Do not fall into the hands of the mafia]. *Pravda* (Moscow), N 269, p. 6.

Levada, Yu. (1991, January 6). Ot bessiliya k vlasti sily? [From powerlessness to the power of force?]. *Moskovskiye novosty, 1,* p. 6.

———— (Ed.). (1990a, July 8). Trust is falling. *Moscow News, 27,* 5.

————. (1990b, November 4). The Russian revolution: As judged by its descendants. *Moscow News, 44,* 8-9.

Morozova, G. (1989). Trudoizbytochna li Srednyaya Aziya? [Is there a work force in excess in the Central Asia?]. *Sotziologicheskiye issledovaniya, 6,* 74-79.

Narodnoe khoziaistvo SSSR v 1988 godu [USSR national economy in 1988]. (1989). Moscow: Finansy i Statistika.

Ogonyak. (1990, January, vol.5).Obeschaniyami syt ne budesh' [Many words will not fill a bushel] (p. 1).

————. (1989a, November, vol. 43). Za i protiv [Pro and contra] (p. 5).

————. (1989b, December, vol. 48). Za i protiv [Pro and contra] (p. 3).

————. (1989c, December, vol. 49). Za i protiv [Pro and contra] (p. 1).

Obeschaniyami syt ne budesh' [Many words will not fill a bushel]. (1990, January). *Ogonyok, 5,* 1.

Obschestvenny vybor: peremeny v sotzial'noi psikhologii v zerkale obschestvenno-politicheskikh diskussy 1989 goda [The public choice: Changes in social psychology mirrored by socio-political disputes in 1989]. (1989). *Kommunist, 12,* 28-35.

Otnoshenie naselenia k radikal'noi economicheskoi reforme [Population attitudes toward the radical economic reform]. (1990). *Voprosy Ekonomiki, 1,* 137-139.

Otnosheniye naseleniya k razvitiyu kooperatzii [Population attitudes toward the coop enterprises]. (1989). *Voprosy Ekonomiki, 11,* 129-134.

Otnosheniye naseleniya k sostoyaniyu potrebitel'skogo rynka [Population attitudes to the state of consumer market]. (1990). *Voprosy Ekonomiki, 1,* 76-80.

Perekhod k rynku. Kontzeptziya i programma [Transition to the market: Concept and program]. (1990, August). Moscow: Arkhangel'skoe.

Pischulin, N. (1990, January 1). Vtoroi S'ezd narodnykh deputatov SSSR: Ozhidaniya, mnenia, otzenki [The second Congress of the USSR People's Deputies: Expectations, opinions, guesses]. *Izvestiya,* (Moscow), N 1, p. 2.

Pischulin, N., & Alferov, V. (1990, December 13). Kogda politika obgonyaet ekonomiku [When politics outruns the economy]. *Moskovskaya Pravda,* N 285, p. 3.

Pokrovskaya, M. (1990). Sotzial'naya spravedlivost' v potreblenii i ego stereotipy [Social justice: in consumption and its stereotypes]. *Sotziologicheskiye issledovaniya, 3,* 46-53.

Pravda (Moscow). (1990, February 16). Chk 'ya ty, zemlya? [To whom does the land belong?] (p. 3).

Pravitel'stvenny vestnik. (1990, February, vol. 9). Tenevaya ekonomika: portret na fone perestroiki [The shadow economy: A portrait against perestroika] (pp. 6-7).

Protzenko, A. (1989, December 8). Tovary i talony [Goods and rations cards]. *Izvestiya* (Moscow). N 343, p. 2.

Pushkar, A. (1990, February 14). Kto est' kto v derevne [Who is who in the village]. *Izvestiya* (Moscow), N 46, p. 3.

Rimashevskaya, N. (1990). Uzlovaya problema perekhodnogo perioda [The crucial problem of the transitional period]. *Voprosy ekonomiki, 1,* 33-36.

Rutgaizer, V., Kinsburgsky, A., & Kirichenko, N. (1990). I vnov' o reforme roznichnykh tzen [Once again about the reform of retail prices]. *Ekonomika i organizatziya promyshlennogo proizvodstva, 4,* 87-91.

Rytov, Yu. (1990, October). 500 dney [500 days]. *Pravitel'stvenny vestnik, 41,* 3.

————. (1989). Sotzial'naya spravedlivost': emotzii i proza zhizni [Social justice: Emotions and the prose of life]. *Pravitel'stvenny vestnik, 17,* 12.

Shashnov, S. (1990a, January 3). My, kooperatziya, ITD [We, cooperative and individual labor activities]. *Ekonomika i zhizn', 3,* 18.

————. (1990b, September). V ozhidanii peremen [Waiting for changes]. *Pravitel'stvenny vestnik, 39,* 5.

Shatalin, S. (1990, September). Kakim putyom pereidem k rynkuz? [Which way to the market?]. *Argumenty i fakty, 37,* 1-2.

Sinilov, G., & Golovnin, S. (1990, October). Novye metamorfozy kriminal'noi nazhivy [The new metamorphoses of criminal greed]. *Ekonomika i zhizn', 40,* 17.

Sobol, N. (1990). Kriminogenny defitzit [Crime-provoking scarcity] *Ekonomika i zhizn', 50,* 7.

Sogomonov, A., & Tolstykh, A. [1989, June]. O nashikh zabotakh [On our troubles]. *Kommunist, 9,* 74-76.

Sokolov, B. (1990). Rabota i zarabotok: azy sotzial'noi spravedlivosti [Work and earnings: The ABC's of social justice]. *Sotziologicheskiye issledovaniya, 2,* 74-80.

Sotziologichesky opros [Sociological survey]. (1990, August). *Argumenty i fakty, 34,* 3.

Telyukov, A. (1989). Ekonomicheskiye prioritety v sotzial'noi sfere [Economic priorities in the social sphere]. *Sotziologicheskiye issledovaniya, 6,* 3-13.

Tenevaya ekonomika: portret na fone perestroiki [The shadow economy: A portrait against perestroika]. (1990, February). *Pravitel'stvenny vestnik, 9,* 6-7.

Tikhonov, V. (1990a, February). Tekhnologiya nischety [Technology of poverty]. *Ogonyok, 7,* 8-9.

_____. (1990b, August 8). A vsyo-taki ona vyzhivet [Still it will survive]. *Literaturnaya gazeta, 32,* 10.

Umneye zhizni byt' nel'zya [One cannot be more clever than life itself]. (1989). *Kommunist, 18,* 28-39.

Voprosy ekonomiki. (1990a, vol 1). Ekonomika SSSR: Vyvody i rekomendatzii [USSR economy: Conclusions and recommendations] (p. 6-72).

_____. (1990b, vol. 1). Otnosheniye naseleniya k sostoyaniyu potrebitel 'skogo rynka [Population attitudes to the state of consumer market] (p. 76-80).

_____. (1990c, vol. 1). Otnoshenie naseleniya k radikal 'noi economicheskoi reforme [Population attitudes toward the radical economic reform] (pp. 137-139).

_____. (1990d, vol. 1). Zabastovki: otnosheniye naseleniya i vzglyad iznutri [Strikes: population attitudes and a view from inside] (pp. 92-98).

_____. (1989, vol. 11). Otnosheniye naseleniya k razvitiyu kooperatzii [Population attitudes toward the coop enterprises] (pp. 129-134).

Voronov, A. (1990). O problemakh preodoleniya defitzita i metodakh regulirovaniya potrebitel'skogo rynka [On the problems of overcoming scarcity and methods of regulation of the consumer market]. *Voprosy ekonomiki, 1,* 26-32.

Vtoroi s'ezd narodnykh deputatov SSSR [The Second Congress of the USSR People's Deputies]. (1989, December 17). *Izvestiya* (Moscow), N 351, pp. 2-15.

Yanitsky, O. (1989). Ekologicheskoye dvisheniye [The ecological movement]. *Sotziologicheskiye issledovaniya, 6,* 26-37.

Za i protiv [Pro and contra]. (1989a, November). *Ogonyok, 43,* 5.

Za i protiv [Pro and contra]. (1989b, December). *Ogonyok, 48,* 3.

Za i protiv [Pro and contra]. (1989c, December). *Ogonyok, 49,* 1.

Zabastovki: otnosheniye naseleniya i vzglyad iznutri [Strikes: population attitudes and a view from inside]. (1990). *Voprosy ekonomiki, 3,* 92-98.

Zaslavskaya, T. (1989). Podlinny optimizm osnovyvaetsya na realizme [The real optimism is based on realism]. *Sotziologicheskiye issledovaniya, 6,* 92-95.

Zhelnorova, N. (1990, August). Programma maksimal'nogo soglasiya [Program of maximum solidarity]. *Argumenty i fakty, 32,* 2.

Zorkaya, N. (1990, February 25). Idealy'i prioritety [Ideals and priorities]. *Izvestiya* (Moscow), 57, p. 2.

CZECHOSLOVAKIA: FACING THE ECONOMIC REFORM

Jadwiga Šanderová and Aleš Kabátek

As a result of forced political, economic, and ideological dependence on the Soviet Union and the concomitant totalitarian regimes of individual Communist parties, the Soviet-bloc countries developed many features in common. Each of those regimes, however, had its distinctive features of economic development and its own degree of political oppression. Searching for typical features of so-called real socialism in Czechoslovakia, that is, socialism as it was actually practiced in daily life, one must go back through the country's history at least to the period immediately preceding World War II.

HISTORICAL DEVELOPMENT

Basic Characterization

Czechoslovakia was established as an independent state in 1918, uniting Czech lands (Bohemia and Moravia), which had been one of the most advanced industrial parts of Austro-Hungarian Empire, with agrarian Slovakia. In 1937, Czechoslovakia, unlike the other Soviet-bloc countries except the former GDR, ranked among Europe's most advanced countries. In the Czech part of the country, the economic standard per capita approached that of France and was comparable to that of Germany. Czechoslovakia retained this position immediately after World War II, for war damage was not enormous. Postwar restoration was swift, with the GNP of 1937 being equaled again as early as 1948. It is this strong start that starkly contrasts with the country's condition after years of irrational political decisions that deformed the structure of economy, employment, and property relations. Today, Czechoslovakia is the only one of the above-mentioned countries in which international comparison between her prewar and her current economic standard makes economic failure quite apparent. Since the so-called socialist revolution, Czechoslovakia has fallen from the front ranks to become one of the backward European countries.

This economic deterioration stems from basic deformations connected with the concept of so-called socialist industrialization and collectivization. For example, the concept of industrial independence imposed by the USSR stunted the growth of Czechoslovak machine-building and metallurgy, mainly in heavy machinery. Stressing heavy industry, the character of this restructuring ran against the grain of the country's traditions. The process was carried out rapidly and pursued mainly through augmentation of the work force and massive investment in new steel works, mines, power plants, factories for building heavy machinery, and the corresponding infrastructures. Czechoslovakia had already been among the 10 most advanced industrialized countries in the 1930s, when she was producing "only" 1,400,000 tons of iron and 1,900,000 tons of steel. By the end of the 1950s the production of iron had tripled (to 4,200,000 tons), and the production of steel had expanded even more (totalling 6,200,000 tons). In the early 1960s Czechoslovakia produced far more iron and steel per capita than the leading industrial superpowers—the United States, the Soviet Union, Great Britain, France, Italy, and Japan (*Světový almanach*, 1965).

The "socialist restructuring of agriculture" appears to have been equally irrational. After 1948, both Czechoslovak agriculture and industry alike became an economic paradox. Well-established and successful spheres of the economy were gradually replaced by new, unsuitable, and ineffective methods. Traditional cooperative associations dating back to the nineteenth century serve as a case in point. After World War II, functioning and well-developed manufacturing associations, cooperative distilleries, dairies, associations of mechanics, and credit associations were eliminated by the communists' scheme of co-ops. Associations were forcibly dissolved even when they had historical roots and pertinently complimented the existing structure of the economy, in which small and medium-size family enterprises had prevailed. The importance of those small intermediate businesses grew with the two land reforms that followed both World War I and World War II. By contrast, cooperative associations were created by force under adverse economic, social, and psychological conditions.

By the late 1950s, it had become apparent that the system of economic functioning and control needed reform. The first program of economic reform was launched in 1958 but was never completed. The conviction that economic restructuring was necessary prevailed again in the mid-1960s.

Development during the 1970s and 1980s

The military invasion of Czechoslovakia on August 21, 1968, had a number of negative consequences on the country's fate. First, it halted economic reform and restored rigid centralization of management. The economic system reverted to its ineffective, labor-intensive, and often irrational character, which had been abandoned only briefly and indifferently.

The period after August 1968, which the communist leadership referred to as one of normalization and consolidation, primarily meant political oppression, for which the leaders of the Communist Party tried to compensate by promoting relative well-being. As part of the central strategy for regulating the standard of living, which, in the 1960s was still comparable in some respects to that of developed European countries and much higher than the standard of the other East-bloc countries, there appeared a strong trend towards the leveling of the living standard of different social groups. By sustaining or augmenting the living standard while leveling it, the leaders meant to create the impression that the living standard was good if the level of material consumption was not worse than in the past and if the poorest groups gradually disappeared.

From 1970 to 1984, salaries and wages in Czechoslovakia rose quickest among social groups in which people had originally earned lower incomes in 1970. For example, the incomes of workers grew by 60%, whereas the incomes of administrative staffs and intellectuals grew by less than 50%. And by the mid-1980s, cooperative farmers, whose incomes were below average in 1970, were making more money than workers in industry. During the 1970s and 1980s, remaining differences between remuneration for skilled and unskilled labor were eliminated, with demanding intellectual work by people with a college education often being rewarded less than manual labor (Bondyová & Petrášková, 1977, pp. 51-53). Moreover, wages only loosely corresponded to effort, so it was an exception to earn a decent income through active hard work and superior qualification on the official labor market.

Within the former Soviet bloc, Czechoslovakia's reputation for having a high living standard is connected with the practice of leveling it. Czechoslovakia differs from Hungary and Poland, for example, mainly in that she has fewer people living in poverty (Beskid & Tuček, 1990). However, Czechoslovakia achieved a relatively high GNP and standard of living only by liquidating existing resources and cutting investments. The price has been high. Over the last 20 years, and mainly in the 1980s, domestic debt (i.e., necessary, but lacking investment in machines, technical equipment, buildings, and other elements of the infrastructure) has soared. In the sector of fuel and energy production, which is a new component of Czechoslovak industry, 40% of the machines and equipment are obsolete. In light industry, the traditional domain of Czechoslovakia, this figure often exceeds 70%. The domestic debt is manifested as low productivity and often unbearable working conditions in factories.

Nature, too, has suffered. Northwestern Bohemia's environment has gradually become one of the most endangered in the world. Czechoslovakia now occupies second place in Europe in sulphur fallout per square kilometer. Two-thirds of Bohemia's and one-third of Slovakia's entire forest area have been damaged by industrial fumes. Seemingly good results were achieved in Czechoslovak agriculture through exploitation of nature, and that mismanagement has impaired her biological systems and self-regulating capacity.

Deterioration of the environment and working conditions has been reflected in the population's health. Since the early 1960s, life expectancy, the most general indicator of the population's health, has stagnated and, recently, even declined. Among European countries, Czechoslovakia fell in this regard from 10th place to 24th. For example, health care and care for the elderly and the handicapped are far below the world standard because investment in material consumption was long given priority.

The costs of achieving a high GNP and standard of living in Czechoslovakia have disrupted other aspects of life as well. During the period of normalization and consolidation, the power of high party officials increased so much that political and economic arbitrariness resulted. The number of measures, regulations, and directives steadily rose, obscuring the legal system more and more, thereby eroding the population's sense of right and wrong and breeding corruption. Of course, the growth of corruption and speculation was promoted by economic stagnation, for shortages of goods and services were worsening. Ever more articles were obtainable only through personal connections or bribes, that is, outside the official market. In about the 1970s, the "parallel economy" began to operate. It represented a well-organized and established part of the economic structure and existed at the expense of both state and cooperative property. By the end of the 1980s, it was operating at the expense of consumers as well. The parallel economy was used by practically all Czechoslovaks to satisfy needs not met by the official (state) market and services.

Deterioration in the field of education cannot be overlooked, either. Whereas the number of secondary school and university students doubled in advanced Western countries and even in some Eastern countries during the 1970s and 1980s, the figure in Czechoslovakia was significantly lower. Between 1970 and 1986, the number of secondary school students grew by 22%; the number of university students, by only 7%. The number of students attending secondary technical schools dropped by 8% (Hochmaulová, 1987, p. 87). A reorganization of education, prompted by a temporary, demographically related reduction in the labor supply, did irreparable damage. Instead of taking advantage of the widespread shortage of labor by rationalizing organization and production, the authorities shortened secondary school study by one year for most teenagers.

An additional cause of economic dislocation in Czechoslovakia was "personnel screening" at the beginning of the 1970s, a practice that forced an estimated 200,000 people to leave their qualified jobs and work in unskilled occupations. Lastly, Czechoslovakia has lost an estimated 510,000 of her intellectual and educated elite through emigration, waves of which have afflicted Czechoslovakia three times in the last 50 years (World War II, the communist *coup d'état* in 1948, and consolidation after 1968).

THE BEGINNING OF ECONOMIC REFORM

Czechoslovakia was one of the last Eastern European countries to face mass political unrest and subsequent upheaval. As in the former GDR, however, the Communist Party's monopoly on power was eliminated practically overnight. Compared to, say, Poland or Hungary, Czechoslovakia now has the advantage of learning from their experience with the slow pace of political changes and difficulties in reforming the socialist system. As a result, the Czechoslovak government intends to move as quickly as possible to a full market economy and to minimize the unproductive period associated with attempts to combine the market economy with central planning—the route that Hungary, for example, had to take.

The reintroduction of the market economy will be an arduous process in Czechoslovakia. The distortion of property and market relations there was unprecedented. After 1948, extensive nationalization was pursued, a process that deeply influenced all small businesses and self-employed entrepreneurs. The private sector ceased to exist in agriculture, services, and the crafts. Self-employment as a person's main form of occupation was restricted to several art professions, the so-called free-lancers. Private services were prohibited but were occasionally provided illegally as a "side-line."

After 1986, a regulation supporting private enterprise was issued. With few exceptions, however, it failed to lead to the opening of small businesses such as private stores, repair shops, and family construction companies. It only gave support and legalized a small share of the existing side-lines. Most people practicing side-lines saw no advantage in independence. As employees of state or cooperative companies, they not only avoided the hardships caused by bureaucracy but were also able to use, albeit illegally, state-paid hours, state material, state equipment, and so forth. Therefore, only 51,000 workers were officially registered as private entrepreneurs by December 1, 1988, approximately 2% of them performing private services as a full-time job (Kaňa, 1990).

In 1990, the Czechoslovak parliament passed legislation making all forms of ownership and enterprise (state, cooperative, and private) formally equal.

The parliament also passed the Restitution Act, enabling the return of property expropriated after 1948. At the same time, legislation on the privatization of small businesses was enacted. It allows for state-run small businesses in trade, services, tourism, and the like to be auctioned. Both these processes commenced in January 1991. The privatization of large businesses is in preparation. Most state property is expected to be denationalized, first in the sphere of light and consumer industries, and later in that of heavy machine-building and metallurgy. The state is supposed to retain control over basic elements of the infrastructure such as railways, communications, and the utilities. The scheme for privatizing large businesses includes a unique experiment, a system of investment coupons that can be traded for shares of specific businesses to be privatized.

Actual economic reform began in January 1991, and it was decided to make it radical. From the macroeconomic point of view, the situation seems quite good. The exchange rate of Czechoslovak currency is stabilizing and the structure of the economy is improving. The two most typical`features of the previous bureaucratic system of distribution—production for production's sake rather than for consumption, and chronically unsatisfied market demand—seem to be slowly disappearing. At the same time, however, production is declining. From the ordinary person's point of view, the situation is a sort of shock, with "price liberalization" (the cutting of subsidies) having the strongest influence. On average, prices have doubled since 1990, whereas the incomes of most people have remained unchanged. About 20% of the respondents representing the adult population in Czechoslovakia claimed that they have to withdraw from their savings to meet everyday needs (*Institut pro výzkum veřejného mínění,* 1991, p. 2). This situation will inevitably become much worse in the near future, when the price of energy and rents are raised as planned.

The main problem is generally seen in the fact that the privatization of small business continues to lag behind price liberalization, although the two processes commenced at exactly the same time. The privatization of small business has been fairly rapid, but it is not expected to be completed until mid-1992. Compounding the difficulties are the new legal and economic issues posed by the coupon scheme for privatization of large factories and businesses. Mainly because of these problems, the privatization of large businesses has not yet begun (spring 1991).

Price liberalization is thus taking place at a time when state plants still have a powerful monopoly, choking off competition. To cope with the new economic conditions, producers have pursued a simple strategy: compensate for higher prices of raw materials and energy by increasing the prices of their products instead of improving their productivity. The consumers, not the producers, thus suffer from inefficient production. These circumstances inevitably influence people's perception of both the economic situation and the reforms. In April

1991, for instance, 62% of the respondents representing the adult population in Czechoslovakia claimed that "the start was good, but it is somehow getting worse now" (*Institut pro výzkum veřejného mínění*, 1991, p. 1).

Because of the country's favorable position before World War II, many people tend to believe that the current transformation of the Czechoslovak economy will be relatively easy. The main message of the following text is that this is not necessarily the case. The Czechoslovakia of the 1980s can be described as a materially and spiritually devastated society not only in comparison with developed countries but also with its own condition 42 years ago. The position of this country is obviously much better than, say, that of the Soviet Union. But the comparison with Poland and Hungary is not so straightforward. In addition to economic factors that are actually better in Czechoslovakia than in those two neighbors, one must consider people's frames of mind, attitudes, and behavior. From this point of view, the situation in Czechoslovakia does not differ significantly from that in the other ex-socialist countries, as we try to demonstrate below.

VALUE ORIENTATIONS

The system of values and the moral fiber of the nation, especially in recent years, has often been characterized by (a) estrangement from society and escape towards privatism, (b) spiritual marasmus and orientation to material aspects of life, (c) deep rooted, even aggressive egalitarianism, and (d) erosion of work values. At the same time these characteristics are often considered the most serious obstacle to the transformation of Czechoslovak society.

This description of the nation's morality is based on everyday experience of the quality of life rather than on quantitative analysis of representative data, which are often at odds with experience. It is difficult to decide which diverges from reality—one's sense of quality or the data.

Exact analysis of value orientation entails a number of theoretical and methodological problems. In trying to compare value systems over the course of time even within one cultural and social environment, one is stepping on thin ice. For example, what use are research results based on identical sets of values when the social context of their functioning or their indices has changed? Furthermore, it can be assumed that a number of value orientations conflict with possibilities for their practical applications. This conflict is then reflected in responses to questions about priorities. When answering questionnaires, some people speak only about values that they believe are attainable, whereas others tell about their dreams. Unfortunately, one never knows which is which. In other words, in Czechoslovakia these data can signify anything because the context for the "operationalization" of particular values is changing both over time and across individuals.

Despite these problems, however, we believe that the data at our disposal indicate that the actual situation is not as one-sided as it would appear at first glance, particularly in terms of morality.

Escape towards Privatism

Without doubt, the value orientation conveying an escape to family or private spheres of life grew stronger in Czechoslovakia during the 1970s (see Table 1). The top four values ranked in Table 1 are also closely related. Through factor analysis, an independent factor interpretable as "being independent of society" or "living a calm life without tensions and risks" was formed. This value ("living a calm life") was operant in sets of values studied in several research works conducted in the 1970s and 1980s. Secondary analysis of the results reported in these works (unfortunately, primary data are no longer available) showed that the most profound shift in value orientations since 1975 was centered precisely on this value. Among 21 values, "living a calm life" moved from 10th position in the 1970s to 4th in the 1980s (Slejška, 1990).

Nevertheless, it would be rather oversimplified to see this trend as a mere lack of interest in public affairs that is deeply rooted in the system of values. It is true that such values as "influencing public affairs" or "taking an active part in the development of socialism" (here, the phrase "development of socialism" has a negative influence) have greatly lost credit, but this change should be attributed to the fact that activities in official, formal, and bureaucratic state and political institutions were understood in scarcely any other terms. After all, unofficial public life had been practically unthinkable because of political oppression.

At the same time, however, data on the value orientations of young people, who are the most sensitive barometers of the change in "the social and political involvement" value, show that the young did not lose their interest in public affairs. For example, "working for the protection of the environment" or "contributing to peace and disarmament" were considered some of the most important values by every second young person (Czechoslovak Academy of Sciences, 1988).

The decrease in the "social and political involvement" value in the 1970s and 1980s should therefore also be seen as a result of Czechoslovak society's growing criticism of the system. Accordingly, a high level of passivity in the population can be interpreted as a form of passive resistance and an expression of a certain helplessness rather than as a manifestation of extreme individualism. Research conducted among the economically active population in Bohemia in 1983 can serve as a suitable illustration. Half of the respondents were of the opinion that "one cannot change society oneself, but everyone should try to improve the situation, at least in local terms" (Czechoslovak Academy of Sciences, 1983). This basically active approach was, however, thwarted by the formalism of public life—and certainly not by accident.

Table 1.   Value Preferences as Ranked by
Czechs and Slovaks in 1984 (in percentages)

Values	Important	Unimportant
Setting an example to one's children	96	4
Being able to adapt oneself	91	9
Being able to do everything oneself	88	12
Living in a small way	87	13
Physical resistance	86	14
Having no conflicts	86	14
Equality of people	85	15
Actively contributing to the development of socialist society	72	18
Achieving top work performance	73	27
Having enough money and living well	61	39
Acquiring high education	56	44
Influencing public affairs	40	60
Being independent of people, society	35	65
Being knowledgeable in natural science	39	61
Having opportunities for private enterprise	18	82

Source: Survey *Třídní a sociální struktura v ČSSR 1984* [Class and social structure in Czechoslovakia 1984].
(1984). Carried out by the Institute for Philosophy and Sociology, Czechoslovak Academy of Sciences;
authors' own calculations.

Orientation toward Material Aspects of Life

The orientation of Czechoslovaks to material consumption is indisputable at first sight, but examination of survey data reveals a fair number of inconsistences. Material consumption as a clear proclivity to a consumption-oriented way of life, is, along with other variables, highly relevant only for one third of the population. Moreover, secondary analysis of research from the 1970s and 1980s has shown that the value labeled "existence, money, and earnings" dropped from 4th to 7th position during those two decades (Slejška, 1990, p. 318). Nonetheless, we are reluctant to interpret this data as a trend toward postmaterialist values. A more likely explanation seems to be that such values are unrealistic for most people (in a manner and extent they consider appropriate for a European at the end of the twentieth century) and that, for the sake of their emotional health, they therefore consider a consumption-oriented way of life unimportant.

In our opinion, a preoccupation with consumption in Czechoslovakia is apparently born more of the economic circumstances than of progressive spiritual emaciation. Although the life standard there is higher than in many ex-socialist countries, it is much lower than in Western countries, meaning that most things are available "only a little bit." A number of commodities one cannot really do without (unless one gives up the standard of civilization) must be hunted for. One has to be patient and persistent to obtain them. Such hunting turns into a stereotype or sometimes even a hobby. After all, it was one of the few spheres where people could freely exercise their inventiveness and entrepreneurship.

Egalitarianism

Special attention should be given to egalitarianism, which, according to some authors, has a long tradition in Czechoslovakia, especially in Bohemia (Filipcová, 1990). This feature of the nation's spirit is being explained by centuries of struggle against the German element in the country, a fight in which all the strata of the nation stood together. This "natural wavelength of the people" was further enhanced by the official ideology, which interpreted social progress as the overcoming of social inequality. As mentioned previously, income leveling played an important role in these efforts, the result being that the quality and amount of work was dissociated from the level of one's official earnings. Consequently, one third of all economically active youngsters who were surveyed believed that the level of earnings had nothing to do with one's performance, initiative, or qualification, and about one half of all young respondents believed that an above-average worker had the same chances for promotion as an under-average worker (*Institut pro výzkum veřejného míně ní*, 1987). These beliefs, along with various privileges of powerful individuals and the enormous illegally accumulated property of speculators, have led to a common view that honest work does not earn money and that those who earn a great deal do not deserve respect. From this perspective any income differentiation is seen as basically unfair.

Work Values

Poor economic conditions have been reflected in working environments, mainly those of manual laborers in factories. Much obsolete, often unfit, and environmentally damaging equipment is still in use. Managerial incompetence and frequent supply shortages undermine the organization of work, resulting in considerable variation in workloads, increased overtime, and stoppages. Such conditions influence work values, especially among industrial workers.

Although the level of earnings is still usually the most important value for this social group, competent organization of work, the use of modern equipment, and sound working conditions have become important to them as well, sometimes even more so than earned income. We cannot however, interpret this response as a shift of interest from financial aspects to the content and character of work. In most cases, it is rather a reflection of the previously mentioned undignified and inhumane working conditions and unsatisfactory standard of technical equipment and management. Furthermore, the level of wages is also influenced by such factors as the use of modern technologies and the professional organization of work. Finally, we can offer two more interpretations of the relatively low importance that some people accord earned money. First, this attitude could result from the fact that, until recently, earning was a matter of course for the productive population of Czechoslovakia. Second, the relative lack of interest in income could be reinforced by wage leveling and by the growing importance of other sources of income, such as the parallel economy.

Speaking about "official" work, we have a great deal of empirical evidence clearly indicating estrangement from work. For instance, research conducted in 1975 showed that one fifth of all employees were not interested in economic and other types of problem-solving at their work places. One third of the respondents in a 1982 survey identified with this attitude (*Institut pro výzkum veřejného mínění*, 1990a). On the basis of the data at our disposal, we can conclude that most people in Czechoslovakia perceive their "official" work as an instrument rather than a target.

But official paid employment is not the only realm of work in Czechoslovakia or anywhere else. A comprehensive area of unofficial, more-or-less private work has developed in Czechoslovakia, as we try to demonstrate in the next section. Unfortunately, we have no empirical documentation of work values in this area and cannot come to any conclusions about the value of work in general.

Returning to the obstruction of social transformation in terms of Czechoslovakia's morality, we do not believe that the ethics of the people are the main problem at present, as is commonly complained in Czechoslovak intellectual circles. Seemingly rooted in the life philosophy of the people, their activities stem first and foremost from their circumstances and the character of the system. But it is hardly possible to change the system without changing the people's activities, and that remains a conundrum.

CHANGES IN INDIVIDUAL EXPERIENCE

It is typical that people will desire to "keep up with the Jones's" rather than be satisfied knowing that they are better-off than their poorer relatives. To have their lives appear even roughly similar to those of their richer Western neighbors, people in Czechoslovakia were willing to exert considerable effort, as shown in the next section. Making every effort to maintain or improve the living standard of their families and to preserve their spiritual health, Czechs and Slovaks often considered their standard of living adequate.

The mood has changed, though. Since the early 1970s, when 49% of the respondents in a public opinion poll believed their living standard had increased over the previous five years and 38% expected it to continue improving over the next five years, the optimism has slowly declined. By December 1989, only 32% of the respondents assumed that their living standard would improve during the subsequent five years (see Table 2).

Table 2.   Czech and Slovak Evaluation of Their
Living Standard, 1970, 1985, and 1989 (in percentages)

	1970	1985	1989
Question: "In comparison with the situation five years ago the current standard of living in Czechoslovakia is:"			
Much better	13	9	5
A bit better	36	35	33
Comparable	28	31	32
A bit worse	18	20	23
Much worse	4	3	6
No answer	1	2	6
Question: "In comparison with the present situation the standard of living in future five years in Czechoslovakia will be:"			
Much better	6	6	4
A bit better	32	28	28
Comparable	40	35	36
A bit worse	15	20	21
Much worse	2	3	4
No answer	5	8	11

Source: *Názory občanů na vybrané problémy životní úrovně* v *ČSSR* [Public opinion of select life standard problems in Czechoslovakia]. (1989). Prague: *Institut pro výzkum veřejného mínění,* p. 12.

Although the 1989 survey was conducted immediately after the November Revolution, one must consider that people's consciousness at that time still reflected the situation prior to the revolution. Hence, the overall situation before the revolution was assessed quite optimistically in that more than one-third of the respondents considered it stabilized, only one-quarter feared deterioration, and nearly one-third even expected the living standard to improve. Table 3 offers a similar picture. Apart from the environment, which is remarkably bad in Czechoslovakia, the situation as seen by roughly three-quarters of the respondents was either stabilized or even hopeful.

At the same time, elementary disorders in all spheres of life, having become more striking, could not be overlooked even though the true situation of the national economy, namely, the exhaustion of resources, was deliberately hidden from the population. Czechs and Slovaks had no illusions about the condition of their society, more and more of them realized the deterioration of the economy. Whereas only 12% of the respondents in 1987 considered the preceding year to have been bad, this figure stood at 21% only a year later (*Institut pro výzkum veřejného mínění,* 1989).

After *perestroika* (restructuring) was launched in the Soviet Union, cautious discussion of certain shortages began in the mass media, but no solutions were found. "Double-speak" emerged, not allowing one to say that something was

Table 3. Czech and Slovak Expectations for
Their Living Standard, December 1989 (in percentages)

Particularly in	Better	Same	Worse	No Answer
Question: "In comparison with the present situation, the livingstandard in Czechoslovakia in the next five years will be :"				
Earnings	32	43	20	5
Housing	24	69	6	1
Accommodation	23	65	9	3
Health care	22	62	11	5
Social security	21	54	12	13
Food supply	25	54	16	5
Clothes supply	27	52	18	3
Other goods supply	25	48	22	5
Services	24	54	11	11
Transport	21	61	12	6
Environment	25	38	34	3

Source: *Názory občanů na vybrané problémy životní érovně v ČSSR* [Public opinion of select life standard
problems in Czechoslovakia]. (1989). Prague: *Institut pro výzkum veřejného mínění,* p. 25.

disastrous or even bad. One was allowed to refer only to "reserves." For
instance, if an enterprise was said to "have reserves" in production quality,
it meant that spoils were being made there. The word "reserve" entered into
public opinion surveys, which subsequently documented what the population
knew—that "the reserves" were ballooning. Of the respondents in a 1973 survey,
42% mentioned "reserves" in machinery and equipment usage. This figure had
risen only slightly to 44% by 1981, but by 1989 it had leapt to 80%. During
that period, the respondents criticized work discipline most. Whereas 64% of
them mentioned "reserves" in this sphere in 1973 and 67% in 1981, it had
reached 97% by 1989 (*Institut pro výzkum veřejného mínění,* 1990a).

Nevertheless, Czechs and Slovaks probably did not expect the system to
break down and assumed they could compensate for its deficiency by relying
on their own power (see next section). It is possible that the November
Revolution of 1989 came as a surprise for most of the people, despite the fact
that they took part in it. In spring 1990, when the total failure of the system
became apparent and it became necessary to build a new one, 52% of the
respondents in a survey (Czechoslovak Academy of Sciences, 1990a) declared
their fears about economic development and their insecurity. Within a few
months, the situation deteriorated to the degree shown in Table 4.

We could thus interpret the data in the Tables 2, 3, and 4 as saying that
people's optimism about the living standard was, in a way, greater before the
revolution than at present. In fact, it would be more suitable to speak about
a "lack of realism" than about "optimism." As we see it, the lack of realism
is rooted mainly in the fact that, before November 1989, Czechs and Slovaks

Table 4. Czech and Slovak Expectations for Their
Living Standard, December 1990 (in percentages)

	Question 1	Question 2

Question 1: "Do you expect your standard of living to improve in the next two years?"

Question 2: "Thinking about economic development, are you apprehensive about the future? Do you have the feeling of insecurity?"

	Question 1	Question 2
Strongly agree	6	40
Agree	16	35
Disagree	39	18
Strongly disagree	39	8

Source: Survey *Ekonomická očekávání a postoje II* [Economic Expectation and Attitudes II]. (1990b). Carried out by the Center for Empirical Researches, Institute of Sociology, Czechoslovak Academy of Sciences; authors' own calculations.

were not aware enough of the true state of the country's economy, particularly of the depletion of resources. They were thus able to believe that they could compensate for the system's shortcomings by tried-and-trusted coping strategies.

INDIVIDUAL COPING STRATEGIES

A typical feature of the previous regime was that it provided for needs that were not felt, and ignored or failed to meet those that were felt. Moreover, the regime promoted the consumer orientation of people. Unfortunately, it did so under conditions of general insufficiency, "general" not in the sense that nothing was available but that there was no sphere of life without shortages. Unable to control the producer through the market, consumers had to seek additional and provisional ways to meet their needs or adjust them to given circumstances. Both possibilities meant loss of money and time. Satisfying one's need became time-consuming, complicated, and costly. People began to strive to adapt themselves as much as possible and searched for their individual solutions, often to the detriment of their own future or that of others. The exploitative "strategy" of the macrosystem thus penetrated the microsphere of ordinary people's everyday lives.

The Parallel Economy

To bridge the gap between needs and incomes, the parallel economy began to operate. The definition of the parallel economy is not clear. It is difficult and often inexact to differentiate between the parallel and the official economy because the two spheres are intertwined. Most spheres of the parallel economy are directly dependent on the official economy, but there are spheres of the official economy where contrary dependence exists.

The parallel economy consists, first, of after-hours work or part-time jobs usually performed for someone other than the main employer (be it the state or a cooperative). Although formally legal, this type of income is often connected, for example, with string-pulling, bribery, hidden reciprocity in providing such jobs, and "easement" from the main job. After-hours work also often serves to compensate for work stoppages, disorders in supplies, bad organization of work, and so forth. The parallel economy, second, involves work for private persons. This source of income supplementing that from one's main job consists primarily of so-called side-lining, usually artisan or maintenance work carried out partially illegally (without licence or taxes) and partially legally (under state authorization). Work for the immediate satisfaction of the needs of one's family comprises the third sphere of the parallel economy and is a source of income, in this case of material character, consisting of so-called do-it-yourself and self-provisioning. The final source of income through the parallel economy is connected with more-or-less illegal activity within the main job. It includes cheating employers and customers, stealing state property, abusing power, bribing, corrupting, and pulling strings.

These four forms of the parallel economy gave rise to two basic overlapping coping strategies. The first one was based on string-pulling, corruption, bribery, abuse of power, and a network of mafia connecting the high party and economic "elite" with state police and a wide-spread underground. The whole system functioned as a conglomerate of archaic elements of barter, privileges of the powerful, criminal practices, and modern market elements. Unburdened by written regulations of morals, it operated reliably and flexibly, enabling people with access to it to satisfy even immodest needs with little or no effort.

The 1979 and 1989 public opinion polls (*Institut pro výzkum veřejného míně ní*, 1990b) showed that the number of people claiming to have given a bribe in the course of one year grew from 32% to 52%. At the same time, the sum of the bribe went up, with 10% of the respondents admitting to having given a bribe exceeding 1,000 crowns in 1989 (i.e., about one-third of an average monthly salary). In the same period the total volume of bribes doubled. The estimated sum of money transferred by bribery ranged from 2.3 to 2.9 billion crowns in 1979 and from 4.7 to 7.7 billion crowns in 1989. It is not, however, only a matter of bribery. The same polls indicated that people commonly encountered smuggled goods (61%), cheating in stores and services (51%), theft of state property (44%), and abuse of power (43%), among other things.

Nevertheless, most of the population had to adopt the second strategy, which was based mainly on do-it-yourself. Because of a lack of goods and services and/or their financial inaccessibility, people relied on home production and home supply. According to research results from the mid-1980s, 72% of the survey respondents were involved in the upkeep of a house, a summer house, or a car; 83%, in the preserving or sterilizing of food at home; 59%, in knitting and sewing for children; and 47%, in knitting and sewing for adults. People became used to the fact that do-it-yourself is essential in a number of spheres. With state or cooperative companies being unreliable and/or too expensive, people preferred the cheaper do-it-yourself solution (Miková, 1989, pp. 53-54).

The coping strategy pursued by most of the population in Czechoslovakia thus stemmed from a necessity to satisfy one's needs from one's official salary. Extra income, if there was any, had only a supplementary function and did not exceed the official income. Naturally, people took recourse to the first, mainly illegal strategy as well. There are reasons to presume that the degree of the occasional and partial use of this first strategy played a more important role in social differentiation (stratification) than education, profession, and other social and economic characteristics.

Passive Attitudes toward the Reform

Czechoslovak society at the turn of the 1990s faces the problem that the old strategies of social and economic behavior are not supposed to be functional and new ones have not yet been created or adopted. Obviously, the new reality is looked upon with old views, and people are attempting to enter it over "well-trodden paths." Given the choice of several strategies for the near future (Association for Independent Social Analysis—AISA, 1990a), people favored private enterprise least. Instead, they gave priority to other approaches: being economical; making more money at one's existing job or finding a better-paid one; and being able to make, maintain, and repair everything at home. As it turns out, then, tried-and-tested strategies were preferred. Similarly, several months later (in December 1990) nearly three-quarters of the respondents believed that neither extra income nor do-it-yourself activities would diminish in importance (see Table 5).

Only 18% of the respondents representing the adult population in Czechoslovakia in March 1991 were interested in taking part in auctions arranged in connection with the privatization of small businesses. Not more than 2% intended to buy, others just intended to watch (*Informace IVVM,* 1991a). More than three-quarters of the respondents expressed outright disinterest in the auctions. Czechoslovaks do not seem any keener on the privatization of large businesses. The interest of workers or other staff members in buying the factories in which they work (by using investment coupons) is negligible at present (spring 1991) mainly because the outlook for most plants is unclear. Although 25% of the respondents in December 1990 intended to buy investment coupons (Czechoslovak Academy of Sciences, 1990b), by March 1991 only 15% were intending to do so (*Informace IVVM,* 1991b).

Table 5. Presumed Importance of Extra
Incomes and Do-It-Yourself Activities
in Czechoslovakia (in percentages)

	Question 1	*Question 2*
Question 1: "Do you think that the importance of extra income will gradually decrease?"		
Question 2: "Do you think that the number of people who repair their flats and cars themselves or who build their houses and cottages themselves will gradually decrease?"		
Strongly agree	10	12
Agree	17	16
Disagree	32	29
Strongly disagree	41	43

Source: Survey *Ekonomická oekávání a postoje I* [Economic
Expectation and Attitudes I]. (1990a). Carried out by the
Center for Empirical Researches, Institute of Sociology,
Czechoslovak Academy of Sciences; authors' own
calculations.

Based on research results from May 1990, the Association for Independent Social Analysis (AISA) identified four types of attitudes toward the planned transition to the market economy and accompanying difficulties (AISA, 1990a, pp. 15-17). According to AISA, nearly 10% of the respondents were likely to play an active role in the reform. They were people determined to start their own businesses and willing to economize and take over responsibility for their lives. Their motivation was positive, and they looked to the future with optimism and confidence. A second group, one-quarter of the respondents, expressed active support for the reform. Most of them (nearly one-fifth of all the respondents) were motivated by the fear of the future. Therefore, these respondents had a high tendency to strike. They showed exceptional readiness to deal actively with deteriorating living conditions: 43% were willing to change jobs, 76% intended to start working harder, and 88% wanted to advance to the top level in their field.

The third group, representing about one-third of the respondents in May 1990, also expressed their support for the reform but in a rather passive manner. They had the least fear of the future and were willing to accept negative consequences of the transition period: 72% of them could cope with higher prices; 67%, with the loss of their present jobs; and 76%, with a broader differentiation of rents. This group manifested little tendency to strike, but neither did they indicate an inclination to try to compensate for the negative impact of the economic transition. The main reason was their passive willingness to restrain themselves. A good example was a letter from a reader of a Czechoslovak daily. The author wrote: "My wife and I were willing to tighten our belts and wait for the results to come even if it should take several years." To these people, the reform is something beyond them, something that will bring prosperity automatically after a short period of hardship.

The mood of the largest group of respondents in May 1990 (40%) was clearly antireformist. Their aversion resulted, first, from their pessimism about future living standards and from their dissatisfaction with the country's overall political development. A great share of this group consists of supporters of the Communist Party. They also appeared to be the most passive of the respondents. Only 7% were willing to change jobs; 6%, to start working harder; and 17%, to advance to the top in their profession. At the same time, these people were ready to go on strike if the living standard were to decline or the social safety net limited.

The attitudes in spring 1990 thus showed the prevalence of passive and defensive life strategies. In this connection, the relation between the former economic system and the population can be characterized as one of mutual exploitation. General leveling (of incomes, the supply of goods and services, and the satisfaction of needs), total absence of criteria for work performance, and the lack of interest in innovation activities resulted in substandard work performance. Lack of creativity and inventiveness in official jobs, together with insufficient technological support, led to low productivity in both state and cooperative sectors. This, however, does not mean that people's abilities were paralyzed. People's activity made up for irrational functions of the state, but in order to carry out these activities, people were taking what they needed from the state. This kind of behavior could be called stealing, yet the immorality implied by such word does not fully capture Czechoslovak circumstances. People rendered impotent by the system were forced to adopt a well-known attitude: "He who does not steal state property, steals from his family." The failing system thus drove most Czechs and Slovaks to compensate for low productivity in the state and cooperative sectors by engaging in extra activities in the unofficial private sphere and by using virtually illegal strategies. Paradoxically, these responses kept the system going.

The prognosis based on the results presented above, together with other AISA research data, appeared to be rather bleak in 1990-1991. People clearly tended to believe that the economic situation would worsen only briefly—two to three years at the most—and that deterioration was not going to be alarming. They expected initial signs of improvement during the first year of the reform and were ready to tolerate a 20% decline in the standard of living (AISA, 1990a, p. 26). As time progresses, the first setbacks in the reform are therefore likely to result in the disillusionment and helplessness of many people. Such a reaction would come uncomfortably close to a change of heart that could prompt people to stick to well-trodden paths, a detour that could circumvent the efforts to create a market economy. People might prefer to look for ways to avoid the new rules rather than try to make them effective. Their activities could thereby support the old economic order instead of the emerging one. Additionally, a warped sense of political reality and citizenship could play a negative role.

POLITICAL ATTITUDES AND ACTIONS

The high percentage of the population who were members and/or functionaries of official political and social organizations was touted by the Czechoslovak totalitarian regime as evidence of people's active and positive relation to the establishment. Therefore, the political authorities carefully saw to it that the preferred social and political organizations, such as trade unions, the Socialist Union of Youth, the Union for Czechoslovak-Soviet Friendship, and the Women's Union, had large memberships, which the communist leadership could manipulate through these organizations.

Political Participation before November 1989

The Czechoslovak population's relatively high membership rate in official organizations of the totalitarian regime may appear to contradict the previous statements that "being socially and politically active" ranked low in the system of values and that activity was on the decline in the 1970s and 1980s. Though official political activity did lose all significance for the legitimate pursuit of collective and individual needs and interests and for democratic dialogue leading to consensus, it did not lose its instrumental function. Having membership or functions in the Communist Party or other officially preferred social and political organizations was an important prerequisite for one's access to education, good jobs, high posts, travels abroad, and so forth.

Every tenth economically active citizen was therefore a member of one of the representative bodies, every fourth was a member of the Communist Party, every second young person was a member of the Socialist Youth Union, and practically everyone was a member of trade unions. According to the surveys of the late 1970s and early 1980s (Czechoslovak Academy of Sciences, 1978; 1984), only about 4% of the adult population, in most cases retired people, were not members of any organizations. Most of the adult population (54%) were members of three or more organizations.

Most of the Czechoslovak population was thus directly or indirectly forced to become members or functionaries of organizations they were ambivalent about. They did not identify with the ideology and political aims of those organizations but were using them as a means of dealing with numerous important concerns and needs. Political life itself, both within and outside organizations, was ritualized and void of any realistic content.

Mutual economic exploitation between the state and its citizens as described in the previous section was thus paralleled by mutual cheating in civic and political life. The political leadership simulated the existence of pluralistic democracy while the population simulated their active participation in public and political life. Passivity, by which we mean lack of activity to influence the system, was juxtaposed with the cheating of the system at the level of the individual. This created one of the typical features of an individual's estrangement from Czechoslovak society, estrangement closely related to a common perception of the social structure. On one side were ordinary people, *us*; on the other, there was *them*, the communist bureaucratic leadership, or the state. *They* were to blame of *our* hopeless situation, so *we* have the right to circumvent their laws and regulations and take from *them* (i.e., from state property) all *we* need.

The individual's estrangement in Czechoslovak society grew so great that by the end of the 1980s macroeconomic problems were seen as *their* problems, and the individual stood by idly watching with little or no interest in how they coped with them. Their failure became a target of folk humor and sometimes even a subject of absurd and perverted satisfaction.

Political Attitudes after November 1989

The political situation has changed radically since November 1989. How has this change altered people's attitude towards Czechoslovak society, the state, and the political establishment? Because of the general simulating and pretending before November 1989, empirical documentation of any change in attitudes is practically impossible. Our data do not differentiate formal, pretended activities from any others. Nevertheless, the seemingly "astute" attitude to the system described above has been developing for 40 years on the basis of actual life experience. Cheating the system has become an integral part of one's survival, and it would be naive to anticipate any quick remedies and changes, particularly if one considers the inevitable economic problems that lie ahead.

It is beyond doubt that a thumping majority of the population rejected the old system quite spontaneously and vehemently. As conveyed by one of the main preelection slogans—"Whoever does not vote, votes for evil" (i.e., the communist regime)—the general elections had a demonstrative character. Fully 96% of the electorate turned out, and the Communist Party received only 13% of the votes. The local elections in November 1990 had a turnout of approximately 70%, which, however, cannot be interpreted merely as a decline in interest on the part of the population. The fundamental question of the general elections, "whether to restore the old system," was relatively simple to answer. In the local elections, on the other hand, the electorate faced a more complex question: "which system, which means, and which people to choose in specific local conditions." We are of the opinion that the lower turnout at the local elections stemmed from the fact that many voters were not able to answer this question. First, they were not in the habit of dealing with such issues, and the preelection campaign did little to clarify who was going to enforce what and by which means.

The complexity of the problems ahead, together with a complete lack of experience with activities of public life, also dampens the desire of people for public office. In September 1990, only 2% of the respondents in the Czech republic and 4% in the Slovak republic, were ready to run for a public office such as that of a parliamentary deputy (*Lidové noviny,* 1990a, p. 2), as compared to 40% in both republics immediately after the November Revolution (AISA, 1990b).

Discussing political attitudes and activities, one cannot disregard the nationality-related issues that complicate the whole development in Czechoslovakia. Such matters include the dispute over the very name of the state, the powers of the two republics versus the federal government, and speculations over the possible separation of Slovakia. Nationality problems have reemerged as issues in practically all countries of the former Soviet bloc, though they admittedly have quite a different and perhaps less dangerous character in Czechoslovakia than, say, in Yugoslavia and the U.S.S.R. In Czechoslovakia, the heart of the matter has political and economic dimensions, the analysis of which is beyond the scope of this contribution. In no case are mass nationalistic feelings involved.

A survey in November 1990 (*Lidové noviny,* 1990b, p. 2) showed that 74% of the inhabitants of the Czech lands and 70% in Slovakia considered the federal question a grand game of the politicians, not a matter reflecting the concerns of ordinary people. In an opinion poll two months later, 81% of the respondents in Czech lands still believed that ordinary people in Slovakia desired to live together with Czechs in a common state, and vice versa: the response was the same in Slovakia (*Informace IVVM,* 1991c, p. 2).

Nevertheless, there are reasons for some dissatisfaction on both sides. The scheme of equalization of Czech and Slovak economic standards gave priority to investment in originally backward Slovakia, where nowadays the technological base is more modern than in Czech lands. Therefore, the Czechs tend to consider the Slovaks ungrateful and even express a "let-them-go-if-they-want-to" attitude. For their part, the Slovak politicians quite rightfully argue that Prague has controlled economic policy since 1918 irrespective of Slovakia's specific character in terms of labor force and natural resources and that the manufacture of finished products tends to take place in Bohemia rather than Slovakia, where production is focused mostly on spare parts for Czech industry. The situation is further complicated by the fact that a large part of the Czechoslovak armaments industry, which is being drastically reduced, is situated in Slovakia. In general, one can say that fears of the transition period's negative impact on the economy are greater in Slovakia than in Czech lands. This anxiety has certainly contributed to a conviction that Slovaks must solve their problems themselves, independently of Czechs. In one survey conducted in November 1990, 65% of the respondents in Czech lands and 58% in Slovakia believed that their respective republic pays for the other (*Lidové noviny*, 1990b, p. 2). But because of an overzealous campaign run by Slovak politicians and supported by the mass media, the reverse ratio was registered three months later: 68% of the respondents in Czech lands and 71% in Slovakia believed that the other republic enjoyed the advantage (*Respekt*, 1991, p. 5).

"Separatist" attitudes are, for the time being, held only by a minority in both republics. The continual nationalistic campaign in Slovakia clearly suggested a dangerous outcome. In January 1991 only 3% of the Czech respondents and 9% of Slovak respondents expressed support for the creation of two independent states, but by February 1991 the figures had increased to 9% and 22%, respectively (*Informace IVVM*, 1991c, p. 2).

As a result, part of the population feels disappointed and suspicious that those in leading positions were only reshuffled while everything remained the same for *us*. According to research of September 1990s, 29% of the respondents in the Czech republic and 43% in the Slovak republic were of the opinion that "since November 1989, new people have taken power and have occupied profitable posts and positions, but otherwise nothing has changed" (*Lidové noviny*, 1990a, p. 2).

We found this skepticism again two months later, when only 18% of the respondents declared that they would be willing to protest a government's measure if it jeopardized the interests of most citizens. More than half of respondents chose the answer: "I would like to do something in such a case but I can't" (*Informace IVVM*, 1991d, p. 1). Deeply rooted disillusionment about making a positive contribution to political and public life is evident again. Helplessness and hopelessness are creeping back.

* * *

We find the situation in Czechoslovakia dangerous. Many representatives of the previous communist regime are still in power in various spheres of economic and political life. The social consciousness of many people as described in this chapter is the very condition that supporters of the previous regime long for because it would aid their efforts to make the transition to a market economy as difficult as possible. We believe that the socialist regime in its most oppressive form is defunct now. But, unfortunately, that does not mean that the bureaucratic system itself has been overcome as well. The tendencies to maintain central control are still quite alive. Together with people's stereotypes refined over the last 20 years, they appear to be a danger that should not be ignored. From this point of view, we do not find that Czechoslovakia is significantly better off than her neighbors.

REFERENCES

AISA. (1990a). *Československo-květen 1990: zpráva z vězkumu* [Czechoslovakia—May 1990: Research report]. Prague: Association for Independent Social Analysis.

AISA. (1990b). *Československo-leden 1990: zpráva z výzkumu* [Czechoslovakia—January 1990: Research report]. Prague: Association for Independent Social Analysis.

Beskid L., & Tuček, M. (1990). Sociální diferenciace v materiální situaci obyvatel Polska a Československa [Social differentiation of the material situation of citizens in Poland and Czechoslovakia]. *Sociologický časopis*, No. 1-2, 91-109.

Bondyová J., & Petrášková V. (1987). K vývoji životná úrovně Československa [The development of the standard of living in Czechoslovakia]. *Statistika*, No. 2, 49-60.

Czechoslovak Academy of Sciences. (1990a). *Ekonomická očekáváni a postoje I* [Economic expectation and attitudes I]. Survey carried out by the Center of Empirical Researches STEM, Institute of Sociology, Prague.

Czechoslovak Academy of Sciences. (1990b). *Economická očekávani a postoje II* [Economic expectation and attitudes II]. Survey carried out by the Center of Empirical Researches STEM, Institute of Sociology, Prague.

Czechoslovak Academy of Sciences. (1988). *Hodnotové orientace mládeže* [Preferences of young people]. Survey carried out by the Institute for Philosophy and Sociology, Czechoslovak Academy of Sciences, Prague.

Czechoslovak Academy of Sciences. (1984). *Třídní a sociální struktura v* ČSSR 1984 [Class and social structure in Czechoslovakia 1984]. Survey carried out by the Institute for Philosophy and Sociology, Czechoslovak Academy of Sciences, Prague.

Czechoslovak Academy of Sciences. (1983). *Diferenciačná procesy a perspektivy rozvoje naši společnosti* [Processes of differentiation and prospect of societal development]. Survey carried out by the Institute for Philosophy and Sociology, Czechoslovak Academy of Sciences, Prague.

Czechoslovak Academy of Sciences. (1978). *Třídní a sociální struktura v* ČSSR 1978 [Class and social structure in Czechoslovakia 1978]. Survey carried out by the Institute for Philosophy and Sociology, Czechoslovak Academy of Sciences, Prague.

Filipcová, B. (1990). Československo—výkonová společnost? [Czechoslovakia—An achievement society?]. *Sociologický časopis*, No. 5, 284-289.

Hochmaulová, D. (1987). Studium na středních školách ČSSR očima statistiky [Grammar school students in Czechoslovakia from the statistical point of view]. *Statistika*, No. 2, 86-89.

Informace IVVM. (1991a, March). *Zájem o aukce v rámci malé privatizace.* [Interest in auctions in terms of the privatization of small business].

Informace IVVM. (1991b, March). *Zájem o investiční kupóny* [Interest in investment coupons].

Informace IVVM. (1991c, January). *Názory čs. veřejnosti na vztahy* Čechu· a Slováku· na a federaci [Public opinion on the relations between Czechs and Slovaks and on the federation].

Informace IVVM. (1990d, January 20). *Chtějí u nás lidé vystupovat radikálně?* [Do people in this country want to act radically?].

Institut pro výzkum veřejného mínění. (1991, April). *Názory* na liberalizaci cen [Public opinion poll on price liberalization]. Prague: Institut pro vzkum veejnho m!nn!.

Institut pro výzkum veřejného mínění. (1990a). *Názory ekonomicky aktivních občanů na rezervy v Československé ekonomice* [Economically active citizens' opinion on reserves in the Czechoslovak economy]. Prague: Institut pro výzkum veřejného mínění.

Institut pro výzkum veřejného mínění. (1990b). *Názory na úplatkáství* [Public opinion on bribery]. Prague: Institut pro výzkum veřejného míněmi.

Institut pro vyzkum veřejného mínění. (1989). *Názory občanů na vybrané problémy životní úrovné v* ČSSR [Public opinion on specific life standard problems in Czechoslovakia]. Prague: Institut pro vyzkum večejného mínění.

Institut pro výzkum veřejného mínění. (1987). *Názory mladých na jejich perspektivy a uplatně ní při řízení* [The opinion of youth on their perspectives and possibilities to participate in management]. Prague: Institut pro výzkum veřejného míněmí.

Kaňa, M. (1990). Lidi pro lidi [People for people]. *Hospodářské noviny,* No. 1, 5.

Lidové noviny. (1990a, October). *Pokles du˙veřy pokračuje* [The decline in confidence continues] (pp. 1-2).

Lidové noviny. (1990b, November). *Chceme silnou federaci* [We demand a powerful federation] (pp. 1-2).

Miková, Z. (1989). Strategie ekonomického chování domácností [Economic behavior strategies of households]. In M. Tucek et al. (Eds.), *Společenské třídy, sociální vztahy a sociální aktivity v současné československé společnosti* (pp. 42-75). Prague: Institute for Philosophy and Sociology, Czechoslovak Academy of Sciences.

Respekt. (1991, No. 16). *Jiná společnost, jiné tužby* [Different society, different cravings] (pp. 5-6).

Slejška, D. (1990). Hodnotová sféra pod vlivem stagnace a tendence jejího vývoje od listopadu 1989 [The realm of values under the influence of stagnation and trends in its further development after November 1989]. *Sociologický časopis,* No. 4, 317-320.

Světový almanach [World almanac]. (1965). Prague: Státní nakladatelství politické literaturs (SNPL).

STRUCTURAL, ECONOMIC, POLITICAL, AND SOCIAL CHANGE IN EASTERN GERMANY, AND SHIFTS IN INDIVIDUAL VALUE SYSTEMS

Toni Hahn and Irene Zierke

In the 1980s, a clear contradiction between the necessity for social action and the possibility for public debate in the social system of the German Democratic Republic (GDR) crystallized. Granted only limited political and material maneuvering room, many GDR citizens concentrated increasingly on their private lives. Individual and group-specific niches emerged in the different spheres of life, and identification with socialism as it was actually practiced in the GDR diminished. These changes were ultimately reflected in the majority vote for unification with the Federal Republic of Germany (FRG) in March 1990.

MAJOR ASPECTS OF POLITICAL, ECONOMIC, AND SOCIAL STRUCTURE IN THE GDR

Structural shifts in the GDR and their interpretation must be seen in the context of developments after 1945, in particular, the integration of the GDR into the system of socialist states. An important factor was the interest of the western state system in the existence of two German states, and in corresponding policies towards the GDR.

An early structural change in the GDR occurred in mid-June 1953. By that time, the necessary payment of reparations to the Soviet Union and the administrative manipulation of work rates had caused stagnation and had exacerbated living conditions. The motives behind the uprising that resulted on June 17 were thus mainly economic. The corrections made in the thrust of some policies eventually eased the hardships somewhat (see Mayer, 1991).

But on the whole the 1950s, a time when open borders and full freedom of travel still existed, and the 1960s were characterized by the reliance upon the persuasive power of normative values and the behavior-modifying role of socialist ideas (the "Ten Commandments of Socialist Morals and Ethics"). The failure of this concept, which for all intents and purposes was admitted in the political and military act of closing the borders between the GDR and the FRG and between East and West Berlin on August 13, 1961, forced a reorientation, especially since stopping the "demographic drain" did nothing on its own to spur the desired economic upturn. Beginning in the 1970s, the leadership of East Germany's ruling political party, the Socialist Unity Party of Germany (SED), hoped to activate commitment to socialist values in order to cultivate politically and economically supportive behavior. This goal was to be achieved by promoting loyalty, particularly through greater orientation to people's social needs and to improvements in their social and material circumstances. The approach did have a measure of success, at least up to the late 1970s and early 1980s.

Despite steady improvements in the standard of living, however, the modification of strategy and its concomitant structural measures ultimately could not achieve the intended stabilization and culmination of everyday socialist conditions. The nature of the changes undertaken led to the destabilization and, finally, the dissolution of the social system. Indeed, the collapse was promoted by the system's production of official ideology and values, and by the increasing contrast between them and the changing experiences of the citizens in their economic and political roles in East German life.

Internal political obstacles to structural change were reinforced by the external conditions and constraints of the conflict between systems, which was shifting ever more to economic aspects. Other essential factors were the GDR's political commitments to and dependence on the socialist countries, especially the Soviet Union. What did these inconsistent changes involve, and what effect did they have?

1. Initially, conditions improved, but the orientation to economic growth and acceleration of scientific and technological progress did little to boost efficiency and productivity. First, the economic strategy was not aimed at facilitating necessary changes in economic or employment structures according to market principles, and it was not conceived to ensure efficiency and a relation

between commodities and money. Second, it never resulted in an international division of labor, especially an economic integration of the socialist countries. In addition, the political strategy underlying the development of the socialist state steadily expanded the share of human and material resources that were unproductively, even destructively, invested in the security, state, and party apparatuses. In short, the economy was not subject to self-regulation based on economic criteria. It was politically guided without adequate economic expertise, particularly at the higher echelons.

2. Structural change in the economy stalled because democratization of the economy never took place. "Ownership by the people" existed only in formal terms; in reality, the state controlled both the type and scope of production (see Wielgohs, 1988). Despite the state's affirmations of democratic production, producers never exercised real control over their production conditions. Democratic participation in decisions about production targets and concepts was, at best, only partial in the country's economic units. Little or no creative opportunity was given to improve efficiency. The workers' indisputable identification with the firm was based less on experience as owners than on collegial bonds and the advantages accruing from the firm's fringe benefits. There was no public forum for the articulation of diverging economic visions, strategies, and interests. No such mechanism existed for exploring the consequences of policy variations. Effective forms of organization for shaping democratic opinion and expression among the "common owners" were unable to develop on any level.

The results of many sociological studies over the last two decades have verified this lack of economic and industrial democracy. Although opportunity to participate in formal discussion about the plan, to promote competition, and to make new suggestions were always shown to be high, the majority of people had little say in decisions concerning work and production conditions, particularly about the introduction of new technology. Even less opportunity for participation existed when it came to deciding on the economic, social, and ecological strategies to be pursued in society.

3. Aimed at "perfecting" the socioeconomic system, the "unity of economic and social policy" for the improvement of the living conditions of all members of society elicited less and less support in the population from the mid-1980s on. This policy gradually failed to live up to its original purpose, which had been to prove the superiority of the socialist system in forging humanistic social relations and to draw on these social relations to release superior forces for economic growth. Influenced in part by changes in social structures in other socialist countries (*perestroika* and *glasnost*), the population of the GDR became increasingly aware that the country's economic policy was neither economically effective (and so could not effectively widen society's scope) nor sufficiently compatible with social or ecological needs. The social policy neither achieved its social objectives (more social justice and a better quality of life

for all) nor became effective as a driving force for improvements in performance and economic growth. Positive interaction of economic and social policy remained elusive.

4.   The effort to achieve the desired unity of economic and social policy entailed decisions affecting the relations between savings and consumption; investment priorities; the relative share of social and individual consumption; and the structural, material, and human aspects of subsidies for prices, rents, and tariffs. Those decisions all had two decisive aims: To tie the citizens to the state and its dominant organ of power—the SED—and to activate the population for the fulfillment of the party's policies. The circumstances worked against this intention. The beneficiaries of this social policy were treated as the mere objects of a system of measures magnanimously bestowed from above. The stable prices, housing programs, secure jobs, and other things that members of society had made possible through their own work were supposed to be seen by them as a munificent gift. They were expected to reward this generosity with committed and efficient work behavior. In fact, citizens could not feel themselves to be the ones shaping their own social relations. They saw less and less reason to be grateful for basic social rights and benefits provided under circumstances with which they were increasingly dissatisfied.

5.   The commitment to ensuring basic social rights and a basic level of social existence for all was only partially realized. To be sure, a number of basic human rights that could not be taken for granted in other social systems were everyday reality in the GDR. For instance, there was no homelessness, no indications of accumulated poverty that marginalizes people in society. Everyone was guaranteed vocational training and a job, albeit not always in a person's desired field. Public child-care facilities, specially funded access to education, and special working-hour arrangements enabled women to avoid interrupting their careers, become economically independent, and develop their sense of self-worth. Nevertheless, the structural changes in the economic and social system that were initiated in the 1970s were never more than partial, because they did not extend to the political system.

Specifically, certain human and legal rights (freedom of travel, freedom of information, freedom of expression, and protection from arbitrary administrative actions) were largely absent as a basic premise for dignified existence in socialist society. Further, there was little opportunity to influence one's current or future living conditions and social status through one's own efforts. Although a job was guaranteed to everyone, there were no universally accepted conditions for job performance and the use of one's skills. The principles of evaluating a person's work according to specific performance criteria and paying workers according to their needs was similarly ignored. The performance principle—remuneration according to work actually done—functioned only partially, if at all. The effect was that hard work did little or nothing to influence one's social advancement. In this way, personal interest in performing well was dampened. For some people, sources of income other than one's primary occupation played a dominant role in determining living standards.

Economic and social policy proved unable to achieve the goal of increasing social justice (meaning across-the-board equalization of life's basic social conditions, alongside a variety of social differentiations based on performance). On the contrary, being deprived of the "right to social inequality based on performance" reproduced a constant tendency toward leveling in social life. This leveling, however, did not create any real equality of opportunity in life. Unjustified social differences increased because, first, not everyone had equal opportunity to take advantage of social benefits intended for all. State subsidies (*die zweite Lohntüte*) were received by everyone regardless of economic and social position. For example, each household's share of rent subsidies ranged from 0 to 400 East German Marks per month. Second, outright abuse of the social safety net contributed to distortions in the system. Third, some groups and individuals had privileged access to goods and services, and even to certain personal freedoms such as the freedom to travel. Fourth, there were conditions that limited and even precluded fundamental opportunities for development among certain social groups (low achievers, the handicapped, a large share of the GDR's senior citizens, single parents, the socially endangered, dissenters, and people leading alternative lifestyles). Furthermore, some individuals happened to have access to the second currency in Germany, while others did not, and only some people were able to take part in the shadow economy. Finally, social mobility had more or less ended in the 1980s.

6. To increase productivity in the national economy, a decision was made to stress basic innovation and high technology, especially through the development of microelectronics. This approach did not lead to new technological production methods or boost productivity, however, because traditional East German industries such as machine-building, chemicals, and agriculture were almost impervious to change.

One reason for the bottlenecks was a contradiction within the system. In terms of skills and education, the main resource of economically and socially effective structural change—the work force—was very advanced. By the end of the 1980s, only 10% of the country's employed persons had not completed vocational training, 11% were college graduates, and 15% were graduates of technical schools. However, this expertise was inadequate for meeting the demands of the modernization that was necessary. It often lay fallow for lack of organizational and material essentials for innovation and its subsequent translation into productivity.

A second obstacle to improvement in the national economy was a lack of resources to replenish capital funds. Between 1982 and 1986, 88% of the GDR's investment went into maintaining basic infrastructure. After 1970, only 1% of the country's capital funds was renewed annually. In the 1980s, the conditions for maintaining the national economy eroded further. The growth rate in the GNP (an annual average of 4.6%) was used mainly to stabilize foreign trade. Accumulation and gross investment stagnated and/or declined increasingly at the cost of the natural environment and working conditions.

Although many obstacles in the working world were eliminated after 1970, the trend reversed itself after the mid-1980s. In fact, new burdens developed, particularly the growing exposure to health hazards at many work places. In 1988, nearly one-quarter of East Germany's work force was employed in hazardous jobs. Among production workers the share was 37%. Environmental damage worsened dramatically, particularly given the methods of energy production and the structure of the chemical industries. In other words, structural developments since the 1970s not only led to declining rates of growth in the 1980s, but also undermined the sources of growth and the foundation of social existence in general.

Over and above these internal conditions, the GDR's predicament must be seen in the context of a global escalation of problems. The deep contradiction between economic and social interests of the present, on the one hand, and ecological and social interests of the future, on the other hand, is no less dramatic for a society like the old FRG than for the former GDR. For the latter, however, the socioeconomic and political preconditions for stabilizing the system internally proved to conflict with those for meeting the increasing demands of global development, universal productive forces, and the conservation of nature.

It is true that the evolutionary structural change in the 1970s and 1980s had led to certain advances and to an improvement in the condition of the population, especially in comparison to other socialist countries. But the prosperity enjoyed by a large part of the population in West Germany, the East German's growing awareness of the country's democratic and constitutional shortcomings and social injustices, the stagnation of economic growth, and the visible deterioration in the GDR's infrastructure and natural environment led to growing dissatisfaction and diminishing loyalty among the citizenry and, finally, to the crisis in the legitimacy of the East German system. In view of the need to carry out widely desired reforms, the ignorance and rigidity reflected in the existing policies only worsened the problems.

SIMILARITIES AND DIFFERENCES IN SYSTEMS OF VALUES AND NEEDS

The development of GDR society was accompanied by a strong ambivalence toward socialist values. Ever greater difficulty in achieving personal aspirations in life was rooted, for example, in a daily inability to satisfy basic needs, the limitations that the political system placed on opportunities to articulate these shortcomings, and the constraints that the economic system placed on the individual's attempts to cope with them. The officially proclaimed "Basic Values of Socialism," which were politically anchored in the country's educational system, cultural life, and mass media, were an attempt by the party leadership and state to conceal material, intellectual, and political sanctions against a diversified way of life determined by the individual or the group.

Through a shift in the focus of policy, the aspirations of the people were really supposed to become the focal point of the state's objectives. An increase in the satisfaction of people's material, intellectual, and cultural needs was supposed to be the main aim of policy. Basic social rights, guaranteed livelihood, social justice, collectivity, and individuality were supposed to be the determining factors of socialist life. As achievements and merits of socialism, these facets of life were meant to prove the superiority of the system. Pluralism of values was rejected on principle because conflicts of interest between actors in socialism (society, groups, individuals) and within one and the same individual were ignored.

The social dissemination and individual assimilation of "socialist" values was not uniform, however. There was a more or less tacit agreement to accept officially pronounced humanitarian values (freedom, justice, human dignity) as ideal values, while increasingly doubting their actual validity. Such ambivalence was reinforced by European events such as the invasion of Czechoslovakia by Warsaw Pact troops in 1968, the Helsinki conference for freedom and human rights in the mid-1970s, and the new policies in the Soviet Union in the mid-1980s. The lack of personal freedom and the neglect of democracy as a basic value became the subject of ever wider critical reflection.

Nevertheless, there were no public or official protests against the social structures that caused these shortcomings. They had been put into place in such a way that critics of real socialism could not articulate themselves. Passive and "blackmailed loyalty expressed in social behavior" was created (Hanf, 1991, p. 75). Public action, public expression of one's thought, and pluralistic individual development of cultural capital were thereby limited, and ultimately did little to diversify economic and social positions even when the actors were part of the political system.

It was on this basis that the private sphere blossomed in many different ways, something that should not be simply equated with trends toward individualization. For many people, restrictions on certain values were compensated for by the actual relationships achieved in everyday life and by the existence of various, partly outmoded basic social rights such as work, education, a home, and health (see Institut für Soziologie und Sozialpolitik, 1990a). Some people hoped for a step-by-step expansion of the latitude for action. Others resigned themselves to the situation and withdrew, neither refusing the advantages of the social order nor exposing themselves to the risks of resisting the political order. A significant share of the population had something to lose and professed either formal or sincere support for the system, which some wanted to improve. Only a few attempted to resist the existing social structures through alternative thinking and life styles. Others passively rejected the system, often for both political and economic reasons. Some of these various forms of conformity and resistance were generation-specific (see Niethammer, 1990), and were simultaneously linked with different social milieus.

Empirical studies in the 1980s at least partially support these statements. Socially proclaimed values were not wholly embraced by the general population. This was true of the high value placed on social relations and mutual help (family, work collective, and other social contacts) as well as the preservation of freedom. In other areas of life, living conditions defied attempts to satisfy needs adequately. Specifically, political restrictions on freedom of expression and on organization within nonprofit or other associations, reduced material and financial opportunities, and the lack of supply structures thwarted efforts to meet consumer demand. Lack of opportunity to obtain various kinds of comprehensive information, to clean up the environment, experience self-actualization at one's job, and enjoy modern living were seen as particularly severe (see Institut für Soziologie und Sozialpolitik, 1990b).

In addition, long working hours, the great amount of additional commuting time needed, and the multitude of household tasks to be done—all of which had not changed for two decades—left little genuinely free time for recreation and leisure (see *Sozialreport 1990*). This factor only further frustrated attempts to satisfy needs, the variety of which had continued to grow over the years. Since 1968, daily work time had remained at 8 3/4 hours for most of the population. In 1989, 62.3% of the population worked 43 3/4 hours per week, and 7% worked 42 hours.

Under these living conditions, people adapted to existing circumstances by circumventing them and by developing personal relations in their private spheres, extending their knowledge and skills, and working towards their own goals. This way of life appeared at many levels. Most citizens of the GDR found freedom, family, and work to be personally significant. Only for a minority was it true that "real life begins only with free time." On the average, professional aspirations of the population revolved around a good income, social contact with colleagues, and the use and recognition of one's skills. The feeling of really accomplishing something professionally, having an interesting job, and having work properly recognized was less pronounced than these aspirations.

Measurable structural patterns of subjective value orientations (see Table 1) suggest that "materialist" and "postmaterialist" orientations were closely linked in the minds of GDR citizens, and that there had been a synthesis of career and family, work and enjoyment of life, and achievement and leisure.

Table 1.   Ranking of Value Orientations in the Personal
Lives of East German Citizens Between 1973 and 1990

Value Orientation	LIS 73[a]	Wohngebiete 81[b]	WiTAL 83[c]	BED 88[d]	Leben 90[e]
Love/family	1 (1)[f]	1 (2)	1 (2)	1 (3)	2 (7)
Material affluence	2 (2)	5 (7)	4 (9)	...[g]	5 (15)
Career/work	3 (4)	2 (3)	2 (5)	4 (12)	1 (5)
Friends/contacts	4 (5)	3 (5)	3 (8)	2 (10)	...[g]
Social involvement	5 (7)	4 (6)	7 (13)	5 (20)	...[g]
Education	6 (8)	6 (8)	5 (11)	3 (9)	4 (12)
Democratic influence	7 (9)	7 (9)	6 (12)	...[g]	3 (8)
Upward social mobility	8 (10)	8 (11)	8 (14)	...[g]	...[g]

Notes: [a] Employed persons in Berlin, 10 indicators.
[b] 1,000 respondents in 7 residential areas, 11 indicators.
[c] 1,000 employees in the science and industry, 14 indicators.
[d] Approximately 500 persons employed in industry, 21 indicators.
[e] 2,000 respondents in the German Democratic Republic, 17 indicators.
[f] Rank of the value orientation in the entire sequence of indicators used in the respective studies.
[g] Not asked in study.

Such an assumption would be premature and overgeneralized. From the 1970s on, East German society was characterized by a "self-contained" social structure (see Niethammer, 1988; Thomas, 1989), very limited economic and material potential, and political restrictions. Differentiations between groups with distinguishable value priorities were, therefore, less developed, or at least less effective, than in the FRG. Presumably, however, a concentration of postmaterialist orientations was detectable among the actors in the grass-roots movements in the former GDR (see Schulz & Wielgohs, 1990). An analysis of the biographies of these citizens could provide insight into determinants of such value structures (see Schweigel, Segert, & Zierke, 1992).

Given the methods used in the social sciences in the GDR, empirical documentation of value and need structures remained at the phenomenological level—that of consciously manifested aspirations, expectations, and effort. Internalized patterns of values and priorities were scarcely registered (see Hahn, 1985). Relatively poor conditions for actually realizing certain value orientations can effect shifts in *observable* expressions of value priorities. For example, job insecurity or unemployment can enhance the value one attaches to a job without there being any real change in one's values or their interrelations. The dominant value repeatedly accorded the environment in recent years did not necessarily mean that environmental orientations were central in the organization and structure of the individual's way of life. Such methodological problems make it difficult to portray different value types. It is only possible to convey priorities within value structures.[1]

In various empirical studies, it has been noted that achieving "a higher position in society" was not a value in most cases. This finding must be interpreted as an expression of social equality that had led to leveling, and that precluded a distribution of social positions according to performance or competence. In addition, managerial functions and the higher positions associated with them generally entailed political connections and responsibilities that not everyone was prepared to accept.

Moreover, the subjective value attached to democratic participation in shaping society was low on the whole, a rank that pointed to lack of identification and legitimation. Although much work was done in neighborhood and parents' associations, value patterns reflected the experience that the individual and community were impotent against entrenched power structures, and that many socially oriented initiatives were ineffective. Most citizens derived little benefit from "socialist" democracy even though the concept of having the individual shape his or her own life was firmly anchored in it. As a result of the system's increasing lack of responsiveness—expressed in the late 1980s in the slogan "Socialism in the Colors of the GDR"—political structures remained sacrosanct. Official proclamations about the population's participation and self-determination starkly contrasted with restrictions on those very values, and the gap between propounded and actual value conceptions and norms of everyday behavior continued to widen perceptibly.

Simultaneously, the latitude for achieving one's chosen goals in life narrowed. With respect to the equality of the sexes and equal rights for women, there was a certain agreement between the societal vision and the value conceptions adopted by the individual. For all the inequalities that remained between the genders in the GDR, a progressive shift was made in the understanding of gender roles in recent decades. At the same time, sociological studies showed discrepancies, as in women's self-confident demands for their rights. The way in which women were supported frequently led to a consolidation or reinforcement of old patterns in household and family routines, making professional advancement for women more difficult. It also often meant that women with qualifications equal to those of men occupied less demanding positions with inferior pay. To enable women to deal with the wide range of demands in various areas of life, the state granted them special concessions that did not encroach fundamentally upon the patriarchal family structure (see *Frauenreport,* 1990, p. 138).

Let us summarize the results of quantitative and qualitative research in the GDR. With the system's increasing isolation, the blocking of distinctions between social positions, an administrated economy based on scarcity, and political patronization, there was a consolidation of ways of thinking aimed at establishing and maintaining basic social rights, basic livelihoods, material prosperity, and meaningful fulfillment at work and in the family. Simultaneously, certain developments in West Europe were copied. There were isolated cases in which the exigencies of modernization in different spheres of life promoted aspirations for individual mobility, the opportunity to exert influence on society, and a universal solution of global problems.

CHANGE IN INDIVIDUAL LIFE STYLES AND GOALS

For all the distinctions between the GDR's social groups, this constellation of disillusionment, aloofness, or rejection spawned by the official value system became predominant in the final years of the country. As a result, many people began to pursue their own goals in life and developed their own life styles. The noticeable retreat into the circle of family, friends, and relations stemmed from unfulfilled expectations of work and from the sociopolitical reality of the GDR. In these circles social policy was discussed, supply shortages were dealt with, social contacts were nurtured, and privacy was achieved. Identifiable trends toward individualization sprang in part from these unmet social needs. They were also due to the growth and differentiation of education, skills, and cultural experience and the pluralization of life styles.

The way in which former citizens of the GDR are dealing with their new situation in life shows that for the last 20 years they had been embedded in a system offering limited alternatives for action. Despite all the variations on the theme, one particular contradiction seems to be typical in the social biographies of most GDR citizens. On the one hand, everyday life was determined by the fact that one had a guaranteed job, that one's basic material needs were met relatively well regardless of one's work or initiative, and that one actually experienced and was increasingly aware of the individual's impotence in the face of social structures both on and off the job. In various ways, then, these citizens are unprepared for the context of social risk into which they have been thrust. In a social system that provides for one's needs, the awareness of the importance of the individual's efforts and personal responsibility for one's own social perspective was not well developed. Now that the social protection once guaranteed by the state can no longer be taken for granted, various sections of the population rank it—limitations and all— ahead of partnership and family for the first time (see *Sozialreport* 1990).

On the other hand, it was precisely because of the limited room for maneuver that everyday life in the GDR, both on and off the job, created the challenge to develop a certain amount of flexibility, ingenuity, initiative, and a certain type of solidarity. The purpose was to satisfy many nonbasic material needs and to realize various intellectual aspirations. This "training" could promote independence and self-initiated action of former East German citizens in the unified Germany.

There are indications of a consistent pattern in GDR experiences and behavior that cannot be simply ignored: a willingness to learn in general; among women, in particular, a willingness to become involved; the social acceptance of this attitude; and a reluctance to abandon the comfort, immobility, and risk-shy life styles that had become habit (see Hahn & Ehrhardt, 1990). But along with the punishment that their country's demise is inflicting upon them, there is a return to an awareness of the self. Features of individual and group ego are becoming increasingly pronounced in life plans and value orientations. Alternatives are being more consciously considered and embedded in plans of action.

Differences will emerge. Just as certain value structures and patterns of behavior dominated among individuals and social groups in former East German society, different patterns of behavior and life styles will develop under the new conditions. Depending on their previous life styles, individuals will find their own place or rebel against the system, some more actively or more passively than others, some acting on their own volition and others acting at the behest of others. In this way, certain patterns of behavior rooted in experience with the GDR will continue having an effect under the new conditions.

WORK

For citizens of the former GDR, the area of life to have undergone the greatest restructuring thus far is that fundamental sphere of everyday experience and activity—work. Most members of the population had to work to support themselves, and for most the right to work was tied just as much to the duty to work.

Empirical studies so far have pointed to inconsistencies regarding work-related needs. For one thing, a key factor in work-related needs was material security. Social connections and recognition were simultaneously linked with this (see Table 2). Past studies have found that the value an individual attached to work was determined essentially by professional demands, social connections, independence, creativity, and opportunities to earn. Unemployment and the risk of losing one's job significantly increase the weight of all work-related aspects. Factors hindering identification with work, such as poor conditions for good work and for the application of one's skills, become less important in a subjective evaluation.

For another thing, groups within the work force had become critical of their working conditions and the content of their work since the mid-1980s. Long, inefficient working hours, lack of professional mobility, traditional and hierarchical production structures, remuneration not based on performance, and mental and physical strain due to obsolete technology and poorly organized work intensified dissatisfaction with work and further limited the willingness to work, especially in industry. The political consequences of these

Table 2.   "What Would You Miss if You Were Absent From the Work Process for a Long Period?" (1983).[a] "As a Result of Losing Your Job?" (1990).[b]

Aspect Missed	Employed Persons 1983		Unemployed Persons 1990	
	Very Much	Pretty Much	Very Much	Pretty Much
Having the accustomed income	37	37	59	30
Having contact with colleagues	25	50	45	34
Feeling useful	22	34	49	32
Having the chance to shape and change something	21	34	35	32
Experiencing success	19	38	33	38
Using my skills	17	40	39	43
Carrying responsibility	11	27	28	33

Notes: [a] Asked of 1,000 persons employed in industry or business in East Berlin and its environs, 1983.
   [b] Asked of 225 unemployed persons in East Berlin, December 1990.

work-related developments, which were also taking in place in other spheres, were largely ignored.

Part of the hope that citizens of the former GDR associated with the introduction of market principles is that efficiency, working conditions, and recognition of work would improve. In January 1990 one-third of the respondents in a representative survey thought that the conditions for work at which one felt good would get better (see *Sozialreport 1990*). The expectations for most other spheres of life were also significantly more optimistic. Long-neglected working conditions will not change overnight. Only 58% of the respondents indicated that they were satisfied or very satisfied on the whole with their work, although here, as in previous studies, the attempt to contribute something oneself was ranked first among a wide variety of desired activities (see *Sozialreport 1990*).

Lastly, a clear ambivalence is registered, especially in the work sphere. Although the centrality of work for citizens of the GDR was documented empirically (see Habich, Landua, & Priller, 1991), it was precisely in the world of work that a large part of the labor force was patronized, an experience that would make independent action in a market economy more difficult. For example, Kern and Land (1991, p. 16) noted "the divergence between official institutions and the always informal practical actions taken by the work forces in their own interests," "distinct aloofness to political demands," and "attempts at ideological mobilization." Our assumption that the potential for independent representation and defense of one's interests is limited or absent must be discussed in a historical context.

DIFFERENCES IN ECONOMIC ACTION

Under the conditions created by the "unity of economic and social policy," similarities and differences developed in the scope (and alternatives) for action and the strategies of economic action available to the citizens of the GDR. There were five similarities: (a) the socioeconomic structures in society, which, as a rule, consisted of formal ownership by the people, a small amount of cooperative ownership, and little or no quantitative and qualitative latitude for the self-employed; (b) the right and duty to work, which were both reflected in the high employment rate, particularly for women, and in simultaneous hidden unemployment; (c) a basic, albeit low, level of social existence; (d) the fact that the producers had little influence on individual and social productivity even though they were formally the owners and, therefore, their own employers; and (e) the limited opportunities to determine one's standard of living legally through one's professional efforts or initiative.

Although the structures of this system severely restricted the scope of the economic citizen, a multidimensional range of economic behavior still existed. First, even under adverse conditions, professional commitment could be found in all strata alongside reluctance to work—even absenteeism. "Frequent absence from work" was a crime. Paragraph 249, which defined "criminally asocial behavior," was not repealed until December 1989. Second, regardless of work motivation, one's attitude toward achievement, and the respective working conditions, professional work was important to most employees not only for its economic significance as a livelihood, but also for its role in social integration and the establishment of identity. Economic interests and social needs were closely intertwined in this regard. Third, mobility (geographical, professional, and social) was rudimentary on the whole, but for some groups it was the rule, depending on the profession or function involved. Mobility was sometimes necessary for young people, particularly those from the countryside and towns. Fourth, because of the leveling of wages, significant gaps in services and the supply sectors, and the high value that material consumption had among citizens of the GDR, there arose various forms of paid and unpaid work that was done on the side (see Manz, 1990). For example, artisans and workers in particular frequently did not report income earned from work they performed in addition to their official jobs; and official second jobs were performed at all levels of all professional groups. They included extra work performed in and paid by the plant, handicraft work performed after hours, and work performed for an honorarium. To a greater or lesser extent, almost half of all employed people in the former GDR engaged in such work. Another form of paid or unpaid work done on the side was do-it-yourself activities, which became increasingly widespread in the final years of the GDR because of poor conditions in the service sector. Extensive gardening, building, and general home improvement was part of the weekend or holiday for many people. This work was often arranged for or performed during official working hours. Often paid and unpaid work on the side was also performed by women interested in working part-time in order to reconcile the career, family, and household demands upon them. At the end of 1989, about 30% of the women in the GDR were working reduced hours (see *Frauenreport 1990,* pp. 85-86). Lastly, illicit work in West Berlin and the FRG spread particularly after the border opened.

These various forms of a second economy were primarily an expression of the limited and limiting economic efficiency of the East German system. Ways to increase the economic base were sought both inside and outside the official economy, with the productive power and knowledge of the labor force's different groups being concentrated in peripheral sectors.

Disparities in personal circumstances used to mean that various forms of economic activity by which to improve one's lot in life were closed to part of the population, and that social inequality was increased. Under the new conditions, the premise is that unequal individual factors and past social status will have an even greater role than before in shaping economic behavior and the material situation of society. Moreover, it is assumed that some of the already existing peripheral social groups, whose socialization and capacity to act are limited, will grow. It is said that all economic citizens of the former GDR, through their respective strategies, day-to-day economic behaviors, and modes of integration in the formal and informal economy, sustained the existing economic and social structures. In other words, they also contributed (for the most part unconsciously) to undermining them.

THE CONFLICT-RIDDEN SEARCH FOR A NEW IDENTITY

In the life of the GDR citizen, the objective contradiction between stabilization and destabilization of the political and social system was particularly clear through his or her everyday behavior in and towards the state. Even the supportive behavior of the active citizens who consciously legitimated the state contributed to bringing about its increasing fragility and final crisis. And the citizens who rejected or merely tolerated the system, using their advantages and "accommodating" themselves, actually propped up these structures. Those who left the country were often in search of a higher standard of living.

The majority characteristically pursued their diverse political and organizational ties—membership in parties or mass organizations, social functions at various levels of these organizational structures, participation in competition, discussions of the plan, and further political education—more or less as duties and formalities, without necessarily identifying with what they were doing. In many of these widely cast political or quasi-political forms of organization, there was simultaneously broad commitment, particularly when specific social or cultural matters were concerned.

For many, the constraints on independent political and social organization were a great burden. Specific interests of particular groups could not be addressed. An organization for the handicapped could not be established, the founding of associations was obstructed, and new political parties or movements were not permitted. This rigidity promoted cooperation between dissidents under the roof of the Protestant church and its special role in the advent of the social upheaval in the GDR. Beyond the possibilities provided by the church, Gorbachev's reforms in the second half of the 1980s sparked informal political life in the GDR. Many found the courage to question social theories and strategies, and at least cautiously voiced these matters publicly. They also dared to develop concepts for fundamental change, concepts that not only touched on economic and social questions but also tackled the issue of coming to terms with the country's own history.

At the same time, the lack, or one-sidedness, of the treatment given the fascist past, the denial of the fact that the GDR, too, was a legacy of that part of German history, the consequences of unsolved social problems in the GDR, and the marginalization of certain segments of the population beset with problems of social integration came to be expressed in the development of radical right-wing tendencies. The official wall of silence only aided their reproduction, and prevented East German citizens from dealing with their own past.

On the whole, the degree to which East German citizens identified with the system declined sharply because of a relatively unsatisfactory material standard of living and the recognizable apologetics of the political rulers. For all the disaffection with everyday socialism, however, the expectations of state services were high. The people were used to the state coming to them with demands as well as services.

In a representative survey of East German citizens conducted in December 1989, 70% of the respondents still said they thought highly or quite highly of the idea of socialism (see *Spiegel, 1989*). In January 1990, an almost representative study (Berlin was not included) found that a mere 52% said it was important for them to live in the GDR (see *Sozialreport 1990*). A rapid revelation of economic, ecological, and political problems soon led to a preference for a western life style. Within months of November 9, 1989, the fundamental value structures were not actually altered, but conceptions of the ways to achieve a better society changed rapidly. At first, ideas of an inherent radical transformation of socialism with the perpetuation of two German states dominated, but the majority soon tended to think in terms of the GDR's accession to the FRG and the adoption of its social structures. That alternative was expected, above all, to enhance political participation, the environmental situation, the service system, the trade system, the legal system, and output.

However, this did not mean an unconditional acceptance of all principles of a market economy. The intention was to preserve achievements of formal East German socialism that did not exist in the same form in the FRG—specifically, the right to work, equality of men and women, the option of state-supported child care, different forms of care for the elderly, and a wide range of opportunities to participate in cultural and athletic activities. In the eyes of many people, the possibilities for grass-roots political and economic involvement that existed from November 1989 to March 1990 ought to be preserved and expanded. The new possibilities to determine one's own social existence and material quality of life are seen as particularly important, yet the new risks and limitations (e.g., for the weaker members of society) must not be overlooked.

NOTE

1. Similar methodological problems beset West German sociology. There, too, the relation between value orientations and observable behavior has not been entirely agreed upon. It is merely assumed subjectively by researchers and respondents. In comparison to GDR sociology, however, it has been possible to overcome mutually exclusive sets of value orientations (see, e.g., Diewald, 1989; Hillmann, 1989; Klages, Franz, & Herbert, 1987; Klipstein & Strümpel, 1984; Noelle-Neumann & Strümpel, 1984; and Scholz, 1987).

REFERENCES

Autorenkollektiv, under the direction of R. Weidig. (1988). *Sozialstruktur der DDR* [Social structure of the GDR]. Berlin: Dietz.

Diewald, M. (1989). *Der Wandel von Lebensformen und seine Folgen für die soziale Integration* [The change in ways of life and its impact on social integration] (WZB preprint, P89-104). Working Group on Corporate Social Accounting [*Sozialberichterstattung*]. Berlin: Wissenschaftszentrum Berlin für Sozialforschung.

Frauenreport '90 [Women's report '90]. (1990). Berlin: Verlag Die Wirtschaft Berlin.

Habich, R., Landua, D., & Priller, E. (1991). Geringere Lebenszufriedenheit in der ehemaligen DDR: Erste Ergebnisse der empirischen Wohlfahrtsforschung [Dwindling satisfaction with life in the former GDR: Initial results of empirical research on well-being]. *Informationsdienst soziale Indikatoren (ISI)*, 5, 1-4.

Hahn, T. (1985). *Motivation, Motivforschung, Motivtheorien* [Motivation, research on motives, theories of motivation]. Berlin: Deutscher Verlag der Wissenschaften.

Hahn, T., & Ehrhardt, G. (1990). Arbeitslosigkeit in der früheren DDR: Objektive Gegebenheiten und subjektive Wahrnehmung. Ergebnisse einer Fallstudie [Unemployment in the former GDR: Facts and perceptions from a case study]. *Berliner Journal für Soziologie, 3*, pp. 73-82.

Hanf, T. (1991). Modernisierung der Gesellschaft als sozialstrukturelles Problem [Modernization of society as a sociostructural problem]. *Berliner Journal für Soziologie* (Special Issue), 73-82.

Hillmann, K.-H. (1989). *Wertwandel* [Value change]. Darmstadt: Wissenschaftliche Buchgesellschaft.

Institut für Soziologie und Sozialpolitik. (1990a, November). Positionen zur sozialen Entwicklung in der DDR [Positions on social development in the GDR]. *Initiativeinformation Berlin*, *2*.

Institut für Soziologie und Sozialpolitik. (1990b). *Strukturelle Aspekte der Bedürfnisentwicklung in der ehemaligen DDR* [Structural aspects of the development of needs in the former GDR] (Unpublished Research Report). Berlin, Akademie der Wissenschaften.

Kern, H., & Land, R. (1991, 13 February). Der "Wasserkopf" oben und die "Taugenichtse" unten. Zur Mentalität von Arbeitern und Arbeiterinnen in der ehemaligen DDR. Im Mittelpunkt des Alltagslebens: Der Betrieb [Bloated at the top and good-for-nothing at the bottom: On the mentality of workers in the former GDR, with a look at the focus of life—The plant]. *Frankfurter Rundschau*, No. 37, pp. 16-17.

Klages, H., Franz, G., & Herbert, W. (1987). *Sozialpsychologie der Wohlfahrtsgesellschaft* [Social psychology of the welfare society]. Frankfurt on the Main: Campus.

Klipstein, M. v., & Strümpel, B. (1984). *Der Überdruss am Überfluss. Die Deutschen nach dem Wirtschaftswunder* [Great wealth, great weariness: The Germans after the economic miracle]. Munich: Günter Olzog.

Manz, G. (1990). "Schattenwirtschaft" in der DDR [The "shadow economy" in the GDR]. *Wirtschaftswissenschaft*, *2*, 219-229.

Mayer, H. (1991). *Der Turm von Babel, Erinnerungen an eine Deutsche Demokratische Republik* [The tower of Babel: Memories of a German Democratic Republic]. Frankfurt on the Main: Suhrkamp.

Niethammer, L. (1990). Das Volk der DDR und die Revolution. Versuch einer historischen Wahrnehmung der laufenden Ereignisse [The people of the GDR and the revolution: An attempt at a historical perception of ongoing events]. In C. Schüddekopf (Ed.), *Wir sind das Volk! Flugschriften, Aufrufe und Texte einer deutschen Revolution* (pp. 251-279). Reinbek: Rowohlt.

————. (1988). Annäherung an den Wandel. Auf der Suche nach der volkseigenen Erfahrung in der Industrieprovinz der DDR [Rendezvous with change: In search of the people's own experience in the backward industrial world of the GDR]. In A. Lüdtke (Ed.), *Alltagsgeschichte. Zur Rekonstruktion historischer Erfahrungen und Lebensweisen* (pp. 19-66). Frankfurt on the Main: Campus.

Noelle-Neumann, E., & Strümpel, B. (1984). *Macht Arbeit krank? Macht Arbeit glücklich?* [Work: Pathogen or pleasure?]. Munich: Piper.

Scholz, J. (1987). *Wertwandel und Wirtschaftskultur* [Value change and economic culture]. Munich: C.H. Beck.

Schweigel, K., Segert, A., & Zierke, I. (1992). Alter Wein in neuen Schläuchen? Lebensstil- und Milieuforschung in Ostdeutschland [Old wine in new bottles? Research on life styles and milieu in East Germany]. In M. Thomas (Ed.), *Abbruch und Aufbruch. Sozialwissenschaften im Transformationsprozess. Erfahrungen–Ansätze–Analysen* (pp. 303-318). Berlin: Akademie Verlag.

Sozialreport 1990. (1990). Berlin: Verlag Die Wirtschaft Berlin.

Spiegel. (1989). 98 Prozent gegen die Funktionäre [98 Percent against the functionaries]. Spiegel-ZDF (Second German Television Channel) Surveys in the GDR and Public Opinion on Politics, Parties, and Perspectives. No. 51, pp. 86-89.

Thomas, M. (1989). Soziale Struktur—Soziale Subjekte. Marxistische Sozialstrukturtheorie in der aktuellen Diskussion [Social structure—social subjects: Marxist theory of social structure in the current discussion]. *Deutsche Zeitschrift für Philosophie, 8*, 759-770.

Wielgohs, J. (1988). *Produktivkraftentwicklung-Eigentumsverhältnisse-Lebensweise* [Development of productive forces—relations of ownership—way of life]. Ph.D. Dissertation. Berlin: Akademie der Wissenschaften.

THE YEAR AFTER:

LABOR MARKET AND WORK ORIENTATIONS AFTER THE SHIFT (WENDE)

Michael Schlese, Peter Pawlowsky, Florian Schramm and Irene Zierke

In the following pages, we deal with our subject in four steps. First, we examine the period of transformation in the German Democratic Republic (GDR) from summer 1989 to spring 1991. We then attempt to show the extent of the change on the territory of the former GDR by focusing attention on the labor market. Third, we regard the perception of this change as an upheaval in various spheres of life. Lastly, we describe the structural and motivational characteristics of this transformation in the system. Our point of view is selective and can deal only with certain aspects.

It is important to keep in mind parallels and differences between the changes taking place in the other countries of the East Bloc, the most important difference being the GDR's renunciation of sovereignty. Thus, the transformation from a socialist planned economy to a capitalist money economy is characterized by a process of national integration on a massive administrative scale. Five relatively autonomous federal states (*Länder*) have been created from the territory of the former GDR. Their position is exceedingly weak, so they depend on transfers of western knowledge, money, and technical expertise with which to manage the creation of structures like those in the West. We wish to speak of a structural transfer in which changes in the social order are coming about through the imposition of more or less ready-made West German solutions.

It is clear that this approach is problematic. The colonization of East Germany by West Germany has been criticized in the East German media. However, one should not forget which scenarios were conceivable for the future of East Germany after the regime shift (*Wende*) in the autumn of 1989 and how they must be evaluated.

Given what we know of economic developments in the GDR from the mid-1980s to the country's accession to the Federal Republic of Germany (FRG), the first scenario, which envisaged an economically independent GDR, was not promising. Although a reasonably high standard of living had been achieved in the GDR, it is very doubtful whether the level of well-being could have continued improving in view of the renewal and restructuring that was irrefutably necessary as the 1990s began. Further, with the FRG as a reference point, it is fairly certain that any government the GDR could have had would have failed to master the problems of legitimating the East German social order.

The second scenario, which was initially pursued, was a confederation of the two German states. This arrangement provided for independent political structures but close economic cooperation, with the FRG lending support to the GDR. Experience since the currency union in July 1990 seems to show that this option had two crucial flaws. First, it is doubtful whether a politically independent government in East Germany could have held to a course of economic renewal for long. Any such government would have been faced with an erosion of its legitimacy, the possible continuation of mass migration to the West, and even civil disorder. Secondly, the very nature of a confederation would have limited the extent to which citizens of the former GDR could have affected the FRG's decisions democratically. If it can be assumed that the transformation of the system in the GDR is linked with a variety of conflicts, then the GDR's accession to the FRG must be welcomed in the sense that it allows East German citizens to influence the politics of the enlarged FRG. East Germany's citizens are thus able to articulate their interests without having to negotiate on the basis of the fictitious sovereignty that a confederation would have meant.

The third scenario was the accession of the GDR to the FRG as provided for in the West German constitution, the Basic Law (*Grundgesetz*). This has had grave consequences for the economy of the former GDR, has greatly strained the FRG's political system, and has meant at least a temporary erosion in the standard of living enjoyed by East Germans. The advantages of accession are that it guarantees the pace necessary for the adaptation process, provides at least minimal social safeguards, and, through the mechanism of political integration, ties the interests of politicians from the old FRG to those of the citizens of the former GDR.

At the same time, it should not be overlooked that rapid accession has entailed extreme psychological strain for those affected. Moreover, there is currently a difference between the resolute actions of the West German government in the wake of unification and the authority to shape the political and economic context for the territory of the former GDR. A further problem with the third scenario is that the economy of the former GDR has yet to find its place in the international division of labor, and is forced to operate under the monetary conditions prevailing in the FRG. In view of the discrepancy between the population's high expectations and the manifest, massive, and widespread economic crisis that has developed, the central political problem of unification is to sustain the motivation for and legitimacy of the "shock therapy" to which the *Länder* on the territory of the former GDR are being subjected.

THE STAGES OF CHANGE

The political change that transformed the GDR into the federal *Länder* can be divided into three stages: (a) migration and political protest within the GDR (summer to November 1989), (b) the Modrow government, Round Table, and coalition (November 1989 to June 1990), and (c) economic, currency, and social union leading to the GDR's accession to the FRG as provided for in the Basic Law (July to October 1991).

Stage 1

In 1989 the political, cultural, and material limitations imposed on the people of the GDR led to mounting dissent. The increasingly obvious denial of basic rights eventually prompted the peaceful revolution of autumn 1989. While the leadership and the Socialist Unity Party (SED) attempted to "continue cementing the cracks in the encrusted structures," tens of thousands of people left the country, and new forces of opposition resisted the rulers (see Bahrmann & Links, 1990, p. 5). The political activities of a few small groups grew into the demand by millions for changes in fundamental spheres of life.

As late as June 1989, the SED was still calling the results of the local elections a mandate for their policies (see Hermann, 1989, p. 7). This assessment crassly contrasted with the displeasure the population had voiced at the time of the elections and in the actual vote. The democratic process that had already begun in the Soviet Union, Poland, and Hungary encouraged demands for a political forum commensurate with the real situation and the measures required to deal with it. While the SED leadership made a point of giving its approval to the violent suppression of the student democracy movement in the People's Republic of China, many citizens openly turned their backs on the politics of the East German government, rejecting the direction shown for socialist development.

The opening of the border between Austria and Hungary triggered decisive action among thousands of weary and embittered citizens, whose only wish by then was to leave. Each day after September 10, 1989, one thousand people, most of them young, left the country via Hungary or the FRG's embassies in Prague and Warsaw (see Bahrmann & Links, 1990, p. 7). The government proved to be powerless to stop the flood. In the days around the 40th anniversary of the GDR (October 7), open confrontations erupted on the streets. All across the country, mass demonstrations were staged in support of political reform ranging from free elections to official recognition of political groups. The series of "Monday demonstrations" in Leipzig culminated on October 23, when 300,000 people gathered in what was then the largest protest ever seen in the GDR (see Bahrmann & Link, 1990, p. 42).

The SED leadership tried to respond by reshaping the Politburo. On October 18, 1989, the East German head of state, Erich Honecker, finally stepped down, and the power center associated with him collapsed. An era in the history of the GDR had come to an end (see Bahrmann & Link, 1990, p. 33). At the same time, the ideas and demands of different grass-roots groups became increasingly varied and specific. The masses, resigned by this point, pinned their hopes on the *Neues Forum*, a loose coalition of opposition groups. On November 4, 1989, another milestone was reached when more than 1 million people protested in Berlin in support of press freedom, the right of assembly, and radical reforms. Simultaneously, East Germans continued to leave the country at the rate of about one thousand a day for political and economic reasons and out of dissatisfaction with the environmental and general living conditions. By opening all borders to the FRG on November 9, the government had hoped to stem the tide of migrants heading westward, but almost 100,000 had relocated in the FRG during the first weeks of November alone. By the end of the year the total stood at about 350,000 (see Speigner & Dorbritz, 1989, p. 3).

Stage 2

Modrow's government reshuffle on November 17, 1989, was supposed to herald a new policy of reform. His government declared itself to be in favor of improving socialism within the framework of a confederation between the two German states. Government support for a "Round Table," which was formed on November 22, 1989, established a context in which the old parties and the new political forces were to discuss electoral and constitutional reform. The move was both a concession to the opposition and an attempt to regain the initiative (see Schulz, 1991, p. 26). The Round Table turned to the public with proposals for surmounting the crisis and rapidly became a key force in steering political change (see Thaysen, 1990, p. 263).

In November and December 1989, the economic problems of the GDR worsened. No tenable concepts for a gradual transition to an efficient economy had emerged. Young qualified workers had continued to resettle in the FRG, and the value of the East German currency had plummeted because of the open borders. Economic aid offered by the West German government was forthcoming only if a range of political demands were acted upon. Helmut Kohl's "Ten Point Plan" made the gradual development of relations between the two Germanies contingent on the holding of free elections, the SED's renunciation of the leading role it claimed, the release of political prisoners, and the dismantling of the planned economy.

Under these political circumstances, the expectations that various social groups had of the future diversified. Some of them built on ideas for independent democratic development, as expressed in the slogan *Wir bleiben hier!* ("We're staying here!"). Others wanted rapid reunification as a radical, short-term solution to existing and predicted economic hardships. The main argument among advocates of this path was certainly not the impoverishment of the population. On the contrary, the intention was to sustain the relatively high East German standard of living and to improve it in the medium term. Supporters of unification feared that any solution involving an independent state would mean a long delay of any noticeable improvement in material living conditions.

An opinion poll taken at the end of November 1989 showed that just under 50% of the citizens of the GDR more or less favored reunification, whereas 50% more or less strongly opposed the idea (see Bahrmann & Links, 1990, p. 178). Similar results were reached by polls in December. In early January 1990, the GDR government was still clinging to the concept of a confederation between the two states. Only after Moscow had signaled approval did the East German government change its position to one that can be summed up in the phrase *Deutschland einig Vaterland,* or "Germany, A United Fatherland" (see Schulz, 1991, p. 50).

The headlong development that followed was determined essentially by a reassessment of the efficiency and potential of the East German economy, a debate exacerbated by discussion in the media about the country's looming insolvency. The majority vote for the conservative Alliance for Germany (*Allianz für Deutschland*) in the elections to the People's Chamber (*Volkskammer*) held in March 1990 was widely interpreted as a majority wish for rapid reunification. The Alliance, which received most of the vote, did particularly well in the south of the GDR and among workers.

Stage 3

After the elections to the People's Chamber, a government led by the conservative Lothar de Maiziere (CDU) was formed. In close cooperation with the Bonn government, he set about preparing the GDR's accession to the FRG. The de Maiziere government agreed with the ruling coalition in West Germany to introduce "economic, currency, and social union" on July 1, 1990, a decision that began to slow the mass exodus to the West. The union proceeded on three levels. Economic union involved the introduction of civil law, reprivatization of state industries, and restoration of a single German market. Currency union called for the exchange of the East German Mark for the West German Mark and the transfer of monetary sovereignty to the West German Central Bank, the *Bundesbank*. Social union meant the adoption of the West German social welfare system, with all the transfers this entailed.

Economic, currency, and social union was the key to transforming the planned economy into a money economy while integrating the two states (see Herr & Westphal, 1990). In this way, the system's inherent shortages of goods have become shortages of money. New microeconomic restrictions have resulted, some of which have had to be relaxed somewhat for macroeconomic and sociopolitical reasons. The economic actors have had to learn how to deal with the new kinds of shortages. The currency union's massive upward revaluation of the East German mark has been "shock therapy" for the economy of the former GDR because many of its enterprises have not been competitive on Germany's domestic markets, and because products have become too expensive for the former GDR's traditional trading partners in the East. Since the creation of a single domestic market through the currency union, the main task has been to reprivatize state industry, a process that is proving to be complicated and contradictory. In addition, many difficulties of making the transition to a new economic system were underestimated.

In terms of economic policy, the currency union was a risky venture. It was, above all, politically motivated. The structural problems it entailed for the national economy of the former GDR, which intensified the pressure for economic policy action and social protection of those affected, were more or less consciously accepted as the price that had to be paid. Immediately after the currency union, de Maiziere declared the GDR's willingness to accede to the FRG as provided for in West Germany's Basic Law, and to hold elections in December 1990 for the first all-German parliament. Acting within the framework of the "two plus four talks" (involving the two German states and the four allied powers—the United States, France, Great Britain, and the Soviet Union), the governments of East and West Germany signed the terms for their political union on August 31, 1990. The four Allied powers then ratified them in their own Final Settlement with Respect to Germany, thereby regulating the legal aspects of Germany unity. Those signatures were ascribed in Moscow on September 12, marking the end of the postwar period and the division of Germany. The way was open for German unification on October 3, 1990.

The economic, currency, and social union and German unification were decided upon with the aim of equalizing the living conditions in eastern and western Germany. We assume that this is still the political aim now that unification has taken place. This assumption cannot be taken for granted, however. It can be accepted if the government actively pursues a policy that ensures equal living conditions in the whole of Germany. The principle of equality must also be duly accepted by the West German electorate, a stance that is likely to depend on a variety of factors. After all, the transfers to eastern Germany are regarded by West Germany as an opportunity to profit from the upswing stemming from resulting economic development. An appeal to national sentiment alone is not enough. "Belated disaffection," the psychosocial process by which a feeling of identity takes root despite perceived differences between eastern and western Germany, cannot take place under a siege mentality. True, the perception of a social gap is necessary for solidarity, which is important for the next stage of the unification process. But the gap must eventually be reduced to justify further transfers, and it is precisely that reduction that will undermine solidarity. Moreover, the East German perception of a prosperity gap, combined with long-term transfers and a sluggish economic reconstruction, will block the transfer of knowledge and identification with the new system. Any program to improve living conditions is therefore bound to be set in a complicated psychological context.

A CHANGING LABOR MARKET

In September 1989 the total number of employed persons, including people in training programs and apprenticeships, was officially still 8,883,900, and the average work week was 42 hours. Generally, working people in the GDR were employed on a full-time and permanent basis. The labor force consisted of workers and employees (88.2%), members of cooperatives (9.6%), and self-employed and assisting family members (2.2%). A further 700,000 working people were classified as "X" (police, military, state security, and so forth). They did not appear in the official statistics of the GDR (see Infratest, 1991). Depending on the definition used, the employment rate in the GDR was over 80% as compared to less than 70% in the FRG (see Statistisches Bundesamt, 1989, p. 82). In the GDR 51.2% of all employed persons were men and 48.8% were women. In the FRG the corresponding figures were 61.2% and 38.8%. The share of women in different sectors of the East German economy ranged from 17.2% in construction to 83.0% in health services and 91.7% in social services (see Rudolph, 1990).

Developments on the labor market are now terminating many employed people who, perhaps with new qualifications, will reenter the employment system. Simultaneously, a massive change in the structure of employment is likely. In 1991, at least 3 million redundancies are expected. In 1991 every other person in eastern Germany will be directly affected by unemployment or will be on short time, that is, working reduced hours (see Belwe, 1991, p. 31).

According to the GDR welfare survey conducted in autumn 1990, there were 700,000 unemployed persons and 1 million persons working short-time. Young people made up a disproportionately high share of the unemployed and only slightly more than one-quarter (26.7%) of those on short-time work. The share of skilled workers and master craftsmen among the unemployed (42.6%) and short-time workers (56%) was greater than that for the working population as a whole (Landua, 1991).

An average of 1.1 million to 1.2 million unemployed and 1.4 million to 1.8 million short-time workers was forecast for 1991 (see Autorengemeinschaft, 1990). Expressed in full-time equivalents, the estimated underemployment comes to 1.73 million people. The many movements on the labor market— job loss, short time, early retirement, receipt of temporary old-age assistance, commuting, migration, and participation in various labor market measures will affect nearly 4 million people, or about 40% of the 9.6 million persons employed. To assess the likely reduction in women's employment in eastern Germany, one must consider the income level, which often forced both married partners in a joint household to hold a job.

The dynamics of the labor market cannot be understood through current data alone, however. Two processes must be distinguished. First, the loss of jobs as plants are reorganized and rationalized, the collapse of entire industries, and the drastic reduction in the public sector are straining the labor market. Second, the reduction in the supply of labor is relieving pressure on the labor market in addition to creating jobs. These two processes differ in the following ways—

- Short-time work: An estimated annual average of at least 2 million workers will be on short time in 1991 (See Belwe, 1991, p. 29), entailing an average weekly loss of hours amounting to about 45%.
- Early retirement: Some 290,000 people are expected to take early retirement in 1991.
- Temporary old-age assistance: More than 100,000 cases are expected in 1991 (see Belwe, 1991, p. 33).
- Commuters: In May 1991, about 350,000 employed persons commuted between eastern and western Germany (see Belwe, 1991, p. 33).
- Migration: A total of 100,000 persons is expected for 1991, making a grand total of 550,000 members of the labor force who have resettled in the FRG since 1989 (see Belwe, 1991, p. 33).
- Persons in further education and retraining schemes: A total of 190,000 participants are expected. In May 1991, funding was earmarked for 500,000 retraining measures (see Belwe, 1991, p. 31).
- Persons in general job-creation schemes: An annual average of up to 300,000 participants is expected (see Belwe, 1991, p. 31).

The effective supply of labor can be expected to decline by about 800,000 persons in the new *Länder* in 1991 (see Autorengemeinschaft, 1990). Whether this will be a real and permanent change is unclear. It may only be that a hidden labor force will form.

THE ACTOR IN TIMES OF UPHEAVAL

The presentation in the previous sections leads to the question of what impacts the radical change in eastern Germany is having on the working population. Since 1990 it has been possible to conduct research in eastern Germany. The results of numerous surveys provide information on the orientation of the East German population.

Orientation and Interests in East and West

The effects of the change in terms of concerns, expectations, evaluation, and satisfaction can only be understood in light of the orientation of East German citizens. Relevant studies have shown a great similarity between the East German and West German patterns of orientations, beginning with the significance accorded key spheres of life. Health and family are ranked highest, followed by environmental protection and work. The importance of political influence comes in a distant last in both parts of Germany (see Landua, Spellerberg, & Habich, 1991, p. 8). Conspicuous differences emerge in the greater weight accorded in the new federal *Länder* to "environmental protection," "work," and "income." Given the trying difficult circumstances in those spheres, these results are not difficult to understand. By contrast, the perceptions and expectations that such orientations will prevail diverge sharply. Many people in eastern Germany lack the resources to achieve their aims under current conditions, not only because of the economic crisis but also because of the new and unfamiliar regulatory framework in which they now find themselves—West German society. Psychological barriers exist as well. Presumably, they are to be interpreted as a result of excessive strain caused by the radical change in people's concepts of life and the capacity to realize them. As a result, East Germans feel forlorn more often than West Germans do, derive no enjoyment from their jobs, and feel that they can scarcely cope with the complications in their lives. A large majority of East Germans (78%) share the view that they can do nothing to solve their problems. Likewise, a sizable minority of East Germans are of the opinion that they find it necessary to do things they consider ethically improper (see Landua, Spellerberg, & Habich, 1991, p. 23).

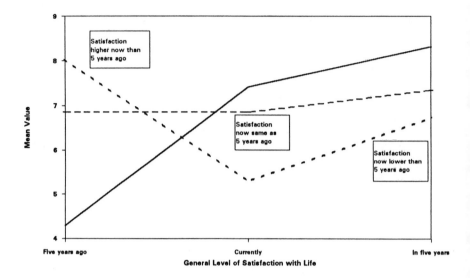

Source: *Der lange Weg zur Einheit–Unterschiedliche Lebensqualität in den "alten" und "neuen" Bundesländern*
[The long path to unity—Differing quality of life in the "old" and "new" federal Länder] by D. Laundua,
A. Spellerberg, & R. Habich (1991) (WZB P91-101). Berlin: Wissenschaftszentrum Berlin für
Sozialforschung, p. 20.

Figure 1.   Perceived Course of Subjective Well-Being

Satisfaction and Concern

In view of such misgivings, the people affected are likely to judge their living
conditions in eastern Germany unfavorably. True enough, satisfaction with life
in November 1990 was found to be far lower in eastern Germany than in
western Germany. Whereas 31% of the population in West Germany were
rather dissatisfied with life in 1988, the figure for the population in the former
GDR in 1990 was 63% (see Landua, 1991b, p. 10). The situation was seen as
poor as early as June 1990, when deterioration in East Germany was not
expected (see Gornig & Scheremet, 1991, p. 33). In West Germany this level
of dissatisfaction is found only among utterly disenfranchised groups with
particular problems, such as retired widows (see Datenreport, 1989, p. 521).

Expectations

The expectations of the East German population are marked by great
skepticism. In June 1990, nearly 40% of employed persons were "very worried"
and a further 40% were "somewhat worried" about losing their jobs. By

contrast, only 40% of the population in the FRG reported such worries in 1984, and the majority had virtually no concern about becoming unemployed (see Statistisches Bundesamt, 1987, p. 464). In the GDR in June 1990, 45% of those surveyed thought that they would lose their jobs, and 35% were sure that would have to change jobs. Data from November 1990, when 1 million people (approximately 10% of the work force) no longer had jobs, reveal a similar pattern of expectations (see Infratest, 1991).

Expectations of future personal well-being are high, however. According to the survey on well-being conducted in East Germany, East Germans—unlike West Germans—expect their satisfaction with life to improve within the next five years. This assessment applies not only to people whom the *Wende* benefited or at least did not hurt, but to the losers in the political and economic developments of 1990. The latter people in particular expect decisive improvements in their lot (see Figure 1). Not surprisingly, this group has a disproportionately high number of people who are members of either the PDS (the political party that succeeded the SED) or the Greens. Those forced out of the employment system—the unemployed, women, and the elderly—are also overrepresented among the "losers" in the process of German unification.

CONDITIONS OF THE TRANSFORMATION

Structural Factors

The economic and production structure in the former GDR had several particular features:

- Pronounced overindustrialization: 50% of the work force (as opposed to 40% in the West) was employed in industry. The service sector was correspondingly underdeveloped, particularly in comparison to the very prominent agricultural sector.
- A one-sided regional economic structure that led to extensive regional monostructures: The chemical industry in the Halle/Bitterfeld region and shipbuilding in Mecklenburg-Pomerania were examples of this structural trend.
- An inadequate infrastructure: Telecommunications and the transport system increasingly failed to meet the demands of modern society.
- Obsolete and worn-out machinery in the plants: This problem contributed to low productivity, especially since a relatively high share of indirect production activity such as maintenance and repair was necessary. Moreover, the percentage of workers exposed to unhealthy working conditions remained high. These rates of exposure coincided with high rates of work-related illness in the GDR (see Sozialreport, 1990, p. 20).

- A Taylorist concept of work organization: The use of new technology for flexible specialization in the production area was not widespread. More than 90% of the work force was employed in traditional jobs. Ways of restructuring or broadening work tasks or making the organization of work partly autonomous were practically unheard of. The work done by most employed people, especially women, was characterized by monotonous manual tasks (see Sozialreport, 1990, p. 86). The feeling of not being able to use existing qualifications to the full and not being intellectually challenged was a major problem particularly among the GDR's "technical elite." College graduates and master craftsmen in particular were overqualified for their jobs (see Sozialreport, 1990, p. 88).

- A labor-intensive, time-wasting economy: Employed persons in the GDR, especially women, worked longer hours than those employed in most other western and eastern European countries. Comparing the daily, yearly, and lifetime working hours of the average GDR citizen to his/her West German counterpart, the East German spent about one third more time on the job. By contrast, the amount of the East German's discretionary time had stagnated for about 20 years, with a great amount of time being required for running a household and satisfying basic consumer needs.

- Small income differentials: Measured against the usual standards, highly qualified persons were disadvantaged (see Stephan & Wiedemann, 1990). The difference between the net income of production workers and that of graduates of universities and technical colleges narrowed from 22% to 15% between 1984 and 1988 (see Sozialreport, 1990, p. 20). The high remuneration for qualified workers in comparison to master craftsmen or foremen also had a demotivating effect in terms of promotion and performance. Women earned an average of 30% less than men in 1989 (see Stephan & Wiedemann, 1990).

Motivational Factors

As far as structural and functional adaptation is concerned, one must decide whether to study the impacts that East Germany's past is having on the former GDR's integration into the economic realm of West Germany or whether to examine the socioeconomic and sociopsychological side of that process.

Even if East German qualifications and socialization were the same as in West Germany, would East Germany have comparable levels of unemployment? The question arises not only because of the structural weaknesses of the East German economy (which do not stem from the planned economy alone), but also because of constraints on autarchy and the economic link with the Soviet Union. This issue is raised here merely to show that one must consider not only the innovation-inhibiting mentalities of East German citizens but also the framework of an individual's economic and political actions.

How is one to evaluate the work ethic of the working population of the former GDR? The predominance of existing judgments (and prejudices) about work and performance motivation in planned economies seems to render the question almost superfluous. However, empirical evidence to substantiate the assertion of a "poor" work ethic in the former GDR is hard to come by. Statements supporting allegations of a poor work ethic among East Germans scarcely go beyond armchair politics. In the following section, a few of the available studies from before and after the *Wende* are examined.

To come to the point, the pattern that emerges is one of clearly declining satisfaction with work and initiative in the former GDR. The grievances of the working population centered on material working conditions and, especially, on the lack of industrial and political democracy. Behind this frustration with work, it seems that the people in East Germany are marked by a basic, deeply rooted, ethical sense of duty, as suggested by recent comparisons of the population's goals in life and values in the new and old federal *Länder*. These findings and their interpretation contradict the frequently heard assertion that the working population in the eastern part of Germany has a "poor work ethic" and an instrumental attitude toward work.

Let us look at the findings (see Stollberg, 1988, 1990). With the proviso that the relevant studies involve limited samples of production workers in the chemical industry in Halle, three trends are clearly visible: a long-term erosion in unconditional, verbally declared commitment to work; a reduction in the identification with one's work; and dwindling satisfaction with work. Interestingly, poor material working conditions, serious stress, and inadequate income were not the only factors constituting the dissatisfaction of the employed in the GDR (see Pawlowsky, 1990). The criticisms were directed primarily at nonmaterial working conditions (see Sozialreport, 1990, p. 21). As stated by Stollberg (1990):

> The expectations people have of their jobs and working conditions have risen continuously in recent decades. In other words, the work situation is being evaluated according to new and ever stricter standards. This is especially clear with the expectations people have of their jobs. The number of those who attach great motivational importance to work content rose by 10 percentage points between 1977 and 1987. As the subjects saw it, the critical indicators were the degree of interest and the possibility to contribute ideas. Additional factors were improved industrial democracy—more effective mechanisms of democratic decision-making in the plants. The growth in these aspirations makes it clear that many people are interested in better ways to ensure that they can take the lead in shaping their professional lives. (p. 120).

The claim of having a "socialist relation to work," by which work becomes increasingly important in the life of the individual, contradicts the respondents' subjective reality, which suggests resignation at the place of work. Inadequate income and opportunities for advancement, the feeling of lacking information, insufficient participation in decisions, and a limited range of options for organizing work have plainly shifted the potential for motivation and led members of the work force to save themselves effort and protect themselves from occupational hazards. This attitude was obviously supported by the work collectives and thus did not contradict the existing informal work culture (see Voskamp & Wittke, 1990, p. 11). Perhaps it was not consumption and the cultural excess of capitalism that led to a hedonistic, leisure-oriented erosion of Protestant work virtues, as critics of postmaterialism have argued (see Noelle-Neumann & Strümpel, 1984); perhaps it was socialism's economics of scarcity that blocked initiative and identification with the occupational activity in which the individual was involved.

The central place accorded to work in eastern Germany is anchored as much in a traditional Protestant work ethic as in the socialist work ideal. It can be seen as an expression of the economic crisis and uncertainty surrounding jobs and income. The central importance of work may presently be increasing, but this interpretation seems inadequate, possibly even misleading. The centrality of work in the lives of East German citizens before the *Wende* and the intrinsic demands for information, participation, and involvement in decisions all suggest that the importance of work did not result solely from instrumental interest. To put it positively, people were concerned with actively shaping their professional lives. The question as to the origin of the central position of work among the employed in the new *Länder* is not only of analytical importance; it is highly relevant in shaping production concepts and organizing work in the future.

Let us formulate this view rather pointedly. If work motivation and the central importance of work among the employed population in the new *Länder* facilitates a revitalization of motivation and initiative, and if there is a strong work ethic beneath the surface of frustrated work motivation—and we sense this is the case—then the necessary motivation to adopt new production concepts is bound to be considerably stronger than if decay of the work ethic and performance has spread to the very core of the values held by the working population of the former GDR. A reconsideration of the empirical evidence indicates that the rapidly increasing job-related and income-related vicissitudes of life may be enhancing the instrumental significance of the work place among many employed persons in the new *Länder*.Discriminating examination of the findings, however, indicates that the value "work" is anchored in a traditional ethos of duty and acceptance (see Klages, 1984; Pawlowsky, 1986; Stollberg, 1990).

This assumption is not unfounded. In early and mid-1990 a number of indicators used over the last three decades to observe "changes in work values" in the old FRG (see Pawlowsky, 1986) were used to gather data in what used to be the GDR. This survey included a "dialogue question" designed to elicit information about plans that people were making for their lives. Two contrasting ideal-type principles were presented, and the respondents were asked which one they agreed with. One statement reflected a middle-class, Protestant perspective; the other, a rather "hedonistic" attitude. The results for the FRG showed that the number of respondents who saw life as a task and focused on achievement was declining, whereas the "hedonistic" attitude of wanting to enjoy life had become important for an increasing number of people since 1963 (see Figure 2). The responses received in the new *Länder* in mid-1990 (see Figure 3) revealed a view of life oriented to traditional middle-class Protestant virtues ("life as a task"), a finding very similar to that for the survey item about the respondents' most important goals in life. The percentage of respondents in the former GDR who accepted this view of life in 1990 was even greater than that in the FRG in 1963.

Let us look at another indicator (see Pawlowsky, 1986, p. 108). Since the early 1960s, West Germans have been asked "Which hours do you enjoy most in general: the hours during work, the hours when you are not working, or both?" If the response "when I am not working" is interpreted as an indication of a preference for discretionary time, and if the responses "I like both" and "I prefer work time" are interpreted as an indication of a preference for work, then the preference for discretionary time has been increasing (see Figures 4 and 5).

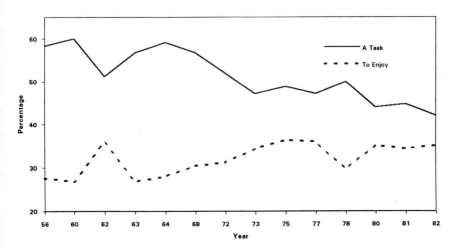

Source: *Arbeitseinstellungen im Wandel* [Changing attitudes toward work] by P. Pawlowsky (1986). Munich: Minerva, p. 31.

Figure 2.   Life as a Task or Life as Something to
Enjoy? The Federal Republic of Germany, 1956-1982

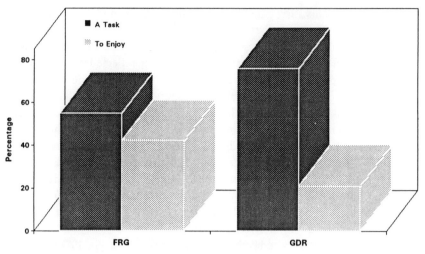

Source: *Der Spiegel* (1991). Das Profil der Deutschen [The profile of the Germans], special edition, p. 69.

Figure 3.   Life as a Task or Life as Something to Enjoy?
Comparision between the Federal Republic of Germany
(FRG) and the German Democratic Republic (GDR), 1990

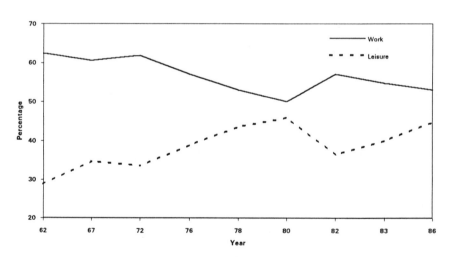

Source: *Arbeitseinstellungen im Wandel* [Changing attitudes toward work] by P. Pawlowsky (1986). Munich: Minerva, p. 108; and unpublished survey data.

Figure 4.   Orientations to Work and Leisure Time
in the Federal Republic of Germany, 1962-1986

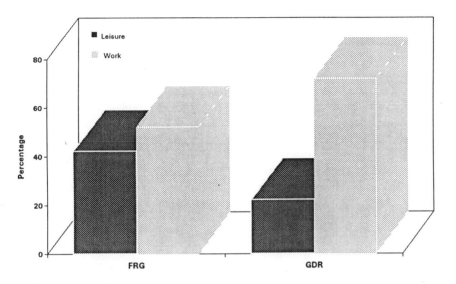

Source: Arbeitseinstellungen im Wandel [Changing attitudes toward work] by P. Pawlowsky (1986). Munich:
          Minerva, p. 108; and unpublished survey data.

Figure 5.   Orientations to Work and Leisure: Comparison
between the Federal Republic of Germany (FGR) and
the German Democratic Republic (GDR), 1990

If the pattern of responses from the first survey of employed persons in the
GDR (February-March, 1990) is added to this picture, it becomes clear that
the working population of the GDR in 1990 answered the survey items about
the same way as West Germany did in the early 1960s. Approximately 70%
of the employed tended to be "work oriented," and only 23% showed a
preference for discretionary time. These findings make it plausible that there
is more behind the centrality of work in the new *Länder* than just instrumental
importance stemming from the current "shortage" of paid work.

CONCLUSION

In the former GDR, people are experiencing and expecting societal change
that seemed impossible even as recently as 1989. This change is propelled less
by East German actors than by the exigencies of Germany's East-West
integration. The population of the GDR accepted reunification in the hope
of preserving or increasing their relatively high standard of living, a prospect
that seemed impossible under socialism as it was actually practiced in their

country. To many people, though, the standard of living seems instead to be threatened by the crisis brought about by that very unification, a crisis rooted as much in the old economic system as in the process of drastic adaptation. The expectations that arose after the *Wende* are frequently unsatisfied both politically and economically. In contrast to the gloomy assessment of the present situation, however, most people have high expectations for the future.

Citizens of the former GDR are compelled to reformulate their goals and identify the appropriate means for achieving them. Coping with the contradiction between present reality and expectations of the future and progressing through various learning processes sorely tests the capacity of people to feel that they can control their situation in life. One way of managing these demands is to emphasize values such as the appreciation of work and family and to create a new identity as a former citizen of the GDR. This identity can help East Germans avoid wholesale debasement of their past and can allow them to feel themselves on a par with the West German population. The East Germans will not escape their past by returning to these values, however. The pressures to be different and behave differently conflict with the tendency to fall back on what is familiar in order to cope with what is new.

What does this mean for the work orientation in eastern Germany? Various impacts are conceivable. A positive outcome (see Pawlowsky, Schlese, & Schramm, in this volume) is the revitalization of a traditional sense of duty that had merely been buried by the everyday world of work in the GDR. A less positive possibility is that political and economic disillusionment and traditional orientations will lead to patterns of behavior that thwart concepts of flexible work organization. One should not underestimate the danger that just such a scenario could evolve, for the orientation to work is, in our judgment, a decisive factor in the economic prosperity of eastern Germany.

REFERENCES

Autorengemeinschaft. (1990). Zur Arbeitsmarktentwicklung 1990/91 im vereinten Deutschland [On the development of the labor market in the united Germany, 1990/91]. *Mitteilungen aus der Arbeitsmarkt- und Berufsforschung, 23,* 455-473.

Bahrmann, H., & Links, C. (1990). *Wir sind das Volk. Die DDR zwischen 7. Oktober und 17. Dezember 1989. Eine Chronik* [We are the people: A chronological of the GDR between October 7 and December 17, 1989]. Berlin: Aufbau-Verlag.

Belwe, K. (1991). Zur Beschäftigungssituation in den neuen Bundesländern [On the employment situation in the new federal *Länder*]. *Aus Politik und Zeitgeschichte* [Bonn], *29,* 27-39.

Gornig, M., & Scheremet, W. (1991). Die erwartete Arbeitsmarktdynamik [Expected dynamics on the labor market]. In G. Wagner, B. v. Rosenbladt, & D. Blaschke (Eds.), *An der Schwelle zur sozialen Marktwirtschaft* (pp. 33-36). Nuremberg: Bundesanstalt für Arbeit.

Herr, H., & Westphal, A. (1990). *Die Transformation von Planwirtschaften in Geldwirtschaften. Ökonomische Kohärenz, Mindestschwelle der Transformation, außenwirtschaftliche Strategien* [The transformation of planned economies into money economies: Economic coherence, minimal threshold of the transformation, and strategies of foreign trade] (WZB Paper FSI 90-9). Berlin: Wissenschaftszentrum Berlin für Sozialforschung.

Herrmann, J. (1989, June 29). Aus dem Bericht des Politbüros an die 8. Tagung des ZK der SED [Excerpts from the report by the Politburo to the 8th conference of the Central Committee of the Social Unity Party]. *Neues Deutschland* [Berlin].

Infratest [Munich]. (1991). *Arbeitsmarkt Monitor für die neuen Bundesländer. Schnellbericht: Daten für November* [Labor-market monitor for the new federal *Länder*]. Unpublished manuscript.

Klages, H. (1984). *Wertorientierungen im Wandel: Rückblick, Gegenwartsanalyse, Prognosen* [Value orientations in flux: Review, analysis of the present, forecasts]. Frankfurt: Campus.

Landua, D. (1991). *Statusmerkmale von Befragten bis 64 Jahre: Erwerbstätigen, Kurzarbeitern und Arbeitslosen: Datenbasis DDR-Wohlfahrtssurvey 1990* [Characteristics of the status of interviewees 64 years old and younger: Employed persons, short-time workers, and the unemployed]. Unpublished manuscript.

Noelle-Neumann, E., & Strümpel, B. (1984). *Macht Arbeit krank? Macht Arbeit glücklich?* [Work: Pathogen or pleasure?]. Munich: Piper.

Pawlowsky, P. (1990). *Arbeit in der DDR: Wie aus Betroffenen Beteiligte der industriellen Modernisierung werden* [Work in the GDR: How the disenfranchized become participants in industrial modernization] (FSA print 8/90). Free University of Berlin, Forschungsstelle Sozialökonomik der Arbeit.

————. (1986). *Arbeitseinstellungen im Wandel* [Changing attitudes toward work]. Munich: Minerva.

Rudolph, H. (1990). Beschäftigungsstruktur in der DDR vor der Wende. Eine Typisierung von Kreisen und Arbeitsämtern [Employment structure in the GDR before the regime shift: A description of districts and employment offices]. In *Mitteilungen aus der Arbeitsmarkt- und Berufsforschung, 23,* 474-503.

Schulz, M. (1991). Neues Forum [New forum]. In H. Müller-Enbergs, M. Schulz, & J. Wiegohs (Eds.), *Von der Illegalität ins Parlament. Werdegang und Konzept der neuen Bürgerbewegungen* (pp. 11-104). Berlin: Links Druck.

Speigner, W. & Dorbritz, J. (1989). *Die Deutsche Demokratische Republik–ein Einwanderer- und Auswandererland? Sozialpolitik konkret* [The German Democratic Republic—A country of immigrants and émigrés? Social policy in detail]. Berlin: Akademie der Wissenschaften.

Spiegel [Hamburg]. (1991, special issue). Das Profil der Deutschen [Profile of the Germans].

Statistisches Bundesamt. (1989). *Datenreport 1989. Zahlen und Fakten über die Bundesrepublik Deutschland* [Information report, 1989. Numbers and facts about the Federal Republic of Germany]. Bonn: Bundeszentrale für politische Bildung.

————. (1987). *Datenreport 1987. Zahlen und Fakten über die Bundesrepublik Deutschland* [Information report, 1987. Numbers and facts about the Federal Republic of Germany]. Bonn: Bundeszentrale für politische Bildung.

Stephan, H., & Wiedemann, E. (1990). Lohnstruktur und Lohndifferenzierung in der DDR. Ergebnisse der Lohndatenerfassung vom September 1988 [Wage structure and wage differentials in the GDR: Results of the wage survey of September 1988]. *Mitteilungen aus der Arbeitsmarkt- und Berufsforschung, 23,* 550-562.

Stollberg, R. (1990). *Arbeitseinstellungen und Arbeitszufriedenheit bei Produktionsarbeitern der DDR* [Work attitudes and work satisfaction]. Unpublished manuscript.

————. (1988). *Soziologie der Arbeit* [Sociology of work]. Berlin: Die Wirtschaft.

Thaysen, U. (1990). Der Runde Tisch: Wer war das Volk? [The round table: Who were "the people"?]. *Zeitschrift für Parlamentsfragen* [Opladen], No. 2, p. 263.

Voskamp, U., & Wittke, V. (1990). *"Fordismus in einem Land." Das Produktionsmodell der DDR* ["Fordism in a country": The production model of the GDR]. SOFI-Mitteilungen.

THE PARADOX OF TRANSFORMATION:

ON SOCIAL CHANGE IN EAST GERMANY

Peter Pawlowsky, Michael Schlese, and Florian Schramm

In the German Democratic Republic (GDR), the end of real socialism, or socialism as it was practiced in everyday life, also spelled the end of the GDR. The public demonstrations that were mounted on the fortieth birthday of the second German state were followed barely a year later by that state's accession to the Federal Republic of Germany. In the wake of the collapse of GDR society, the integration of the two states has entailed the attempt to import the social order of the Federal Republic. This transfer of the West German system to eastern Germany has created a paradox, however: The foundations required for a successful transfer will not exist until the transfer succeeds first. This circumstance is what we call the transfer paradox. The problems arising from rapid unification cannot be solved quickly, nor is there any one way to solve all of them. It will take longer than first anticipated until it can be said that major political and economic renewal has been achieved. We assert that this success will depend partly on how possible it is to identify clearly defined regions facing similar problems, and to use their special characteristics in producing an economic policy tailored to the needs of specific areas. One of the vehicles of this regional revitalization could be the model of "diversified quality production." Regional revitalization can be the core of a scenario for eastern German development that does not copy the Federal Republic, leave the new *Länder* with only unskilled or semiskilled jobs, or perpetuate the acute economic crisis.

FOUR IDEAL-TYPE SCENARIOS FOR DEVELOPMENT

Four ideal-type scenarios for industrial modernization appear to be conceivable for the future development of the economic structure in Germany's new federal *Länder* (Marz & Pawlowsky, 1990). They can be briefly summarized as the "Zero Scenario," the "Workbench Scenario," the "Transfer Scenario,", and the scenario of "Innovation-Oriented Regional Revitalization."

The "Zero Scenario"

Given the lack of economic perspective in the eastern Germany, the lack of consensus on western Germany's willingness to make sacrifices, and both the functionalist conservatism and crude materialism in the former GDR, Germany's western *Länder* become resigned and turn away from the new *Länder*. Active reorganization is dropped from the agenda, the blame for the problems is attributed to the failure of individuals to adapt, and the conflicts are postponed until the next generation.

The "Workbench Scenario"

The West German economy, which is oriented to productivity on the basis of highly skilled labor and diversified quality manufacturing, would be complemented by an economic structure designed to achieve a Tayloristic division of labor that would leave the region with jobs that could be performed by unskilled or semiskilled workers. To ensure viability, such a strategy would be flanked by a low-wage labor policy and a neoliberal policy for increasing flexibility (e.g., external flexibility, fixed-term employment contracts, and reduced protection against dismissal). According to this model, such asymmetrical cooperation would make possible a complementary economic structure based on traditional work values under the motto "work hard, or Korea will be cheaper." The likely gap between the resulting level of welfare and the expectations of the population in eastern Germany, the required development in products and production processes, and the exigencies of international competitiveness all indicate that the workbench scenario would degenerate into the zero scenario or would be superseded by an independent economic development in eastern Germany.

The "Transfer Scenario"

The western German model would be adopted, the welfare state buttressed, and production strategies adapted accordingly to those in the west. The basic assumption of this model is that the corresponding transfers of capital, technology, and know-how will, admittedly, entail frictional losses and the costs of social adaptation, but that modernization resulting in a western-style work and economic culture will come about within a foreseeable period.

The Scenario of Innovation-Oriented Regional Revitalization

This scenario would involve the development of an appropriate modernization strategy of flexible specialization that promotes adaptable cooperation networks through concerted industrial policy in order to cultivate buried qualifications, identification, and motivation.

In the following sections, we sketch the developments to date (section 2); the concomitant problems of social change in eastern Germany, that is, the transfer paradox (section 3); and an alternative development scenario aimed at regional revitalization (sections 4 and 5).

THE PATH SO FAR: TRANSFER INSTEAD OF TRANSFORMATION

The restructuring of eastern Germany is presently a transfer of the more-or-less ready-made and ostensibly superior order of the "old" Federal Republic to the territory of the former GDR. Departures from the copy are unintentional results of adapting the "West German" model to the conditions of the former GDR and not consequences of purposeful political action.

By contrast, transformation is more than mere transfer. We understand transformation to be a change that is sustained by the internal forces of society. That change includes the adoption and modification of elements of west German society. But the special path down which German unification is moving continues to be marked by outside (west German) pressures to change and adapt rapidly, something one could call shock therapy. The path is also marked by massive economic support from the *Länder* of the old Federal Republic—transfers of money, expertise, and personnel that, somewhat like a heart-lung machine, have a stabilizing effect in the midst of change.

However, transfer, too, requires certain things before it can proceed. The changes in the East cannot be set rolling if the people affected are not willing to cooperate and communicate. It is essential to prevent the affected people in the East from withdrawing within themselves, and from perpetuating comfortable and familiar routines that are inappropriate from today's point of view. Consolidation of their earlier mentalities must be avoided. Given the new conditions, a certain measure of opportunism is actually one of the conditions for success. But this opportunism must not undermine the identity of the people in eastern Germany in a way that incapacitates them for pursuing social change as independent actors. Such contradictions are not limited to motivation and willingness to learn; they are also found on a general level as a characteristic of the transfer process. In the following section, we indicate paradoxes that the unification process entails for the economy as a whole, the legal system, labor management, and orientations toward work.

THE PITFALLS IN THE PATH THUS FAR: THE TRANSFER PARADOX

By transfer paradox we mean a situation in which the conditions for successful transfer depend on the very process that is supposed to make them possible. To put it provocatively, only the old Federal Republic would be in a position to bring about everything that is necessary in the new *Länder* to make them productive and equally entitled parts of the united Federal Republic of Germany. This problem can be illustrated by examining four fields of action.

A Macroeconomic Dilemma

The objective of restructuring the economy is to create a social market economy. The rules of the game are the "free play of market forces" and governmental moderation of this play of forces when it approaches the limits of social acceptability or social compatibility. Private ownership and private initiative are seen as crucial motors of development. It follows that the state should largely refrain from intervening to steer economic development, for government intervention would constantly counteract the stated objective. Reality looks different. The economic crisis in eastern Germany makes it necessary for the state to intervene increasingly in the economic process at the very time it is striving to create a new economic order based on non-interventionist principles. The crisis demands that the social costs of the upheaval be cushioned through compensatory measures on the labor market. One way of doing so is to provide support for the unemployed. Thus far, some of the dominant instruments for accomplishing this have been job-creation schemes and "early retirement" plans, none of which can be described as active labor-market policies. Another way of cushioning the social costs of the upheaval in the former GDR is to pursue an active industrial policy, which is necessary if the modernization of firms is to take precedence over their sale or liquidation and if local measures to promote innovations are required. We will return to, this point under the heading of "regional revitalization." The present development, however, only perpetuates the economic dilemma. Privatization continues to be flanked with cushioning economic and social policies.[1]

A Dilemma of the State Based on Due Process

The capacity of the political actors to take action is based on a legal system, which is an expression of a certain stage of social development. Every western German modification of the legal system of the *Länder* formed on the territory of the former GDR requires legitimation and becomes less and less likely as time passes in the unification process. There are discrepancies in the adoption and application of West German law, as can be seen, for example, in the work being done by legal specialists and the courts to sort out the past. Certain cases must be ruled upon according to the laws of the former GDR. That legal system is thus given partial recognition, which according to the FRG's legitimate view of the GDR as an "illegal state," cannot be justified.[2]

The procedures for regulating industrial relations in the FRG are another example of ongoing development. The equilibrium in industrial relations in the FRG, which exists on all levels of the exchange process from the individual's work status to the relation between the partners in the collective-bargaining system, is the result of a historical process. Building on a postwar coalition oriented to productivity, that process has repeatedly brought management and labor together despite their different stances. Despite, or because of, years of wrangling with each other in the collective-bargaining process, these opposing parties have come to a fundamental understanding and acceptance of each other's rights, obligations, and positions. This system has now been extended to the five new federal *Länder*, although the economic situation there is the result of a different development. There is no normative and psychological basis for honoring "implicit contracts," which must always go hand in hand with the explicit provisions of the employment contract. The old law must be built into the legal system of the new states. West German law cannot be established there without eventually conflicting with rights protecting employees or with environmental legislation, for example. The new laws must be applied in a context still determined by the former GDR. This practice conforms to the principle of equality as laid down in the Basic Law, but in individual cases it is quite controversial because of the contradictory situation. Here, too, simply transferring a system or practice leads to deadlock.

The Dilemma of Labor-Market Policy

The reconstruction of viable enterprises in eastern Germany cannot take place without structural innovations and new kinds of skills. These changes have motivational preconditions that are expressions of an industrial, cultural, and working world that, in part, has yet to be created. The possibilities for realizing production concepts and modern service enterprises are a function of financial constraints, the concepts on which the enterprises are based, and the professional and social skills of the people employed. However, the availability of that labor force is, in turn, a function of the economic success resulting from successful realization of a production concept. Which comes first—the chicken or the egg?

The Psychological Dilemma

The "objective" dilemmas at the economic, legal, and labor-policy levels have their subjective counterparts. This subjective realm embraces the psychological dynamics of rapid social change that does not express inner forces of change, and that is not sustained from the outset by groups of actors it affects. Sixteen million people are to be "retrained," as Meier (1991) put it. But mentalities and cultural identities cannot be technocratically created. They result from a subjective process of coming to grips with the new situation, a process that is unpredictable in many ways.

Beginning with the prelude to the shift of regime, let us try to follow some of the experiences arising from this "psycho-logic." Since at least the 1970s, economic success had been recognized officially and unofficially as an aim of the socialist economic model. Comparison with West Germany revealed the relative failure of the former GDR in this respect. The people of the GDR were confronted with the knowledge of having lived and worked in an unsuccessful system and, in part, of having committed their lives to it. Because integration in society is a function of paid work, the insinuation is that the individual's own performance is to blame for the failure. Accordingly, one either sees oneself as unsuccessful or re-evaluates one's biography and achievement. Because people tend to avoid holding a low opinion of themselves (the degree of avoidance depending on various personal traits such as age and professional identity), the implication is that former East German citizens have begun to re-evaluate their own achievements and those of their former society.

Their revised assessment is sobering. Since the initial "unification euphoria," "belated disaffection" has been building. It has resulted from a backlash expressed in the phrase "not everything was all that bad" and from a perception of the differences between East and West Germans. This backlash is heard in relation to certain subjects. "A job for every person who wants to work" and "sufficient child-care facilities" were rated high by people surveyed in the former GDR. The government guarantee of a job and the nationwide provision of child-care facilities in the GDR are expressed in these results. "The willingness of people to help each other" was evaluated by 85% of the respondents as good or very good (Landua, Spellerberg, & Habich, 1991, p. 26). Together with "equality between man and woman" and "stable prices," these responses constitute the essence of a retrospective GDR identity, and simultaneously define potential political demands.

This belated disaffection ranges from the feeling that communication between the members of the two parts of Germany is insufficient and unequal in the sense that one's identity as a reborn "citizen of the former GDR" is a relevant concept that can be acted upon. The "citizen of the GDR" did not seem to emerge in the thinking of the "political citizen" until the demise of "his" state.

FROM TRANSFER TO TRANSFORMATION

The dilemmas in the social economy, the treatment of social problems according to the rule of law, the design of labor policy, and the degree to which socio-psychological aspects condition the transfer of the system cannot be solved by temporarily abolishing the structures and processes that cause them. To explore the possibility of solving the transfer paradox through step-by-step mitigation, we would like to address two elements. One of them is the time factor. The attempt to sort out seemingly incompatible things through interactive learning processes requires time. This realization will cease being taken for granted if it is incorporated into policy-planning and social programs of the restructuring process.

The second element is "regionalization," by which we mean the classification of problems and the drafting of solutions for comparatively small regions. As obvious as this idea may be, one must bear in mind the problem of centralized structures and the economic weakness of the regions involved. This strategy requires interregional willingness to accept redistribution. Let us take a closer look at these two elements.

The Time Factor

In order to form an idea of the temporal dimension of the transformation process and economic reconstruction in the former GDR, it is helpful to take a look at the Federal Republic at the time of its greatest growth. Even if the "economic miracle" of the 1950s and 1960s were to be repeated now in eastern Germany, it would be decades, not years, before one could expect a balanced labor market with western-like wages and productivity and, hence, a comparable per capita gross domestic product. Despite the massive flow of capital from West to East, the relatively slight employment effect of investment nowadays (see Herr & Westphal, 1990) is just one indication seeming to suggest that eastern Germany might well not reach the same level of prosperity by the end of this century. Attention should be paid not only to the trends of average living conditions, but also to their distribution. The possibly long-term exclusion of many former GDR citizens from the employment system, which sustains the individual's welfare, leads one to expect the number of hardship cases in the former GDR to increase beyond levels previously known in either part of Germany.[3] The lean period that disadvantaged actors must endure is ever more clearly a problem of transfer and economic reconstruction.

Regionalization

The general problem with regionalization is that concerted, regionally oriented economic action is both politically and materially demanding. The technical dimension of regionalization can be better understood if one recalls the basics of regionalization. From various examples of regional policies that promote flexible networks, Hatch (1991) extracted a few principles for designing a strategy of regional revitalization that emphasizes innovation. Concepts of regional modernization build upon the identification of strategic market opportunities. Initially, the focus is not on technology transfer but on product or service innovation, which is not supported with the relevant technology until a second stage is reached. Through systematic analysis and observation, an optimal match between market opportunities and regional products is worked out.

The strategy is thus based on potential demand, not on supply. Governments must spread investment around to many enterprises instead of concentrating on a few key industries. In bodies for regional cooperation, the task is to define development profiles that are flanked by training measures, investment in technology, and joint marketing concepts whose implementation would involve and benefit as many enterprises as possible. Corporate networks establish fields of cooperation such as the purchasing, design, and execution of training courses, research and development, and marketing.

However, the economy in eastern Germany is typified by two main drawbacks: (a) a completely outmoded economic structure based primarily on mass production and single-product industries that dominate entire regions[4] and (b) sectorial deformations manifested as a lack of services and crafts and the absence of a small business sector. These shortcomings, which plague fundamental areas such as transport and telecommunications as well, also determine the impact of regional policy oriented to innovation. This fact makes "diffuse industrialization" (Hatch, 1991) particularly urgent. In addition, there is a need for new kinds of ties that reduce the migration of labor, particularly of young and qualified workers. Human potential is an important foundation of strategies for regional revitalization.

A final essential element in the dynamics of regional development is the identification of a common economic culture and craft tradition that can serve as a vision. It is not even necessary for the actors revitalizing these visions to have experienced them personally. It is a matter of creating a regional identity that can be effective as a motivational motor and a kind of social glue.

An orchestrated campaign involving the *Treuhand* (the holding company established by the Federal German government to sell off or liquidate the state-owned businesses and property of the former GDR), local bodies, the unions, employers, training institutions, and potential investors is required for planning sectorial industrial policy and ensuring its decentralized implementation. Innovation can be promoted in two ways: (a) through measures to increase the innovation potential of existing companies (particularly in what exists of the small business sector); and (b) through measures to establish enterprises of various sizes in specific locations.

One could also consider writing flexible working arrangements into regional wage agreements in order to give businesses and their work forces greater room for maneuver.[5] The structure of the *Treuhand* could also enable it to serve as a linchpin of regional differentiation and flexible working arrangements. To do this the *Treuhand* must come to stress greater sectorial and political differentiation between the regions. Each of these regions has its own characteristics (production structure, territorial and historical ties, main problems, and so forth). Measures for regional revitalization could be flanked by limited protectionism and debt relief granted by government creditors to, say, local authorities. Systematic debt relief must not be decoupled from the monitoring of new loans to local authorities. That control is intended to prevent long-term structural effects that could result from renewed insolvency. One of the political necessities for revitalization is to change the image of the process of economic transformation as symbolized by the *Treuhand*. A quasi-Keynesian program of economic transformation billed in its own words as consistent and socially responsible privatization must be converted to a program of active industrial policy. As previously indicated, this industrial policy is based on a corporatism of the participating actors.

MEZZO GIORNO OR SILICON VALLEY? OPPORTUNITIES FOR REGIONAL REVITALIZATION

The regional revitalization model seems to us to be a vehicle for increasing the adaptability of solutions that are transferred. It also seems to be a vehicle for motivating the appropriate actors to take advantage of the transfer of knowledge and directly involve themselves in the process of modernization. The broad perspective provided by the paradoxes we have pointed out makes it plain that the model helps break down the existing problems into manageable units, and forge a consensus on the inevitable sacrifices to be made in dealing with them. Regions are conceivable not only as suitable abstract entities (i.e., definable problem areas), but also as units in which revitalization can actually be experienced and sociopsychologically reinforced. Regions that may well have diffuse identities simultaneously symbolize a pattern of life that can be held constant despite change. One should also remember the theoretical lessons that the planned economy taught about control. The ultimate failure of East

Germany's economy makes centrally directed revival highly unlikely in the *Länder* that have been formed in what was once the GDR.

Starting points for the regional revitalization model are the definition and identification of problematic regions, political federalism, fledgling regional programs, and a regional focus in the organizational structure of the *Treuhand*. The objective of regionally oriented industrial policy should be to reorganize existing structures and create incentives to attract new companies. Low wages, preferential federal aid, and cheap land can function only temporarily as incentives in decisions on the siting of new settlements. Later, other siting factors come into play, and they are presently already being considered where large plant investments are concerned. In the medium term, special regional characteristics are a key factor of competition.

Let us examine this point more closely. The dual integration of the enterprise—at the local level (the region) and the global level (world markets)—is a central aspect in this regard. Ekstedt and Henning (1988) even saw "local mobilization" as essential for effective global competitiveness. How can these interrelationships be explained? Competitive pressure at the international level is increasing. The main thrust of this development is an internationalization of markets and a globalization of business activity, which have made for keener competition in a growing number of industries and firms. Strategy discussions focus on the goal of opening up new markets either through the establishment of production facilities abroad or mergers with foreign companies. A common variation of this internationalization is for companies to cut costs by shifting production to low-wage countries while centralizing knowledge-intensive spheres such as research and development in "think tanks" located in highly industrialized locations. It is not only that German firms are not alone in pursuing such strategies; foreign firms, too, especially ones outside the European Community, feel forced to operate globally.

Competition is therefore intensifying because of the growing number of suppliers in international markets and because of the different cultural, geographical, and political contexts involved. For example, emerging nations compete against the long-established industrialized countries; low-wage countries against high-wage countries. Countries with elaborate protective social and labor legislation are pitted against countries in which the risk rests largely on the individual. Countries with flexible night and weekend working hours compete against countries with relatively rigid working time arrangements. And all of them are competing with their products increasingly on the same markets (see v. Dohnanyi, 1989). But intensified international competition, particularly from low-wage countries, cannot be met primarily by price wars, whose limits, at least in the Federal Republic of Germany (including its new *Länder*), are evident from the costs of maintaining the social safety net.

Certain elements suggest that it would be appropriate for the Federal Republic of Germany to develop a corporate strategy of deriving competitive advantage from the quality of human resources and a high-quality synergistic environment that promotes innovation. One of those elements is the German labor force, which by world standards is relatively skilled in both the old and new federal *Länder*. Another is the social protection offered by German labor law. A third is the system of collective bargaining, which greatly stabilizes the environment in which firms must plan and operate. To improve competitiveness through "intelligent" products and services and "diversified, high-quality products," one must have considerable flexibility in production technology, organization, and planning (see Meffert, 1969; Osterloh, 1988). These prerequisites can be achieved, in particular, through a concept of "flexible specialization." As Piore and Sabel (1985) see it, technological possibilities and the economic exigencies of the market will enable the strategy of diversified quality production to supplant mass production, which has hitherto dominated all industrial nations. According to Sydow (1991) and Piore and Sabel (1985), the strategy is based primarily on small and medium-sized companies that—

- form a closely knit network of subcontracting and client companies;
- produce a specialized program of products in small runs;
- increasingly use flexible automation technology; and
- feature a craft-based organization of work.

The preconditions for the development of regional structures amenable to such flexible specialization differ greatly. The examples of successful regional modernization in machine-building in Baden-Württemberg (see Sabel, Herrigel, Deeg, & Kazis, 1987); the chemical industry in the northern part of the Ruhr District (see Grabher, 1988, 1989; Ewers, Wettmann, Kleine, & Krist, 1990); the "subcontracting networks" of the textile industry in Northern Italy (see Piore & Sabel, 1985; Regine & Sabel, 1989, Marciani, 1991); the models of flexible specialization in the small firms of the tool and craft industry in Småland, Sweden (see Ekstedt & Henning, 1988); and the network program of the Danish government in the furniture industry (Hatch, 1991) point to a renaissance of regional spheres of influence and the success of producer networks. In certain regions of the *Länder* in eastern Germany, are there elements and planning opportunities that offer what it takes for regional modernization oriented to innovation? To what degree can a transfer of regional revitalization models serve as an option for modernization?

One example to examine is the Emilia-Romagna region, which Piore and Sabel (1985) cited as the source and prototype of regional development models. Which conditions have been crucial for the development of structures of flexible specialization there? At the end of the 1960s, Emilia Romagna was torn by bitter labor disputes. Productivity plummeted, reducing the ability of large companies to act and react as required by changes in world markets. The oil crisis of the early 1970s and the mounting indebtedness of developing countries hit particularly hard among producers of agricultural machinery, the largest employers in the area. The domestic footwear industry came under more and more pressure from foreign firms. Investment dropped sharply, and unemployment rose. Large firms geared to mass production consequently decentralized their operations and relocated them in other regions to escape union pressure. Employment in these industries subsequently declined dramatically. Nevertheless, this collapse in the economic base of the region was offset by the explosive growth of small companies in the most important towns—Bologna, Modena, Reggio, Parma, and Carpi.

The keys to the economic boom in the region lay in the spread of production networks established with government support. The economic problems of the area brought local-level representatives from government, union, and employers to the "table" to launch networks of cooperation between small and medium-sized companies. One such initiative is CITER, the hub of a network. In Carpi, the economist Lorendana Ligabue developed an integrated service concept for textile manufacturers. The essential features were—

- transfer of information;
- joint financing of detailed market analysis that individual companies could not have financed alone;
- a product-upgrading policy;
- market expansion; and
- development of new joint sales channels and marketing concepts.

Today, CITER offers technical services and international market analysis in the field of fashion to over 600 companies in the region. Hatch (1991) reported that small firms in numerous industries of the Emilia-Romagna region routinely network their resources with new synergistic effects. The *terza Italia* model in currently characterized by—

- networks of small and medium-sized companies;
- close cooperation and mutual help between companies;
- a coalition between unions and employers for the purpose of sustaining increased productivity;
- systematic promotion and support of the network through the local government, including the provision of consultants and market research; and
- limited competition between firms (Marciani, 1991).

   It seems that the "economic crisis" in Emilia Romagna has indeed given rise to a cooperative concept of flexible specialization that can bring the flexibility of modern production concepts fully to bear, one that is especially responsive to the growing dynamics of markets.

In the meantime, similar networks have formed in numerous European regions under widely differing conditions. It would be useful at this point to examine these various contexts for perspectives that could shape the framework of regional support in parts of Germany's new *Länder*. Our intention is not to give the impression that the Federal Republic's new *Länder* offer ideal terrain for transformation based on concepts of flexible specialization. For example, in discussing the problems of innovation-oriented regional policies, Ewers et al. (1990) mention location factors (p. 42) and measures for their improvement (p. 60). In regional terms, say the authors, locational factors include the level of wages; the distribution of relatively high-quality basic infrastructure; the distribution of universities, technical schools, external R&D institutes, advisory offices, and information banks; regional industry and competitive relations; the transport infrastructure; the degree of diversification in the economic structure; and the regional distribution of banks. The authors also point to an international level at which synergistic effects arise from the interplay of the factors mentioned. Finally, there is the corporate level (qualification of personnel, the amount and quality of information, management style, entrepreneurial qualifications, and financial resources), which determines the capacity and willingness to innovate.

It is no exaggeration to say that the regions of the former GDR are deficient on almost all counts. The aim of industrial policy must be a concerted effort to overcome these shortcomings. The opportunity for the new *Länder* lies in completely modernizing their run-down infrastructures—and in using the latest technology and know-how to do it. The human potential must be retained, for it would no longer be possible to compensate for a long-term brain drain.

CONCLUDING OBSERVATIONS

In many respects the initial context for regional revitalization in other places was similar to that now prevailing in eastern Germany (impending industrial action, predominance of mass production, and a sudden change in the competitive conditions). Other facets of the situation (changes in the system of allocation, employee expectations, and the psychosocial conditions governing the transfer of the western order) cannot be so clearly categorized. But if our assumptions are correct, then the incipient upturn in the new *Länder* can be promoted by a regionally oriented policy of economic support, which must be pursued in a way that does not reinforce subjective and psychosocial obstacles to innovation.

By their very nature, many of the problems to be faced can be gradually eliminated only through compromise. There will be setbacks, too. The paradox of development policies in eastern Germany is that the conditions normally required for success, whether achieved by conventional or unconventional means, have yet to be created. Sustained consensus on the acceptance of temporary austerity is needed, for new disaffection, resignation, or unfocused protest is incompatible with the communicative routines underlying diversified production of high-quality goods and services. And precisely that concept of production is the point behind the transfer of basic economic structures. Combined with the restructuring of big industrial companies, the establishment of flexible, specialized production, and networks of cooperation that build on the existing pool of skilled labor, discipline, motivation, and optimism could be eastern Germany's *own* way out of the crisis in the foreseeable future.

NOTES

1. In the winter of 1991, the most prominent example of this approach was the privatization of the metal-working plants in Brandenburg. Faced with the intended sale to Riva, the organizations collectively representing the interests of the workers attempted to win flanking job-creation measures. The most recent example is the privatization of the shipyard industry in the spring of 1992. The process triggered massive protests by the population of Mecklenburg-Pomerania.

2. Can former East German border guards who fired on would-be escapees successfully defend themselves by claiming only to have been "following strict orders"? Is the western legal system a "just" standard by which to rule on their actions?

3. In the meantime, however, the level of social equality could stagnate at a point lower than that in the old Federal Republic.

4. The best-known example is the high concentration of production sites oriented solely to the chemical industry, as in Halle, Bitterfeld, and Magdeburg.

5. Two instruments appear to be suitable: (a) the creation of wage-contract options between which enterprises can choose according to the conditions in the company, and (b) graduated wage-contract agreements explicitly spelling out improvements in employee income and other future measures.

REFERENCES

v. Dohnanyi, K. (1989). Gesellschaftspolitische Wirkungen des partnerschaftlichen Unternehmensmodells. In C. Bertelsmann-Preis (Ed.), *Symposium 1989* (pp. 79-88). Gütersloh: Bertelsmann Stiftung.

Ekstedt, E., & Henning, R. (1988). *Globalization and local mobilization* (FA radet 1988-02-18). Unpublished. Stockholm.

Ewers, H.-J., Wettmann, R., Kleine, J., & Krist, H. (1990, March). *Innovationsorientierte Regionalpolitik* [Regional policy oriented to innovation] (WZB Discussion Paper FS-4). Berlin: Wissenschaftszentrum Berlin für Sozialforschung.

Grabher, G. (1989). *Industrielle Innovation ohne institutionelle Innovation?* [Industrial innovation without institutional innovation?] (WZB Discussion Paper FS-I89-7). Berlin: Wissenschaftszentrum Berlin für Sozialforschung

———. (1988). *Unternehmensnetzwerke und Innovation* [Corporate networks and innovation] (WZB Discussion Paper FS-I88-20). Berlin: Wissenschaftszentrum Berlin für Sozialforschung.

Hatch, R. C. (1991). The power of manufacturing networks. *TransAtlantic, 22*, 3-6.

Herr, H., & Westphal, A. (1990). *Die Transformation von Planwirtschaften in Geldwirtschaften. Ökonomische Kohärenz, Mindestschwelle der Transformation, außenwirtschaftliche Strategien* [The transformation of planned economies into money economies: Economic coherence, minimum threshold of transformation, international economic strategies] (WZB-Print FSI 90-9). Berlin: Wissenschaftszentrum Berlin für Sozialforschung (WZB).

Landua, D., Spellerberg, A., & Habich, R. (1991). *Der lange Weg zur Einheit–Unterschiedliche Lebensqualität in den "alten" und "neuen" Bundesländern* [The long road to unification: The gap in living standards in the "old" and "new" federal Länder] (WZB- Print P91-101). Berlin: Wissenschaftszentrum Berlin für Sozialforschung (WZB).

Marciani, F. (1991). *Das Konzept der flexiblen Spezialisierung am Beispiel innovationsorientierter regionaler Wirtschaftskulturen im nördlichen Italien* [The concept of flexible specialization: The example of innovation-oriented regional economic cultures in Northern Italy]. Unpublished masters thesis. Berlin: Free University of Berlin.

Marz, L., & Pawlowsky, P. (1990). Moderne (De)Modernisierung? Über die Unmöglichkeit einer sozialmarktwirtschaftlichen Reorganisation der neuen Bundesländer. *Journal für Sozialforschung, 4, 5.*

Meffert, H. (1969). Zum Problem der betriebswirtschaftlichen Flexibilität. *Zeitschrift für Betriebswirtschaft, 39*, 779-800.

Meier, C. (1991, March 5). Wie das Lernen blockiert wird. Ein Plädoyer für mehr Großzügigkeit [How learning becomes blocked: A plea for more tolerance]. *Frankfurter Allgemeine Zeitung*, p. 34.

Osterloh, M. (1988). Methodische Probleme einer empirischen Erforschung von Organisationskulturen. In E. Dülfer (Ed.), *Organisationskultur* (pp. 139-154). Stuttgart: Poeschel.

Piore, M. J., & Sabel, C. F. (1985). *Das Ende der Massenproduktion. Studie über die Requalifizierung der Arbeit und die Rückkehr der Ökonomie in die Gesellschaft* [The end of mass production: The requalification of work and the return of the economy to society]. Berlin: Wagenbach.

Sabel, C. F., Herrigel, G. B., Deeg, R. & Kazis, R., (1987). *Regional prosperities compared: Massachusetts and Baden-Württemberg in the 1980s* (WZB Discussion Paper ILM-LMP 87-106). Berlin: Wissenschaftszentrum Berlin für Sozialforschung (WZB).

Sydow, J. (1991, March). Strategische Netzwerke in Japan. *Zeitschrift für betriebswirtschaftliche Forschung, 3*, 238-254.

SOCIOECONOMIC CHANGE IN ISRAEL:
POLICY, RHETORIC, AND PUBLIC OPINION

Ephraim Yuchtman-Yaar and Avi Gottlieb

POLITICAL CONTEXT AND ECONOMIC STRUCTURE

Israel is a young and small country molded under unique historical circumstances, which have profoundly affected the country's political and socioeconomic development. Israel's foundations were laid during the first-half of this century by eastern and central European Jewish immigrants who had been motivated to leave their countries by the fear of antisemitism and by the Zionist vision of establishing a Jewish state in Palestine.

After gaining independence in 1948, Israel made the absorption of immigrants a major national goal. Within ten years, the Jewish population grew from 650,000 to over 1,800,000, mostly because of the mass immigration of survivors of the Holocaust and of Jews from the Arab countries in North Africa and the Middle East. This policy has endured ever since without heed to its immediate costs. By the end of 1989, the Jewish population totaled 3,717,000; 77.6% are first- or second-generation immigrants.

Since the change in the Soviet government's restrictive emigration policies, Israel has embarked on the monumental task of assimilating a large part of the Russian Jewry. In 1990 alone, 200,000 immigrants from the Soviet Union arrived; approximately one million are expected by the end of the century. The economic and social integration of this vast population and the satisfaction of its basic needs necessitate the commitment of substantial national resources, at least during the early phases of absorption.

The private sector could not possibly accomplish this task. Thus, the absorption of immigrants has been critical in shaping Israel's centralized and government-controlled political economy. Indeed, the state's economic dominance is so pervasive[1] that the prospects of all economic sectors and private households depend in one way or another on government dictates—ranging from terms of credit and the price of goods and services to wage increases. With the demise of "real socialism" and the transition in eastern Europe, Israel's economic system remains one of the most highly controlled and highly centralized in the world.

Yet there are other, no less significant grounds for the government's commanding economic position. Ever since the founding of Israel, she has been in a continuous state of conflict with the Arab world. The dispute has erupted into several major armed confrontations, as well as numerous more minor clashes. This state of affairs has, among other things, direct economic repercussions, which are most clearly reflected in Israel's national budget. Expenditures for national defense typically consume over 20% of the GNP; in times of war, that share may even surge to 40%. Only in the past decade did the government succeed in reducing the share of the defense budget in the GNP somewhat. In 1989 it comprised an average 18.8% of the GNP (Bank of Israel, 1990), and the trend is downward. Nevertheless, such an apportionment of national resources accounts not only for the government's extraordinary economic prerogatives but also for some of the economic difficulties confronted by Israel.

The Arab-Israeli conflict is costly in other ways. Israel is denied access to regional markets, handicapped by the Arab boycott in many other business transactions, and, because of the frequent outbreak of hostilities, regarded as an inferior investment opportunity by much of the business world. Local and foreign investments have been discouraged further since the 1987 eruption of the Intifada, which has generated an atmosphere of uncertainty and low expectations. The Palestinian uprising has also curtailed the supply of labor from the occupied territories and has reduced Israeli business output.[2] Bruno and Meridor (1990) estimated the total costs of the Intifada as equivalent to an annual reduction of about 4% of the GNP.

There is little doubt that Israeli society will continue to bear the double burden of economic hardship and a state controlled economy as long as the regional conflict persists. Nevertheless, Israel's centralized economic management should not be mistaken for political totalitarianism; on the contrary, its political system is firmly grounded in principles of Western democracy. The government, which is formed on the basis of free national elections, typically comprises several coalition partners.[3] This arrangement has been a source of political instability and disputes; in fact, several governments have fallen because of changing alignments between coalition and opposition parties. However, this system has also served to limit governmental power and impede drastic measures and policies.

Israel's powerful labor federation, the Histadrut, constitutes an additional restraint on the government's sovereignty. It is a unique institution. Its trade union represents the interests of most Israeli employees and workers and offers diverse welfare and cultural services. On the other hand, the Histadrut also encompasses some of the country's largest conglomerates, accounting for some 25% of the labor force. Its organizational structure is akin to that of the state. Its nation-wide elections—also based on the system of proportional representation—encompasses Israel's entire political spectrum. Thus, the Histadrut combines the often conflicting roles of employees' representative and employer. Its sheer size renders it a pivotal economic force, second only to the government (Shalev, 1984), and its executive committee is often considered Israel's "second government," without whose cooperation no major economic policy can be undertaken.

Israel's private sector, which is hampered by its dependence on government policies and regulations and by the power of the Histadrut, has traditionally played a relatively weak role in this peculiar triangle of corporatism. Nonetheless, its slice of the business-sector and industrial pie is growing steadily. In 1989, the private sector accounted for nearly 70% of the labor force in industry (Central Bureau of Statistics, 1990, pp. 334-335). Despite this impressive growth, its degree of freedom remains severely circumscribed. The government continues to impose onerous fiscal and monetary regulations, while the Histadrut attempts to dictate inopportune wage and employment programs.

As delineated in the following pages, these dynamics were expected to change after the 1977 elections, which for the first time brought the politically conservative and market-oriented Likud party to power. In practice, however, the Likud followed the policies of previous socialist-oriented governments headed by the Labor party and did little to liberalize Israel's economic structure.

THE ECONOMIC CRISIS

While the government, "aided" by the labor federation, continued its strong-arm economic management, Israel's economy slid into a deep recession. The acute decline began in the mid-1970s, after the 1973 Yom-Kippur War and the sharp increase in defense expenditures associated with it. The global economic slowdown caused by the 1973 oil crisis did not improve Israel's economic prospects and preempted any chance of a quick and easy recovery.

The malfunctioning and, ultimately, the virtual collapse of the Israeli economy is easily demonstrated. Economic growth rates, which had been quite impressive during most of the 1960s, started to decrease rapidly in the early 1970s. The gross domestic product had actually frozen by the early 1980s (Figure 1). At the same time, the rate of inflation accelerated at an

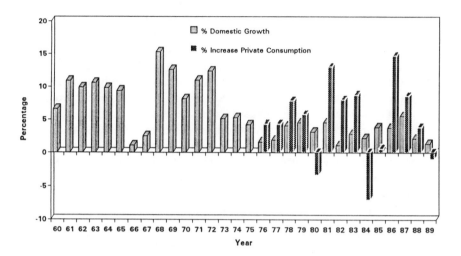

Source: Central Bureau of Statistics (Israel). (1990). *Statistical Abstracts of Israel, 41,* Abstracts nos. 6.1 and
6.2 (pp. 192-197), Resources and the use of resources. Jerusalem: Keter (in Hebrew).

Figure 1. Israel's Gross Domestic Product (GDP),
1960-1989, and Private Consumption Expenditures, 1976-1989:
Percentage of Annual Change (at constant prices)

unprecedented pace, reaching three-digit figures in 1980. By 1984, it had shot
up to hyperinflationary levels (Figure 2).

Whereas productive capacity came to a virtual standstill, the public's
standard of living (per capita private consumption) continued to rise, creating
a growing gap between economic revenues and expenditures (Figure 1).
Although foreign trade suffered (because currency exchange rates were not
adjusted to inflation), the local market continued to expand.

The Histadrut played a central role in these developments. It succeeded in
negotiating both excessive wage increases and a more advantageous
implementation of the "indexation method"[4] with public and private employers.
The government proved itself helpless not only in preventing these processes
but also in restricting its own expenditures. The spreading hole in the public
pocketbook was stitched with loans from abroad. By 1984 external debt had
reached $19.7 billion, a fourfold increase within one decade (Figure 3).

Before long, these predicaments had become grave enough to constitute a
serious threat to Israel's entire social and economic fabric. Yet the Israeli public,
which in the past had evinced only scant concern about the country's economic
performance and prospects, was not quite convinced. In 1982, when economic
growth was at a standstill and the annual inflation rate over 100%, only 60.2%

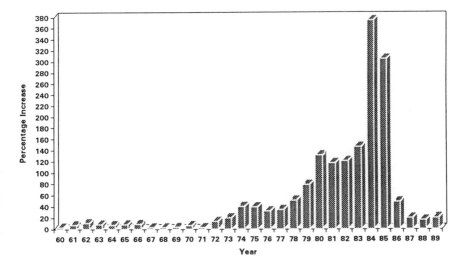

Source: Central Bureau of Statistics (Israel). (1990). *Statistical Abstracts of Israel, 41,* Abstracts nos. 10.2 (p. 282), Resources and the use of resources. Jerusalem: Keter (in Hebrew).

Figure 2. Israel's Consumer Price Index (Rate of Inflation), 1960-1989): Percent Annual Change (at constant prices)

regarded the economic crisis as "serious" or "very serious."[5] Those acknowledging the urgency of the situation appeared to be troubled. Most expected a prolonged impasse (80.7%), and only a small minority (22.9%) foresaw a possible aggravation of economic conditions in the near future.

When the data of the first survey were collected in 1982, the country's economic predicaments already constituted a highly salient issue in political discourse and received broad coverage in the news media. Thus, the 40% minority of people who displayed indifference can hardly be excused on the grounds of ignorance. The more probable explanation for these casual attitudes is that they were inspired by personal experience rather than societal concern. The dissociation of wages from productivity and their adjustment to the cost of living constituted protective devices, which rendered employees virtually invulnerable to economic vicissitudes. Entrepreneurs often used government loans and credits, which were obtained at below-inflation interest rates, to procure swift profits (e.g., by "playing the stock market") rather than investing them in production.

Paradoxically then, the dire economic difficulties on a national level were matched by a widespread sense of material well-being on the personal level— a prosperous population residing in a destitute country. Under these circumstances, the public's nonchalance about the economic crisis is hardly

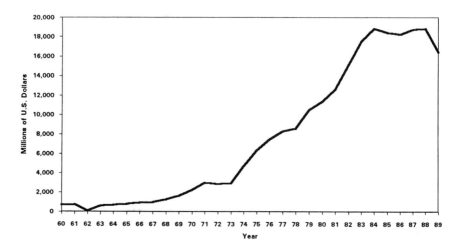

Source: Central Bureau of Statistics (Israel). (1990). *Statistical Abstracts of Israel, 41,* Abstracts nos. 7.4 (pp. 234-235), Israel's foreign liabilities, Jerusalem: Keter (in Hebrew).

Figure 3. Israeli Foreign Liabilities, 1960-1989
(in millions of constant US dollars)

surprising. In the final analysis, even those acknowledging these predicaments may have merely demonstrated abstract awareness rather than authentic concern.

The precarious drift of economic affairs was not arrested until 1985, over 10 years after the backslide had begun. Deadlocked after the 1984 elections and motivated by the already menacing crisis, Israel's two largest political parties, the right-wing Likud and the left-wing Labor Party, formed a "national unity" government, which was joined by several smaller parties. This wall-to-wall coalition also served to ensure the cooperation of the Histadrut, which itself has traditionally been dominated by the Labor party, and of the private sector, as well as broad public support. Thus reinforced by an almost unanimous national consensus, the new government devised and implemented its rather bold "Plan for Economic Stabilization."

THE ECONOMIC STABILIZATION PROGRAM AND ITS AFTERMATH

The economic stabilization plan could have succeeded only in the unique sociopolitical context that had evolved at that point in time. The virtual tie between Likud and Labor in the 1984 elections had essentially compelled the two parties to form a coalition government, which was bolstered by a substantial parliamentary majority.

Once the new government had secured the vitally important cooperation of the Histadrut, it could proceed to wrest concessions from the working public. The program called for a reduction of both the active work force and real income, the latter cut to be accomplished by a wage freeze and a rescinding of wage indexation. The private sector joined the "package deal," and the program gained the implicit support of the Israeli public, which, having just witnessed the spectacular collapse of the stock market, had become genuinely concerned. Thus, the government could operate in an environment virtually devoid of opposition either inside or outside the Knesset.

The general objective of the program was to ameliorate the four principal problems then afflicting the national economy: lack of economic growth, the three-digit inflation rate, and excessive private consumption and public expenditures. The strategy was based chiefly on drastic fiscal and monetary restraints.

Two years after the program had been implemented, the economy appeared to be well on its way to a successful recovery (Bruno & Meridor, 1990). Annual output of the business sector had grown by an average of 6%; the inflation rate had dropped from close to 400% in 1985 to an annual 15% to 20%; the government budget, which in the preceding decade had run an average deficit equal to 15% of the GNP, had been balanced and even showed a slight surplus; foreign currency reserves had increased impressively as Israel regained its position on international money markets; and even some repercussions of the program itself had been recovered, for unemployment had returned almost to the pre-1985 level of 5%.

However, the deep economic recession recurred in mid-1987 (see Table 1 for the change in relevant economic indicators between 1980 and 1989). Annual GNP dropped once again to 1%, and unemployment gradually increased to 9.5% by mid-1989. Instead of approaching the envisioned one-digit level, inflation has stabilized at an annual rate of 20% or less.

This economic decline is partially attributable to the previously mentioned detrimental effects of the Intifada, which commenced in 1987. However, it is probably the diminishing profitability of the business sector that is at the root of these difficulties. Business profits have declined because of an increase in taxation (from 38% in 1982-84 to 48% in 1988) and interest rates. The change was due mostly to the government's failure to devaluate the Israeli Shekel against foreign currencies in accord with the rising cost of living and to the renewed wage explosion,[6] which substantially escalated the cost of labor. Not until 1989, with the notable increase in unemployment, did real wages decrease even modestly relative to labor productivity (Neubach, Razin & Sadka, 1988).

Moreover, as the stabilization program and the process of recovery commenced, the business sector's previous adjustment to the economic

Table 1. Indicators of Economic Development in Israel, 1980-1989

	Percentage Annual Change					
	1980-84	*1985*	*1986*	*1987*	*1988*	*1989*
Real growth rates:						
Gross domestic product	2.8	5.3	5.8	7.2	1.5	1.5
Private consumption	5.5	0.5	14.2	8.4	3.0	-1.0
Gross domestic investment	2.7	-10.6	10.4	2.9	-1.9	-2.7
Gross real income	16.2	5.9	-0.4	-9.0	7.9	6.2
Cost of living	189.2	304.6	48.1	19.9	16.3	21.0
Unemployment rate	5.1	6.7	7.1	6.1	6.4	8.9
Real interest rate	23.0	100.0	33.0	39.0	26.0	11.0
Labor cost per hour:						
Business sector	91.0	88.5	100.0	104.7	108.7	105.1
Tax rate, nonlabor income:						
Business sector	24.9	27.5	33.3	31.0	30.0	26.0
	Percent of Annual GNP					
Public sector deficit	10.9	-1.1	-3.5	-0.1	1.9	6.1
Gross tax rate	43.1	45.0	47.7	47.1	45.1	41.1
Internal debt	128.8	129.5	116.8	109.6	103.7	105.1
External debt	65.2	80.0	63.3	53.2	45.1	38.4

Source: Adapted from: "The costly transition from stabilization to sustainable growth: Israel's case" by M. Bruno and L. Meridor, 1990, *The Economic Quarterly, 145,* 99-129. Tables 1, 2, and 7. (in Hebrew)

conditions prevailing during the crisis evolved into a series of inevitable handicaps. During the era of hyperinflation, business firms had relied on unrealistically cheap government credits and on financial manipulations to make profits without necessarily being efficient. The drop in inflation rates and the more costly lines of credits that accompanied those lower rates exposed widespread inefficiency and dictated structural reorganization. These adjustments are yet to be implemented.

Lastly, the business sector was traumatized by the government's effort to balance the budget. Public expenditures were curtailed significantly, and the government rejected most bids to support inefficient, unprofitable, and failing industries. These policies resulted in a dramatic threefold increase in the number of bankruptcies. Only the few firms that adjusted quickly by augmenting their productivity and efficiency managed to expand their output and labor force.

In sum, the main causes of the current recession in Israel are rooted in the slow pace of recovery from the distortions of the inflationary era and the curtailment of public expenditures, in the consequences of the recently recurring increases in labor costs and rising interest rates, and in the heavier tax burden. The economic crises of the 1970s and the late 1980s and the temporary respite achieved by the stabilization program during the mid-1980s provide the macroeconomic context to which the Israeli public have had to adjust as economic persons[7] and as economic citizens in recent years.

THE ECONOMIC PERSON: EARNINGS, CONSUMPTION, COPING

With few exceptions, the real income of the Israeli labor force grew annually during the past decade. In parallel, there has been a striking increase in private consumption. Nonetheless, the public is far from satisfied with either its personal economic fortunes or the societal distribution of affluence. Only 60.5% of the working population feel that they are getting their "equitable share of comfort and amenities in life compared to other people in this country." Fully 33% believe that they are receiving less or much less than they deserve. The sense of inequity has intensified. Seven years earlier, in 1982, 68% had reported that they were equitably rewarded; 27.6%, that they were receiving less than they thought they deserved.[8]

At first glance, there appears to be little evidence for personal discontent in workers' appraisals of their own job and work commitment: 37% report being very satisfied or satisfied with their jobs; another 47.7% are "quite satisfied." This distribution closely resembles ratings of job satisfaction typical of most Western nations.

Israelis express a degree of commitment to their work that is even higher than that usually found among comparable work forces: 66.6% assert that they would enjoy working even if they did not need the money (versus less than 60% in the United States and Britain and less than 50% in Germany and Italy[9]); 47.6% claim that "work is [their] most important activity" (a statement rejected by most of the public in all Western nations); and a significant minority of 39% maintain that they work as required even if it interferes with other activities.

However, this image of the highly committed and content Israeli worker vanishes under closer scrutiny, especially in terms of satisfaction with the availability and allocation of work incentives. Frustrated expectations and demands are particularly evident with respect to the inadequate level of income and the discrepancy between the preferred and the actual determinants of salaries and wages at the work place.

As may be observed in Table 2, the Israeli working population and people employed in comparable industrial nations do not differ appreciably in their assessments of major work incentives. High income, opportunities for advancement, job security, and an interesting job are considered the most important outcomes. The work place proffers mostly job security, an interesting job, independence, and work that aids society. Income and, more marginally, advancement are provided at a level far below expectations.[10] However, this

Table 2.   The Importance and Perceived Realization of Work
Outcomes in Israel and Five Industrialized Countries, 1988

Work Outcome[a]		Israel	Britain	Italy	Germany	USA	Hungary
Job security	Importance	1.36	1.46	1.36	1.54	1.53	1.50
	Realization	2.28	2.47	2.08	1.86	2.09	2.24
High income	Importance	1.89	2.06	1.89	1.99	1.95	1.63
	Realization	3.02	3.40	3.12	2.98	3.20	3.73
Advancement	Importance	1.90	1.85	1.90	2.09	1.68	2.21
	Realization	2.28	3.31	3.48	3.15	3.00	3.77
Leisure time	Importance	2.72	2.70	2.37	2.29	3.00	2.10
	Realization	3.04	3.28	3.02	2.98	3.21	3.62
Interesting job	Importance	1.59	1.54	1.56	1.59	1.65	1.92
	Realization	2.24	2.11	2.19	1.98	2.11	2.40
Independent job	Importance	1.97	2.20	2.03	1.83	2.06	2.11
	Realization	2.48	2.10	2.53	2.03	2.08	2.25
Helping people	Importance	2.21	2.22	2.00	2.37	2.04	2.09
	Realization	2.41	2.29	2.69	2.62	2.06	2.17
Useful to society	Importance	2.10	2.22	1.91	2.25	1.99	1.79
	Realization	2.31	2.44	2.50	2.17	2.15	2.09
Flexible hours	Importance	2.26	2.61	2.21	2.59	2.45	2.24
	Realization	2.79	3.15	3.10	3.50	2.80	3.38

Notes: [a] The subjective importance of job outcomes was rated on five-point scales (1 = very important; 5 = not at all important). The realization of job outcomes was ascertained by asking: "To what extent do you agree or disagree that the following apply to your job?", (1 = definitely agree; 5 = definitely disagree).

Source: International Social Survey Project (Work Orientation Module). 1989. *Zentralarchiv für empirische Sozialforschung* (ZA), University of Cologne.

subjective resemblance between work forces obscures an important objective difference, the fact that the buying power of the average employed person in Israel is significantly lower than in many other Western countries.[11] Thus, despite indexation and the other protective devices discussed earlier, inadequate income remains the economic person's most salient problem.

Not only the amount of remuneration but also the principles that determine wages fail to meet the public's expectations; the relevant data are displayed in Table 3. Israelis and respondents from other nations concur that wages should be determined primarily on the basis of performance; experience, seniority, and education are less important. But perceptions of the structure of remuneration differ. At the Israeli work place, performance counts far less than it presumably should, whereas the value of seniority is inflated.

How does the Israeli public cope with these challenges? The almost continuous increase in private consumption (see Figure 1 and Table 1) certainly does not point to a cutback in consumer demand. In fact, a serious reduction in consumption does not seem feasible. The cost of the basic needs and expenses sustained by an average family, figures that are computed and issued monthly

Table 3. Desired and Perceived Determinants of
Income in Israel and Five Industrialized Countries, 1988

Determinants of Income[a]		Israel	Britain	Italy	Germany	USA	Hungary
Duration of employment	Desirability	.96	1.15	1.21	.93	1.41	1.31
	Attainment	.89	1.15	1.21	1.28	1.46	1.15
Quality of work	Desirability	1.20	1.31	1.16	1.07	1.30	1.24
	Attainment	.79	1.35	1.15	.96	1.28	1.27
Employee's experience	Desirability	1.24	1.72	1.22	1.08	1.77	.76
	Attainment	.97	1.71	1.21	.90	1.72	.89
Equality	Desirability	.53	.63	.20	.55	.34	.46
	Attainment	.42	.68	.30	.57	.43	.88
Employee's age	Desirability	.14	.22	.22	.38	.07	.24
	Attainment	.13	.19	.23	.48	.06	.27
Employee's sex	Desirability	.05	.04	.11	.08	.05	—
	Attainment	.06	.01	.10	.13	.08	—
Family obligations	Desirability	.38	.18	.62	.37	.16	.59
	Attainment	.29	.12	.51	.26	.17	.79
Education, qualifications	Desirability	1.11	.65	1.09	.65	.98	1.36
	Attainment	.84	.71	.92	.53	.95	1.16

Notes: [a] Desired determinants of income were rank-ordered, with the first three ranks being included in the calculations (1 = most important; 2 = second most important; 3 = third most important). Actual (attained) determinants of income were rated on 5-point scales of subjective importance (1 = very important; 5 = not at all important).

Source: International Social Survey Project (Work Orientation Module). 1989. *Zentralarchiv für empirische Sozialforschung* (ZA), University of Cologne.

as an "elementary consumer package" by the Central Bureau of Statistics, already exceeds the average employee's salary.

In view of the prevailing inadequate level of income, only the existence of additional sources of capital can plausibly explain the relatively high level of consumption. Beyond legitimate alternatives of increasing household earnings, such as second jobs and the growing participation of women in the labor market,[12] a considerable portion of the total income generated by the Israeli public is derived from illegal (i.e., untaxed) sources.

The most common, though certainly not the only, source of these considerable cash reserves is a substantial and booming second economy: undisclosed private work by craftsmen, the unregistered retail sale of consumer goods,[13] and extensive moonlighting by salaried workers. Precise figures are obviously difficult to come by. Kondor (1986), who has ventured the only empirical study of tax evasion in Israel known to us, estimates the total amount of undisclosed earnings at 20% of the GNP, not including income from illegal activities such as drug trafficking. Even if we allow for a large margin of error, this rate is well beyond estimates typical of Western nations, except Italy.

Lastly, the consumer market has adopted a variety of techniques to accommodate the scarce resources of potential customers. Banking establishments permit clients to overdraw their accounts far in excess of their salaries, credit cards are widely accepted and used to postpone payments, many consumer products are discounted, and sales are frequently made on installments or against deferred payments not bearing interest.

ECONOMIC CITIZENSHIP AND
THE RHETORIC OF CAPITALISM

At the very onset of the economic crisis, Israeli society also experienced a profound political transformation. After Likud scored its electoral victory in 1977, the party formed the first right-wing government in the country's history. This turn of events was accompanied by a decisive ideological change, which manifested itself both in political rhetoric and in practice. The most explicit reflection of this metamorphosis is the government's uncompromising attitudes and policies vis-à-vis the Palestinian problem (e.g., the Intifada, Jewish settlements, the question of Palestinian sovereignty in general) and the Arab-Israeli conflict (e.g., peace negotiations). On the domestic front, the government has introduced a series of subtle and insidious restrictions on democratic and civil liberties.

The public by and large agrees with this agenda: 73.1% identify with the right, the moderate right, or the political center;[14] 66.5% are willing to relinquish no more than a small part of the occupied territories for peace, and 39.3% reject any territorial compromise; 57.7% do not envision peace with surrounding Arab nations; instead, many expect that the current status quo will prevail, or even that relations will deteriorate further (33.9%).[15]

As is often characteristic of the political right, the public also endorses manifestations of authoritative power. Strong national defense and law and order are regarded as highly important social goals (86.4% and 87.3%, respectively) at the expense of quality-of-life preferences ("a less impersonal society," 79.2%) and democratic values ("greater influence on government decisions," 69.4%).[16] In 1989, 42.7% asserted that Israel was "too democratic"; 57.8%, that security threats justify profound infringements on democratic principles; and 58.3%, that "it is best to have a strong leadership...without having to depend on elections or a majority in the Knesset" (Peres & Yuchtman-Yaar, 1991). In short, the political attitudes of the Israeli public may not appeal to everyone in the society, but they do communicate a considerable degree of internal constraint (e.g., Converse, 1964).

Most observers are probably less acquainted with the socioeconomic elements of the Likud's conservative platform. They are marked by the intent to accomplish a transformation from a centralized, regulated system to mechanisms of a market economy: the reduction of government intervention and its economic role and functions, decentralization and the relaxation of economic control, and privatization—in short, the classic capitalist credo.

There are obvious external and internal constraints delimiting the decentralization of Israel's tightly controlled and highly regulated economy: military expenditures and the cost of immigration on the one hand, and the weak private sector, the political influence of the Histadrut, scarce investment capital, and vulnerable export markets on the other. Nonetheless, a range of liberalization measures, such as the suspension of price controls, subsidies and tariffs, and the privatization of government-owned and controlled companies, are applicable even under these unique circumstances.[17]

Admittedly, decentralization has been severely impeded by the economic crisis and especially by the government's massive intervention in the course of the economic stabilization program. Yet even before and after the implementation of the program, the stated objectives were realized sporadically at best, if indeed the government ever genuinely intended to achieve them. At first glance, relevant indicators appear to document some success, but it is known that statistics sometimes lie.

1. By 1987, the price of about 50% of all goods and services in Israel had been decontrolled. Yet, most basic staples remain subject to price control and subsidization, and many essential nonconsumer products (e.g., water for agricultural use) are still heavily subsidized.

2. Import depositions and levies were reduced gradually and were cancelled in 1988. However, the foreign currency market is still strictly regulated. The repeal of many statutes benefitted private individuals (e.g., tourists) more than business enterprises.

3. The sale of government-owned companies is the best known aspect of Israeli economic liberalization. Of these 210 firms owned by the government, 50, including several large corporations such as Bezek/Telephones and Communications, the Israel Oil Refineries, and the Israel Chemical Company, are currently at various stages of privatization (Katz, 1988). Yet in practice, little has changed. In some sectors (e.g., defense industries) the number of public firms has actually doubled during the last decade; their total number is now virtually identical to that in 1977, and their work force of more than 60,000 has been reduced by a mere 400 persons.

THE PARADOX OF PUBLIC OPINION

It is hardly shocking that politicians often fail to fulfill their promises, yet one is puzzled by the discovery that the public not only condones these contradictions but even reproduces them. On the one hand, most economic citizens identify themselves with a capitalist orientation, which should in principle imply support for economic decentralization; on the other hand, the government is increasingly charged with the responsibility for resolving the country's most fundamental economic problems.[18] In short, with or without faith in the precepts of a market economy the public continues to regard interventionism as the fundamental collective remedy for Israel's economic ills.

In line with the conservative rhetoric of the Likud party, the general ideological label "capitalist" has become increasingly popular over the last decade. In 1982, only 41.1% identified themselves as capitalists (as opposed to "socialists") or as persons inclined toward this value orientation; by 1989, 55.6% embraced this credo.

At first glance, diverse positions on socioeconomic issues appear to validate these self-identifications. For example, the factors viewed as responsible for the country's economic problems can be categorized into two clusters:[19] (a) government policies and performance (excessive economic intervention, flawed tax legislation, the imprudent accumulation of national debt, ineffective crisis management—in short, the prevailing economic system) and (b) the working public (low productivity, efficiency, work discipline, responsibility, and work ethic; excessive wage demands; the exclusive profit motivation of entrepreneurs).

Whereas a large majority used to believe and continues to assert that the government and the public share the responsibility for the country's economic afflictions, the *relative* apportionment of blame has shifted decisively. In 1989, the government and its interventionist policies were viewed as considerably more liable, whereas the work force's performance was perceived to be a significantly less central catalyst of economic problems (Table 4).

Table 4.   Ascriptions of Responsibility for Israel's
Worsening Economic Conditions: 1982 and 1989

		Ascriptions [in Percentages] [a]		
Affect Economic Deterioration	Year	*1*	*2*	*3*
Unions demands for excessive wages	1982	41.3	13.2	54.5
	1989	37.2	38.3	65.5
Entrepreneurs only seeking profit	1982	46.5	20.9	67.4
	1989	46.5	20.5	67.0
Economy too dependent on foreign aid	1982	38.9	49.0	87.9
	1989	43.3	34.2	77.5
Entrepreneurs' taxes too high	1982	36.9	16.4	53.3
	1989	43.2	22.7	65.9
Too much government intervention	1982	44.0	17.0	61.0
	1989	47.8	19.5	67.3
The "economic system"	1982	44.5	33.4	77.9
	1989	50.5	29.6	80.1
Work ethic too low	1982	41.2	48.7	89.1
	1989	45.5	34.2	79.7

Notes: [a] 1 - "has some effect"; 2 - "has much effect"; 3 - has either "some effect" or "much effect".
Source: *National representative surveys conducted by the authors in 1982 and 1989 (N = 1,800 and N = 1,200, respectively).*

Paradoxically, even though the blame for economic predicaments is increasingly shifting toward the government, support for its policies of intervention and centralization is expanding rather than diminishing. Table 5 presents a comparison of responses to the question of the extent to which "an important role" in various socioeconomic domains is sought for the public and the private sector, or both cooperatively. Much of the support previously accorded the cooperation between the two sectors has shifted to the government, which had traditionally exercised substantial economic control in any case. Not only is the government now expected to perform an even more pivotal role in the most vital spheres of economic activity, these expectations pertain to functions traditionally delegated to the state (e.g., "equality") as well as to those typically considered a classic domain of the private sector (e.g., economic growth).

It is only the government's economic functions that engender such internal contradictions. As the public gains a more positive image of its own productive role, other self-assessments are becoming more favorable as well. Thus, confidence in workers' productive contributions, though far from copious, is mounting. In 1989, 48.1% asserted that "the average Israeli worker" is inclined to accept discipline (versus only 37% in 1982); 54.2%, that she or he demonstrates responsibility toward the work place (47.3%), and 35.2% that she or he is highly productive (29.8%).

Moreover, the public is now more inclined to espouse measures designed to enhance productivity and efficiency at work, even at the expense of job security.[20] When these two dimensions are juxtaposed (Table 6), most Israelis

Table 5.   Desired Role of the Government and the Private
Sector in Diverse Economic Activities in Israel: 1982 and 1989

Activity/Involvement	Year	"An Important Role" Desired for....[a]			
		1	2	3	4
Increase Employment	1982	38.3	11.2	50.5	88.8
	1989	46.6	19.9	33.5	80.1
Increase Economic Growth	1982	39.2	11.2	49.6	88.8
	1989	52.0	18.0	30.0	72.0
Reduce Social Inequality	1982	58.6	6.8	34.6	93.2
	1989	65.0	12.5	22.6	87.6
Fight Inflation	1982	56.6	3.8	39.6	96.2
	1989	66.7	8.9	24.4	91.1

Notes: [a] 1 - government sector; 2 - private sector; 3 - government sector and private sector together; 4 - either government sector, or government sector and private sector together.
Source: National representative surveys conducted by the authors in 1982 and 1989 ($N = 1,800$ and $N = 1,200$, respectively).

Table 6.   Preferences for Work Efficiency Versus Job Security: 1982 and 1989

Statement	1982	1989
Technological innovations[a]	68.0*	64.8
Fire workers[b]	57.3	63.8
Continue tenure system[c]	44.6	45.2
Wages based on productivity[d]	82.9	77.3

Notes: * Percentage of respondents agreeing with the efficiency statement, which was juxtaposed with a corresponding assertion favoring job security.

[a] "Technological innovations should be encouraged to increase efficiency, even if workers will be fired as a consequence" vs. "Technological innovations for greater efficiency should not be encouraged, as this will lead to the discharge of workers."

[b] "It is justified to fire workers and to close plants, even if it causes higher unemployment" vs. "It is the government's responsibility to ensure work for all, even if this necessitates the continued operation of failing industries."

[c] "The current tenure system should be continued, as it grants the worker security at his or her work place" vs. "The current tenure system should be changed, for it may discourage workers from making an effort."

[d] "Workers' wages should be based primarily on their productivity and less on seniority or social considerations" vs. "Workers' wages should be based primarily on seniority and social considerations and less on their productivity."

Source: National representative surveys conducted by the authors in 1982 and 1989 ($N = 1,800$ and $N = 1,200$, respectively).

advocate that wages and salaries be made contingent upon productivity, that technological innovations be introduced even if layoffs will ensue, and that inefficient industrial plants be closed even at the risk of higher unemployment. The line is drawn only at the suggestion to abolish the sacrosanct tenure system.[21] Needless to say, these speculations do not necessarily reflect a firm commitment to sacrificing job security for higher productivity.

Lastly, there is little evidence to suggest that the ideological transformation and the changing views of the public about its own economic performance and that of the government have also generated a parallel shift in the public's traditional and solid support for welfare policies and income redistribution. These principles have consistently been endorsed by a large majority of Israelis. Thus, 75% or more invariably endorse welfare benefits for socially vulnerable groups (e.g., the elderly, young couples, the indigent, army veterans). Immigrants, who had been less favored earlier (57.4% in 1982) have gained more support since the Jewish exodus from the Soviet Union (67.3% in 1989). The increase in backing for the unemployed (45.2% in 1982 versus 58.4% in 1989) is probably due to the current hazards of the labor market. It is noteworthy, however, that the unemployed receive only qualified public support. For example, they are expected to make substantial adjustments in order to regain employment, and these demands are becoming more and more stringent (Table 7). Only the requirements that the unemployed accept worse physical working conditions or change their place of residence are routinely rejected.

Table 7. Concessions Demanded of the
Unemployed Seeking a Job: 1982 and 1989

	"…than in the Previous Job"[a]	
	1982	1989
More Distant From Home	76.7	81.5
Earn Less	62.7	65.6
Less Convenient Hours	74.8	71.6
Lower Status	64.2	63.6
Worse Physical Conditions	43.7	44.6
	Other	
Work Below Abilities	52.1	52.2
Require Retraining	75.6	78.4
Temporary Job	58.5	63.0
Change Residence	35.3	35.4
Earn Less Than Unemployment Benefits	24.5	—

Notes: [a] Percentage of respondents agreeing with the demand.
Source: National representative surveys conducted by the authors in 1982 and 1989 ($N = 1,800$ and $N = 1,200$, respectively).

UNRAVELING THE CONUNDRUM

In sum, the central paradox relates to the apparent contradiction between the Israeli public's growing dissatisfaction with government policies on the one hand and its burgeoning dependence on a centrally controlled, managed, and regulated economic system on the other hand. In other words, the government is both *the* cause of the country's economic problems and *the* actor to be entrusted with their rectification. These presumably incompatible views call to mind the negation between the government's rhetoric about economic liberalization and the unabated practice of a highly controlled, state-dominated economy.

One needs little sophistication to account for the contradiction between what the government says and what it does; such inconsistencies are hardly uncommon (remember "read my lips"?). At best, the government is vacillating between the acknowledged need to institute mechanisms of a market economy and recognition of the objective constraints on such a transformation. At worst, its statements of intent are insincere. It does not take a misanthrope to recognize the contribution that the current centralized system can make to the political power held by the government and the party dominating it. This appraisal would hardly lead one to conjecture that the government would ever be inclined to relinquish economic control, capitalist rhetoric or not.

The paradox between the public's critical stance on economic policies and the growing support for government regulation and intervention is more convoluted. The accord between *political* attitudes and regional policies is not altogether surprising. The issues involved are sufficiently salient to determine the outcome of most elections, and the government's related rhetoric and policies by and large coincide. This, of course, is not the case in the economic sphere. The government expounds deregulation but continues its control of the economy; the public endorses capitalism and criticizes the government's performance but yearns all the more for the persistence of the same old system.

Conventional explanations—Israel's Zionist tradition or the fostering of a dependency syndrome during 40 years of socialist rule—do not adequately account for this growing reliance on the government. The most probable answer lies in two recent, critical, and highly important economic events in which the government played a pivotal, and presumably successful, role. The first of these episodes, the economic stabilization program, has already been touched on; the second is known as "the banking crisis."

The crisis evolved because private banking establishments had illicitly, though with the government's tacit approval, subsidized their own shares on the stock market. When the banks collectively decided to discontinue this practice because of difficulties with cash flow, shares dropped instantly by 35%, and trading was suspended. Low-income groups and business firms, which had made massive purchases of these shares as a conservative investment during inflation, suffered the heaviest losses. To prevent an avalanche of bankruptcies, the government was forced to purchase all shares in circulation;[22] consequently, it is currently holding the majority of shares in all banking establishments.

During the banking crisis and the implementation of the economic stabilization program, the government showed considerable skill in managing critical economic processes and averting some of the potential risks involved. However, both events also failed to manifest some of the limitations of intervention. The stabilization program achieved only part of its objectives, and even those accomplishments were short-lived and costly. As for the banking crisis, it had been precipitated in collusion with the government in the first place, and the ensuing state control of most private banks can hardly be considered a desirable outcome. Nonetheless, these ventures are typically presented to, and accepted by, the public as a demonstration of the success of government policies and of economic intervention. Criticism of and belief in the capitalist doctrine aside, "big brother" remains the Israeli public's ultimate savior and protector.

ACKNOWLEDGMENTS

We would like to thank Yasmin Alkalai and Yael Har-Even for contributing their useful ideas and aiding in the data analysis.

NOTES

1. Spending by governmental and quasi-governmental bodies has often exceeded the gross national product (Sharkansky, 1987).

2. These effects are due to the decline in tourism, the Palestinian boycott of Israeli goods and services, and so forth.

3. About a dozen political parties typically partake in national elections. Because the electoral system is based on proportional representation, no single party has ever won a majority in Israel's parliament (Knesset); hence, the routine establishment of coalition governments.

4. Indexation is a method for partially neutralizing the reduction of real income due to inflation. In Israel, these corrections were typically made trimonthly and amounted to a 70% adjustment of wages to the average increase in the cost of living during the preceding three months. Under conditions of hyperinflation, this three-month delay obviously constitutes a penalty for employed persons. The Histadrut accomplished a further compensation of this erosion by compelling the government to institute a monthly indexation of wages at the rate of 80% of inflation.

5. Unless otherwise noted, the subjective data cited in this chapter are derived from two national representative surveys conducted by the authors in 1982 and 1989 ($N = 1,800$ and $N = 1,200$, respectively). The surveys partially overlapped in content. Some items (e.g., the assessment of the economic crisis reported here) were not replicated in 1989.

6. Between 1986 and 1988, average real income exceeded the rate of inflation by some 7.5% annually.

7. The terms *economic man* and *economic citizen* were originally introduced along by Strümpel and Yuchtman-Yaar (1986). Here, we use the nonsex ist term *economic person* for *economic man.*

8. This change coincides with a factual, albeit moderate, trend toward greater socioeconomic inequality. In 1982, the upper 20% of the population received 38.8% of total earned income after income transfers and taxes. By 1989, their share had increased to 40.1% (Ginny Index: .22 versus .29).

9. The data on Western countries reported here are based on an international comparative study of 10 nations (the United States, Britain, Germany, Italy, Austria, the Netherlands, Norway, Denmark, Israel, and Hungary) conducted under the auspices of the International Social Science Program (1989).

10. On the other hand, leisure is considered neither as important nor as discrepant with expectations as in other countries. It appears to be of little concern to Israelis altogether. For example, the opportunity to make changes in work time so as to gain a day off each week or to prolong vacations is rejected by 28.1%. Another 20.9% claim that these options do not apply to their work.

11. In 1985, for example, *real* wages in Israel increased by 2.5%; in Sweden, 5.7%; in Britain, 6.7%; and in Italy, 7.6%. Workers in the United States sustained a 4.7% decrease in real wages.

12. In the course of the last two decades, the share of women actively participating in the labor force grew by one-third, from 29.4% to 39.8% (Central Bureau of Statistics, 1990).

13. Consumers are often compensated by a waiver of value-added tax.

14. In the context of contemporary Israeli politics, there are only trivial differences between right and center, especially with respect to policies vis-à-vis Palestinians and the Arab world.

15. These beliefs are more typical of Israel's Sephardic community and the more religious and the less educated sectors of the population. These groups identify with the same nationalist ideology represented by the Likud and by the smaller right-wing and religious parties and are willing to tolerate many of the economic hardships imposed by a government they consider "their own."

16. These items are adopted from Inglehart's (1977) materialism/postmaterialism measure; 5-point scales ranging from "goal very important" to "goal not at all important" were employed.

In 1982, support for "a strong national defense" (93.2%) and "law and order" (97%) had been somewhat higher.

17.   Given Israel's volatile security situation and the frequent demand for major public efforts (e.g., immigration), some measures typically used as indicators of the functioning of market economies, (e.g., the share of the private sector in the GNP, private and public construction) are irrelevant here.

18.   This finding is also in line with trends observed in other Western countries (e.g., Dalton, 1988).

19.   A third cluster (marginal groups, especially Palestinians) suspected of constituting potential competition for employment is less germane to the present analysis. The amount of blame attributed to members of this cluster depends primarily on changes in the volatile employment situation.

20.   Self-defined capitalists do differ from socialists on some of these dimensions. They are more critical of both government involvement and worker productivity, more likely to demand that employees sacrifice job security for efficiency, and more determined to confine government functions to redistribution. However, both capitalists and socialists evince the common contradiction of growing more skeptical of government economic performance while asking that the government play a more prominent role in key areas of the economy.

21.   Most firms and organizations in both the public and the private sector award life-long employment after a trial period of 6 to 10 months. Tenured employees are rarely discharged, and even then only at considerable compensatory cost.

22.   To recompense investors, the government issued secure bonds at a value corresponding to the price of shares at the closing of the stock market (i.e., at a 35% loss). These bonds are tied to the U.S. dollar and thus constitute a relatively safe investment, but they can be traded only after 10 years.

REFERENCES

Bank of Israel. 1990. *Annual report*. Jerusalem: Government Printing Office. (In Hebrew)

Bruno, M., & Meridor, L. (1990). The costly transition from stabilization to sustainable growth: Israel's case. *The Economic Quarterly, 145,* 99-129. (In Hebrew)

Central Bureau of Statistics (Israel). (1990). *Statistical Abstracts, 41,* Abstracts nos. 6.1, 6.2, 7.4, 10.2, 12.9. Jerusalem: Keter. (In Hebrew)

Converse, P. E. (1964). The nature of belief systems in mass publics. In D. Apter (Ed.), *Ideology and discontent,* pp. 206-261. New York: Free Press of Glencoe.

Dalton, R. S. (1988). *Citizen politics in western democracies.* Chatham, NJ: Chatham House.

Inglehart, R. (1977). *The silent revolution: Changing political styles among western publics.* Princeton: Princeton University Press.

International Social Survey Project (Work Orientation Module). (1989). *Zentralarchiv für empirische Sozialforschung* (ZA). University of Cologne.

Katz, I. (1988). Privatization in Israel: Unique characteristics. *Management [Israel's Manager's Magazine], 63,* 7-11. (In Hebrew)

Kondor, Y. (1986). *Tax evasion in Israel: 1975-1983.* Discussion paper No. 13-86, Tel Aviv University, Pinchas Sapir Center for Development.

Neubach, A., Razin, A., & Sadka, E. (1988). *Economic growth: Embarking on the 1990s.* Tel Aviv: Ma'ariv Library. (In Hebrew)

Peres, Y., & Yuchtman-Yaar, E. (1991, spring). Public opinion and democracy after three years of Intifada. *Israeli Democracy,* 21-25.

Shalev, M. (1984). Labor, state, and crisis: An Israeli case. *Industrial Relations, 23,* 362-386.

Sharkansky, I. (1987). *The political economy of Israel.* New Brunswick, NJ: Transaction Books.

Strümpel, B. & Yuchtman-Yaar, E. (1986, July). *Germany and Israel: Contrasting cases in popular culture*. Paper presented at the 6th Annual Meeting of the International Society of Political Psychology, St. Catherine's College, Oxford, England.

SWEDEN:
STILL THE MODEL?

Axel van den Berg and Ryszard Szulkin

THE RISE OF THE "SWEDISH MODEL"

In several respects, Sweden is an outlier in the advanced industrialized world. Its process of industrialization was both relatively late and exceptionally rapid. From around 1870 to 1950, Sweden may have enjoyed the highest sustained economic growth rates in the world. As a result, by 1950 it had metamorphosed from one of the poorest countries in Europe in the late 19th century to the second richest in the world (after the United States) in terms of GNP per capita. A large part of this successful record is no doubt due to Sweden's ability to stay out of both World Wars (see, e.g., Bergman, Bjürklund, Jakobsson, Lundberg, & Söderström, 1990, pp. 16-19; Horváth & Daly, 1989, pp. 16-17).

Naturally, such rapid industrialization implies an equally rapid transformation of the occupational structure. Whereas in 1870 almost three quarters of the Swedish labor force was still employed in agriculture, that figure has dwindled to less than 4% in recent years. Similarly, manufacturing employment grew from 12% of the labor force in 1870 to a high of about 33% in the early 1950s, only to decline again to less than 25% in recent years (see De Geer et al., 1987, p. 24; Furåker, 1990, p. 10; SCB, 1989a, pp. 87-94).

Sweden's rapid, and no doubt at times brutal, industrialization partly accounts for the other major feature setting Sweden apart from most other advanced capitalist countries: the extraordinary strength of the Swedish labor movement. From their very beginnings in the late 1800s, the blue-collar labor union central *Landsorganisationen* (LO) and the Social Democratic Party (SAP, for *Socialdemokratiska Arbetarepartiet*) closely cooperated to strengthen each others' positions in the labor market and political arena. Already by 1907 some 48% of Swedish industrial workers belonged to a union. Although the Swedish union movement suffered a disastrous setback in the 1909 General Strike, from which it did not recover until 1917 (Einhorn & Logue, 1989, pp. 237-238; Forsebäck, 1980, pp. 7-8), it continued to grow thereafter to achieve the highest union density anywhere in the advanced capitalist world, representing over 80% of the labor force in recent years (see, e.g., Kjellberg, 1983, pp. 36, 51).

Similarly, the SAP, after early electoral successes leading to participation in a number of coalition governments as junior partner in the late 1910s and early 1920s, suffered electoral defeats during the later 1920s, which prompted its leadership to shed the earlier radicalism and adopt a firmly reformist program (Heclo & Madsen, 1987, pp. 7, 254-257). In 1932, at the height of the Great Depression, the SAP finally won enough votes to become the dominant party in the government. The election platform included a far-reaching proposal by party theorist Ernst Wigforss for an economic recovery policy foreshadowing what was later to become known as "Keynesianism"— including the idea of countercyclical aggregate demand stabilization by means of deficit spending while balancing the budget over the business cycle rather than annually. The program also called for a massive expansion and liberalization of public works projects. The apparent success[1] of these policies is one of the major reasons for the subsequent decades of SAP dominance in Swedish politics (Barkin, 1977, pp. 9-11; Ginsburg, 1983, pp. 111-112; Jangenäs, 1985, pp. 10-11; Korpi, 1978, pp. 80-81; Martin, 1984, pp. 193-195; Öhman, 1974). SAP-dominated governments ruled Sweden from then until 1991, except for the brief spell of "bourgeois" government from 1976 to 1982 (see Einhorn & Logue, 1989, p. 313).

In addition to the unrivaled power of the country's labor movement, Swedish employers are unusually well-organized in the highly centralized *Svenska Arbetsgivarefreningen* (SAF). The SAF's early and relatively aggressive use of the lockout in response to the LO's actions was in part responsible for the eventually very high degree of centralization in Swedish collective bargaining. Until the late 1930s, Swedish industrial relations were marked by a great deal of conflict, with frequent and bitter strikes and lockouts. When the Social Democratic government threatened to intervene to regulate labor relations, however, the LO and the SAF were able to arrive at the famous 1938 "Basic Agreement" at Saltsjöbaden. The Saltsjöbaden agreement set the ground rules for collective bargaining between employers and unions without state intervention. It produced an almost immediate and dramatic drop in the incidence of industrial conflicts, transforming Swedish labor relations from among the most strife-torn to one of the most peaceful in the industrialized world.

During the early 1950s, both the SAF and the LO pushed toward further centralization of industrial relations. By the mid-1950s, yearly country-wide collective agreements between the SAF and the LO, later joined by the white-collar union central (*Tjänstemännens Centralorganisation,* TCO) and the union of academics (*Sveriges Akademikers Centralorganisation,* SACO), became the norm (see Fulcher, 1988, pp. 130-133; Heclo & Madsen, 1987, pp. 115-116). This process of centralization culminated in 1970, when economists of the LO, SAF, and TCO came to an agreement—the so-called EFO model (after the three economists' last names)—according to which wage increases in the rest of the economy were to be made dependent on what the export industries could bear without loss of competitiveness. The model was applied to some extent throughout the 1970s (see Forsebäck, 1980; pp. 70-73; Heclo & Madsen, 1989, pp. 109-120; Horváth & Daly, 1989, p. 26).

From the 1950s on, the LO pursued its "solidaristic wage policy." It was part of an ingenious combination of policies originally proposed in a 1951 policy statement entitled *Trade Unions and Full Employment,* which became famous as the Rehn-Meidner Model, named after the two union economists who were its main authors. The package was intended to secure rapid economic growth while avoiding both unemployment and inflation and strengthening union solidarity.

Rehn and Meidner proposed that the LO insist in its wage negotiations on the principle of equal pay for equal work irrespective of the employers' productivity and profitability. Wages would be set at such a level as to cause difficulties for the least profitable firms but, by implication, generally at a level somewhat below what the most profitable companies might be able to pay. At the same time, the government was to observe a policy of strict fiscal restraint. With this combination of wage and fiscal pressure, less efficient firms would be gradually squeezed out of business while the most efficient ones would be encouraged to expand faster than they otherwise would. If properly fine-tuned, Rehn and Meidner argued, such a policy would thus stimulate rapid economic restructuring without necessarily leading to high levels of "frictional" unemployment. Moreover, unemployment as well as the inevitable inflationary effects of crude Keynesian aggregate demand stimulation could be avoided, they argued, by a massive program of *selective* "active" labor-market policies to create and promote the creation of jobs where necessary, while encouraging the rapid flow of labor from declining to expanding industries by a system of efficient employment services, retraining programs, and mobility allowances.

These programs would simultaneously serve to make the overall strategy more palatable to the workers who would be forced to move and would help keep down inflationary pressures by eliminating possible bottlenecks in the labor market. Moreover, while reinforcing internal solidarity within the LO, the labor movement's power would be strengthened to the extent that the policies would succeed in maintaining near full employment. Rehn and

Meidner also foresaw that their proposed policies would eventually lead to a general profit squeeze in the private sector, necessitating increasing amounts of public funds to maintain investment levels, introducing a form of "creeping socialism" (for the best available summary, see Martin, 1984, pp. 202-208; see also Björklund, 1986a, pp. 4-6; Erixon, 1985, pp. 5-6; Esping-Andersen, 1985, pp. 228-230; Ginsburg, 1983, p. 114; Jangenäs, 1985, pp. 12-13; Lundberg, 1972, pp. 471-473; McBride, 1988, pp. 307-308).

The government was at first rather reluctant to adopt the Rehn-Meidner plan, hoping it could instead continue to pressure the LO into "voluntary" restraint so that the government might continue to pursue the popular expansionary policies that would otherwise cause inflation. But in 1955 the unions flatly refused any longer to play the role of an "apparatus for keeping down the money wages of their members" (Rehn, 1984, p. 6), which they saw as "contrary to their natural way of functioning." This stance finally convinced the government it had no other choice. From then on, labor-market policies expanded very rapidly (Rehn, 1984, p. 7). Expenditures grew from less than 0.5% of GNP in the early 1950s to between 2% and 3% in the early 1970s (Rehn, 1984, p. 7), and the number of people affected grew from 0.5% of the labor force to over 2% as well (see Barkin, 1977; Jangenäs, 1985, p. 13; Johannesson & Persson-Tanimura, 1978, p. 8; Martin, 1984, pp. 217-218; Rehn, 1984, p. 7).

An integral part of the model was the so-called work line (arbetslinjen), meaning that the "goal of employment policy is 'work for everyone'" (Larsson, 1988, p. 3; see also Dahlberg, 1988, pp. 98-99; Jangenäs, 1985, p. 32; Jonzon, 1988, p. 140; Leijon, 1988, p. 92; Sou, 1975; Van Den Berg & Smucker, 1988, pp. 11-13).[2] This commitment to full employment, originally promoted by the labor movement and Social Democratic Party (see, e.g., Martin, 1984; Therborn, 1985, pp. 102-104), now seems to have become accepted without question across the Swedish political spectrum, a consensus from which not even "bourgeois" politicians can permit themselves to deviate. In Sweden, "a job is considered a basic right" (Ginsburg, 1983, p. 123). Few observers would contest that "Sweden is distinguished from other developed countries by the extraordinary lengths to which it has gone to hold down unemployment" (McBride, 1988; Rivlin, 1987, p. 6).

The other major pillar of the Swedish Model and major Social Democratic commitment consists of the construction and consolidation of the world's most comprehensive welfare state. Although most of Sweden's welfare policies and social insurance programs can be found in other advanced countries in one form or another, none has implemented a whole system of programs of the comprehensiveness, universality, extent, generosity, and redistributive effect as Sweden has. Swedish benefit levels and replacement ratios tend to be higher (most social insurance programs seek to replace up to 90% of the average industrial worker's wage), maximum payment periods longer (parental leave support may be taken for up to a year and a half), eligibility rules more generous, and coverage more universal than in other countries. With a whole array of more or less universal transfer payments, from housing allowances to child support, the attempt is made to guarantee a relatively high minimum standard of living for all Swedes and to reduce inequality in disposable incomes. Social insurance programs (including health care, sickness benefits, unemployment insurance, and pensions) are also mildly redistributive in that they replace income up to a fixed, and relatively modest, maximum.

In addition, there is a broad variety of policies more or less specifically intended to benefit women and support their participation in the labor force. These include the 1971 tax reform, which treats all individuals as separate filers—greatly increasing the progressivity of income tax rates—and provides for generous parental leave support, a massive system of subsidized day care for young children, and the deliberate hiring of women by the burgeoning public sector, frequently on a part-time basis.

Whereas this edifice of social policies was put into place over a long period of time beginning in the 1930s, the greatest expansion of the Swedish welfare state took place from the mid-1960s on (see Olsson, 1990, pp. 125-128, 193-195). In fact, Swedish social spending grew from about 10% of GNP in 1950 to 33% by the late 1970s (Einhorn & Logue, 1989, p. 195; Elmér, 1989, p. 36; Olsson, 1990, p. 30), the highest level among the OECD countries (see Gordon, 1988; for comprehensive reviews of the history and extent of the Swedish welfare state, see Elmér, 1989; Olsson, 1990, chap. 3; Olsson, 1989; see also Einhorn & Logue, 1989, chap. 9; Esping-Andersen, 1990).

THE GOLDEN AGE: SWEDEN UNTIL THE OIL CRISIS

For the quarter century leading up to the 1973-74 oil crisis, the "Swedish Model" appeared to deliver exactly as promised. Unemployment rates remained among the lowest of all OECD countries, rarely rising above the 2% "full" employment rate. Moreover, this was accomplished while women, responding to deliberate incentives, joined the labor force in greater numbers than in any other advanced country. The female labor force participation rate rose from 59.3% of all women aged 16 to 64 in 1970 to over 80% in the late 1980s, the highest level anywhere (SCB, 1989a, p. 46). At the same time, inflation was kept hovering around a modest average of 3% per annum. Moreover, the Swedish government also seemed to have succeeded in smoothing out the business cycle by means of a combination of countercyclical labor-market policies and investment incentives. The Swedish economy continued to grow steadily during the 1950s, 1960s, and early 1970s, albeit at somewhat modest rates, slightly below the OECD averages (see e.g., Einhorn & Logue, 1989, p. 195; Erixon, 1985; Horváth & Daly, 1989, pp. 24-26).

As a result of the massive expansion of social services and welfare programs, the public sector grew much faster than the economy as a whole during this period. Consequently, public sector expenditure as a proportion of GNP grew dramatically. Whereas it still stood at an unremarkable—as compared to other industrialized countries—26.% in 1950, the public sector accounted for more than half of GNP as early as 1975, when only Holland's proportion (54.3%) was higher. The size of the Swedish public sector in relation to GNP went on to reach a peak of 68% in 1982, exceeding that of any other noncommunist country (see Einhorn & Logue, 1989, p. 216; Furåker, 1987; Horváth & Daly, 1989, pp. 17-18 and 32; SCB, 1985).

Employment in the public sector grew correspondingly, from less than 20% of the labor force in the early 1960s—a figure not very different from that in many other OECD countries at the time—to over 30% by the mid-1970s (see Esping-Andersen, 1990, p. 203; SCB, 1989a, p. 138). The overwhelming majority of the new state employees were women filling traditional "women's" positions as health, education, social, or clerical workers. Moreover, a very large proportion of them worked part-time only. Thus, somewhat ironically, the success in drawing women into the labor force was in part bought at the price of a very high degree of occupational gender segregation in terms of type of occupation, sector (public versus private) and part-time versus full-time status (see, e.g., Åberg, 1987; Esping-Andersen, 1990, chap. 8; Flanagan, 1987, p. 128; Standing, 1988, pp. 23-30).

In order to finance this huge public sector without abandoning their policy of fiscal prudence, Social Democratic governments have had to impose a very heavy tax burden on the Swedish economy as well. The overall burden has grown from 20% of GDP in 1950 to over 60% of GDP in the early 1980s, the highest of any industrial country. Whereas about half of government revenue is raised through a tax on goods and services (having just recently been increased to 25% in the 1990-91 tax reform) and social security contributions, over 40% comes from income taxes alone. Swedish maximum marginal income tax rates have risen continuously since the 1950s and reached an all-time high of over 80% in the early 1980s. The marginal tax rates facing the household of the average production worker rose from 26% in 1965 to 59% in 1975, while average income taxes paid by the family of the average Swedish worker rose from 22% to 33% (see Esping-Andersen, 1990, p. 177; Gramlich, 1987, pp. 268-276; "Swedish Economy," 1990, pp. 9-10), the highest in the OECD (see also OECD, 1989).

At the same time, virtually all Swedes benefited to an increasing extent from the myriad transfer payments and entitlements offered by the Swedish welfare state. In the mid-1960s, transfer payments accounted for a little over 10% of household income. By 1975, this proportion had doubled (see Jansson, 1990). As a result of this combination of taxes and transfers, by the early 1970s the family of the average Swedish production worker ended up with about 75%

of original gross earnings as disposable income (see Marklund, 1988, p. 61), a proportion not all that different from that in other industrialized countries.

Whereas an increasing proportion of Swedish disposable incomes was thus being determined by governmental agencies, actual employment earnings were increasingly set centrally by the annual negotiations between the union and employer centrals. By the mid-1960s they seemed to have worked out a well-worn routine of annual country-wide negotiations, setting the terms within which local wage rates could be settled relatively easily. They seemed to have struck a successful bargain, trading overall moderate wage increases and labor peace for a gradual reduction of wage differentials.

The results of this highly centralized collective bargaining system were quite remarkable. Although Sweden had endured very high strike volumes by international standards during the 1920s and 1930s, the Swedish industrial relations arena was almost strike free from the early 1950s on. Swedish relative strike volumes have remained among the lowest among the OECD countries ever since (see Einhorn & Logue, 1989, p. 230; Ingham, 1973; Korpi, 1983, chap. 8).

At the same time, the unions' "solidaristic wage policy" helped drastically reduce wage differentials among blue-collar workers in the 1960s. As can be seen from Figure 1, the spread between the highest paid and the lowest paid decile of workers in the sectors covered by the LO-SAF collective agreements, expressed as a percentage of average pay, was squeezed from more than 45% in 1970 to about 30% in the early 1980s (see also Åberg, 1987, p. 8; Åberg, 1984, pp. 216-217; Björklund, 1986b; Flanagan, 1987, pp. 131-133; Forsebäck, 1980, p. 80; Hibbs, 1990; Standing, 1988, pp. 41-47).[3] This was accomplished in spite of the fact that there has been a considerable amount of "wage drift," consistently wiping out between half and two-thirds of the reductions of wage dispersion negotiated by the LO (Bosworth & Lawrence, 1987, pp. 39-41; Flanagan, 1987, p. 140, also pp. 166-169; Hibbs, 1990; Martin, 1984, p. 213).

Taken together, then, these trends produced a considerable reduction in income inequality, especially of after-tax and after-transfer income, throughout the period until the mid-1970s (see Åberg, Selén, & Tham, 1987; Fritzell, 1991; Korpi, 1983, pp. 195-198; Olsson, 1990, pp. 181-185). By the end of the 1970s, the Swedish after-tax and after-transfer income distribution had become the least unequal in the capitalist world (see, e.g., Fritzell, 1991, chap. 6).

The available evidence on public opinion about welfare state reform and on attitudes toward work suggests that throughout the period there has been a solid consensus in support of the Social Democrats' policies of full employment, redistribution, and promotion of labor-force participation, in spite of some hard political battles over these policies, particularly over the introduction of the general pension system (ATP) in the late 1950s (see, e.g., Heclo & Madsen, 1987, pp. 161-163; Olsson, 1990, pp. 117-119).

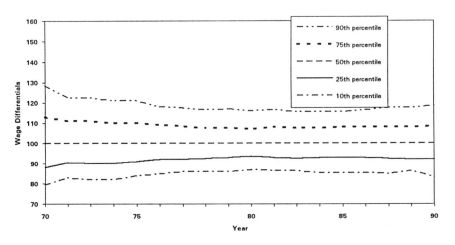

Source: LO.

Figure 1.   Wage Differentials between Percentiles of Swedish
Blue-Collar Workers in the Sector Negotiated by the Blue-Collar Labor
Union Central (LO) and the Swedish Employer's Association (SAF)

Most Swedes, it seems, would agree with former AMS director and Minister
of Finance, Alan Larsson, that "work is an important part of a good society:
Everybody who is willing and able to work should be given a chance to do
so" (Larsson, 1988, p. 4; see also Dahlberg, 1988, pp. 98-99; Jangenäs, 1985,
p. 32). In public opinion surveys and in their voting behavior, Swedes continue
to view maintaining full employment as a top political priority even though
they clearly have very little experience with unemployment by international
standards (see Jonung & Wadensjö, 1981; Smucker & van den Berg, 1991).
By all accounts, support for the core welfare state programs has been solid—
if not spectacularly stronger than elsewhere—with very little change over time
throughout the post-World War II period (see Korpi, 1983, pp. 199-204;
Olsson, 1990, pp. 234-241; Svallfors, 1989, chap. 3). Moreover, in a 1980
international comparison of attitudes toward work, Swedish attitudes came
out as unremarkable, if anything. Swedish employees' commitment to their
jobs, instrumental as opposed to intrinsic interests in work, and so on,
consistently fall somewhere in the middle when compared to the answers of
employees in other countries (see Yankelovich et al., 1985; Yuchtman-Yaar,
1989; Yuchtman-Yaar & Gottlieb, 1985; Zetterberg et al., 1983).

But in 1969-70 a sudden rash of wild cat strikes, beginning with a walkout
and bitter strike at the government-owned iron ore mines in the northern town
of Kiruna in December 1969, rudely disturbed this picture of apparent

industrial peace and political consensus. The strikes were widely interpreted, especially by the union leadership, as an indication of growing rank and file concern with more "qualitative" concerns, and as a protest against the unions' overly technocratic "moving van" policy promoting labor mobility to suit the needs of industry (see Einhorn & Logue, 1982, p. 13; Ginsburg, 1983, p. 146; Heclo & Madsen, 1987, pp. 52-53; Martin, 1984, pp. 224, 227-228, 255-256; Rehn, 1984, p. 10; Wadensjö, 1986, p. 7). But it is certainly possible that the wild cat strikes were at least partly motivated by resentment of diminishing wage differentials and of the centralized process of wage-setting on the part of better paid workers (Leion, 1987, p. 39).

At any rate, in response to these signs of apparently widespread discontent among the union rank and file, the government and the LO began to shift their policy emphasis from industrial restructuring to issues of job security, industrial democracy, and occupational health and safety. A flurry of laws was passed in the early 1970s such as the 1974 Security of Employment Act; the 1977 Codetermination Act, requiring consultation with the unions before any major managerial decision; and the 1973 revision of the Work Safety Act (see Edlund & Nyström, 1988; Ginsburg, 1983, pp. 151-153; Jangenäs, 1985, p. 15; Martin, 1984, pp. 248-264; Standing, 1988, pp. 73-74). In addition, the LO began to push for the ultimate incursion into managerial prerogative in the form of proposed Wage-earner Funds that would be used to gradually increase the unions' control of capital (see below).

Although the actual results produced by this "legislative explosion" (Edlund & Nyström, 1988, p. 13) have, according to most reports, been rather disappointing (Berggren, 1986a; 1986b; Broström, 1982; Edebalk & Wadensjö, 1989, p. 194; Edlund, Hellberg, Molin, & Nyström, 1989; Edlund & Nyström, 1988, pp. 45-63; Fulcher, 1988, pp. 135-136; Hart & Hörte, 1989; Hellberg & Vrethem, 1982, part 3; Standing, 1988, pp. 77-80), they did provide the average Swedish worker with a greater degree of security and the Swedish unions with more legal power of obstruction than that enjoyed virtually anywhere in the industrial world (see Emerson, 1988, pp. 794-797).

THE CRISIS OF THE 1970S: THE FALL AND RISE OF THE SWEDISH MODEL?

At first, it seemed as though the Swedish economy might escape the worst effects of the 1973-74 oil crisis, in spite of the country's heavy dependence on imported oil. After a brief stay of execution, however, a number of fateful factors combined to produce "the most severe crisis in its history" (Horváth & Daly, 1989, p. 1). The Swedish economy was particularly hard-hit because the oil shock coincided with the rise of sharp low-cost competition for some of Sweden's core industries, ship-building, iron and steel, and forest products.

In addition, the Swedish government's brief success in shielding the economy from the crisis with a strong expansionary policy only made things worse when the crisis finally did hit in 1976. The policy fueled a virtual wage explosion in the collective agreements of 1974-1976, which, in combination with slow productivity growth, caused unit labor costs to soar out of control to the second-highest level (after Great Britain) in the OECD by 1980, rapidly pricing Swedish products out of the international market (Horváth & Daly, 1989, pp. 35-38). Furthermore, in 1976 the last thing the freshly elected "bourgeois" government felt it could afford to do under the dire economic conditions was to abandon the long-standing commitment to full employment. Thus, instead of letting declining industries die, as was prescribed by the original Rehn-Meidner model,[4] the government started to subsidize the ailing ship-building, steel, textile, and forestry industries to the tune of some 4 billion Kronor per annum to maintain employment (see Carlsson, 1983; Lawrence & Bosworth, 1987, pp. 70-75). As a result, support for industry had escalated by the end of the decade to the highest level in Europe as a proportion of GDP (Horváth & Daly, 1989, p. 56). In addition, the government ran up enormous deficits, and its expenditures grew to two-thirds of GDP, the highest in the OECD. The overall tax burden and marginal tax rates also became the highest in the OECD. None of this was particularly helpful in promoting the necessary restructuring of the Swedish economy or bringing inflation and production costs under control. Eventually, economic growth stagnated, and real incomes stagnated or even declined until well into the 1980s. Despite all efforts to contain unemployment, it rose to levels far above those considered acceptable, to a peak of 3.5% of the labor force in 1983 (for the above see Bosworth & Rivlin, 1987; Heclo & Madsen, 1987, chap. 2; Horváth & Daly, 1989, chaps. 3 and 4; Lundberg, 1985; "Swedish economy," 1990).

When the SAP regained power in 1982, it was clear that drastic measures were needed. Rejecting both further subsidization of declining industries and Thatcherite deflation, finance minister Kjell-Olof Feldt embarked on a "third way." First, the Krona was devalued by 16% (it had already been devalued in 1977 and 1981, amounting to a total devaluation of nearly 50%). Second, for the year 1982-83 the ailing industries were offered one last and huge support package, but on the clear understanding that after this subsidies for declining industries would be rapidly phased out—which they were. Finally, the government returned to a tight fiscal policy by drastically curbing public spending to reduce the budget deficits (see Carlsson, 1983; Horváth & Daly, 1989, chap. 5; Jangenäs, 1985, p. 15; Lawrence & Bosworth, 1987, pp. 70-75; Wadensjö, 1986, pp. 7-11).

The "third way" initially seemed to be remarkably successful. Sweden was ready to profit from increased world demand with the waning of the deep recession of 1981-82. It experienced an export-led boom that lasted until the late 1980s. Public-sector spending was curbed without further tax increases, so that by 1984 the first decline of public-sector spending as a proportion of GDP was achieved since World War II. And unemployment finally began to decline again after the 1983-84 peak of almost 4% of the labor force.

In fact, during the later 1980s, labor markets were becoming very tight indeed, for the unemployment rate hovered around 1%. "Wage drift" once again was taking on alarming proportions, putting pressure on the centralized bargaining process. Fears of a new cost-crisis were widespread. The government tried a number on things to dampen down the overheated economy, including heavy arm-twisting of the labor market organizations to moderate wage increases and the introduction of an extremely unpopular temporary, repayable tax known as "forced saving." In early 1990, the leaders of the LO and the government actually agreed on a moratorium on industrial action to cool the situation down. This provoked an uproar among union activists, forcing the LO leadership to back down and the Carlsson government to resign. But as the Riksdag could not produce a viable alternative, Carlsson once again formed a Social Democratic government, albeit without Kjell-Olof Feldt, the vociferous minister of finance who is credited with having pulled Sweden out of the crisis of the 1970s, but who was considered to be too right-wing by many rank-and-file members of the labor movement.

In the course of 1990, however, conditions changed with remarkable speed. Whereas labor shortages were among the most serious problems at the beginning of the year, by year's end Sweden was clearly being dragged into the international recession. Ever since, there has been an atmosphere of crisis provoking some of the most acrimonious debates in years about what policies to follow (see OECD, 1990).

In several respects, the new economic policies of the 1980s constituted a departure from the redistributive orthodoxies of the earlier Swedish Model. With a view to encouraging a larger supply of labor, the government began to lower the maximum marginal income tax rates gradually (Gramlich, 1987, p. 268). In 1990 it began to implement the "tax reform of the century," which will eventually lower the maximum marginal rates to 50%. The reduction in tax revenue is to be compensated for by increased indirect taxation, abolition of various deduction possibilities and of certain subsidies such as those on employer-subsidized lunches (see OECD, 1990, pp. 11-13). In addition, whereas the Swedish welfare state was not cut back as drastically as was the case in some other countries during the 1980s, the period was definitely marked by stagnation and retrenchment in welfare spending (Marklund, 1988, pp. 41-43).

Changes in post-1974 industrial relations were more dramatic. The LO's campaign for "qualitative" change during the early and mid-1970s already constituted a challenge to the principle of managerial prerogative that had been a major pillar of the "Historic Compromise" of Saltsjöbaden. But to add insult to injury, it launched a campaign for its much more radical proposal of "wage-earner funds" as forwarded by Rudolf Meidner. For the LO, the introduction of these funds, giving the unions a gradually increasing voice in the management of business, was to be the culmination of the campaign for "qualitative" change in the work place. But it never really managed to get wholehearted support for its more radical proposals from either the other union centrals or its Social Democratic allies. By contrast, the SAF and the "bourgeois" parties united to conduct an extremely forceful crusade against the LO proposals. In an often uncharacteristically acrimonious campaign, the LO's proposals were eventually defeated in favor of a much watered-down version of wage-earner funds (see Heclo & Madsen, 1987, chap. 6).

More generally, relations between the SAF and the unions became considerably more confrontational from the late 1970s onward. Eventually, this led to the collapse of the centralized, LO-dominated system of collective bargaining. Behind this collapse lay a number of factors. The labor movement itself had become more fragmented because of the growth of white-collar occupations and the corresponding growth of white-collar unions (TCO and SACO), independent from the LO and the SAP and less or not at all committed to wage equalization and other socialist principles.

Second, its victory in the battle over the wage-earner funds seems to have emboldened the SAF into taking a more confrontational position toward other old LO goals as well. The increasingly uncompromising stance of both the SAF and the LO came to a head in the great showdown of 1980, Sweden's largest strike/lockout ever (De Geer et al., 1987, pp. 45-46; Forsebäck, 1980, pp. 133-135; Heclo & Madsen, 1987, pp. 129-31). Although the overall average annual strike volume did not increase dramatically after the peak of 1980 (Einhorn & Logue, 1989, p. 230), year-to-year changes clearly became more erratic, reflecting the new, much more volatile industrial relations (see SCB, 1989a, pp. 219-221).

This increased volatility was partly the result of an increasing tendency toward decentralization in the collective-bargaining process. The growth of powerful white-collar and public-sector unions, as well as restiveness in the LO's own ranks (particularly the metalworkers' unions), undermined the LO's ability to dominate and centralize the annual negotiations. The SAF, in turn, energetically sought to exploit these divisions in order to force the decentralization of negotiations it was pursuing then. In 1983, for the first time since the 1950s, both the blue-collar and the white-collar centrals were unable to prevent separate settlements by member unions. Ever since, the centrifugal forces, strongly encouraged by the employers' side, have made centralized bargaining increasingly tenuous. More and more often the government has had to participate in order to keep central bargaining alive, and more and more these efforts have failed. This tendency toward decentralization has clearly reduced the effectiveness of the LO's "solidaristic wage policy" (see Ahlén, 1989; Elvander, 1990; Heclo & Madsen, 1987, pp. 131-135).

RESULTS OF THE CRISIS AND ITS AFTERMATH

Roughly speaking, the main effect of the crisis for the average Swede has been a stagnation of his/her disposable income. Whereas there was some fluctuation in the interim, the 1983 per capita real disposable income was only 1% higher than in 1975 (SBC, 1987, p. 8). But during the same period, *factor income* per capita actually declined. The relative stability of disposable incomes is explained by the growing importance of transfer payments, which grew by 50% from 1975 to 1985 (Esping-Andersen, 1990, p. 56; Fritzell, 1991, chap. 4; SBC, 1987, chap. 2; Vogel, Andersson, Davidson, & Häll, 1988, pp. 107-111).

But while average disposable incomes have remained more or less stable, the *distribution* of disposable incomes continued to become more equal until 1980. This was primarily due to the equalizing effect of transfer payments and taxes because, as can be seen in Figure 1, the compression of LO-negotiated wages virtually halted after the late 1970s and earnings of others seem to have become more *un*equal (see Hibbs, 1990; Olsson, 1990, pp. 181-184; SBC, 1987, chap. 3). After 1980, however, transfer payments, although still growing in importance, failed to stem the unequalizing effect of diverging factor earnings and tax reductions combined. Since then, the Swedish distribution of disposable incomes has started to become more *un*equal (see Jansson, 1990, p. 49 and Table 5.1).

Thus, in terms of income, the post-1975 period marks a major reversal for the average Swede: From a period of steady growth and increasing equality to one of stagnation and increasing inequality. On the other hand, as far as employment is concerned, the Swedish experience has been one of continued security, with the unemployment rate never rising above 4%, although there have been considerable regional differences (see SBC, 1989a, pp. 74-75).

At the same time, the number of hours worked by the average employee has declined somewhat as a result of various legislative changes and collective agreements (longer vacations, parental leave, sick-leave, early retirement) and of the increasing importance of part-time work (Elmér, 1989; Furåker, 1990, pp. 6, 14; Olsson, 1990; SBC, 1989a, pp. 153-172). In a sense, the combination of little or no growth in real wages, overall reduction of hours worked per average worker, and rise in the rate of labor-force participation amounts to something of a de facto work-sharing scheme. This would seem to be confirmed by the fact that the number of hours worked per person in the population (i.e., whether in the labor force or not) has remained virtually unchanged (see Furåker, 1990, p. 11; Helliwell, 1990).

On the whole, then, the individual economic experience of the average Swede during this period has probably been somewhat less discontinuous than in most other countries. Employment shifts between declining and growing sectors of the economy and of the country have continued, but within a framework of a very high degree of employment and income security (though not necessarily job security). Also, the position of workers vis-à-vis their employers has remained relatively strong as a result of a continued tight labor market, and has even been significantly strengthened by the far-reaching job security legislation of the mid-1970s.

On the other hand, the labor-force participation of women has become increasingly indispensable in maintaining the family's living standard. Much of this increased participation has taken the form of part-time employment, primarily in the public sector. There is some evidence that a sizable minority of women currently in part-time jobs would prefer to work longer hours (SBC, 1989a, p. 165).

PLUS ÇA CHANGE...: CHANGE AND STABILITY IN SWEDISH ATTITUDES AND OPINIONS

In short, in comparison to the other industrialized countries, Sweden stands out for the extremely high degree to which its population has been sheltered from economic insecurity for an extraordinarily long period of time. Even during the gravest economic crisis since the 1930s, few Swedes have had to worry about losing their jobs and even fewer about losing their incomes. In the process, the levels of their disposable incomes have become more and more market-independent, and their distribution egalitarian to a degree unmatched anywhere else. This has been accomplished by means of an extreme degree of centralization and stability in both the industrial-relations and political arenas. What effect would one expect from this rather eccentric set of experiences on Swedish attitudes and values?

There are several competing predictions. On one side, there are the critics from the right who have long argued that the cradle-to-grave security and the far-reaching dissociation between effort and reward produced by the Swedish Model would inevitably lead to the undermining of the Swedish work ethic. Somewhat paradoxically, all the way at the other end of the political spectrum some Neo-Marxists have taken this kind of argument one step further. Growing sectors of society, these authors reason, are being "decommodified" in that their disposable income is governed not by the anonymous dictates of the capitalist labor market but by politically determined transfer payments and taxes. As a result, conflicts over income shares between different groups become naturally more and more politicized, and justifications of income differentials in terms of economic "market forces" lose their legitimating power. Moreover, so the argument goes, by reducing the workers' subjection to market forces, "decommodification" reduces the intensity of competition *between* workers, which both increases solidarity and strengthens the hand of labor vis-à-vis capital. The prediction, then, is that "decommodification" will lead to increasing radicalization among large strata of the population in an anticapitalist direction (see, e.g., Esping-Andersen, 1985; Offe, 1972, 1973a, 1973b, 1984).[5]

On the other hand, one might expect a growing polarization between different sectors of society as their competing claims on their shares of the economic pie turn into an increasingly visible zero-sum game (e.g., Blumberg, 1980; Esping-Andersen, 1990; Thurow, 1980). Cleavages between social classes throughout the period after the mid-70s might be predicted to sharpen, reflecting the stagnation of real incomes, the reversal of the historical trend toward the equalization of economical rewards, and the (consequently?) more confrontational style of Swedish politics and collective bargaining. In addition to, and partly instead of, class conflict, several authors foresee a growing rift between those employed by the public sector and those working in the private sector (Dunleavy, 1980; Hoel & Knutsen, 1989). Other aspects of social inequality, such as income, education, and sex, may be expected to exert stronger influence on attitudes on socioeconomic issues during the period discussed.

Finally, there is the now famous "postmaterialism" thesis of Ronald Inglehart, which, given its emphasis on material security, would seem to be particularly applicable to the Swedish case. The long period of stable economic development and experience of comprehensive welfare policies that eliminate, or at least greatly reduce, the hazards of economic misfortune should exert a strong influence on values and speed up the shift from materialist to postmaterialist value priorities.

The problem with all such predictions is that they are far more long-term in scope than the attitudinal data that are usually available—not least because by the time a theory's long-term scope is achieved, researchers have lost interest in it and therefore stop asking the questions that would enable one to test them conclusively. This is, unfortunately, also the case with the Swedish data we were able to find. In the following sections, we will only be able to bring some suggestive pieces of evidence to bear on the questions raised, not provide any conclusive answers.

The Work Ethic

Are there any clear signs of a deteriorating work ethic among Swedish workers? First, in the international comparative study conducted in the early 1980s mentioned earlier, the work ethic of Swedish respondents turned out to be not especially weak. Whereas on some measures the Swedes' commitment to work appears to be in the lower end of the middle range when compared to countries such as Great Britain, the United States, West Germany, and Israel (see Hondrich, 1989, p. 145; Yankelovich et al., 1985, p. 399; Yuchtman-Yaar, 1989, p. 169; Zetterberg et al., 1983, pp. 153-154), on other measures Swedes appear to have a stronger work ethic than any of the other populations, with the possible exception of the Japanese (see Yankelovich et al., 1985, p. 398).[6]

But, of course, these are cross-sectional data that do not tell us anything about trends over time. It is entirely possible that the Swedish work ethic was higher still in the past and that it has been declining. There is no way to disprove this possibility conclusively until the same questions are asked again. However, the results of a recent study replicating a classic 1950 community study in the industrial town of Katrineholm do suggest remarkable long-term stability in basic attitudes toward work as well as other basic life values (see Åberg, 1990). In fact, if anything, a slight shift toward a less instrumental attitude toward work may have occurred from 1950 to 1988 (see Johansson, 1990, p. 188). This change may also be behind the growing proportions of workers, particularly manual workers, who, according to the annual Living Conditions Survey conducted by the Swedish Central Bureau of Statistics, report that their jobs give them personal satisfaction rather than just pay.[7]

In the recent, increasingly heated public debate (see Lindqvist, 1989, pp. 91-93), one phenomenon that has been taken as a sign of flagging work commitment is the allegedly alarming increase in rates of absenteeism due to illness. It is true that the number of insured sickness days per year per insured employee has risen from a low of less than 13 in the early 1960s to 25.3 in 1988 (Lindqvist, 1989, p. 87; SBC, 1989a, p. 178). The increase is clearly due to increased frequency rather than duration, for the latter has actually declined quite considerably (SBC, 1989a, p. 178). Moreover, while the number of sick days per year for women has increased from fewer than 19 in 1970 to 28.7 in 1988, for men it hardly changed at all (SBC, 1989a, and our own calculations). There is also a strong correlation between the number of sick periods and age, young employees being sick considerably more often than older employees (see *Riskförsäkringsverket*, 1990).[8]

There is also some evidence that the ups and downs of the sickness rate follow fairly closely on changes in the rules and benefits introduced from time to time (Lindqvist, 1989, p. 89).[9] But does this mean the system is too lax and undermines the work ethic, as critics charge? In view of the other data on the relative strength of the work ethic in Sweden, it seems to us that one has to be cautious with such interpretations. True, the Swedish rates of absenteeism due to sickness are relatively high by international standards (Kangas, 1991). On the other hand, the issue is at least partly of a moral-ideological nature: Does the reduction of sick days upon a reduction in benefits mean that the workers were not sick in the first place, or that they are now being forced by economic need to go to work sick?

Decommodification without Radicalization

Next, are there any signs of anticapitalist radicalization of political attitudes of Swedes in the wake of the process of a moderating and weakening of the forces of the market economy? Data from the Swedish Election Studies[10] can

Table 1. "Social Reforms Have Gone so far in This Country
That in the Future the Government Ought to Reduce rather
than Increase Allowances and Assistance to Citizens"

Year	Disagree completely	Disagree on the whole	Agree on the whole	Agree completely	Don't know	Total	Excess "Left" answers
1964	17	16	36	27	4	100	-30
1968	25	26	25	17	7	100	+9
1970	17	19	31	27	6	100	-22
1973	13	20	32	28	7	100	-27
1976	11	21	34	27	7	100	-29
1979	10	17	35	32	6	100	-40
1985	9	21	38	24	8	100	-32
1988	9	21	39	22	9	100	-31

Sources: *Svenska väljare* [Swedish voters] (p. 250) by S. Holmberg, 1981. Stockholm: Liber Förlag; *Väljare och val i Sverige* [Voters and elections in Sweden] (p. 127) by S.Holmberg and M. Giljam, 1987. Stockholm: Bonniers. Also based on our own calculations.

be used to address this issue. Table 1 shows the trend of public opinion toward social reforms from 1964 to 1988.

Rather than any trend toward overall radicalization, the responses display trendless fluctuation over time. The number of "excess leftist" answers is virtually the same in 1988 as it was in 1964. If anything, a slight amount of deradicalization may be occurring, for the proportion of those *completely* disagreeing seems to be declining over time. We found a similar pattern in responses to a statement endorsing control by "society" over private enterprise to curb the excessive influence of business leaders from 1964 to 1988 (not shown).[11]

Election results for the past decades do not indicate anything in the way of radicalization of public opinion, either. For the first time since 1932, the "bourgeois" parties defeated the Social Democrats in the 1976 election, but then lost power to them again in 1982. During the past decade, electoral support for the Social Democrats has oscillated between 43% and 45%, while the communists have received around 5% of the vote—no obvious trend toward radicalization. There are, however, signs that the political system is losing its former stability. In the elections of 1988, the Greens were the first new political party to enter Parliament since 1917. In the elections of September 1991, the Greens lost their toehold in the Riksdag, unable to obtain the 4% electoral support necessary for entry. On the other hand, two new "bourgeois" parties, the Christian Democrats and a rightist populist party were able to enter parliament, producing a slim overall bourgeois majority. The Social Democrats, on the other hand, suffered their severest electoral loss since the 1920s. Although these developments can hardly be interpreted as radicalization

Table 2.   "The Political Parties are only Interested
in People's Votes but not in Their Opinions"

Year	Agree completely	Agree on the whole	Disagree on the whole	Disagree completely	Don't know	Total	Alienation excess
1963	14	23	32	24	7	100	-19
1973	12	34	36	12	6	100	-2
1976	11	38	38	8	5	100	+3
1979	24	39	25	7	5	100	+31
1982	18	43	26	8	5	100	+27
1985	23	43	23	6	4	100[a]	+37
1988	22	43	25	6	4	100	+34

Notes: [a] Because of rounding, these figures do not add up exactly to 100.
Sources: Svenska väljare [Swedish voters] (p. 164) by S. Holmberg, 1981. Stockholm: Liber Förlag; Rött blått
          grönt [Red, blue, green] (p. 114) by S. Holmberg, and M. Giljam, 1990). Stockholm: Bonniers. Also
          based on our own calculations.

in any conventional sense, they may signal rising discontent with, and distrust toward, the political establishment.

There is some evidence in the Swedish Election Studies to support this interpretation. Political alienation, as measured by answers to questions about whether political parties and members of parliament are at all interested in the opinions of ordinary people, has been on the increase in Sweden at least since 1968. By some measures, particularly when one looks at the trend in the answers given by the most alienated respondents, the decline of confidence accelerated sharply from 1976 to 1979, after which the degree of political alienation seems to have stabilized at a historically relatively high level (Table 2). In addition, election participation in Sweden has decreased during the most recent elections, although the decline appears to have halted in 1991.

Another fact worth noting in this context is that membership in political parties and participation in political meetings has stagnated for at least two decades. At the same time, participation in so-called "opinion-shaping activities" (speaking at meetings, writing articles, and participating in demonstrations) steadily increased from 1968 to 1987 (see Szulkin, 1987; SBC, 1988, part 1). One can speculate that the combination of these trends may be a sign of growing dissatisfaction with the political situation.

But maybe one should not read too much into these findings. These trends in political alienation do not differ much from what happened in other countries during the same period (see Miller & Listhaug, 1990). Swedish election participation is still high by international standards, and the decline is not limited to Sweden (see Holmberg & Giljam 1990, pp. 186-187). Moreover, participation in "opinion-shaping" activities could just as well be a sign of the vitality of democracy. The trends described here are also not simultaneous.

The growth in alienation clearly predates the decline in election participation. And neither of them is clearly related to economic crises. But the fact remains that the political scene seems to be undergoing rapid and fairly significant change, at least by Swedish standards.

Group Conflicts and Polarization

Are there any signs of the hypothesized polarization of different segments of Swedish society? As we noted above, the economic changes after 1975 might be expected to have resulted in a sharpening of social and political conflicts. We will try to address this question by examining the relation between various background variables and attitudes toward social reforms and "society's" control over private enterprises over time in the Swedish Election Studies data. These issues seem to tap relatively deep-seated values with great relevance for the left-right political division in Swedish society. The polarization postulated here should be observable in such a longitudinal analysis.

The impact of a set of variables on attitudes toward social reforms is shown in Table 3. The analyses cover three points in time: one before 1975 and two after. Variables included are class, education, after-tax family income, and some standard demographic variables (age, sex, marital status, and children, if any). The statistical technique is regression analysis with dummy variables.[12]

Looking at the statistical effects of different variables, as shown in Table 3, the first thing one should note is a very clear and persistent class pattern. The self-employed, farmers, and upper- and lower-white-collar workers were clearly more negatively disposed toward social reforms than blue-collar workers were.[13]

The impact of class on attitude to social reforms was consistently significant and *relatively* strong during whole the period. We emphasize "relatively" because, given the fact that overall variances explained are only around 5%, none of our independent variables can obviously be said to have a *strong* influence on attitudes. Moreover, the strongest effects are to be found among the smallest class categories, that is, the self-employed and farmers. The parameter estimates show some variation over time, but the fluctuations are without any clear trends and thus cannot be interpreted in terms of growing polarization (or depolarization) between social classes. Second, the association between income and attitude toward social reform was quite strong in 1968, but less so in 1979 and in 1985. Thus, there is no evidence for any growing divisions between different income categories, either.[14]

Better educated respondents were more positive toward social reforms. The effect of education on the dependent variable was more or less constant over time. The effects of demographic variables were generally weak or moderate and did not display much variation over time in the direction predicted, with the exception of age. While the effect of age was not statistically significant

Table 3. Regression Analysis of Attitudes toward Social Reform[a]

Respondents	1968			1979			1985		
	b[b]	sign (t)[c]	Beta[d]	b	sign (t)	Beta	b	sign (t)	Beta
Self-Employed	-0.68	.0001	-0.13	-0.67	.0001	-0.13	-0.76	.0001	-0.17
Farmers	-0.86	.0001	-0.15	-0.80	.0001	-0.11	-0.89	.0001	-0.13
Upper-white-collar	-0.63	.0003	-0.09	-0.57	.0001	-0.10	-0.26	.032	-0.06
Lower-white-collar	-0.31	.0001	-0.09	-0.16	.028	-0.06	-0.33	.0001	-0.12
Blue-collar worker	0.00	—	0.00	0.00	—	0.00	0.00	—	0.00
Education (years)	0.03	.057	0.02	0.06	.0001	0.14	.02	.034	0.06
Family income	-1.04E-05	.0001	-0.11	-2.40E-06	.047	-0.05	2.25E-06	.01	-0.06
Age	-1.08E-03	.62	-0.01	-0.0007	.001	-0.08	-0.0005	.027	-0.06
Sex (women = 0, men = 1)	0.15	.013	0.05	0.20	.002	.07	-0.10	.133	-0.03
Married (no = 0, yes = 1)	0.18	.032	0.05	0.02	.79	.001	-0.02	.805	-0.001
Children (no = 0, yes = 1)	0.13	.09	0.04	-0.001	.92	-0.001	-0.02	.744	-0.001
Adjusted R^2	.046			.056			.055		
N	2,377			2,234			2,153		

Notes: [a] "Social reforms have gone so far in this country that in the future the government ought to reduce rather than increase allowances and assistance to citizens:" agree completely = 1; agree on the whole = 2; disagree on the whole = 4; disagree completely = 5.
[b] Unstandardized regression coefficient.
[c] Significance level for t-values.
[d] Standardized regression coefficient.

in the beginning of the period (1968), it became so later (1979 and 1985). In later years, the younger respondents were more positive to social reforms than their older counterparts were. But this is the only evidence of a trend over time in terms of increasing differences between population categories.

We performed the same kind of analysis on a question about the desirability of control by "society" over private enterprise (not shown). Except for some minor differences, the pattern we found was on the whole the same as in Table 3.[15] Thus, we have no evidence so far to support the proposition that the cleavages between different social, economic, or demographic categories has significantly increased in recent decades.

What about any rifts between those employed in the private sector and those working in the public sector, allegedly at the expense of the former? The time series available are too short to permit an assessment of this proposition for a longer period. For 1979 and 1985 we can, however, insert information on sector of employment into our regression equations. The results (not shown) indicate that there was a significant difference between public-sector and private-sector employees with respect to their attitudes to social reforms and "societal" control of enterprises. As predicted, public-sector employees were significantly less favorable toward retreat from social reform and more favorable toward further controls over private enterprise than their private-sector counterparts. The impact of sector was, however, clearly weaker than the effect of class (see Svallfors, in press, for similar results).[16]

Whether this line of cleavage is becoming more important in the long term is, as mentioned, impossible to determine with the data available. The effects of sector observed in our data for the later time points are, however, too modest to make any claims on "new lines of cleavage" and political polarization along these lines and show, at any rate, no signs of overtaking class as the apparently most important variable determining sociopolitical attitudes.

Complexities of Postmaterialism

Finally, as noted, Sweden would seem to be a particularly good test case for the Inglehart argument about the rise of "postmaterialism" in advanced countries. The Swedish population has enjoyed an extraordinarily long period of security and even comfort. The degree of security of employment and income that has been created by the Swedish Model is virtually unmatched in the world. Moreover, Sweden has been less affected by World War II than any other advanced industrialized country (with the possible exception of Switzerland), a factor that Inglehart considers of some importance (Inglehart, 1989, p. 92).

These considerations yield the following two hypotheses: (a) the proportion of "postmaterialists" should be higher in Sweden than in other western countries, and (b) there should be few dramatic cohort differences. The major fault-line between materialists and postmaterialists should occur between those who spent their critical years of socialization during (and perhaps before) the Great Depression and all later cohorts. There should be, furthermore, a moderate and monotonous increase of postmaterialism among later cohorts, reflecting the gradual development of the welfare state. One might, finally, expect a minor period effect for those people who have grown up during the period of "crisis" of 1976-1984. This age cohort is, unfortunately, still too young to be included in our data.

Sweden has not been a part of Inglehart's longitudinal international research project. However, some "Inglehartian" research is now getting under way in Sweden as well, and some results have been reported. When one compares the data presented by Knutsen (1989, p. 233) and Pettersson (1988, p. 123) to those given by Inglehart (1989, p. 95), it appears that the percentage of postmaterialists in Sweden is about the same as the average for other Western European countries. The Netherlands and West Germany have the most postmaterialist populations of Europe, and their proportions of postmaterialists are clearly higher than Sweden's. This result runs directly against the first hypothesis above, which is derived from Inglehart's theory. Knutsen's (1989, pp. 234-235) results also seem to contradict the second hypothesis. The relation between materialism/postmaterialism and age is stronger in Sweden than in any other Nordic country. Three of the four comparative countries, it should be borne in mind, took part in World War II.

On the other hand, results from multivariate regressions on a measure of postmaterialism derived from Inglehart's 4-item scale included in our 1985 data does seem to indicate some significant cohort differences, which are along the lines predicted by the theory (Table 4). Two models are tested in the analysis. Variables included in model A are sex, life-cycle position of respondent, respondent's economic status, class, and age cohort. In model B the number of years of education is added to the model.[17]

As can be seen in model A of Table 4, the results are in agreement with predictions derived from Inglehart's theory. The effects of age cohort when we control for sex, life cycle, income, and class are significant and point in the direction predicted. There appears to be a clear break in the effect of age on postmaterialist values just about at the cohort that experienced the Great Depression during the formative years considered so crucial by Inglehart (1989, p. 56). Moreover, we have indications of a monotonous increase of postmaterialism among later age-cohorts as postulated above. The latter result is in agreement with the argument about the effects of a gradual development of the welfare state.

One can also see (in model A) that there is no association between respondents' sex and the measure of postmaterialism. The association between life-cycle position and postmaterialism is weak. There is some tendency for people without children to be more prone to accept postmaterialist attitudes. Respondents' economic status does not have any significant effects.[18] On the

Table 4. Multivariate Regression Analysis of the Effects of Sex, Life Cycle, Economic Status, Class, Age, and Education on Values, 1985

	b^a	Sign $(t)^b$
Model A		
Sex (female = 0, male = 1)	0.029	0.48
Married (no = 0, yes = 1)	-0.019	0.69
Children (no = 0, yes = 1)	-0.10	0.06
Income category 1 (lowest income)	0.025	0.76
Income category 2	0.083	0.25
Income category 3	0.028	0.65
Income category 4	-0.012	0.83
Income category 5 (highest income)	0.000	—
Self-employed	0.328	0.0001
Farmers	0.198	0.048
White-collar higher	0.459	0.0001
White-collar lower	0.247	0.0001
Blue-collar workers	0.000	—
18-20 years old	0.435	0.0003
21-30 years old	0.424	0.0001
31-40 years old	0.417	0.0001
41-50 years old	0.320	0.0003
51-60 years old	0.324	0.0002
61-70 years old	0.097	0.264
71 years and older	0.000	—
R^2	0.094	
N	1,107	
Model B		
Sex (female = 0, male = 1)	0.012	0.78
Married (no = 0, yes = 1)	-0.028	0.55
Children (no = 0, yes = 1)	-0.094	0.07
Income category 1 (lowest)	0.07	0.38
Income category 2	0.161	0.03
Income category 3	0.072	0.25
Income category 4	0.042	0.48
Income category 5 (highest)	0.000	—
Self-employed	0.264	0.0002
Farmers	0.182	0.069
White-collar higher	0.265	0.0009
White-collar lower	0.155	0.001
Blue-collar worker	0.000	—
18-20 years old	0.274	0.027
21-30 years old	0.254	0.004
31-40 years old	0.290	0.001
41-50 years old	0.252	0.005

(continued)

Table 4. (Continued)

	b[a]	$Sign\ (t)$[b]
Model B		
51-60 years old	0.283	0.001
61-70 years old	0.086	0.31
71 years and older	0.000	—
Education (number of years)	0.043	0.0001
R^2	0.117	
N	1,112	

Notes: [a] Unstandardized regression coefficient.
　　　 [b] Significance level for t-values.

other hand, the association between class and postmaterialism is very strong. Postmaterialism seems to be strongly rooted among the self-employed, and particularly among upper-white-collar workers as opposed to blue-collar workers.

The positive implications of our analysis for Inglehart's theory change, however, at least partly, when we include education in the regression equation (model B). Education is strongly and positively associated with postmaterialism (better educated people being more prone to postmaterialist values). Education also has some influence on other predictors included. The effect of the experiences of the Great Depression on postmaterialism seems to remain. The cohort effects are, however, in general more moderate, and no gradual increase in postmaterialism can be observed among the younger age cohorts. The effect of class position decreases somewhat, but it still remains an important predictor in the model. Other predictors are not significantly affected.

What, then, are the implications of our analysis for Inglehart's thesis? Is the emphasis on the importance of "formative affluence" for postmaterialist values warranted? Our results, at least to some extent, indicate that this is not the case. Although "formative affluence," measured by age cohort, does seem to play some role in the process of value formation, its impact seems to be limited to a shrinking category of people who were born before the depression (model B).[19] Besides this quite limited long-term psychological process, one can see other (and more powerful) processes that appear to exert a more immediate influence on value formation. The impact of occupational class position and education on postmaterialism (model B) suggests that sociologically rather conventional factors may be more important than Inglehart's "formative affluence" in accounting for value formation.

There is, of course, a large and venerable body of literature documenting and identifying the mechanisms by which occupational class affects attitudes and values, particularly via the intervening variables of working conditions.[20]

Our findings on the significance of class are very much in keeping with that literature. On the other hand, the impact that we found education to have can be interpreted in different ways. Inglehart (1982) himself tried to assimilate such findings by arguing that education is just another measure of "formative affluence" (pp. 471-472) because it reflects the relative prosperity of the family during one's childhood and youth. But, although it is, of course, true that "educational attainment is influenced by one's class origins and affects one's class destination" (Heath et al., 1985, p. 64), Inglehart's rather ad hoc maneuver to disarm a potentially disturbing finding is less than satisfactory. After all, the issue is whether education has a significant effect in addition to that of "formative affluence." This is a matter that can only be settled by controlling for *both*, not by theoretical ukase. Short of such a test, the conventional theory that universities and secondary schools socialize people to cultural and libertarian values that are quite close to Inglehart's postmaterialism appears at least as plausible as Inglehart's alternative.

In conclusion, then, it is reasonable to say that even if the Swedish case does not seem to contradict the Inglehart thesis entirely, it obviously does look as though it might produce some serious complications for the argument.[21]

CONCLUSION

Compared to the upheavals that many of the other countries discussed in this book have suffered in recent times, the Swedish socioeconomic and political situation appears to be extraordinarily stable, not to say dull. But there are several indications that major changes, by Swedish standards at least, are looming. As noted already, in September 1991 the Social Democrats suffered their worst electoral defeat since the 1920s. A new government was formed by a coalition of four "bourgeois" parties, on a joint program promising a "system shift." On the industrial relations front as well, it looks likely that present trends away from centralized bargaining and thus from the LO's wage solidarity will continue unabated. Finally, with the recent turnabout by the Social Democrats on the issue, Sweden is now a candidate for EC membership. It is widely assumed that eventual membership will force Sweden to harmonize many of her policies and programs with those in force in the other member countries, which might mean a significant down-scaling of her more ambitious welfare state policies.

Our survey of socioeconomic and attitudinal developments may provide some of the ingredients for making some sense out of this. The extraordinary political strength of the Swedish Social Democrats has traditionally rested on two main pillars, their apparent expertise at managing the Swedish economy and their commitment to and gradual implementation of the world's most comprehensive welfare state. These earned them the support of a very broad spectrum of the electorate. But left-wing Social Democrats have always assumed that they would be mere stepping stones for building a constituency for much more radical reform. Such reform was expected to lead eventually to the kind socialization of the capitalist economy envisaged in the more radical proposals for wage-earner funds. But, as we have seen, the expected radicalization of the population failed to materialize and the radical proposals were eventually defeated in the great wage-earner funds campaign.

With this defeat, socialism effectively disappeared from the Social Democrats' political agenda. Meanwhile, the "bourgeois" parties, mindful of the persistent and solid popular support for the welfare state, have, on the whole, accepted it. Thus, the Social Democratic Party is effectively deprived of all of its distinctively "socialist" appeal. It must now rely entirely on its reputation for superior economic management to retain the support of the electorate. Significantly, recent debates between the defenders and opponents of the SAP have revolved entirely around the question of whether or not the Swedish economy's productivity is falling behind that of its major competitors (see Bergman, Jakobsson, Persson, & Söderström, 1990; Erixon, 1991; Korpi, 1990a, 1990b).

Thus, partly because of its own success at forging a broad popular consensus supporting "its" welfare state—a consensus so wide that the "bourgeois" parties had little choice but to join it—and because it has been forced to drop its more radical socialist aims, the SAP is now just another political party claiming to be able to deliver the goods (mostly economic) better than its competitors. And now that the SAP's "third way" seems to have foundered in recession, the electorate is apparently willing to let the "bourgeois" parties have a go at it. Thus, the era of stable Social Democratic dominance appears to be over, giving way to shifting alliances and governments for the foreseeable future.

On the other hand, much of the Social Democratic legacy of comprehensive and mildly redistributive social security seems likely to survive. No doubt, future "bourgeois" governments will try to tighten up some of the more generous programs and privatize some of the services now provided by the public sector. But given the persistently solid support for the institutions of the welfare state, not even the most right-wing of the "bourgeois" governments is likely to embark on any wholesale dismantling of the Swedish welfare state in the near future. Plus ça change.

ACKNOWLEDGMENTS

We thank Robert Erikson, Carl le Grand, Michael Tåhlin, and our colleagues in the international project of which this book is the product for their valuable comments on an earlier draft of this chapter. We are indebted to Johan Fritzell for generously providing us with data on the Swedish income distribution. We also thank Miljan

Vuksanović for his computer programming help and expertise and Consuelo Quesney and Janet Logan for their able research assistance.

NOTES

1. There is some question about the degree to which the program was actually carried out. It could, therefore, be credited with having brought about the economic recovery of the late 1930s (see Heclo & Madsen, 1987, p. 48; Martin, 1984, p. 195).

2. Larsson is the former director of the *Arbetsmarknadsstyrelsen* (AMS), the huge bureaucracy implementing and overseeing labor market policy, and was Minister of Finance in the last Carlsson cabinet; Leijon is the former Minister of Labor.

3. Although initially seeking merely to ensure equal pay for equal work irrespective of interfirm or interindustry differences in profitability, the aims of the solidaristic wage policy became more egalitarian in the 1960s, now seeking to reduce pay differences between workers in different occupations as well (Flanagan, 1987, p. 131). It has been suggested that this approach was largely a matter of convenience (Heclo & Madsen, 1987, p. 117) because the measurement of comparative worth necessary for implementing the original policy proved too complicated.

4. Whether the Social Democrats would have done anything different had they been in power at the time is a moot point. Obviously, however, the marked shift from assisting individuals to move to assisting companies to survive had already begun during the early 1970s and partly at the behest of the LO.

5. For a highly critical review of such arguments, see van den Berg (1988, chaps. 5 and 6).

6. In the comparison referred to, three of the other five countries had higher scores for the "strong" work ethic position, but when one compares proportions endorsing both the strong and the weak work-ethic statements with those endorsing either of the two money-motivated statements, Sweden's response is by far the most favorable to the work ethic (84% versus 12%). Moreover, the Japanese data are not strictly comparable, for the question was posed quite differently there.

7. The percentages of all employees choosing this over the alternative statement ("This job is like any other job. You do your part, but the only thing that really matters is the pay.") grew from 67 in 1975 to 76 in 1986-87, and for manual workers from 56 to 66. There are, however, a couple of caveats with respect to the possible interpretation given here. First, the answers refer to the respondents' present jobs, not to work in general. Second, they may simply reflect the improved working conditions reported by the same respondents over the same period (see SBC, 1989b, p. 54; 1982, p. 172; and 1978, pp. 134-135).

8. Of workers 20-24 years of age in 1988, 18% take six or more days sick leave a year, whereas the corresponding figure for those over 30 was 8.2% (*Riksfrösäkingsverket,* 1990, p. 9).

9. In early 1991, benefit levels for the first sickness days were reduced in an effort to tighten control and counteract alleged abuse. The change reportedly caused an immediate reduction in sick leaves.

10. Unless indicated otherwise, the data presented in the following tables are from the Swedish Election Studies, 1956-88, conducted by Statsvetenskapliga Institutionen, University of Gothenburg, under direction of Sören Holmberg. The data were made available to us by the Svensk Samhällsvetenskaplig Datatjänst (SSD). Neither the SSD nor the original researchers bear any responsibility for the interpretations or translations presented here.

11. Neither should the question of possible anticapitalist radicalization of political attitudes among Swedes be used to infer anything about the absolute amounts of support for "progressive" policies. In Table 1 there is a huge excess of "rightist" answers. The opposite applies for the table not shown here. This difference can probably be explained by the differences in the wording of questions.

12.   See Pindyck and Rubinfield (1981) for methodological details. The coding of the dependent variable is explained at the bottom of the table. The class has been transformed into dummies. The variable "self-employed" has, for instance, a value of 1 when the respondent belongs to the category and 0 otherwise. Analogous codes have been assigned to the variables "farmers," "upper-white-collar," "lower-white-collar," and "blue-collar workers." In the case of after-tax family income, respondents were assigned an income equal to the midpoint of the income range they reported being in. The highest range, which has no upper limit (e.g., "100,000 Kronor and over") was converted by multiplying its lower limit by a factor of 1.3 (e.g., 130,000 Kronor). The only other continuous variables in the analyses are respondents' age and education. The latter has been recorded from a category variable to number of years of education.

13.   The parameter estimates for the class dummies are negative and significant at the 99% confidence level in all regression equations, with the single exception of higher-white-collar workers in 1985, which is statistically significant at the 95% level only. "Blue-collar worker" is the point of reference for the class dummies in the equations, meaning that its parameter estimate is assumed to be equal to zero.

14.   See footnote 11, above, for the coding of our family income variable. Some tests with other classifications were performed. The overall results remained unchanged.

15.   The impact was somewhat weaker and less systematic. The effect of education was highly significant throughout, indicating absence of any trend. Moreover, in terms of the traditional left-right continuum at least, the effect was the opposite of the relation shown in Table 3 above. Better educated respondents were *less* favorable toward a curbing of the excessive influence of business leaders than the less educated were. The effect of age was statistically significant in 1985 only, but again in the "opposite" direction; that is, older respondents tended to be more favorable toward "societal" control of big business. Thus, here, too, we find some indication of a growing age gap, although the impact of the age variable was rather moderate when compared to that of education and class. It is also worth noting that, whereas the effect of class on position on the left-right continuum seemed to be consistent across issues, the effects of age and education were not.

16.   Betas in 1979 and 1985 for the social reforms question were 0.09 and 0.06, respectively, both significant at the 99% level.

17.   The measure of postmaterialism is based on a subsample of our 1985 data set. Of the respondents, 25% were classified as materialists and 16% as postmaterialists. All remaining cases are included in the mixed category. Materialists are assigned the value 0; the mixed category, 1; and postmaterialists, 2. Respondents' life-cycle position is measured by variables indicating whether the respondent is married and whether he/she has children. Economic status is family income after taxes (five categories).

18.   We tested the effects of different measures of economic status like share-holding, wealth, and home ownership. None of these measures showed any significant effect on the dependent variable.

19.   Inglehart's measure of economic security during formative years is indirect. A more straightforward measure like the class of origin would be a better approximation of "formative affluence" (see Heath, Jowell, & Curtice, 1985, p. 63). The association between class of origin and postmaterialist values is, according to Heath, fairly weak. Unfortunately, class of origin is not included in our data.

20.   For a plausible explication of the mechanism connecting work and attitudes, see Kohn and Schooler (1983).

21.   None of this should, moreover, be construed as support for the overall notion of a "postmaterialist" revolution as presented by Inglehart, about which we remain, to say the least, skeptical.

REFERENCES

Åberg, R. (Ed.). (1990). *Industrisamhälle i omvandling* [Industrial society in transformation]. Stockholm: Carlssons.

_____. (1984). Market-independent income distribution: Efficiency and legitimacy. In J. N. Goldthorpe (Ed.). *Order and conflict in contemporary capitalism* (pp. 209-230). Oxford: Clarendon Press.

_____. (1987). Employment and working hours. In R. Erikson & R. Åberg (Eds.), *Welfare in transition: A survey of living conditions in Sweden 1968-1981* (pp. 78-100). Oxford: Clarendon Press.

Åberg, R., Selén J., & Tham, H. (1987). Economic Resources. In R. Erikson & R. Åberg (Eds.), *Welfare in transition: A survey of living conditions in Sweden 1968-1981* (pp. 116-152). Oxford: Clarendon Press.

Ahlén, K. (1989). Swedish collective bargaining under pressure: Inter-union rivalry and incomes policy. *British Journal of Industrial Relations, 27*, 330-346.

Barkin, S. (1977). *Swedish active manpower policy*. Amherst, MA: Massachussetts Labor Relations Research Center.

Berggren, C. (1986a). Top management and codetermination in Swedish companies: Greater union influence results in better decisions. *Economic and Industrial Democracy, 7*, 99-108.

_____. (1986b). *Fack, företagsledning och besluten om företagens framtid* [Unions, management, and decisions regarding the future of business]. Stockholm: Arkiv.

Bergman, L., Björklund, A., Jakobsson, U., Lundberg L., & Söderström, H. T. (1990). *I Samtidens Bakvatten? Konjunkturrådets Rapport 1990* [In today's backwater? Business cycle report, 1990]. Stockholm: SNS förlag.

Bergman, L., Jakobsson, U., Persson, M., & Söderström, H. T. (1990). Sveriges tillväxt. Replik till Korpi [Sweden's growth: A reply to Korpi]. *Ekonomisk Debatt, 7*, 660-665.

Björklund, A. (1986a). Policies for labor market adjustment in Sweden (IUI Working Paper No. 163). Stockholm: Industriens Utredningsinstitut (The Industrial Institute for Economic and Social Research).

_____. (1986b). Assessing the decline of wage dispersion in Sweden. *IUI Yearbook 1986-1987* (pp. 101-111). Stockholm: Industriens Utredningsinstitut (The Industrial Institute for Economic and Social Research).

Blumberg, P. (1980). *Inequality in an age of decline*. New York: Oxford University Press.

Bosworth, B. P., & Lawrence, R. Z. (1987). Adjusting to slower economic growth: The domestic economy. In B. P. Bosworth & A. M. Rivlin (Eds.), *The Swedish economy* (pp. 22-54). Washington, DC: The Brookings Institution.

Bosworth, B. P., & Rivlin, A. M. (Eds.). (1987). *The Swedish economy*. Washington, DC: The Brookings Institution.

Broström, A. (1982). *MBLs Gränser–Den Privata Äganderätten* [The limits of codetermination: Private property rights.] Report No. 32 Stockholm: Arbetslivscentrum.

Carlsson, B. (1983, September). Industrial subsidies in Sweden: Macro-economic effects and an international comparison. *The Journal of Industrial Economics, 32*, 1-23.

Dahlberg, Å. (1988). Sweden's labour market policies: Programs and costs. In G. M. Olsen (Ed.), *Industrial change and labour adjustment in Sweden and Canada* (pp. 95-107). Toronto: Garamond Press.

De Geer, H., Ekstedt, E., Elvander, N., Henning, R., Lyttkens, L., Norgren, L., Sjölund, M., & Wikström, S. (1987). *In the wake of the future: Swedish perspectives on the problems of structural change*. Aldershot: Avebury.

Dunleavy, P. (1980). The political implications of sectoral cleavages and the growth of state employment: Part 2, Cleavages, structures, and political alignment. *Political Studies, 28*, 527-549.

Edebalk, P. G., & Wadensjö, E. (1989). Contractually determined insurance schemes for manual workers. In B.A. Gustafsson, & N. A. Klevmarken (Eds.), *The political economy of social security* (pp. 195-210). Amsterdam: Elsevier.

Edlund, S., & Nyström, B. (1988). *Developments in Swedish labor law.* Stockholm: The Swedish Institute.

Edlund, S., Hellberg, I., Molin, T., & Nyström, B. (1989). *Views on co-determination in Swedish working life.* Lund: Juristförlaget.

Einhorn, E. S., & Logue, J. (Eds.). (1982). *Democracy on the shop floor? An American look at employee influence in Scandinavia today.* Kent, OH: Kent Popular Press.

————. (1989). *Modern welfare states: Politics and policies in social democratic Scandinavia.* New York: Praeger.

Elmér, Å. (1989). *Svensk socialpolitik* [Swedish social policy]. Stockholm: Liber.

Elvander, N. (1990). Incomes policies in the Nordic countries. *International Labor Review, 129,* 1-21.

Emerson, M. (1988). Regulation or deregulation of the labour market: Policy regimes for the recruitment and dismissal of employees in the industrialised countries. *European Economic Review, 32,* 775-817.

Erixon, L. (1991). Styrfel—inte systemfel—orsak till Sveriges eftersläpning? [Steering errors—not systematic defects—The cause of Sweden's falling behind]. *Ekonomisk Debatt, 1,* 47-52.

————. (1985). *What's wrong with the Swedish model? An analysis of its effects and changed conditions 1974-1985.* Meddelande 12. Institutet for Socialforskning, Stockholm.

Esping-Andersen, G. (1990). *The three worlds of welfare capitalism.* Princeton: Princeton University Press.

————. (1985). *Politics against markets.* Princeton: Princeton University Press.

Flanagan, R. J. (1987). Efficiency and equality in Swedish labor markets. In B. P. Bosworth and A. M. Rivlin (Eds.), *The Swedish Economy* (pp. 125-174). Washington, DC: The Brookings Institution.

Forsebäck, L. (1980). *Industrial relations and employment in Sweden.* Stockholm: The Swedish Institute.

Fritzell, J. (1991). *Icke av marknaden allena: Inkomstfördelningen i Sverige* [Not by the market alone: Income distribution in Sweden]. Stockholm: Almqvist & Wiksell International.

Fulcher, J. (1988). Trade unions in Sweden. *Economic and Industrial Democracy, 9,* 129-40.

Furåker, B. (1990, July). Labor markets and labor market flexibility in Canada and Sweden. Paper presented at the 12th World Congress of Sociology, Madrid, 1990.

————. (1987). *Stat och offentlig sektor* [The state and the public sector]. Stockholm: Rabén and Sjögren.

Ginsburg, H. (1983). *Full employment and public policy: The United States and Sweden.* Lexington, MA: D.C. Heath.

Gordon, M. S. (1988). *Social security policies in industrial countries: A comparative analysis.* Cambridge: Cambridge University Press.

Gramlich, E. M. (1987). Rethinking the role of the public sector. In B. P. Bosworth and A. M. Rivlin (Eds.), *The Swedish economy* (pp. 250-288). Washington, DC: The Brookings Institution.

Hart, H., & Hörte, S. Å. (1989). *Medbestämmandets stagnation: medbestämmandets utveckling 1978-1985* [The stagnation of codetermination: The development of codetermination, 1978-1985]. Göteborg: Arbetsvetenskapliga Kollegiet.

Heath, A., Jowell, R., & Curtice, J. (1985). *How Britain votes.* Oxford: Pergamon Press.

Heclo, H., & Madsen, H. (1989). *Policy and politics in Sweden: Principled pragmatism.* Philadelphia: Temple University Press.

————. (1987). *Policy and politics in Sweden.* Philadelphia: Temple University Press.

Hellberg, I., & Vrethem, M. (1982). *Lagen om anställningsskydd: tillkomst och tillämpning* [*The job-security law: Origins and application*] (Monograph No. 27). Göteborg: Göteborg University, Institute of Sociology.

Helliwell, J. F. (1990). Globalization and the national economy. In K. Newton, T. Schweitzer, & J.P. Voyer (Eds.), *Perspective 2000: Proceedings of a conference sponsored by the Economic Council of Canada* (pp. 121-139). Ottawa: Ministry of Supply and Services.

Hibbs, D. A., Jr. (1990). *Wage compression under solidarity bargaining in Sweden* (Economic Research Report No. 30). Stockholm: FIEF.

Hoel, M., & Knutsen, O. (1989). Social class, gender and sector employment as political cleavages in Scandinavia. *Acta Sociologica, 32,* 181-202.

Holmberg, S., and Giljam, M. (1990). *Rött blått grönt* [Red, blue, green]. Stockholm: Bonniers.

Hondrich, K. O. (1989). Value changes and the economic experience of mass publics. In B. Strümpel (Ed.), *Industrial societies after the stagnation of the 1970s* (pp. 131-158). Berlin: de Gruyter.

Horváth, D. J., & Daly, D. J. (1989). *Small countries in the world economy, what Canada can learn from the Swedish experience.* Halifax, NS: The Institute for Research on Public Policy/L'Institut de Recherches Politiques.

Ingham, G. K. (1973). *Strikes and industrial conflict: Britain and Scandinavia.* London: Macmillan.

Inglehart, R. (1989). *Culture shift in advanced industrial society.* Princeton: Princeton University Press.

_____. (1982). Changing values in Japan and the West. *Comparative Political Studies, 14,* 445-479.

Jangenäs, B. (1985). *The Swedish approach to labor market policy.* Stockholm: The Swedish Institute.

Jansson, K. (1990). *Inkomst och förmögenhetsfördelningen. Bilaga 19 till Långtidsutredningen* [Income and wealth distribution: supplement 19 to the long-range investigation]. Stockholm: Finansdepartementet.

Johannesson, J., & Persson-Tanimura, I. (1978). *Labor market policy in transition studies about the effects of labor market policy.* Stockholm: Delegation for Labour Market Policy Research (EFA).

Johansson, M. (1990). Arbetsförhållanden och solidaritet. In R. Åberg (Ed.), *Industrisamhälle i omvandling* [Working conditions and solidarity]. Stockholm: Carlssons.

Jonung, L., & Wadensjö, E. (1981). The effect of unemployment, inflation and real income growth on government popularity in Sweden. In S. Strom (Ed.), *Measurement in public choice* (pp. 202-212). London: Macmillan.

Jonzon, B. (1988). Evaluation of labour market policy measures: Some short reflections. In G. M. Olsen (Ed.), *Industrial change and labour adjustment in Sweden and Canada* (pp. 133-151). Toronto: Garamond Press.

Kangas, O. (1991). *The politics of social rights.* Stockholm: Sofi.

Kjellberg, A. (1983). *Facklig organisering i tolv länder* [Union organization in twelve countries]. Lund: Arkiv.

Knutsen, O. (1989). The priorities of materialist and post-materialist values in the nordic countries—A five-nation comparison. *Scandinavian Political Studies, 12,* 221-243.

Kohn, M. L., & Schooler, C. (1983). *Work and personality: An inquiry into the impact of sociological stratification.* Norwood, NJ: Ablex Publishing Corporation.

Korpi, W. (1990a). Halkar Sverige efter? Vår ekonomiska tillväxt och produktivitet i jämförande belysning [Is Sweden falling behind? Our economic growth and productivity in comparative perspective]. *Ekonomisk Debatt, 5,* 455-470.

_____. (1990b). Sveriges tillväxt följer de andra rikaste västländernas. Svar till SNS Konjunkturråd [Sweden's growth follows that of the other richest nations in the West: An answer to the business cycle council of the association for the study of the economy and society]. *Ekonomisk Debatt, 7,* 666-674.

────────. (1983). *The democratic class struggle.* London: Routledge and Kegan Paul.

────────. (1978). *The working class in welfare capitalism: Work, unions and politics in Sweden.* London: Routledge and Kegan Paul.

Larsson, A. (1988, May). Flexibility in production, security for individuals: Some aspects of Sweden's active labor market policy. *Working Life in Sweden, 35,* 1.

Lawrence, R. Z., & Bosworth, B. P. (1987). Adjusting to slower economic growth: The external sector. In B. P. Bosworth and A. M. Rivlin (Eds.), *The Swedish Economy* (pp. 55-88). Washington, DC: The Brookings Institution.

Leijon, A. G. (1988). The Swedish approach to labour market policy. In G. M. Olsen (Ed.), *Industrial change and labour adjustment in Sweden and Canada* (pp. 91-94). Toronto, Garamond Press.

Leion, A. (1987). *Själfränskap och medlemskap: Facket på 80-talet* [Soulmates and members: the union in the 1980s]. Stockholm: SIFO Frlag.

Lindqvist, R. (1989). Sjukförsäkring och sjukfrånvaro [Sickness benefit insurance and absenteeism]. In B. Furåker, (Ed.), *Välfärdsstat och lönearbete* (pp. 24-53). Lund: Süudentlitteratur.

Lundberg, E. (1985). The rise and fall of the Swedish model. *Journal of Economic Literature, 23,* 1-36.

────────. (1972, March). Productivity and structural change: A policy issue in Sweden. *Economic Journal, 82,* 465-485.

Marklund, S. (1988). *Paradise lost? The nordic welfare states and the recession 1975-1985.* Lund: Arkiv.

Martin, A. (1984). The shaping of the Swedish model. In P. Gourevitch, A. Martin, G. Ross, C. Allen, S. Bornstein, & A. Markkovits (Eds.), *Unions and economic crisis: Britain, West Germany, and Sweden* (pp. 190-359). London: Allen and Unwin.

McBride, S. (1988). The comparative politics of unemployment: Swedish and British responses to economic crisis. *Comparative Politics, 20,* 303-323.

Miller, A. M., & Listhaug, O. (1990). Political parties and confidence in government: A comparison of Norway, Sweden and the United States. *British Journal of Political Science, 20* (Part 3), 357-386.

OECD. (1990). *Economic surveys: Sweden.* Paris: OECD.

────────. (1989). *The tax/benefit position of production workers: 1985-1988.* Paris: OECD.

Offe, C. (1984). *Contradictions of the welfare state.* London: Hutchinson.

────────. (1973a). The abolition of market control and the problem of legitimacy I. *Kapitalistate,* No. 1, pp. 109-116.

────────. (1973b). The abolition of market control and the problem of legitimacy II. *Kapitalistate,* No. 2, pp. 73-75.

────────. (1972). *Strukturprobleme des kapitalistischen Staates* [Structural problems of the capitalist state]. Frankfurt on the Main: Suhrkamp.

Öhman, B. (1974). *LO and labor market policy since the Second World War.* Stockholm: Prisma.

Olsson, S. O. (1990). *Social policy and welfare state in Sweden.* Lund: Arkiv.

────────. (1989). Social welfare in developed market countries: Sweden. In J. Dixon & R. P. Sheurell (Eds.), *Social welfare in developed market countries* (pp. 264-308). London: Routledge.

Pettersson, T. (1988). *Bakom dubbla lås* [Behind double locks]. Stockholm: Institutet für framtidsstudier.

Pindyck, R.S., & Rubinfield, D. L. (1981). *Econometric models and economic forecasts.* New York: McGraw-Hill.

Rehn, G. (1984). *Cooperation between the government and workers' and employers' organisations on labor market policy in Sweden.* Stockholm: The Swedish Institute.

Riksförsäkringsverket (National Social Security Board). (1990). *Sjukskrivningsmönstret bland ungdomar och unga vuxna: översiktlig kartläggning* [The pattern of reported sickness among youth and young adults: A synoptic survey]. Statistical Reports Is-R, 1990:1. Stockholm: Riksförsäkringsverket.

Rivlin, A. M. (1987). Overview. In B. P. Bosworth & A. M. Rivlin (Eds.), *The Swedish economy* (pp. 1-21). Washington, DC: The Brookings Institution.

SBC. (1989a). *Arbetsmarknad i Siffror* [The labor market in numbers]. Stockholm: SBC.

SBC. (1989b). *Arbetsmiljö 1986-87, Rapport 61. Levnadsförhållanden* [Work environment 1986-1987, Report 61: Survey of living conditions]. Stockholm: SBC.

SBC. (1988). *Almänna valen 1988* [The general elections]. Stockholm: SBC.

SBC. (1987). *Levnadsförhållanden, Rapport 54: Ett decennium av stagnerande realinkomster* [Living conditions report 54: A decade of stagnating real incomes]. Stockholm: SBC.

SBC. (1985). *Offentliga Sektorn: Utveckling och Nuläge* [The public sector: Development and current situation]. Stockholm: SBC

SBC. (1982). *Arbetsmiljö 1979, Rapport 32. Levnadsförhållanden* [Work environment 1979, Report 32: Survey of living conditions]. Stockholm: SBC.

SBC. (1978). *Arbetsmiljö 1975, Rapport 12. Levnadsförhållanden* [Work environment 1975, Report 12: Survey of living conditions]. Stockholm: SBC.

Smucker, J., & Van Den Berg, A. (1991). Some evidence of the effects of labour market policies on workers' attitudes toward change in Canada and Sweden. *Canadian Journal of Sociology, 6,* 51-74.

Sou. (1975). *Arbete åt Alla* [Work for all]. Government Public Inquiries, 1975:90. Stockholm: Department of Labor.

Standing, G. (1988). *Unemployment and labor market flexibility.* Geneva: International Labor Office.

Svallfors, S. (in press). The politics of welfare policy in Sweden: Structural determinants and attitudinal cleavages. *The British Journal of Sociology.*

_____ . (1989). *Vem älskar välfärdstaten? Attityder, organiserade intressen och svensk välfärdspolitik* [Who loves the welfare state? Attitudes, organized interests, and Swedish welfare policy]. Lund: Arkiv.

Swedish economy: On a different tack. (1990, March 3). *The Economist,* special 22-page insert.

Szulkin, R. (1987). Political resources. In R. Erikson & R. Åberg (Eds.), *Welfare in transition: A survey of living conditions in Sweden 1968-1981* (pp. 193-215). Oxford: Clarendon Press.

Therborn, G. (1985). *Why some peoples are more unemployed than others.* London: Verso.

Thurow, L. C. (1980). *The zero-sum society: Distribution and the possibilities for economic change.* New York: Basic Books.

Van Den Berg, A. (1988). *The immanent utopia: from Marxism on the state to the state of Marxism.* Princeton: Princeton University Press.

Van Den Berg, A., & Smucker, J. (1988, June 8). Labour markets and the state: Individualist versus cooperativist visions in Canada and Sweden. Paper presented at the conference on Social Progress and Sociological Theory, Jagiellonian University, Cracow, Poland.

Vogel, J., Andersson, L.-G., Davidsson, U., & Häll, L. (1988). *Inequality in Sweden: Trends and current situation, living conditions 1975-1985* (Report No. 58). Stockholm: SBC.

Wadensjö, E. (1986). Labour market policy and employment growth in Sweden. *Labour, 1,* 3-23.

Yankelovich, D., Zetterberg, H., Strümpel, B., Shanks, M. Immerwahr, J., Noelle-Neumann, E., Sengoku, T., & Yuchtman-Yaar, E. (1985). *The world at work: An international report on jobs, productivity, and human values.* New York: Octagon.

Yuchtman-Yaar, E. (1989). Economic culture in post-industrial society: Orientations toward growth, technology and work. In B. Strümpel (Ed.), *Industrial societies after the stagnation of the 1970s* (pp. 159-184). Berlin: De Gruyter.

Yuchtman-Yaar, E., & Gottlieb, A. (1985). Technological development and the meaning of work: A cross-cultural perspective. *Human Relations, 38,* 603-621.

Zetterberg, H., Busch, K., Crona, G., Frankel, G., Jönsson, B., Sönderlind, I., & Winander, B. (1983). *Det osynliga kontraktet: En studie i 80-talets arbetsliv* [The invisible contract: A study of working life in the 1980s]. Vällingby: SIFO Förlag.

ECONOMIC PERFORMANCE, GOVERNMENT POLICIES, AND PUBLIC OPINION IN ITALY

Anthony C. Masi

In a provocative analysis of the Italian economy, Giavazzi and Spaventa (1990) noted that "[o]ver the past 15 years, the Italian economy has experienced rather uncommon developments, by comparison with the rest of Europe" (p. 133). Indeed, the performance of the Italian economy has not been easily or satisfactorily explained or predicted over that time period by either Italian or foreign observers. According to Giavazzi and Spaventa (1990, p. 133), most analysts have been prone to look at Italy in terms of near-collapses, miracles, or impending bankruptcy. In these analyses, three aspects of the Italian case have been cited with some regularity. First, for a variety of reasons, and until very recently, Italy's industrial sector has shown remarkable structural strength. Second, huge internal and external imbalances, record fiscal deficits, and mounting debt indicate a rare, if not unique, case of macroeconomic weakness among the advanced industrial democracies. Third, the underground economy and its concomitant "black labor market" have achieved dimensions in Italy that are well beyond those found in the rest of the industrialized world.

However, although no one can simply dismiss the underground economy in Italy (see Masi, 1987, for a review of a seven-volume series on moonlighting that involved a research effort by over 40 Italian social scientists; Blim, 1990; Bruno, 1979; Deaglio, 1987; Redivo, 1983), "the popular explanation of Italy's growth in terms of the strength of its underground economy is...wholly unsatisfactory" (Giavazzi & Spaventa, 1990, p. 135). In other words, that phenomenon alone cannot "reconcile structural strength and macroeconomic weakness"(Giavazzi & Spaventa, 1988, p. 2). In fact, in the analysis of Giavazzi and Spaventa (1988, 1990; see also Britton, Eastwood, & Major, 1986; Hughes, Hallet, & Petit, 1988; Ranci, 1990), the economic policies pursued by various Italian governments over the last two decades go much farther than facile recourse to the "underground" economy in explaining Italy's relative success in the face of oil shocks, wage shocks, and staggering inflation (Zandamela, 1989).

In the first section of this chapter, I deal with the objective indicators of economic performance that have characterized the Italian case since 1970 or so. Reference, however, is also made to earlier periods in order to place these more recent trends (as well as contemporary policies) in perspective. In the second section I explore descriptively the kinds of policies that have been pursued to deal with short-term problems and longer-term goals. I argue there that Giavazzi and Spaventa (1990) were indeed correct in their characterization of Italian economic policies and concomitant (if not resulting) economic performance as "unconventional."

However, even without entering into the merits of the case that can be made for viewing Italy as a "success" (both in relative and absolute terms) and for characterizing its approach to economic policy as "unconventional," one can explore the reactions of the Italian people to the changes that they have experienced over the last 20 years. In light of the policies and instruments that Italian governments have used in attempting to create the appropriate conditions for economic growth, these individual (and collective) reactions and responses become even more significant to explore. Indeed, as shown below, many of these policy instruments have had consequences that could be anticipated only in light of their unconventional nature. In the third section of this chapter, I therefore broadly outline some of the more striking features of contemporary Italian public opinion and attitudes in comparison with several other national groups and discuss some of the more significant changes that have occurred in those opinions and attitudes in the course of the 1970s and 1980s.

Obviously, by putting together objective indicators of economic performance, descriptions of economic policies, and the subjective reactions of the Italian public, I hope to provide insight into the ways in which Italians have experienced the policies and lived the changes that their economy has undergone spontaneously (on its own) and/or as a possible result of explicit government policies. In the concluding section of this chapter I explore and speculate on the extent to which the Italian case is unique or can be generalized to other contexts.

OBJECTIVE CHANGES IN THE ITALIAN
ECONOMY AND LABOR MARKET

The performance of the Italian economy, as measured by the percentage of change in real domestic product (annual averages) has been consistent with that of the other six largest industrial democracies since around 1970 (see OECD, 1989, 1986). Of course, Italy was considered an economic miracle in the decade from 1955-1964, when its real growth rates were on the order of 8% annually. The oil shocks and a continuation of the strike activity of the late 1960s that continued well into the 1970s seem, however, to have put Italy slightly out of phase with her other partners in the group of seven. Italy's upturns have tended to be higher and her downturns lower (Masi, 1989, p. 131). In fact, there was a significant, one could even say dramatic, upward trend in Italian gross domestic product (in constant 1980 lire) from 1951 to 1989 (OECD, 1989, 1986; *OECD Economic Outlook,* various issues; *OECD Economic Surveys,* various issues).

During the late 1970s and early 1980s, manufacturing continued to account for a larger share in the creation of gross domestic product in Italy than it did in other industrialized nations. Its continued growth paralleled that of overall gross domestic product and by the end of the 1980s had recovered the ground lost during the serious recession of 1981-82. However, the Italian industries that have done best have tended to be concentrated in traditional sectors such as textiles, clothing, and footwear (the so-called TCF sectors) and in heavy industry such as steel production. Notwithstanding the strong performance of selected industrial districts in northern and central Italy that specialize in TCF (cf. Blim, 1990, for a dissenting view on the performance of at least one such manufacturing network), and the massive restructuring of the public steel sector (Masi, 1990), both of these sectors can be expected to come under increasing pressure from the newly industrializing nations (cf. Viesti, 1990, for a more optimistic appraisal). Italy has, however, tended to concentrate on the high value-added end of both of these markets, a practice that has provided a buffer from the low-end competition that the newly industrializing countries currently create. The continued importance of industrial output in the Italian economy, a part of what Giavazzi and Spaventa (1990) noted as the country's remarkable structural strength, has also carried over into Italy's ability to maintain relatively high levels of employment in the manufacturing sector (see Figure 1).

Measured and reported unemployment in Italy reached 12% of the labor force in 1988-89, and according Murat (1989) "there is no evidence that the tendency should substantially change in the near or medium term" (p. 2). Figure 2 shows the trend in Italian unemployment from 1951 to 1986. I should like to point out that the series on which the graph is based has undergone several modifications, but the OECD standardization procedures allow for a margin

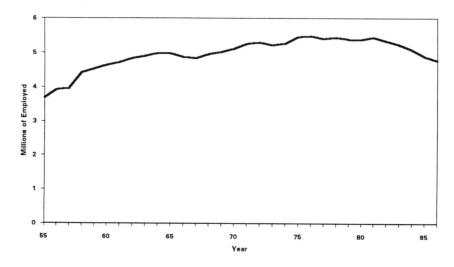

Notes: Adapted from *OECD Economic Outlook* (various issues); and *OECD Economic Surveys, Italy* (various
           issues).

Figure 1.   Total Employed in Italian Manufacturing Sector, 1955-1986

of faith to be placed in the levels reported over the long time period in question.
The significant downturn in unemployment starting around 1956 coincides
with two major migratory experiences: a wave of international migration to
North America and Australia that lasted for approximately a decade, and
significant shifts of rural populations from southern Italy to its northern
"industrial triangle" of Torino-Milano-Genova. At present, although there has
been some noticeable increase in unemployment due to layoffs (the effects of
which are sometimes masked by the "wage integration fund," see below), the
phenomenon is particularly widespread among women, young people, and
those living in the south (D'Antonio, Colaizzo, & Leonello, 1988; Faustini,
1988; Padoa Schioppa, 1990). Industry layoffs have not been compensated for
by absorption in the services sector, at least not as officially recorded. Although
it has been possible in the manufacturing sector to maintain a higher proportion
of value added than elsewhere in the industrialized world, productivity in the
Italian service sector has lagged considerably, at least on the basis of qualitative
accounts. Moreover, self-employment has remained very high in Italy and even
grew from 18.7% of the labor force in 1975 to 20.6% in 1984 (*OECD Economic
Surveys,* various years; see also, De Caprariis, 1988; Rosti, 1989).

In the 1980s at least four major structural transformations were characteristic
of Italy's developments, according to Brunetta (1988): (a) job losses in large
enterprises due to innovation and rationalization in industry (see also Masi,

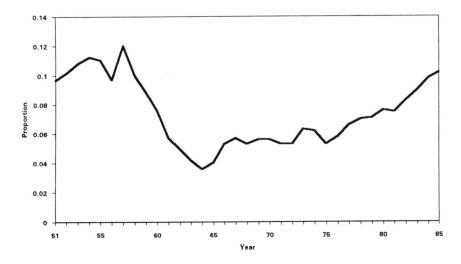

Note: Adapted from *OECD Economic Outlook* (various issues); and *OECD Economic Surveys, Italy* (various issues).

Figure 2.   OECD Standardized Unemployment Rates, for Italy, 1951-1985

1990), (b) an overall increase in employment levels due to the growth in the services sector (De Caprariis, 1988), (c) a rise in "irregular employment" concomitant with the increasing importance of the underground economy (Redivo, 1983), and (d) growth in self-employment and small business that partly offset labor-shedding by large firms (De Caprariis, 1988).

Brunetta (1988) noted that there were also changes in the labor market as a consequence of these structural transformations: (a) diversified behavior of the labor force (see also Neri, 1988), (b) search for job stability and the capacity to adapt to precarious positions (see Torelli & Trivellato, 1989), (c) heightened youth unemployment problems (see Padoa Schioppa, 1990), (d) segmentation of the labor force (see Bruno, 1979; Torelli & Trivellato, 1988), and (e) higher female participation (see Faustini, 1988).

As a cautionary note, however, I should like to point out that the way in which unemployment is measured in Italy causes difficulties in comparing her to other advanced countries. The standard labor force concept is in use in Italy (as is the case elsewhere in the OECD), but as far as Italy's National (formerly Central) Institute of Statistics is concerned, to be considered unemployed one has only to indicate a desire to work. In Canada and the United States, at least, one must not only indicate a desire to work but must also have undertaken specific action to search for work in the month prior to being interviewed. Thus, all other things being equal, the Italian rate of unemployment would be reported as considerably lower than its current level if the American or Canadian definition were applied (see Accornero & Carmigliano, 1986). Another potential difficulty is the way in which Italians most likely conceive of "employment." Whereas American teenagers who work for a small business, even off the books, are likely to report their activities as a "job," Italian young people in similar situations will almost certainly not consider such activities as real employment. The specifics of Italian unemployment also indicate that the phenomenon is particularly sharply felt among women, the young, and those living in the southern regions of the country (Chiarello, 1988; Murat, 1989; Padoa Schioppa, 1990).

ITALIAN ECONOMIC POLICIES, 1970-1987

Italy has no general system of unemployment benefits comparable to either the unemployment insurance schemes popular in North America or the massive retraining efforts of the Scandinavian countries, especially Sweden. Consequently, one of the most important elements in Italy's social and economic programs, particularly during the period of massive industrial restructuring in the early 1980s, was the introduction of a "layoff wage" in the form of the *Cassa Integrazione Guadagni* (Wage Integration Fund) (see Schweke & Jones, 1986). Although it is true that this fund was extremely important and useful to big businesses in their rationalization, reconversion, and restructuring efforts, middle-size firms in all sectors of the Italian economy took recourse to it (Cipolletta, Heimler, & Calcagini, 1987; Zanetti, 1987).

Another interesting feature of the Italian panorama of economic policies was a "wage indexation scheme" that had very noticeable effects in the 1970s (*Scala Mobile*) (Zandamela, 1989; see also Masi, 1989, Figure 8.2, p. 134). During that decade, this institution covered nearly 100% of the price increases, but it was not used in that way in the 1980s, particularly because the Italian public voted in a referendum in 1985 to curtail the automatic nature of its "contingency points" (Biorcio & Natale, 1989; Uleri, 1989). In fact, according to Uleri's (1989) calculations based on data provided by Italy's National Institute of Statistics, 54.3% of the valid votes cast in the 1985 referendum were for the "No" option, which upheld the law limiting the wage indexation scheme. Murat (1989) claimed that "the mechanism had also been implemented with the purpose of smoothing wage differentials between different kinds of jobs" (p. 3).

Brunetta (1988) also claims that Italy engaged in an incomes policy and established guidelines for a labor-market policy during the 1980s. The explicit incomes policy included measures to curb inflation and income growth, diffuse the labor conflicts that dominated from the late 1960s to the end of the 1970s, introduce more flexible labor-market rules (and attempt to avoid labor-market rigidities, see Dore, 1988), and try to design some job-creation measures (Brunetta, 1988, p. 8). Tripartite bargaining was the mechanism chosen to arrive at and implement these policies. One feature that several analysts have noted in the Italian case was the flattening of wage differentials during the period of most rapid economic growth. However, this was accomplished without the help of tripartite bargaining and may have been simply the result of strong union pressure on sectoral and local bargaining units. (This goes well beyond the scope of the present research and deserves to be explored further. See, for example, Paci, 1989.)

There were, however, also implicit attempts to arrive at an incomes policy. They included (a) control of public spending to curb inflation, and (b) more direct government intervention in disputes between business and labor, in particular, the centralization of the bargaining processes.

In the late 1970s, labor-market policies in Italy dealt mainly with problems of the entry of young people into the world of work (Law 285/1977) and with the urgent need for industrial restructuring (Law 675/1977). There was also legislation aimed at equal rights for women (Law 903/1977) and for vocational training for young people (Law 845/1978). The wage indexation system was also modified in the late 1970s. The early 1980s saw a continuation of these policies and, in addition, measures to help individual industries and even firms during the restructuring process: regulation of resort to the Wage Integration Fund and the introduction in some regions of employment agencies (to supplement the old-fashioned labor exchanges—the *Uffici di collocamento*). Only after 1984 did an explicit set of guidelines emerge for general employment problems: regulation and deregulation, in particular of cost-of-living allowance points; job-creation schemes, such as the seasonal employment of youth (Law 79/1983), which allowed hiring by name rather than number on the list at the labor exchange; and the reform of the apprenticeship law (Law 863/1984) to include trainee contracts and flexible (and part-time) working hours. Of course, the above-noted referendum approved the cut-backs in the indexation scheme in 1985. Subsidies to employers were approved in Law 113/1986, and in May of that year a business-labor accord approved further cost savings for employers. Entrepreneurship was favored, particularly in the southern regions, with the De Vito Act (Law 44/1986). Law 160/1988 also instituted a fund to finance enterprises by young people. Early retirements were also encouraged and seem to be on the increase. Reform of the state employment service (Law 56/1987) established regional observatories for labor-market conditions (and provided a not indifferent source of integrative income for Italian labor-market specialists).

At the level of the economy as a whole, subsidies in the form of reduced social security contributions seem to have played a significant role in Italy around the time of the second oil shock. But there was also a rise in direct taxes—the result of a 1974 tax reform that introduced steeply rising marginal tax rates—coupled with high inflation (Giavazzi & Spaventa, 1988, p. 13). Of course, it can also be argued that high inflation can erode old debt for enterprises, especially if such debt was contracted at fixed nominal interest rates. Italy's monetary policy in this period also accommodated new debt by effectively permitting negative real interest rates. The consequent real depreciation of the Italian lire seems, also, to have "allowed a more aggressive price competition on export markets" (Giavazzi & Spaventa, 1988, p. 15). It is also worth noting that Italy has engaged in a variety of industrial policies (Adams Malerba, 1983; Ranci, 1978) that have been designed to facilitate industrial reconversion and restructuring and to provide subsidies, particularly for exports, to specific sectors.

PUBLIC OPINION IN ITALY, 1973-1988

In 1987, the International Social Survey Program (ISSP) conducted an international, comparative data collection in nine countries, including Italy, on the general topic of equality in income, wealth, and opportunity. The survey instrument included questions on the perceived extent of inequality in the various countries and attempted to measure support for government programs to reduce inequality. The Italian portion of the survey was conducted by Eurisko (Milan) and was a probability-with-quota sampling design that, when appropriately weighted, can be considered broadly representative of the Italian population aged 18 years and older.

Because this survey is cross-sectional, it cannot provide information about changes and adaptations in which the Italian public has engaged in response to the objective changes in their economic circumstances as outlined in the first two sections of this chapter. However, some of the data do provide an interesting snapshot perspective of the way in which Italians think about economic behavior and government's role in economic life. In what follows I briefly discuss the raw percentage point differences between Italy and three other countries that were also part of the cross-national effort of ISSP— Hungary, Great Britain, and the United States. Hungary and Britain were chosen because they are an Eastern European and Western European nation, respectively. The United States was chosen as a reference because it is often taken to represent the case of extreme individualism in value orientations.

Table 1 presents the percentage of respondents in the four countries who responded that each of a series of factors was "essential" or "very important" in achieving economic success in their countries. Some of the results are striking. For example, whereas two-fifths of the Italians thought it was very important or essential to come from a wealthy family, only one-fifth of the Britons and Americans felt that was the case, and one-third of the Hungarians. Nearly 9 out of 10 Americans thought that ambition and hard work were very

Table 1.   Perceptions of the Requisites for Success (in percentages)

"Essential" or "Very Important"	Italy	Hungary	Britain	U.S.A.
Wealthy family background	40.1	34.2	21.6	20.2
Well-educated parents	44.8	26.6	27.0	39.0
Good education for oneself	78.9	38.1	72.2	84.1
Ambition	48.6	72.8	79.6	88.5
Natural ability	75.3	70.6	57.7	59.3
Hard work	56.6	61.2	83.6	89.4
Contact with the right people	75.0	41.3	39.2	40.1
Political connections	55.2	30.2	7.1	16.1
Region from which one comes	12.2	3.8	7.9	7.3
One's sex	13.8	12.1	12.7	14.6
Political beliefs	22.3	25.4	5.3	9.1
Sample Sizes	1,027	2,606	1,212	1,285

Source: Adapted from *Social Inequality, 1987* by the International Social Science Program, September 1990, International Social Survey Program, Inter-university Consortium for Political and Social Research (ICPSR) 9383.

important or essential for success, but only about half of the Italians were of that opinion. About three out of four Italians thought that possessing natural ability and knowing the right people were important. But only two out of five Americans, Britons, and Hungarians shared the view that knowing the right people was a determinant of economic success. Three out of five Britons and Americans responded that natural ability was an important factor, but seven out of 10 Hungarians thought so. One in five Italians and a similar share of the Hungarians thought that political beliefs were essential or very important for economic success, but only one in 10 Americans and one in 20 Britons responded in that way. Over half the Italians in the survey felt that economic success was linked to one's political connections, but only three out of 10 Hungarians, one out of 10 Britons, and one out of five Americans were like-minded.

The survey also recorded respondents' views on the role of government in regulating the effects of income differences in their countries. Table 2 provides the percentages in the four countries who "agree" or "strongly agree" with specific government actions. While four out of five Italians and Hungarians thought the government should be responsible for reducing income differences, the percentage of Britons who shared this view was about 3 out of 5, and less than one in three Americans agreed. Italians, with 82% agreeing, were second only to the 90% of the Hungarians who thought that the government should provide jobs for those who want them. Only about 60% of Britons and 45% of Americans were of this opinion. With regard to the government's providing a decent standard of living for the unemployed or even a basic guaranteed income, between 60% and 70% of the Italians and Britons shared these beliefs, with only between 20% and 37% of the Americans agreeing with them. Four

Table 2. Perceptions of the Role of Government

	Percentage "Agreeing" or "Strongly Agreeing"			
Action	*Italy*	*Hungary*	*Britain*	*U.S.A.*
Assume responsibility for reducing income differences	81.7	79.5	63.9	28.7
Provide money so that poor children can go to university	90.0	73.8	83.5	75.8
Provide jobs for those who want them	82.0	91.5	59.1	44.5
Spend less on the poor	7.3	10.1	4.4	18.1
Provide a decent standard of living for the unemployed	68.0	—	65.3	36.7
Provide a guaranteed basic income	67.3	79.4	60.7	20.8
Sample Sizes	1,027	2,606	1,212	1,285

Source: Adapted from Social Inequality, 1987 by the International Social Science Program, September 1990, International Social Survey Program, Inter-university Consortium for Political and Social Research (ICPSR) 9383.

out of five Hungarians were in favor of guaranteed basic income (they were not asked about providing a decent standard of living for the unemployed).

Table 3 illustrates the extent to which individuals in the four countries saw conflicts between various social groups. In all these nations, around three-fifths of the respondents saw conflict or strong conflict between the rich and the poor. However, whereas nearly half of the Italian sample and two-fifths of the Hungarians saw conflict between the working and middle classes in their countries, only one-fifth of the American and British respondents thought that was the case. And just under three-fifths of the Italians thought there were conflicts between the unemployed and those who had jobs, whereas less than half of the British and Americans held that view. (The question was not asked of the Hungarians.) About one-quarter of the sample in the three European countries responded that there were conflicts between farmers and city people, whereas almost two-fifths of the Americans believed this to be the case in the United States.

There are interesting anomalies with regard to the level of industrial conflict that Italians have experienced. Figure 3 shows the number of workers involved in industrial conflicts in Italy from 1951 to 1986. Figure 4 illustrates, instead, the actual number of industrial conflicts that occurred in Italy over that same time period. The two trends are by no means identical. Whereas the number of conflicts reached its peak in the "hot autumn of 1969," the number of workers who participated in strikes peaked a full decade later in 1979. I believe these figures need careful re-examination and may shed some light on the changing nature of the demands and modalities of strikes in Italy over the last 25 years. In a very interesting secondary analysis of survey data dealing only with industrial workers, however, Golden (1990) has forcefully argued that the

Table 3.   Perceptions of Conflicts between Groups in Society

Conflicting Groups	Percentage of Perceiving Conflict			
	Italy	Hungary	Britain	U.S.A.
Rich and poor	59.9	55.8	53.1	1.9
Working and middle classes	47.6	39.0	20.4	1.4
Unemployed and employed	58.5	—	40.7	8.0
Management and workers	52.7	43.2	55.5	5.4
Farmers and city dwellers	24.8	26.6	28.3	8.1
Young and old	32.8	41.0	38.6	—
Sample Sizes	1,027	2,606	1,212	1,285

Source: Adapted from *Social Inequality, 1987* by the International Social Science Program, September 1990, International Social Survey Program, Inter-university Consortium for Political and Social Research (ICPSR) 9383.

preferences of Italian workers should not be inferred from their behavior in such activities as strike participation. The data she refers to in her study, in fact, indicated no major shifts in the trade union politics (attitudes) of industrial workers over a nearly 20-year period. However, her analysis did not include data from general social surveys, such as the Euro-Barometers (see below), to gauge any potential changes in the body politic as a whole rather than only in the industrial-labor-force segment.

It was also possible from the ISSP survey to obtain information on the perceived levels of inequality and opportunities for economic success. Table 4 provides data on those who "agreed" or "strongly agreed" with a series of statements measuring those variables. The Italians (33%) and the Hungarians (45%) were much less likely than their American counterparts (72%) to see themselves as having a chance for upward mobility. Whereas 58% of the Americans and over 75% of the Britons and Hungarians thought that income inequalities in their countries were too large, nearly 90% of the Italians believed this to be the case. Italians were also the least likely of the four groups to think that large differences in income were either necessary for prosperity or important to get people to work hard. Interestingly, they were among the most likely to think that "good profits" for businesses was the best way to improve everyone's standard of living (59.5%).

I would like to draw on these descriptive data to make one additional point about Italian perceptions of one other government policy—taxes. In Tables 5 and 6 I have divided Italian respondents into quartiles according to their family earnings (a variable estimated by interviewers). Table 5 presents the percentage breakdowns of their attitudes toward taxes for individuals according to high, middle, and low incomes. Table 6 indicates the attitudes of these income groups to the tax shares of the wealthy. Between 80% and 90% of Italians believed that taxes for the lowest income groups are too high. However, between 60% and 70% of those in the lower three quartiles of family

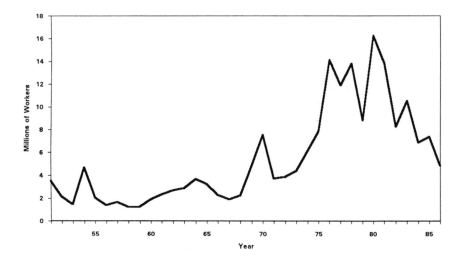

Note: Adapted from *OECD Economic Outlook* (various issues); and *OECD Economic Surveys, Italy* (various issues).

Figure 3.   Millions of Workers Involved in Industrial Conflict, Italy, 1951-1986

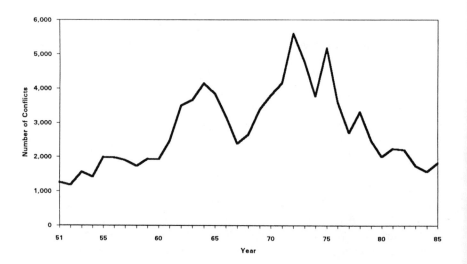

Note: Adapted from *OECD Economic Outlook* (various issues); and *OECD Economic Surveys, Italy* (various issues).

Figure 4.   Number of Industrial Conflicts in Italy, 1951-1985

Table 4.   Responses to Statements Measuring Variables
of Inequality and Opportunities for Economic Success

Statement	Percentage "Agreeing" or "Strongly Disagreeing"			
	Italy	*Hungary*	*Britain*	*U.S.A.*
People like me and my family have a good chance of improving our standard of living	44.6	33.4	37.2	72.2
Differences in income are too large	87.1	76.3	75.7	58.0
People would not want to take extra responsibility at work unless they were paid extra for it	77.5	62.6	82.1	70.5
Workers would not bother to require skills unless they were paid extra for having them	74.1	63.3	70.0	58.3
No one would study for years to become a lawyer or doctor unless he or she expected to earn a lot more than ordinary workers	57.3	56.6	79.8	68.5
Inequality continues to exist because it benefits the rich and powerful	74.7	38.4	62.4	49.4
Inequality continues to exist because ordinary people don't join together to get rid of it	62.4	30.7	42.0	44.2
Large differences in income are necessary for prosperity	18.7	26.5	27.5	32.5
Allowing business to make good profits is the best way to improve everyone's standard of living	59.5	58.5	55.3	47.9
Sample Sizes	1,027	2,606	1,212	1,285
	Percentage Responding with "Absolutely Necessary" or "Probably Necessary"			
Large differences in pay are important to get people to work hard	56.0	73.9	64.8	71.4
Sample Sizes	1,027	2,606	1,212	1,285

Source: Adapted from *Social Inequality, 1987* by the International Social Science Program, September 1990, International Social Survey Program, ICPSR 9383.

income believe that taxes for the high income groups are too low. Remarkably, over 40% of the individuals in the highest family income quartile thought that the rich were not taxed enough. There was, at least for this nationally representative sample in the spring of 1987, virtually no disagreement by quartiles concerning the middle income group: In all income groups, one-third of the respondents thought taxes were about right, and two-thirds thought they were too high.

Table 5.   Attitude of Italians to Taxes for Individuals According to High, Middle, and Low Incomes, by Quartiles of Family Income (in percentages)

Income Group	High	Right	Low	Total Percent	N	Percent in Groups
Taxes for High Incomes						
Lowest	13.3	18.3	68.5	100.1	241	24.4
2nd	12.9	18.0	69.2	100.1	256	25.9
3rd	15.8	22.8	61.4	100.0	259	26.2
Highest	33.9	22.7	43.4	100.0	233	23.6
Overall	18.7	20.4	60.9	100.0	—	—
N	185	202	602	—	989	100.1
Taxes for Middle Incomes						
Lowest	56.6	38.1	5.3	100.0	247	24.6
2nd	60.4	36.2	3.5	100.1	260	25.9
3rd	63.1	31.6	5.3	100.0	263	26.2
Highest	68.8	29.9	1.3	100.0	234	23.3
Overall	62.1	34.0	3.9	100.0	—	—
N=	624	341	39	—	1,004	100.0
Taxes for Low Incomes						
Lowest	88.7	10.5	0.8	100.0	247	24.6
2nd	89.2	8.8	1.9	99.9	260	25.9
3rd	83.6	14.8	1.5	99.9	263	26.2
Highest	79.1	18.4	2.6	100.1	234	23.3
Overall	85.2	13.0	1.7	99.9	—	—
N	856	131	17	—	1,004	100.0

Source: Adapted from *Social Inequality, 1987E by the International Social Science Program, September 1990, International Social Survey Program, ICPSR 9383.*

Not surprisingly, it can be observed from Table 6 that about half of all Italians, regardless of their family income status believe that the rich should pay a larger share of taxes than the poor. In fact, for the three lowest income groups, between one-quarter and one-third of the respondents thought the share that ought to be paid by the rich in Italian society should be "much larger." By contrast, about three in 10 individuals in the highest quartile of family income in Italy thought that paying the same share would be most appropriate.

What can one make of these figures? It must be remembered that these data refer to cross-sectional, nationally representative sample surveys conducted in 1987. Nonetheless, the pattern of responses for Italy provide clear indications that Italians strongly favor government intervention to reduce inequities in income and to improve opportunities for advancement. But they are skeptical of the economic and political system in which they live because they have more faith in natural ability than hard work and in social and political connections

Table 6.   Share of Income that should be Paid by High as
Compared to Low Incomes, by Family Income Groups (Quartiles)

Income Group	Much Larger Share	Larger Share	Same Share	Smaller Share	Totals	N	Percent in Groups
Lowest	34.4	48.2	16.6	0.8	100.0	247	24.6
2nd	32.7	47.3	18.1	1.9	100.0	260	25.9
3rd	26.7	55.0	16.8	1.5	100.0	262	26.1
Highest	17.5	53.0	28.2	1.3	100.0	234	23.3
Overall	28.0	50.8	19.7	1.4	99.9	—	—
N	281	510	198	14	—	1,003	99.9

Source: Adapted from *Social Inequality, 1987* by the International Social Science Program, September 1990, International Social Survey Program, Inter-university Consortium for Political and Social Research (ICPSR) 9383.

than ambition. They see their society as consisting of conflicts between all major social classes, and they are convinced that the economy generates income differences that are too large.

Of course, it would be informative to know the extent to which attitudes in Italy have changed as her economic fortunes have improved. By using the Eurobarometer Studies, which have been conducted yearly in member states of the European Community since 1973, one can gain an insight into this problem. However, there are serious limitations to the sampling frame that has traditionally been used in Italy for those surveys—it has been a quota sample, with weights applied to approximate national representativeness. This does not mean that the sample cannot or should not be used for purposes of statistical description and analysis, but caution must be exercised in interpreting the results.

Figure 5 seems to imply a decreasing level of dissatisfaction among Italians for the way in which democracy works in their country. In fact, over 85% of the Italians polled in 1976 indicated that they were "not satisfied" or "not at all satisfied" with the overall performance of their political institutions. However, by 1986 that level of dissatisfaction had fallen to about 70% of the respondents (and had risen again to just under 75% by 1988). (Because surveys with this question were conducted twice annually except in 1976 and 1985, I have used simple arithmetic averages for each year. In other words, I have pooled the semiannual results into a single yearly sample.)

Figure 6 shows the way in which Italians have cast their votes over the entire postwar period. I have followed Parisi and Pasquino (1979) in classifying the "left" as the Communists, Socialists, and smaller radical and Marxist parliamentary groupings; the "center" as the Christian Democrats and the small lay parties (Republicans, Liberals, and Social Democrats); and the Neo-Fascists, Monarchists, and other smaller nationalist parties as the "right." There does not seem to be a discernible turn to the "right" but rather a slight

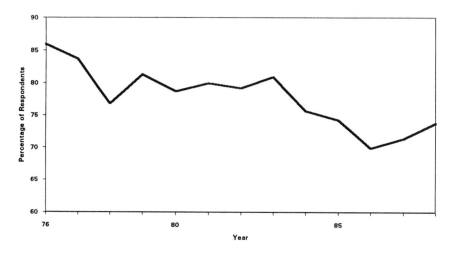

Note: Adapted from Euro Barometer Survey (various issues)

Figure 5.   Percentage of Respondents "Not Satisfied"
with the Way Democracy Works in Italy, 1976-1988

convergence toward the left. Of course, a breakdown of the vote for the left would be most informative. Since its heyday in 1976, however, the Italian Communist Party, which renamed itself the Democratic Party of the Left in 1991, has seen a dramatic decline in its fortunes, whereas the Socialists have significantly increased their share of the votes on the left. This trend may help explain why the Christian Democrats, who have governed Italy but for one short and one longer period since World War II, have been engaged in significant economic policies.

Another very interesting change in attitudes that has accompanied Italy's economic successes has taken place in expressed levels of happiness and overall life satisfaction. For the sake of brevity in this presentation, I deal only with weighted averages for responses to two questions asked in at least four different years in the Eurobarometer Surveys of the 1970s and 1980s.

In the first question, Italians were asked to state whether they felt themselves to be "very happy," "somewhat happy," or "not-too-happy." In the 1970s, those who responded that they were "not very happy" ranged from a low of 33.0% to a high of 52.8%, with a weighted average of 41.1% covering 7,445 individuals. Among the 6,342 individuals interviewed by these semiannual survey interviews in the 1980s, the range of "not-too-happy" respondents extended from 26.9% to 34.2%, with a weighted average of only 29.8%.

Another question that was posed in vitually all the Euro-Barometer surveys dealt with "overall life satisfaction." In the 1970s, 56.1% to 63.4% of the 9,600

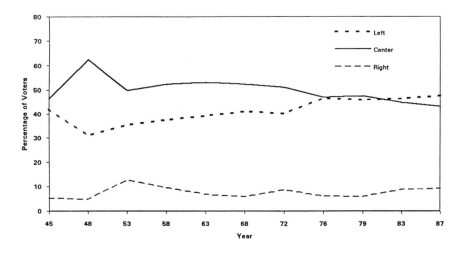

Note: Adapted from Changes in Italian electoral behavior: The relationships between parties and voters, by A. Parisi, & G. Pasquino (October 1979). *West European Politics, 2(3)*, pp. 6-30; ISTAT (Istituto Nazionale di Statistica, formerly Istituto Centrale di Statistics), *Annuario di Statistica*[Italian national statistics yearbook]; and *Compendio di Statistica* [Italian statistical abstracts] (various issues).

Figure 6. Distribution of Italian Voters on the
Political Spectrum (in percentages), 1945-1987

Italians who gave valid responses (with a weighted average of 60.0%) were moderately to completely satisfied with their lives overall. In the 1980s, the weighted average for the 15,242 Italians who gave valid responses had risen to 67.1%, with a low of 61.1% and a high of 71.3%. In Figure 7, the entire series of those who responded that they were either "satisfied" or "very satisfied" with their lives is reproduced, including data for one survey in 1988 (again using simple arithmetic averages for the years in which two surveys contained the question). It seems to indicate an unmistakeable upward trend. As Italians were getting richer, they were not only getting "happier" but also more "satisfied" overall with their lives!

Of more direct concern in terms of value orientations, however, are the responses given to Inglehart's (1977; 1990) "postmaterialism" index. This index, which is a composite of several questionnaire items ranging from economic concerns to issues related to the environment, classifies respondents on a composite scale from "materialist" to "postmaterialist" value orientations. This composite variable has been calculated and reported as a separate variable on all Euro-Barometer surveys since 1976. From 1976 through 1988, Italians with a materialist orientation ranged from 41.3% to 57.3% of the population, with an unweighted average of 45.2%. Those with a clearly postmaterialist value

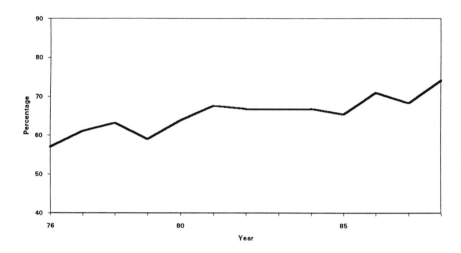

Note: Adapted from *Euro Barometer Survey* (various issues).

Figure 7.   Percentage of Respondents "Satisfied"
"Very Satisfied" with Their Lifes, Italy, 1976-1988

set ranged from 8.8% to 12.3% with an unweighted average of 9.3%. However, a time plot of the various orientations reveals that, as of survey number 21 of April 1984, those of mixed orientations have consistently outnumbered those with materialist values. Over the period in question, those with neither clearly materialist nor postmaterialist values ranged from a low of 38.2% to a high of 57.9%, with an unweighted average of 46.6% of the Italian population that gave valid responses to the Inglehart battery of questions. Figure 8 presents a time-series for 24 Eurobarometer surveys (from 1976 to 1988) on which Inglehart's postmaterialism index was reproduced. While there is no evident trend in Italy toward values that could be unambiguously labeled as postmaterialist, by the mid-1980s a cross-over occurred in which individuals with a "mixed" orientation came to outnumber those who were clearly "materialists." It should be remembered, however, that I have been dealing in the present context only with descriptive percentages and that I have not tried to explain these attitudes.

CONCLUSIONS

As noted above, Biorcio and Natale (1989) analyzed electoral mobility in Italy during the 1980s, and their findings indicated considerable shifts in certain regions and among certain types of voters. These researchers argued that the

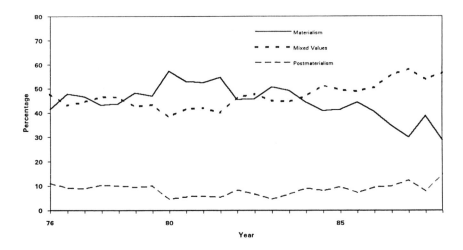

Note: Adapted from *Euro Barometer Survey* [*various issues*].

Figure 8. Distribution of "Postmaterialist"
Values, Italy, 1976-1988 (semiannual surveys)

shifts they had observed in the Italian voting public could be taken as a sign of distrust in the political system and/or as a realignment based on new exigencies and "solidarities." It is interesting to consider their findings and interpretations together with those presented by Golden (1990) and the data included in this chapter. Golden (1990) found no systematic changes in the attitudes that industrial workers have toward trade-union politics, and the information presented above from the Eurobarometer surveys indicates decreasing levels of dissatisfaction with the way democracy works in Italy. At the same time, voters appear to have become more detached from their traditional party preferences. And Italians appear to have been getting happier and more satisfied with their lives as their economic fortunes improve.

But these observations are based on aggregate trends. In the future, research should be directed to analyzing the values and attitudes of the Italian population regarding specific government interventions in the economy (in addition to the general role of the state as indicated above in connection with the 1987 ISSP survey), as well as specific questions on the feelings of Italians about their own and their nation's economic well-being (including reactions to high inflation, a depreciated lire, and continuing difficulties with integrating women, the young, and those from the south into the labor market.

REFERENCES

Accornero, A., & Carmigliano, F. (1986). *I paradossi della disoccupazione* [The paradoxes of unemployment]. Bologna: Il Mulino.

Adams Malerba, P. (1983, June). *Institutional performance and industrial policy in Italy*. Paper presented at the international conference on The Performance of Italy's Institutions, Bellagio (Como), Italy.

Biorcio, R., & Natale, P. (1989, December). La mobilita elettorale degli anni ottanta [Electoral shifts in the 1980s]. *Rivista Italiana di Scienza Politica, 19*, 385-430.

Blim, M. L. (1990, March). Economic development and decline in the emerging global factory: Some Italian lessons. *Politics and Society, 18*, 143-163.

Britton, A., Eastwood, F., & Major, R. (1986, November). Macroeconomic policy in Italy and Britain. *National Institute Economic Review*, pp. 38-52.

Brunetta, R. (1988). *Report '88: Labour and employment policies in Italy*. Rome: Ministero del Lavoro e della Previdenza Sociale and Fondazione Giacomo Brodolini and Centro Europa Ricerche.

Bruno, S. (1979). The industrial reserve army, segmentation and the Italian labour market. *Cambridge Journal of Economics, 3*, 131-151.

Chiarello, F. (1988, April-June). Politiche del lavoro e mezzogiorno [Labor-market policies and the south of Italy]. *Poleis, 1*, 33-41.

Cipolletta, I., Heimler, A., & Calcagnini, G. (1987, September-December). Restructuring and adjustment in Italian industry. *Review of Economic Conditions in Italy*, pp. 341-381.

D'Antonio, M., Colaizzo, R., & Leonello, G. (1988). Mezzogiorno/Centre-North: A two-region model of the Italian economy. *Journal of Policy Modelling, 10*, 437-451.

Deaglio, M. (1987, January-April). Submergence in the Italian economy 1970-85. *Review of Economic Conditions in Italy*, pp. 49-77.

De Caprariis, G. (1988, May-August). Structural changes in employment in Italy. *Review of Economic Conditions in Italy*, pp. 179-203.

Dore, R. (1988, April). Le rigidita' nel mercato del lavoro [Labor-market rigidities]. *Stato e Mercato, 22*, 37-62.

Faustini, G. (1988, May-August). Labour supply in Italy. *Review of Economic Conditions in Italy*, pp. 153-178.

Giavazzi, F., & Spaventa, L. (1990). Italy: The real effects of inflation and disinflation. *Economic Policy, 8*, 133-172.

_____. (1988). *Italy: An unconventional story*. Unpublished manuscript.

Golden, M. (1990). Political attitudes of Italian workers: Twenty years of survey evidence. *European Journal of Political Research, 19*, 305-323.

Hughes Hallett, A. J., & Petit, M. L. (1988). Trade-off reversals in macroeconomic policy. *Journal of Economic Dynamics and Control, 12*, 85-91.

Inglehart, R. (1990). *Culture shift in advanced industrial society*. Princeton, NJ: Princeton University Press.

_____. (1977). *The silent revolution: Changing values and political shifts among Western publics*. Princeton, NJ: Princeton University Press.

Masi, A. C. (1990). The Bagnoli steel complex: Too little too late or too much too soon? In R. Nanetti & R. Catanzaro (Eds.), *Italian politics: A review*, (vol. 4, pp. 71-101). London: Pinter.

_____. (1989). Deindustrialization, economic performance, and industrial policy: British and American theories applied to Italy. In R. F. Foglesong & J. D. Wolfe (Eds.), *The politics of economic adjustment* (pp. 127-152). Westport, CT: Greenwood Press.

_____. (1987). Moonlighting under the Italian sun: A series on multiple-job holding. *Contemporary Sociology, 16*, 485-491.

Moy, J. (1988, April). An analysis of unemployment and other labor market indicators in 10 countries. *Monthly Labor Review*, pp. 39-50.

Murat, M. (1989, April). *Macroeconomic policies for full employment: The Italian case.* Paper presented at the conference on Export Led Growth, Uneven Development and State Policy: The Cases of Canada and Italy. Pisa, Italy.

Neri, F. (1988, May-August). Immigration and the Italian labour market: A contradiction? *Review of Economic Conditions in Italy*, pp. 141-152.

OECD (Organization for Economic Cooperation and Development). (1989). *Economies in transition: Structural adjustment in OECD countries.* Paris: OECD.

————. (1986, December). *Economic Outlook, No. 40* ("Italy"). Paris: OECD.

OECD Economic Outlook. (Various biannual issues). Paris: OECD.

OECD Economic Surveys, Italy. (Various issues). Paris: OECD.

Paci, A. (1989). I problemi sociali, le relazioni industriali e le politiche occupazionali [Social problems, industrial relations, and employment policies]. *Industria e Sindacato*, No. 7, pp. 3-7.

Padoa Schioppa, F. (1990). Classical, Keynesian and mismatch unemployment in Italy. *European Economic Review, 34,* 434-442.

Parisi, A., & Pasquino, G. (1979). Changes in Italian electoral behaviour: The relationships between parties and voters. *West European Politics, 2* (3), 6-30.

Ranci, P. (1990). Does Italy have an economic policy? *Italian Journal: A Bi-Monthly Digest of Italian Affairs, 4,* 11-14.

————. (1978). La legge sulla riconversione come strumento di politica industriale [The law on restructuring as an instrument of industrial policy]. *Economia e Politica Industriale*, No. 20, pp. 21-39.

Redivo, G. (1983). Sistemi produttivi sommersi e mercati del lavoro: Una analisi della letteratura [Hidden productive systems and the labor market: An analysis of the literature]. *Economia e Lavoro, 17* (3), pp. 31-52.

Rosti, L. (1989, April). Self-employment: Stock and flow dynamics in Italy. Paper presented at the conference on Export Led Growth, Uneven Development and State Policy: The Cases of Canada and Italy. Pisa, Italy.

Schweke, W., & Jones, D. R. (1986, October). European job creation in the wake of plant closing and layoffs. *Monthly Labor Review*, pp. 18-22.

Torelli, N., & Trivellato, U. (1989). Youth unemployment and duration from the Italian labour force survey. *European Economic Review, 33,* 407-415.

————. (1988). Modelling job-search duration from the Italian labor force data. Labour: A Review of *Labour Economics and Industrial Relations, 2,* 117-134.

Uleri, P.V. (1989). The 1987 referenda. In R. Leonardi & P. Corbetta (Eds.), *Italian Politics: A Review* (vol. 3, pp. 155-177). London: Pinter.

Viesti, G. (1990). Italian exports: The challenge from the South. *Italian Journal: A Bi-Monthly Digest of Italian Affairs, 5,* 49-54.

Zandamela, R. L. (1989). Wage indexation, openness and inflation uncertainty. The case of Italy. *Applied Economics, 21,* 651-657.

Zanetti, G. (1987, September-December). Structure and financial requirements in the Italian business sector. *Review of Economic Conditions in Italy*, pp. 417-453.

WEST GERMANY:
CHANGING VALUES, RIGID LABOR MARKETS

Florian Schramm

THE FAILURE OF POLICY ON WORKING HOURS

In the following section, two lines of analysis are developed. The first one is based on a comparative view of the development in the FRG over the previous 30 years. There have been two distinct periods. The first period, extending from the early 1950s to the early 1970s, was marked by a low and decreasing rate of unemployment. The second, starting with the oil crisis in 1973, was characterized by a high and increasing rate of unemployment. The transition from the first period to the second is often explained solely in terms of altered economic and demographic factors such as the decrease in economic growth and the increase in the numbers of baby boomers completing school and entering the labor market. Instead, it should be interpreted as a consequence of the diminished capacity of institutions to solve problems. Adjusting to the decreasing supply of labor by reducing the number of working hours and redistributing the volume of working time worked reasonably well before 1970, then ceased to be an effective approach.

The second line of analysis, an international comparison of development in Europe over the past three decades, shows Germany to be an extreme case of what has happened in the European Community (EC) as a whole. The labor pool has shrunk drastically, and the already high rate of productivity is rising. Many jobs with low productivity, which are poorly paid in the United States and are state-run or subsidized in Sweden, have been shed. Therefore West

Germany is extremely vulnerable to unemployment. Faced with a decreasing amount of work, the country must keep reducing working hours massively. If there is a delay, leading to underemployment, labor must be redeployed. Neither alternative was adequately pursued in the 1970s. Unemployment is only one of many characteristics that describe the situation on the market, especially the available or unavailable options for those who are or could be employed. In any case it is necessary to consider both sides of the labor market: employment or the employers' demand for labor on the one hand, and available labor offered by the work force, including "hidden unemployment," on the other hand. The structures described above will be examined in an international context for their development over time.

International comparison allows one to see the range of possible political options. The intertemporal comparison illuminates the structural and institutional dynamics dominating in a country, thereby making it possible to begin formulating realistic political options. Past conditions on the labor market and previous means of regulation are still part of a collective memory. They serve both society and the relevant players as criteria by which to judge present actions. If, for example, the economic statistics show only a weak relation between economic growth and the size of the work force but a distinct relation between a reduction of working hours and unemployment, then the general and institutional acceptance of labor redeployment and a shorter working week would be of great interest.

A Review

Figure 1 shows the well-documented fever curve of unemployment in the FRG. Increasing to the intermediate plateau of the first million in 1973-74, the rate doubled to two million in 1981-1983 and has remained high ever since. Unemployment can be understood as a balance between the supply and demand of labor. The rise in unemployment is generally explained by both supply analysis and demand analysis. The demand-side argument is based on the decrease that the oil embargo has caused in growth. The supply-side argument points to the entry of large numbers of potential workers (baby boomers). Neither of these two explanations is sufficient.

In the FRG economic growth is clearly no protection against a reduction in the total volume of labor. On the supply side, the number of potentially employed persons rose by 11% between 1960 and 1987. The number of people who want to work has increased, but most of them are looking for part-time employment. Another reason why the picture of an increasing labor supply is misleading is that the German labor force reduced its per capita supply of hours worked from 2,150 in 1960 to about 1,900 in 1972, and to fewer than 1,700 hours in 1987 (see Zahlenfibel, 1988, p. 30). Remarkably, and contrary to general perception, the rate at which additional part-time jobs are being

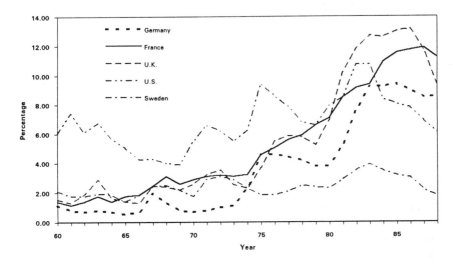

Note: From *Labor force statistics-Statistiques de la population active* (1972-1988), OECD (Ed.). Paris: OECD, pp. 30-32; and *Labour force statistics-Statistiques de la population active* (1960-1971), OECD (Ed.). Paris: OECD, p. 18, pp. 24-26. National differences in the definition of unemployment are reduced on the basis of the OECD definition.

Figure 1.   Unemployment in Five Industrialized Nations, 1960-1988

created has slowed since 1973. The average number of hours worked by all employed persons, including part-timers, has decreased by 12% since 1972, a 1.27% reduction of working hours between 1972 and 1982, the year the center-left government led by the Social Democrats (SPD) was replaced by a center-right government led by the Christian Democratic Union (CDU).

The average reduction of working hours by 0.83% between 1960 and 1972 was also distinctly higher than it was in the 1980s, when working hours were reduced by only 0.5%. In contrast to the 1950s and 1960s, then, the instruments for diminishing the volume of working time, which was regulated in wage contracts, and for creating part-time jobs were not applied strictly enough in the 1980s. It is therefore reasonable to see the slower reduction of working hours in the 1980s as the main reason for the deterioration of the situation on the labor market in West Germany (see Wahl, 1985).

Germany: A Special Case?

In the 1970s and 1980s, all relatively large western industrialized nations registered a rise in unemployment. Internationally, the FRG ranked in the middle, but the surge in West German unemployment in the early 1970s is distinct. In a short time, the star pupil had become the problem child.

Furthermore, the FRG is—with the exception of the last few years—the one big industrial nation in which the number of employed persons has stagnated significantly over the last 30 years. In the United States, the number of employed in relation to the total population rose from 38% in 1960 to 47% in 1988; in Sweden, by 5%, from 47% in 1960 to 52% in 1988. In the FRG, the number dropped by 3%, from 47% in 1960 to 44% in 1988 (see Strümpel & Schramm, 1989, p. 13).

According to available data, the average number of hours worked each year is lower in the FRG than in comparable countries except Sweden. Despite a slowdown, the reduction is still relatively high in comparison to other countries. Given the decreasing and relatively low share of the employed in relation to the total population, this means that the volume of labor in the FRG has fallen. Thus, it is justified to talk about the FRG as special case requiring explanation and, looking to the future, interpretation.

Next, it is worth noting that the decrease in the amount of labor was not accompanied by declining economic growth. Productivity in other western European countries, especially in the FRG, was also high and steadily rising. In other words, rising productivity in the United States and western Europe, especially in Germany, contributed much more to rising economic growth rates than was the case in other industrialized countries (see Figures 2, 3, and 4).

The logical conclusion is that economic growth in the FRG was accompanied, more than was the case in other countries, by a decrease in the number of hours worked. In view of international interdependencies, the differences are perhaps surprising. Dissimilarities in the development of productivity, the amount of labor, and those seeking employment are obscured by similar rates of growth and unemployment, and to explain those dissimilarities it is necessary to take into account the differences in institutions and means of regulation (Therborn, 1985). What, for example, happens to those jobs that are endangered by technical progress, that is, jobs at which productivity cannot be increased by information technologies? This category includes jobs dealing directly with people or things: repair and maintenance, handicrafts, or care of people. Characteristic international differences in this respect are described by Scharpf (1988, p. 107, translated version):

> In the Western world we can observe three different kinds of solutions: Firstly, incomes are determined by job productivity. Thus there are highly productive jobs going along with high income and less productive jobs going along with less income. That is in principle—simplified—the American way.
> Secondly: We insist on the principle that in any job similar income can be earned. At the same time we don't want to do without the less productive public services, so we have to finance them. That is the Swedish way. In Sweden, 30%-35% of employed are engaged in the public services.

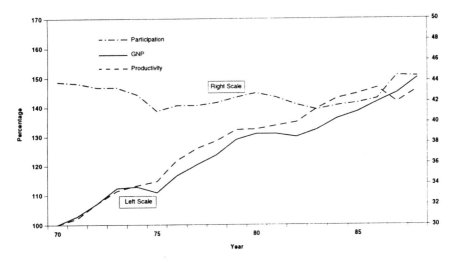

Note: From *Labor force statistics-Statistiques de la population active* (1990), OECD (Ed.). Paris: OECD, pp. 26-27; and *National accounts-Comptes nationaux* (*Main aggregates-Principaux agrégates*) (1990), OECD (Ed.). GNP and productivity are measured in each country's currency in real prices of 1980, with 1970 as the base year. Productivity is computed by dividing GNP by the number of employed.

Figure 2.   Growth, Productivity, and Labor-Market
Participation in the Federal Republic of Germany, 1970-1988.

The third way is that of the FRG: We demand that all jobs offer a similar and reasonable income. If productivity is not sufficient to justify these incomes, the jobs just disappear. In this sense unemployment is high in Germany, much higher than in Sweden or the USA. The services which are not offered by those in low-income employment anymore have to be done in a do-it-yourself procedure.

How is the FRG adapting to the imbalance between the supply of and demand for labor? Has the country started to institutionalize mechanisms of distribution and redistribution that are in keeping with the interests of the potentially employed and their idea of what jobs are acceptable? This was done in the second half of the 1950s when, despite a shrinking labor supply, a determined reduction in working hours made it possible to integrate millions of jobless persons and refugees. Or are the consequences of a surplus supply of labor pushed onto a minority of jobless persons and other employment seekers? What level of inequality is a society prepared to tolerate? In other words, how readily or reluctantly does society correct unequally distributed employment opportunities?

The status-quo scenario looks grim. The trend towards reduction in working hours is robust and has a low elasticity in relation to growth. It can hardly

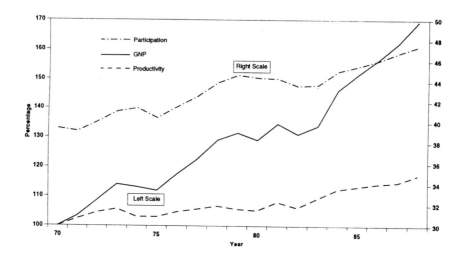

Note: From *Labor force statistics-Statistiques de la population active* (1990), OECD (Ed.). Paris: OECD, pp. 26-27; and *National accounts-Comptes nationaux* (*Main aggregates-Principaux agrégates*) (1990), OECD (Ed.). GNP and productivity are measured in each country's currency in real prices of 1980, with 1970 as the base year. Productivity is computed by dividing GNP by the number of employed.

Figure 3.   Growth, Productivity, and Labor-Market
Participation in the United States, 1970-1988.

be influenced by Keynesian or other macroeconomic strategies aiming at growth promotion even if growth could be achieved. On the supply side, the crush on the labor market continues unabated. The fall in the birth rate has been made up for by women's increased rate of participation in employment, a rise in retirement age, and a growing migration surplus. If the reduction in working hours is not accelerated, then the number of unemployed will remain in the millions into the next millennium (Kühl, 1988).

As shown in the following sections, however, the FRG has the chance to change the status quo and achieve a more appropriate distribution of working time volume, because many job holders have shown a preference for shorter working hours. The combination of large minorities of underemployed (unemployed or those willing to work) and overemployed full-timers leads to a decline in welfare and work options and opens the road to compromise. That compromise can be arrived at, however, only if working hours are made flexible to accommodate a variety of life styles and a modern perspective of gender roles. This means that employment institutions—labor and management (as wage-negotiation partners), regional administrative bodies, and the government (in its regulatory function)—will have to show great flexibility as well.

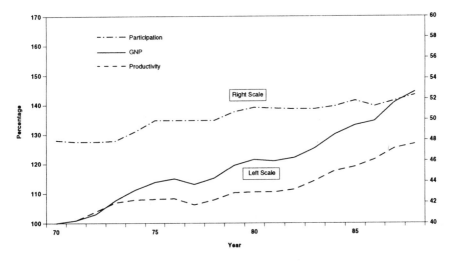

Note: From *Labor force statistics-Statistiques de la population active* (1990), OECD (Ed.). Paris: OECD, pp. 26-27; and *National accounts-Comptes nationaux* (*Main aggregates-Principaux agrégates*) (1990), OECD (Ed.). GNP and productivity are measured in each country's currency in real prices of 1980, with 1970 as the base year. Productivity is computed by dividing GNP by the number of employed.

Figure 4.   Growth, Productivity, and Labor-
Market Participation in Sweden, 1970-1988.

Values, Expectations, Life Styles

Work serves a variety of social functions and aims, creating goods and services and offering the employed a sense of identity and livelihood. As regards the creation of goods and services, work is successful in the West German national economy. As has been shown in the preceding sections, German labor productivity and productivity growth compare favorably in the international context.

But the indications are that work no longer provides the identity and livelihood it once did. The unemployment rate is chronically high, and a high percentage of the unemployed perceive a discrepancy between their wishes and expectations and the reality of their working arrangements (a discrepancy also partly due to changes in the labor market). The young generation of well-educated young women (and men) in particular want to create a balance between familial, personal, and occupational needs. This desire clashes with the working world's demand for total involvement. Obviously, women are the ones mostly affected by the conflict between family and occupation. The manifest crisis in the family and in women's career biographies—low net reproduction rate and forced interruption in women's careers despite women's success in education—is making itself increasingly felt. It is now being publicly debated, and its political significance is growing steadily.

Pluralization of Life Styles

In dealing with the question of underemployment's wider consequences for a variety of people, it would be superficial to look only at the labor market and social statistics. If one wants to know the extent to which the employment pattern offers or denies people welfare, it is necessary to ask to what extent their life styles have changed and how far their needs have been satisfied. Besides the change in the employment situation, one must consider the cultural change in life styles and demands in affluent society. Such changes have been discussed as individualization, differentiation, and pluralization (Zapf et al., 1987). There are a variety of possible family and household models to choose from. The traditional model, in which the head of the family is the only breadwinner, now accounts for only a minority of people on the labor market. Double income earners and singles who are not bound by financial, geographical, or fixed working-time constraints are in the majority. Social relations have become less consistent. A large number of marriages and relationships end in divorce or separation. The life-long security of the unemployed partner is no longer the rule. More and more people find themselves in living arrangements where clear rules of conduct no longer exist. Life styles are thus becoming a matter of conscious decision.

The extension of the system of social welfare and education has considerably widened the behavioral scope of the two population segments that have benefited most—the elderly and the young. The elderly now have the means to live their lives according to their own ideas—an apartment of their own, travel, and entertainment. Young people who remain longer than some of their peers in the educational system may become more economically dependent than they otherwise would be, but the socialization entailed in this educational system has had an emancipating effect. Life styles and goals are being dissociated from individual social backgrounds.

One particular issue that had prompted change in the social roles of women has been addressed. Women were the main beneficiaries of the expansion of the West German educational system in the 1970s. Women attend institutions of higher learning almost as often as men, and are at least as successful there. Women want to use their abilities and skills on the labor market. Many women refuse to be geared only to household and children. They aim to be employed and limit their work within the family, though that area is still considered mainly "their business." They postpone starting a family and put off or avoid pregnancy. Some aspects of this change can be demoscopically investigated as changes in values and expectations. They are extremely pertinent in relation to the working world (see Inglehart, 1989).

Educational principles and the philosophy of life have changed, for example. Values such as human interaction, self-determination, and pleasure have become more important, and conformity, subordination, and achievement have become less significant. Workers' expectations of employment have changed accordingly (Klipstein & Strümpel, 1985, p. 24), in that the significance of values such as interpersonal communication has increased. Creative and interesting occupations and reduced working hours are sought more and more, and high income seems to have become less important.

Professional Work Ethics: From Sacrificing All to Creating the Right Balance

An increasing number of men and women insist on a balance between occupation and private life. The primacy of work, which used to be associated with a high tolerance for stress or a readiness to make sacrifices, is being seriously questioned. Young people in particular emphasize their desire for an autonomous private life unaffected by occupational demands. Germans distance themselves more clearly from work's traditional demands than people of other nations do (Pawlowsky & Strümpel, 1986; Reuband, 1985). But it is not a question of refusing work. "To do one's work properly and conscientiously" is still a central educational aim in Germany (Pawlowsky, 1986, pp. 235-236). In interviews with 170 young people between 19 and 25 years of age, Baethge, Hantsche, Pelull, and Voskamp (1988) identified four distinct concepts of life: "work-oriented," "work and private life in balance," "family-oriented with subordinate, yet high significance of work," and "leisure-oriented with low significance of work." Only the last category, which is applicable to only 1/8 of the young people in West Germany, reflects an alienation from work.

Roughly summarized, demoscopic findings show that jobs have not been adequately adapted to changing demands. As perceived by the employed, working conditions may not have worsened since the 1960s. But apart from easing physical labor, reducing dust particles, and mitigating air and noise pollution, developments have not actually improved working conditions. By contrast, reduced working hours, rising income, and a higher educational level have opened many new possibilities in people's private lives. Work seems to compare poorly with leisure because work offers fewer opportunities to shape one's own life. Cultural change, prosperity, and greater scope in leisure and private life bring new and wider expectations into the work domain. The working world has not accommodated these expectations enough. There is a three-way demand for balance and equilibrium: balance between occupation and private life, equal rights for women at work, and, on the other side of the coin, men's full participation in work within the household and the family. It would be surprising indeed if the massive changes that have taken place in peoples lives—welfare, the social safety net, the broadening of educational opportunity, increased leisure, and smaller families—did not fundamentally alter people's attitude toward work.

PERCEPTION AND IMPACT OF THE SITUATION ON THE LABOR MARKET

The impact of unemployment is not limited to the segment of the unemployed, though this group is the one uppermost in the mind of the public and in discussions among experts. Unemployment also affects those who do have a job, but whose position on the market and toward the employer has weakened. Is the hypothesis correct that unemployment divides and polarizes, or does it unite the many whom it affects? I first examine the broad circle of those affected by unemployment, and then emphasize a few important issues concerning the people more directly affected by it (see Schramm, 1992, for a full treatment of this subject).

Loss of Options

Underemployment has a direct and plausible effect on people's labor-market options. This connection was subjectively reflected in people's assessment of how likely it would be to find a comparable job if the present one were to be lost (see Strümpel & Schramm, 1989, p. 29). The perceived worsening of one's chances on the labor market between 1980 and 1984 corresponded to an objective deterioration of the situation. More remarkable, however, is that conditions on the labor market were perceived to have improved greatly between 1984 and 1988 despite official unemployment statistics that showed no such change. The majority of the working population seemed to express a certain "all-clear signal."

Underemployment allows employers to ignore the described change in people's life situations and aspirations, which means that they adhere to old-fashioned norms, rules of behavior, and role patterns. At least three different mechanisms are involved in this process. The first is the distribution of scarce resources through recruitment and promotions, namely, the preference shown for those "right" employees who have not yet been affected by the previously mentioned cultural changes, or who are hiding or limiting their aspirations. The second mechanism is "overemployment" through regulations that perpetuate inflexible working-time arrangements, mostly overtime in addition to full-time work, thereby increasing unemployment again. The third mechanism through which changes in people's life situations and aspirations are ignored is the discipline expected of and practiced by the employed, who, confronted by the situation on the labor market, compete against each other. Organizational climate, communication, cooperation, co-determination, and self-determination are all undermined in this way. The three areas of impact dealt with in the following section can be seen as originating from one base. The loss of options on the labor market leads to a vicious circle in the world of work: The loss of control and security both sets up and results from the changed position on the labor market and toward the employer.

Recruitment

The employer prefers employees who place work above everything else. When underemployment is prevalent, the employer can recruit from a great number of applicants, a process in which the "selection of values and life styles" (Windolf & Hohn, 1984, p. 134) plays an important part. An uninterrupted work biography, the applicant's life style, and a readiness to subordinate private goals and family life to business interests have become important selection criteria (Windolf & Hohn, 1984, p. 115). The chances of being hired are particularly poor among the "alternatively" committed. Rosenstiel, Nerdinger, Spiess, and Stengel (1989) showed that about a quarter of them were still without employment a year after having finished their studies, whereas only 15% of the career-minded jobs seekers and 20% of the leisure-oriented applicants were still unemployed by that point.

Options for Time Use

The German labor market is ruled by standard employment contracts, which prescribe full-time jobs. Most working women and practically all working men must submit to these arrangements. Holidays are regulated in the wage agreement. Training sabbaticals have not been properly established yet, and the formerly celebrated flexible retirement age has proved to be a noble, but ineffective, experiment. The special regulations that govern older part-timers obviously complicate personnel planning and the representation of employee interests (Deters, Staehle, & Stirn, 1989).

Hopes for occupational success can be entertained only by those who work at least 40 hours a week, and who are able to document uninterrupted employment since leaving the educational system. Those who deviate from this norm must bear the consequences. Part-time work, almost all of which is reserved for women, offers little chance for advancement and is poorly paid. Taking a break from employment is risky, and returning to a job once left is often difficult or even impossible. The other option, a full-time job, is no solution for women with family responsibilities. Their dilemma shows that every third female full-timer would prefer a part-time job, but cannot manage to get one without sacrificing occupational fulfillment.

More and more younger men are confronted with similar conflicts. They are slowly becoming aware that women are at a disadvantage at work but that

Table 1. Actual and Desired Working Time in Hours per Week

	Cases (weighted)	Working Time		Difference
		Actual[a]	Desired[b]	
Dependently employed	814	38.5	33.8	-4.7
Men	522	42.7	37.3	-5.4
Women	292	30.8	27.5	-3.3
Full-time	128	41.1	33.0	-8.1
Part-time	156	22.3	23.4	+1.1
Part-time (1-19 hours)	37	(12.9)	(18.7)	(+5.8)
Part-time (20-36 hours)	120	25.2	24.4	-0.8
Compared to nonemployed women	275	0.0	21.7	+21.7

Notes: [a] Question 1: "If you imagine a normal working week, how many hours do you work in a week?"
   [b] Question 2: "If you think about a normal working week and take necessary earnings into account, and if you and your spouse could choose your working time, how many hours of working time would you like to work?"
   $N = 1,089$ employed women and nonemployed women (who would like to work), 32 to 55 years of age.

Source: *Eingeschränkte Erwerbsarbeit bei Frauen und Männern* [Restricted paid employment among women and men] by H. Bielenski & B. Strümpel, 1988, Berlin: Edition Sigma, p. 50. Reprinted by permission.

they themselves are at a disadvantage in the family. Nevertheless, 10% of employed men, not least the fathers of infants, positively acknowledge the wish for part-time work (i.e., around 30 hours a week). For most of them, that alternative remains wishful thinking (Strümpel, Prenzel, Scholz, & Hoff, 1988).

If the unfulfilled occupational wishes of the officially unemployed and the "hidden unemployed" (housewives not registered as unemployed) are related to the unwanted hours that are worked, two things become evident. First, the amount of overemployment is equal to the amount of underemployment. In other words, underemployment could make up for unemployment and "hidden unemployment." A desire of the employed to work less is an opportunity for those who have no job to find one. Second, men are, on balance, overemployed; women are underemployed despite the great share of overemployed female full-timers (see Table 1).

The amount of available work volume is great. If the employed, as they had desired, had worked an average of five hours less in 1985 (without additional costs for the employer), 126 million working hours would have been available to the unemployed. Even with productivity gains figured in, that is a considerable reservoir in relation to the 77 million working hours demanded by the registered unemployed, taking the desired 34 hours a week as basis for calculation. In the context of this chapter, the coexistence of underemployment and overemployment implies an extensive loss of options. The unfavorable situation on the labor market is one reason for the difficulties that overemployed persons have in reducing hours. Reducing working hours is possible only by neglecting important occupational goals. Thus, the limitation on labor-market options for the overemployed also concerns the underemployed, but in different ways and with different consequences. This artificially maintained imbalance indicates the need for *work redistribution*. In the following sections, I examine the institutional resources and difficulties in effecting such redistribution.

Discipline

Productive interaction between employee and employer becomes more probable when both sides have a common interest in entering into and maintaining the employment contract. According to traditional Marxist analysis, the employee clearly has a structurally weak position not only in periods of underemployment but at other times as well. From the employer's point of view, the employee's services can be replaced with those of another recruited from the "industrial reserve army." Hence, the financially hard-pressed individual employee with little mobility and a limited view of the market is exposed to ever greater competitive pressures. It is difficult to sustain solidarity in hard times when people see their livelihoods endangered, and when the still relatively strong groups of the employed are expected to make sacrifices to help the weaker ones. It is therefore highly appropriate to investigate the suspected weakening of solidarity that accompanied the precarious conditions on the labor market in the 1980s.

"Solidarity" is not only a means by which interests are articulated by labor and management at the political level, it is also a component of the labor climate. It strengthens the employee's self-confidence and self-assertiveness vertically, in relation to superiors, by enabling employees to make use of rights and behavioral options, as has been shown, for example, in the frequency of sick leaves. Horizontally, however—in terms of solidarity among colleagues—are employee relations characterized by trust and cooperation, or are they merely competitive? Social arrangements facilitating early retirement due to illness and disablement and allowing for payment during periods of illness have eased the employees anxieties. They enable people to retreat temporarily or permanently from work in a socially cushioned and accepted way. On the other hand, it has always been suspected that underemployment has a disciplining effect, that it reduces the option of sick leave (see Wacker, 1983). Figure 5, a time series from 1970 to 1987, corroborates that supposition.

Sick leave (the number of hours of absence from work due to illness) and the unemployment rate were parallel. Though less than 10% of the employed (excluding civil servants) felt directly threatened by unemployment (i.e., they expected unemployment in the next 12 months), it becomes evident that many employees experienced an atmosphere of job insecurity at their place of work. For 15% of employees, the statement "Where I work, colleagues worry about their jobs" was "entirely true." For 40% it was "partly true"; for 48%, "entirely

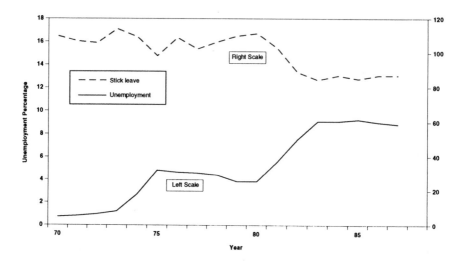

Note: From *Ergebnisse der Arbeits- und Berufsforschungsmärkte in Tabellen* [Tabulated results of labor-
          market and occupational research]. Zahlenfieel (1988). Nuremberg: Eigenverlag, pp. 62-63; and Zur
          Arbeitssituation der Ausländer in der Bundesrepublik Deutschland [On the labor-market situation of
          foreigners in the Federal Republic of Germany], by H.-U. Bach, C. Brinckmann, & H. Kohler (1987).
          Mitteilungen aus der Arbeitsmarkt- und Berufsforschung, 3, pp. 277-287.

Figure 5.   Unemployment and Illness Rate, 1970-1987.

untrue." All in all, 63% of the respondents presumed—more or less—that
absenteeism was on the decline because of fear of job loss (see Table 2).

The perceived weakening of the employee's positions resulted not only in
less sick leave but also in a change of labor climate. Employment insecurity
also had an effect on relations between colleagues and superiors. More than
30% of those who experienced an atmosphere of employment insecurity at their
place of work thought that competition among colleagues had increased in
the last few years. This was the case for only 8% of those working in companies
where a threat to jobs was not perceived to exist.

The change in labor climate from cooperation to competition has meant
a clear deterioration in the quality of work places in the FRG. The aspects
of job security and labor climate are especially important. Because of the trend
on the labor market in the 1980s, job security has become the most important
factor provided by places of work (Pawlowsky, 1986, p. 138).

It is doubtful that competition at least promotes business, for solidarity
among colleagues—a precondition for high efficiency—is also impaired by job
insecurity. Of the people holding secure jobs, 44% counted on their colleagues'
collaboration. That was true for only 25% of those holding insecure jobs. This
finding was confirmed by the impact that job insecurity had on the relation

Table 2. Perceived Organizational Climate
in the Federal Republic of Germany, 1985[a]

Job Security	Competitive Behavior			
	Yes	*Partly*	*No*	*N (Percent)*[b]
Low	36%	40%	24%	136 (14)
Medium	12%	55%	34%	380 (40)
High	8%	34%	58%	428 (44)
N (Percent)	126 (13)	407 (43)	411 (44)	944 (100)
	Decrease in Sick Leave			
	Strong	*Weak*	*No*	*N (Percent)*
Low	58%	34%	8%	140 (15)
Medium	35%	43%	22%	374 (40)
High	9%	30%	61%	412 (45)
N (Percent)	373 (27)	555 (36)	63 (38)	926 (100)

Notes: [a] Statements rated: Job security: "Where I work, some of my colleagues worry about losing their jobs."
Competitive behavior: "Where I work, the competition between colleagues has risen in the last few years."
Sick leave: "Where I work, the employed workers take less sick leave than before."
[b] $N = 1{,}067$ employees. Percentages are rounded.

Source: Survey conducted by the Forschungsstelle Sozialökonomik der Arbeit of the Free University of Berlin in 1985.

between employees and superiors. Only 10% of those employed in a company where jobs were insecure, but 33% of those working in a company where job security was not an issue, thought that they could express their opinions in disagreements with superiors. The implications are evident especially for modern production. Because of the complex technology and extreme division of labor involved, modern production requires well-functioning personal relations among employees and between employees and superiors. Uncooperative behavior is thus a handicap.

The Small Range of "Impact"

Let us now look at underemployment's direct impact on the individual—the length and frequency of periods of unemployment and the personal experience connected with it. Some of this experience includes the unsatisfied employment aspirations of women not registered as unemployed and the psychological stress of worrying about one's job. Unlike the latent consequences of unemployment dealt with in the previous section, such frustration and stress are felt to be directly related to the unfavorable situation on the labor market. Relevant cases all concern minorities of employed or employable persons. Most of the population is unaffected. This fact is reflected, first, in the cumulation of unemployment among the same people, mainly long-term or repeatedly unemployed; second, in the limited occupational opportunities of workers; third, in the labor-market problems that concern mainly women.

The Cumulation of Unemployment

When interviewed, only 15% of the actually employed stated that they had been unemployed at least once during the last ten years (Strümpel & Schramm, 1989, p. 52). Hence, about 85% of them indicated that they had not experienced unemployment. If the potentially employed are taken into account, the percentage of those having been unemployed in the last 10 years rises to about 25%. If one also includes women not registered as unemployed but wanting to work, the percentage of those who were at least temporarily excluded from employment rises to 30%.

In terms of expectations for the future, it was again only 10% who worried greatly about their jobs; 6% thought they would lose their jobs during the next two years (see Strümpel & Schramm, 1989, p. 65). The most significant and most publicly relevant indicator of the segmentation caused by unemployment is the development of long-term unemployment. Since the beginning of the drastic increase in unemployment in the mid-1970s, the share of the working population of those becoming unemployed has varied between 12% and 20%. Since 1984, the rate of new unemployment has settled between 15% and 17%. Although the unemployment rate doubled between 1980 and 1983 and remained at that level, it was not accompanied by an increasing number of newly unemployed. Rather, the average duration of unemployment lengthened from 12 weeks in 1975 to 15 weeks in 1980. By 1987 it reached a total of about 30 weeks, or almost seven months (see Figure 6).

Accordingly, the significance of long-term unemployment increased. By the end of 1988, one in three unemployed persons had been without a job for at least one year; one in six had been unemployed without interruption for two or more years.

Workers in the Shadow of Structural Change

Although literature in industrial sociology describes a new type of skilled worker for the core area of manufacturing industry—a well-paid, possibly privileged employee in high demand (Kern & Schumann, 1984)—and although employers' complaints about the shortage of skilled workers are getting louder, statistical as well as demoscopic trends show that the ranks of the underemployed consist of a disproportionately high share of blue-collar

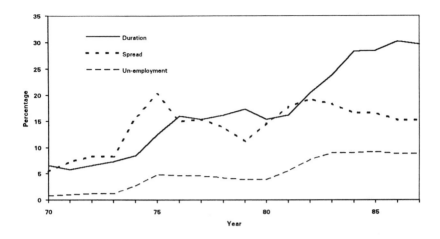

Note: From *Ergebnisse der Arbeits- und Berufsforschungsmärkte in Tabellen* [Tabulated results of labor-markets and occupation research]. Zahlenfiebel (1988). Nuremberg: Eigenverlag, pp. 62-63. The spread of unemployment is measured by the number of entries of unemployment divided by the number of dependently employed persons.

Figure 6.   Duration and Spread of Unemployment
in the Federal Republic of Germany, 1970-1987

workers. First, the blue-collar unemployment rate is not only higher than the white-collar rate, it has also risen more steeply (see Strümpel & Schramm, 1989, p. 68). Second, the percentage of employed blue-collar workers affected by unemployment in the last 10 years has continually risen since 1982, whereas the percentage of white-collar workers so affected has remained almost the same despite the drastically worsening situation on the labor market. The gap is clearly widening (see Strümpel & Schramm, 1989, p. 68) The same is true of the qualification level. The unemployment rate for persons without any qualification have risen in relative and absolute terms more sharply than the corresponding rates of all other qualification categories (Zahlenfiebel, 1988, p. 17).Third, among the employed, blue-collar workers run a greater risk of losing their job than people in other occupational groups. This objective risk also has subjective effects. Up to 8% of blue-collar workers thought it likely or even certain that they would lose their jobs in the next two years, whereas that was the case for only 4% of white-collar workers (Strümpel & Schramm, 1989, p. 54).

The extreme degree to which blue-collar workers are affected by unemployment is not only due to their lower level of qualification. It must also be explained by the conditions within the economic sector in which blue-collar workers are mainly active: manufacturing, that is, industry and crafts. As regards employment, these areas include declining industries, whereas service industries are expanding at an above-average rate. Thus, it is not surprising that the number of employed persons worrying about their jobs is twice as high in manufacturing as in the service industries. A comparison between private service industries and manufacturing industries results in smaller, but still distinct, differences.

WOMEN: THE NEGLECTED PRODUCTIVITY FORCE

For women, the unemployment rate in relation to all employed persons (among whom women are underrepresented) is only slightly higher than that for men. In addition, there is the group of "hidden unemployed" that consists mainly of women. Taking them into account, one finds that the majority of people looking in vain for a job are women. Of unemployed women between 32 and 55 years of age, 55% want to work (almost exclusively in part-time jobs). But these statistics still do not fully describe women's precarious situation on the labor market. Bielensky and Strümpel (1988, p. 52) showed that every second woman who works 20 hours a week wished to work between 20 and 36 hours a week. Schwarze and Wagner's (1989) analysis of the socioeconomic panel led to similar conclusions. According to Schwarze and Wagner (1989, p. 185), 13% of all employed women in the FRG work fewer than 20 hours a week. More detailed analyses (Büchtemann & Schupp, 1988) suggest that the number of women working fewer than 15 hours a week has considerably increased during the last 10 to 15 years. Unemployment's impact on women who are underemployed is especially severe because their family income is below average, and because their retirement is not well provided for (Schwarze & Wagner, 1989, p. 185). Thus, there is strong evidence that women in particular are severely affected by an unfavorable situation on the labor market.

This is especially true for academics. In the wake of educational expansion, women have almost caught up with men. The number of women earning advanced degrees is now about equal to that of men. Accordingly, the number of employed women with academic degrees rose by 107% between 1970 and 1985 (from 286,000 to 555,000) whereas the number of male academics rose by only 58% (from 729,000 to 1,125,000) (Siebert & Schmid, 1988). However, women's unemployment rose more drastically than men's, especially among new graduates. Among 25- to 30-years-olds, unemployment among male academics stood in 1988 at 8%, whereas unemployment among female academics amounted to 15%.

Behind the various ways that unemployment affects the population of the FRG, ideas of what the average employee should be like are changing. On the one hand, these ideals are being adapted to the socioeconomic change; on the other hand, they countervail it. In the traditional industrial system, the factory owner needed a kind of labor force that could be divided into shifts for the purpose of mass production. There was great demand for strong, economically motivated men and unmarried women, including those having little education or job training. The recruitment of foreign workers in the 1960s still followed that pattern. The current ideal of flexible and qualified employees reflects the change in Germany's economy and relations between labor and management. As has been shown, the corresponding system is geared towards technological development, relatively high wages and salaries, and work intensity. Those who are less qualified become victims of increases in productivity, especially in sections of the productive sector where employment is decreasing. Thus, the segmentation to the disadvantage of less or inappropriately skilled workers has resulted from the concept of postindustrial development.

The employers' insistence on standard working hours is harder to explain. Perhaps it is a fossil from the golden age of industrialization. Still, employers fill attractive and promising jobs with fully available, mainly male employees, without considering that this practice blocks their access to women who do not want to sacrifice their family lives for an occupation. The consistent rejection of women's capacities, facilitated by underemployment, not only risks wasting an important productive force. According to my findings, it also affects the individual well-being of women and their families (Lischke, 1985). Individual life-planning is disrupted, abilities and skills erode, and egalitarian life styles fail because traditional role patterns often perceived as unbearable are forcibly maintained.

THE ECONOMIC CITIZEN BETWEEN CONFLICT AND SOLIDARITY

This analysis of unemployment's impact in the FRG indicates that objective and subjective burdens on individual well-being have increased. At the same time, it is claimed that unemployment is not a relevant source of conflict or political instability in Germany (Prisching, 1988). I have reason to pursue this latent contradiction by means of survey research. The question arises as to whether those affected by unemployment are aware that their interests are being hurt, and whether the majority of those who experience little or no affect articulate conflicts of interest. What is the potential for protest from the minority that is extremely affected? And how great is the majority's possible resentment? In the first part of this section, I evaluate the opportunities and risks that may be entailed by politization of unemployment's impact. I examine the consequences of the previous and current situation on the labor market, and how they influence people's feelings and thinking. The second part of the section deals with the acceptance of hypothetical and real problem-solving strategies that are expected to relieve some of the burdens described above.

Potentials for Conflict

Underemployment and its various types of impact have not yet shaken the political system or even the allocation of political power in the FRG. One of the several plausible explanations for such peace on the political front is the social safety net. The unemployed neither starve nor freeze. They are not hit hard enough to remonstrate. Ranging between catastrophic scenarios and the soothing diagnosis that unemployment in an affluent society is not politically explosive and perhaps never will be, the conclusions based on the following findings present a more discriminating picture. Underemployment and unemployment have often exacted no price in the sociopolitical arena because affected persons were not organized enough to be politically mobilized in pursuit of a common goal. The permanently and repeatedly unemployed of the 1970s and 1980s came from heterogeneous marginal groups: the aged, the disabled, people with health restrictions, young people without job training, students of certain fields of study, and women in unskilled occupations. They were without a powerful lobby and were normally not organized in unions. Furthermore, fluctuation in the ranks of the jobless was considerable despite the high rate of long-term unemployment. This also restricts the ability to be organized.

A sensitive indicator for the popular interpretation of underemployment is voting behavior. Full employment is one of the most important and most accepted political goals in pluralistic democracies. Periodic and widely published announcements make the public even more aware of the situation on the labor market than of economic growth. The significance of employment as a criterion for judging government actions varies, however. For example, unemployment was a less important issue in the Bundestag election campaigns of 1972 and 1980 than it was in 1983 and 1987. And in 1990, the classical election campaign issues became irrelevant because of "reunification." A political goal is more important and topical if its realization is threatened. Nevertheless, it is plausible that persistent high unemployment is not good for a government's reputation. A government that fails to solve the country's most important problems also raises doubts about its ability to deal with other political issues (Rattinger, 1985).

The existing literature is unequivocal: Failure to achieve full employment is punished, if not always to the same extent, by the loss of votes (see Krieger, Liepelt, Schneider, & Smid, 1989), and there are no examples where the supposed "winners" on the labor market withdraw their support of the government. There is no evidence that those connected to industry would reward the government for maintaining high unemployment rates. On the contrary, union policy, which in Germany is mainly geared towards overcoming unemployment, is supported by those employees who belong to marginal groups as well as by most of the employed (see Krieger et al., 1989). Though the reaction of unemployed voters must be described as quite mild, the group of those who felt threatened by job loss revealed a certain anxiety. In the 1980s their votes, more than those of people less affected than they, were cast against the ruling parties (first the center-left coalition of the Liberals and Social Democrats, then the center-right coalition of the Liberals and Conservatives), which were blamed for the aggravation or stagnation of the unemployment rate. Krieger (1986) talked of antigovernment sentiment expressed by all regular voters in the first half of the 1980s. The defection from the SPD to the CDU before the regime shift in the GDR and back to the SPD thereafter was more pronounced among those who worried about their jobs.

My tentative conclusion is that unemployment is blamed on the governments under whose leadership the employment situation has worsened. That is true for the people affected by unemployment as well as for the majority of the constituency. In that sense there can be little doubt that unemployment has been politicized. Furthermore, comprehensive data and analyses from election research specify the conditions under which the described general relation between the employment situation and voting behavior becomes either more or less prominent. As shown by an international comparison of the results of 70 elections in 20 industrialized countries, ruling parties have a good chance of remaining in power despite rising unemployment (see Schmidt, 1986).

Resentment and Tolerance

Emotional and informal latent conflicts, which are empirically hard to grasp, are smoldering under the surface of constitutionally channeled voting behavior. Attitudes such as tolerance and scapegoating not only determine a society's social climate, but also limit and define political possibilities and have an impact on the future, through socialization of the young generation.

Some of the questionnaires of the *Institut für Demoskopie* in Allensbach dealt with the population's attitude toward the unemployed (see Strümpel & Schramm, 1989). In the first questionnaire in 1975, every second person expressed a critical opinion. The rejection of the underemployed increased until the end of the decade. In time, the labor-market situation improved again, some people found new jobs, and there was even talk about a shortage of skilled workers, but those who remained outside appeared suspicious. In 1981/82 the stigma receded. The peak of two million unemployed seems to have been a psychological threshold. Nevertheless, the tolerant attitude has declined again since 1986, though only slightly.

It is possible that the sorting and segmentation processes described in the previous section have reduced most people's empathy with those affected by unemployment. Whereas people with higher occupational status express slightly more tolerant opinions (see Strümpel et al., 1988), opinions that blue-collar workers have about the unemployed are especially negative. They find themselves in a conflict. First, there are more actual or potential victims of the labor market situation among them than among other groups. Second, blue-collar workers compare their own situation with that of the unemployed to a greater extent than other occupational groups do. They work hard, and they are aware of that. Thus, they are tempted to regard the unemployed as privileged people who live at the expense of those who have to work for a living.

The question arises as to whether the relatively high tolerance that the different population groups have for each other is due to the segment of educated, mostly younger people who are in fact also quite strongly affected by the situation on the labor market. Indeed, education, by virtue of its high correlation with tolerance towards the unemployed, mitigates intolerance. That effect is also of interest because the share of adults remaining in the educational system for a relatively long time has risen and will rise even more.

In conclusion, the thesis that underemployment is a means of the middle classes to threaten marginal groups and to benefit from their situation cannot be verified.

FINAL OBSERVATIONS

"Continuity within change" is a characterization of West Germany's main trend in economic development over the last 30 years. Growth rates that are around average in comparison to those of western countries are made possible by a high productivity rate. Low-productivity jobs of the sort that exist, say, in Sweden or the United States are being eliminated. This specific "production style" is problematic in two ways. Large minorities of the working population, mainly women, are thus excluded from employment. The number of registered unemployed has just about dropped below the two-million mark since 1983, and decisive improvements cannot be expected. The exclusion from employment is unlikely to result in a threat to social peace, but rather in an extensive loss of welfare for a great share of the employed persons who would prefer to change the numbers of hours they work.

The FRG has by now become an immigration country for eastern Europeans who, because of their different culture, language, or outdated skills, are crowding onto a segment of the labor market whose significance is steadily declining. This points to considerable problems that are perhaps harder to solve in West Germany than in other countries. One possible scenario for dealing with these problems is the "Americanization" of the German labor market. In comparison to other Western industrialized countries, the FRG has a great demand for low-productivity jobs. As a rule these would be "bad jobs," that is, jobs that entail no prospect for advancement, require few skills, pay scarcely enough to live on, and offer no permanent social benefits. The alternative would be to maintain the present course, meaning at the same time even stricter isolation from the surrounding countries. Isolation great enough to enable the labor market to keep offering only high-productivity jobs is undesirable and difficult to achieve.

Internationally, the West Germans have to be the "model pupils" of value change. Besides a general turn away from traditional and/or materialistic values, especially in the 1980s, a drastic individualization and pluralization of life styles and value patterns has taken place. At the same time, the significance of employment remains untouched. The critical opinions of the situation at present do not imply that the value of employment is declining. The end of the "work society" is not at hand. On the contrary, social benefits guaranteed by employment are necessary for individualization.

The impacts that labor-market trends have are diverse, if sometimes latent. In addition to the generally acknowledged effects of unemployment, weaker forms thereof concern a wide range of people. One such secondary effect is a pervasive loss of options. This loss is reflected partly in the employers' value-oriented recruitment strategies. In periods of high unemployment, for example, employers can choose applicants "of the right spirit." Second, the perceived chances of finding new jobs are very small, so employees are highly dependent on their jobs. They consequently adopt many attitudes that are expected of them. Third, the gap between preferred and existing working-hour arrangements is perceivable. Both the unemployed and the overemployed suffer from this impact of unemployment. The effects of unemployment are very unevenly distributed in the FRG. This segmentation results from a selection process, for at the beginning of the 1980s unemployment was something that could concern everybody more or less. Severe effects—the exclusion from employment—are borne by social groups that are not necessarily even granted a right to employment. The main group affected in this way is women. Despite their appropriate qualifications and efforts to gain access to the labor market, they have largely been denied employment in the FRG.

The reactions of the "economic citizen" to trends on the labor market have remained quite moderate in the past few years. Neither the affected nor the privileged are hostile to certain population groups. The unemployed do not question the "system," are fairly well provided for, and supposedly can adopt alternative roles. Furthermore, the movement against unemployment lacks effectiveness. Resentment of the sort expressed in the slogan "He who does not work should not eat either" are not very common. As demonstrated by the success of the right wing under the *Republikaner* at the end of the 1980s, tendencies towards extreme positions do exist in the FRG. But in retrospect, the empirical evidence measuring the significance of that phenomenon is all but conclusive. It is completely open to speculation how the revolutionary processes in central and eastern Europe will effect the labor market in Germany and the social orientation of her citizens.

REFERENCES

Baethge, M., Hantsche, B., Pelull, W., & Voskamp, U. (1988). *Jugend: Arbeit und Identität* [Youth: Work and identity]. Opladen: Leske & Budrich.
Bielenski, H., & Strümpel, B. (1988). *Eingeschränkte Erwerbsarbeit bei Frauen und Männern* [Limited employment among women and men]. Berlin: edition sigma.
Büchtemann, C., & Schupp, J. (1988). Strukturen und Entwicklungsperspektiven der Teilzeitbeschäftigten (Analysen 1987) [Structures and prospects for development (Analyses, 1987)]. In H.-J. Krupp & U. Hanefeld (Eds.), *Lebenslagen im Wandel (Analysen 1987)* (pp. 88-113). Frankfurt on the Main: Campus.
Deters, J., Staehle, W. H., & Stirn, U. (1989). *Die Praxis des gleitenden Übergangs in den Ruhestand-Geht eine sozialpolitische Idee in Rente?* [Flexible transition to retirement—Retirement of an idea in social policy?]. Berlin: edition sigma.
Ingelhart, R. (1989). *Cultural Change.* Princeton: Princeton University Press.
Kern, H., & Schumann, M. (1984). *Das Ende der Arbeitsteilung?* [The end of the division of labor?]. Munich: Beck.
Klipstein, M. v., & Strümpel, B. (1985). Wertewandelung: Wirtschaftsbild der Deutschen [Value change and economic belief systems of the Germans]. *Aus Politik und Zeitgeschichte* (Supplement to the Bonn weekly *Das Parlament*), *B 42,* 19-38.
Krieger, H. (1986). Arbeitsmarktsituation und politische Stabilität (Reaktionsformen abhängiger Beschäftigter auf die Arbeitsmarktentwicklung 1975-1985) [The situation on the labor market and political stability (Reactions of dependent employees to the development on the labor market, 1975-1985)]. *Aus Politik und Zeitgeschichte* (Supplement to the Bonn weekly *Das Parlament*), *B 17,* 3-18.
Krieger, H., Liepelt, K., Schneider, R., & Smid, M. (1985). *Arbeitsmarktkrise und Arbeitnehmerbewusstsein* [Crisis on the labor market and employee awareness]. Frankfurt on the Main: Campus.
Kühl, J. (1988). 15 Jahre Massenarbeitslosigkeit—Aspekte einer Halbzeitbilanz [Fifteen years of mass unemployment—Aspects of an interim review]. *Aus Politik und Zeitgeschichte* (Supplement to the Bonn weekly *Das Parlament*), *B 38,* 3-28.
Lischke, G. (1985). Erwerbsarbeit von Frauen zwischen Lebensunterhalt und Lebensinhalt [Paid work by women: Between earning a living and filling a life]. In M. v. Klipstein & B. Strümpel (Eds.), *Gewandelte Werte-Erstarrte Strukturen (Wie Bürger die Wirtschaft und Arbeit erleben)* (pp. 217-231). Bonn: Verlag Neue Gesellschaft.
OECD (Ed.). (1973). *Labour Force Statistics-Statistiques de la Population Active (1960-1971).* Paris: OECD.
———. (1988). *Labour Force Statistics-Statistiques de la Population Active (1966-1986).* Paris: OECD.
———. (1988). *National Accounts-Comptes Nationaux 1960-1986 (Main Aggregates-Pricipaux Agrégates,* Vol. 1). Paris: OECD.
Pawlowsky, P. (1986). *Arbeitseinstellungen im Wandel* [Changing attitudes toward work]. Munich: Minerva.
Pawlowsky, P., & Strümpel, B. (1986). Arbeit und Wertewandel: Replik [Work and value change: Reply]. *Kölner Zeitschrift für Soziologie und Sozialpsychologie, 38,* 772-784.

Prisching, M. (1988). *Arbeitslosenprotest und Resignation in der Wirtschaftskrise* [Protest of the unemployed and resignation during economic crisis]. Frankfurt on the Main: Campus.

Rattinger, H. (1985). Politisches Verhalten von Arbeitslosen: Die Bundestagswahlen 1980 und 1983 im Vergleich [The political behavior of jobless people: A comparison of the 1980 and 1983 West German parliamentary elections]. In D. Oberndörfer, H. Rattinger, & K. Schmitt (Eds.), *Wirtschaftlicher Wandel, religiöser Wandel und Wertewandel* (pp. 97-129). Berlin: Duncker und Humblot.

Reuband, K.-H. (1985). Arbeit und Wertewandel—Mehr Mythos als Realität? [Work and value change—More myth than reality?] *Kölner Zeitschrift für Soziologie und Sozialpsychologie, 37,* 723-746.

Rosenstiel, L. v., Nerdinger, F., Spiess, E., & Stengel, M. (1989). *Führungsnachwuchs im Unternehmen* [Future managers in business]. Munich: Beck.

Scharpf, F. (1988). *Flexible Arbeitszeit. Die Chance für Mensch und Wirtschaft* [Flexitime: The opportunity for people and the economy]. Unpublished.

Schmidt, M. G. (1986). Wahlen, Parteipolitik und Arbeitslosigkeit [Elections, party politics, and unemployment]. *Aus Politik und Zeitgeschichte* (Supplement to the Bonn *Das Parlament*), *B 17,* 37-45.

Schramm, F. (1992). *Beschäftigungsunsicherheit. Wie sich die Risiken des Arbeitsmarkts auf die Beschäftigten auswirken-Empirische Analysen in Ost und West* [Employment insecurity: How risks of the labor market affect employed persons—Empirical analyses in East and West]. Berlin: edition sigma.

Schwarze, J., & Wagner, G. (1989). Geringfügige Beschäftigung—empirische Befunde und Reformvorschläge [Marginal employment—Empirical findings and proposals for reform]. *Wirtschaftsdienst, 4,* 184-191.

Siebert, D., & Schmid, G. (1988). *Systemanalyse des Arbeitsmarktes für Akademiker/innen (Simulation 1970-2010)* [Systems analysis of the labor market for academics (Simulation 1970-2010)] (WZB Discussion Paper FS I 88-22). Berlin: Wissenschaftszentrum Berlin für Sozialforschung.

Strümpel, B., Prenzel, W., Scholz, J., & Hoff, A. (1988). *Teilzeitarbeitende Männer und Hausmänner* [Part-time working men and "house husbands"]. Berlin: edition sigma.

Strümpel, B., & Schramm, F. (1989). *Arbeitslosigkeit und Arbeitsumverteilung. Betroffenheit, Konflikt, Reformpotential* [Unemployment and redistribution of work: Impacts, conflicts and the potential for reform]. Unpublished expert report for the federal chancellery.

Therborn, G. (1985). *Arbeitslosigkeit (Strategien und Politikansätze in den OECD-Ländern)* [Unemployment (strategies and policy approaches in the OECD countries)]. Hamburg: VSA.

Wacker, A. (1983). *Arbeitslosigkeit (Soziale und psychische Folgen)* [Unemployment (social and psychological impacts)]. Frankfurt on the Main: Europäische Verlagsanstalt.

Wahl, S. (1985). Langfristige Trends auf dem Arbeitsmarkt [Long-term trends on the labor market]. *Aus Politik und Zeitgeschichte* (Supplement to the Bonn Weekly *Das Parlament*), *B 42,* 3-17.

Windolf, P., & Hohn, H.-W. (1984). *Arbeitsmarktchancen in der Krise (Betriebliche Rekrutierung und soziale Schliessung)* [Opportunities on the labor market (Recruitment and social integration in the plant)]. Frankfurt on the Main: Campus.

Zahlenfibel. (1988). *Ergebnisse der Arbeitsmarkt- und Berufsforschung in Tabellen* [Tabulated results of labor-market and occupational research]. Nuremberg: Eigenverlag.

Zapf, W., Breuer, S., Hampel, J., Krause, P., Mohr, H.-M., & Wiegand, E. (1987). *Individualisierung und Sicherheit* [Individualization and security]. Munich: Beck.

CANADIANS:

LOOKING GOOD, FEELING BAD

Joseph Smucker

In May 1991, Canadians learned that a United Nations survey of 160 countries ranked their country second only to Japan as the "best place to live" ("Canada Second", 1991).[1] But according to a comparison of Gallup polls conducted among 33 countries at the end of 1990, only the Hungarians seemed to be more pessimistic about the coming year than Canadians. A comparison of the Canadian results and data available from other countries reported in this volume is presented in Table 1.

According to *The Gallup Report* of January 1, 1991, 63% of Canadians believed that 1991 would be worse than 1990, the highest percentage recorded since at least 1965. This figure far exceeds the 51% who expected the coming year to be worse in 1975, or the 49% in 1980, the eve of the recession of 1981-82.[2] Nor did that percentage increase during 1981-82. Figure 1 reveals a general decline in optimism since 1965, with modest exceptions in 1984 (the year the Progressive Conservative Party was elected to federal office), and in 1986.

Such pessimism, then, is not endemic in the Canadian "character." Indeed, in 1960 a Gallup poll revealed that 95% of Canadian respondents reported that they were "happy," the highest proportion of respondents in similar polls carried out among 11 countries (Gallup Canada, 1960).[3] One might argue, of course, that the discrepancy between the United Nations report and the current pessimism among Canadians is merely a matter of relative standards. Canadians have it good, but they want it better or they do not think what they have will last. But this interpretation explains neither the phenomenon nor the dramatic increase in pessimism.[4]

Table 1. International Comparisons:
"Coming Year to be Better" (in percentages)

Country	Year		
	1989	1990	1991
Canada	47	36	18
Germany	n.a.	n.a.	25
Hungary	n.a.	15	2
Israel	n.a.	62	28
Sweden	47	44	40
USSR-Moscow	54	37	18
U.K.	46	36	43
U.S.A.	61	49	48

Note: N = approximately 1,000.
Source: Gallup Canada (Canadian Institute of Public
           Opinion). (Various Years). *The Gallup Report*
           (January 1, 1991). Toronto: Canadian Institute of
           Public Opinion.

This chapter is an attempt to provide an explanation. It is based on a profile
of economic, behavioral, and attitudinal indices. It begins with an overview
of the economic and political environment during the past three decades. After
presenting aggregate measures of economic performance, I describe the
structural changes that have occurred during the same period of time. Indices
of personal experience and the principle means by which Canadians appear
to have coped with these changes are then presented. Along with these indices,
available survey research is mined to discover the effects of the changes on
Canadian attitudes and perceptions in terms of the economic and social status
of their country, their assessments of their own lives, and their trust in public
institutions. Finally, an effort is made to assess whether there has been a change
in basic values over the past three decades. My conclusion at the end of this
chapter is that Canadians not only have had to endure relatively profound
economic changes, they have also experienced yet another period of political
crisis in the interests of trying to define and achieve a viable national identity.
The unfolding of these events has resulted in a growing mood of exasperation,
expressed by disillusionment with the "open-market" approach of the current
government, and an apparent readiness for a new approach of government
policies. At the same time, Canadians have been taking action either to
minimize the effects of these changes on their personal lives or to maximize
their returns from these changes.

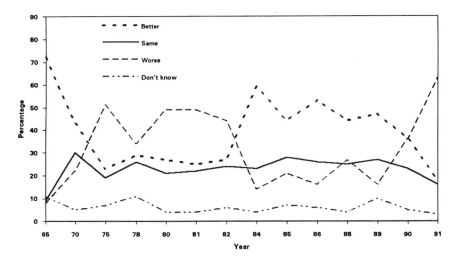

Note: Adapted from Gallup Canada (Canadian Institute of Public Opinion). (various years). *The Gallup Report* (January 1, 1991). Toronto: Canadian Institute of Public Opinion. ($N =$ approximately 1,000).

Figure 1.   Prospects for the Coming Year as Judged by Canadians

CHANGING FORTUNES: AN OVERVIEW

For approximately 25 years after World War II, Canada shared with its neighbor to the south, the United States, economic growth that was unprecedented in its relatively steady rate. Growth during the years from 1960 to the early 1970s was particularly remarkable. Canada's economy went through mild economic cycles, but their effects seemed to be minimized by modestly applied Keynesian countercyclical policies and by continued international demand for its raw materials and partially finished goods.[5]

During that period governments at both the federal and provincial levels created new welfare programs and expanded on those introduced during the prewar years of the Great Depression. These measures included the introduction of universal programs such as the national program of medicare, the old-age pension benefit system, and the program of family allowances. The federal government also expanded the unemployment insurance program, instituted a more generous social welfare system, and embarked on a number of innovative job-training and job-creation programs. Both the federal and provincial governments also funded expansion in postsecondary education, and they supported a variety of urban development schemes, cultural projects, and social services (Doern, Maslove, & Prince, 1988, pp. 2-3; Courchene, 1987, pp. 7-10).

The 1960s and early 1970s also marked the period of the civil rights movement in the United States and the "cultural revolution," initiated by members of the "baby-boom" generation in a number of western countries, including Canada. It was within this context that the various versions of a postindustrial thesis were advanced and that Inglehart perceived the development of a postmaterialist era (Inglehart, 1977; for a now-classic statement of postindustrial society, see Bell, 1973).

Those were heady years for Canada. Social reforms initiated by the populist wing of the Progressive-Conservative government under Diefenbaker were followed by more progressive reforms under the Liberal administration of Pearson and were further consolidated by the charismatic Liberal prime minister, Pierre Trudeau. Trudeau embarked on a program designed to strengthen the central government, reduce dependence upon foreign direct investments, particularly those from the United States, expand social welfare services, and establish an official bilingual and bicultural national identity. However, alongside these developments was the independence movement of French-speaking Quebec, led in large part by its cultural elite.

By 1972 there were signs that the economic foundations for the optimism and social experimentation were weakening. Inflation rates were creeping upward, driven in part by world-wide commodity shortages. Finally, the dramatic oil-price shocks of 1973-74 resulted in a diminishing faith in the ability of the economy and past government policies to sustain what was, in retrospect, an unusual era.

In 1975, "stagflation" attained especially dramatic proportions. Unemployment had climbed to a level of 7%, rates that were unacceptable in an era in which 4% was viewed with some alarm. Wage demands and settlements were increasing by about 19%, and the consumer price index was rising at nearly 11% (Riddell, 1986, p. 13). The federal government first tried to invoke a program of voluntary restraints for both wages and prices but failed to get support from individual unions. Rather than invoke restrictive fiscal and monetary policies, the federal government then tried compulsory controls. They were put into place in 1975 and lasted for three years (Doern et al., 1988, p. 5). Meanwhile government deficits increased, partly because of decreasing revenue from an inflation-indexed income tax, a sluggish economy, and higher expenditures due to increases in unemployment and social welfare support programs.

In the latter half of the 1970s, both federal and provincial governments searched for new economic policies to deal with problems created by increased levels of unemployment, increasing rates of inflation, and increased strife in industrial relations. There were also increased political tensions between provinces and regions as their economic disparities became more apparent. Meanwhile, Quebec, in 1976, had actually elected a provincial government that was avowedly separatist.

Within this milieu of economic and political confusion and after the unusually severe recession of 1981-82, the 1980s were a decade during which the embrace of a more market-centered set of policies grew. The election to federal office of the Progressive-Conservative party led by Brian Mulroney in 1984 symbolized a state of impatience with the failure of previous government policies to maintain economic growth and support progressive social welfare measures while bringing about stronger national identity. An embrace of "the market" seemed to provide new hope for the well-being of the individual in the latter years of the Liberal government's tenure. There had been a growing view that the federal government had become too interventionist and, at the same time, that it had lost its sense of direction.

The policies of the Progressive-Conservative government of Mulroney were inspired by those of the governments of Reagan, elected in 1981 in the United States, and Thatcher, whose government came to power in Britain in 1979. Compared to the United States and Britain, the Mulroney government was less extreme in its advocacy of a minimalist approach, but it did seek economic renewal through a less regulated market. It also announced its opposition to federal centralism and sought to curtail the growth of government bureaucracy. It reasserted the virtues of economic individualism, and it announced an end to past policies that had sought to protect Canadian industry and had attempted to reduce the extent of foreign control of its firms (Doern et al., 1988, pp. 5-8). In practice, the Mulroney government continued the tight money policy instituted by the previous Liberal government; it claimed credit for reducing unemployment;[6] it reduced the growth of deficits through tax reforms, tax increases, and some spending cuts; it curtailed the rate of increase in welfare spending; it privatized a small number of government corporations; it instituted some deregulation, primarily in banking, telecommunications, the trucking industry, and the airlines; and it signed a free-trade agreement with the United States (Doern et al., 1988, pp. 5-8). Uninterrupted economic growth from 1982 through 1989, though somewhat sluggish, seemed to validate the effectiveness of the government's "open-market" policies.

There are now clear signs that these policies do not have the public support they once did. The current recession (1990 through at least the third quarter of 1991), compounded in its effects by the government's restrictive monetary policy, its severe fiscal policy (which includes the introduction of a goods and services tax), and the effects of the Free Trade Agreement with the United States, further detracts from support for the Mulroney government. Indeed, since its re-election in 1988, support for the Progressive Conservatives has fallen from 43% to a record low of 12% in January, 1991 (Gallup Canada, January 17, 1991). The assessment of Mulroney as prime minister has been the least favorable of any preceeding prime minister; only 7% of the respondents in a Gallup poll thought he was either "the best" or "one of the best" (Gallup Canada, November 26, 1990). Further, a social democratic party, the New

Democratic Party, has been elected to head the government in Ontario, the wealthiest and most industrially diversified province in Canada. In addition, the New Democratic Party has come to head the governments of the provinces of British Columbia and Saskatchewan and the Yukon territory.

Equally damaging to the Mulroney government was its inept handling of the so-called constitutional crisis. In reversing the previous Liberal government's commitment to a strong presence of the federal government and attempting to embark on a program of provincial consensus, it has only increased animosities among the geographically diverse province, heightened tensions between the French and English-speaking sectors of the population, and in general exasperated the Canadian public.

CHANGING DYNAMICS OF ECONOMIC PERFORMANCE

General Trends

An insight into the economic changes that accompanied, if not caused, the changes described above can be gained by comparing the three decades from the beginning of the 1960s to the end of the 1980s. These comparisons reveal a number of important shifts in the nature of Canada's economic performance. During the three periods of 1961-71, 1971-81, and 1981-88, the average annual percentage changes in real gross domestic product were 5.5, 4.0, and 3.1, respectively (McKitrick, 1989, Table 13, p. 48). In themselves, these trends indicate quite respectable economic performance for a "mature" industrialized society. It is the relative decline in these rates of growth and the shifts within these trends that have important consequences for the current mood of Canadians.

Average annual rates of increase in compensation per person per hour for all business activity, including farming, were 7.2%, 10.9%, and 5.7% during these three periods. But in real terms these increases were only 4.1%, 1.9%, and 0.3%. Meanwhile, average annual real profits after tax for all industries for the three periods was 3.1%, 6.0%, and 5.0% for these three periods (McKitrick, 1989, Table 13, p. 51),[7] while average annual rates of increase in productivity per person per hour for all business activity are estimated to have been 4.0%, 1.8%, and 1.5% over these three time periods, 1961-70, 1971-80, and 1981-88 (Courchene, 1989, Table 3, p. 11).

Average annual rates of inflation during these three periods were 3.5%, 8.4%, and 5.2% (McKitrick, 1989, Table 7, p. 26). Interest rates as expressed by bank rates climbed steadily from 4.33% during 1961-71 to 7.71% during 1971-81 and finally to 10.37% during 1981-88 (McKitrick, 1989, Table 13, p. 52).

Finally, the curtailment of government expenditures at all levels is reflected in the declining rates of average annual increase. Expressed in constant 1981 dollars, they were 5.8%, 3.5%, and 1.9% over the three periods, respectively (McKitrick, 1989, Table 13, p. 46). These statistics provide initial evidence of change, the costs of which have not been shared either consistently or equally.

Since taking office, the Mulroney government has targeted inflation as the major economic problem and has followed a tight monetary policy at the expense of tolerating relatively high unemployment rates. Unemployment rates of over 11% during the recession of 1981-82 declined, but only to a low of 7%. Since 1988, they have steadily increased, surpassing 10% in the beginning months of 1991. Government policy-makers, influenced by "monetarists," currently regard an annual unemployment rate of 8% as a "natural rate," with any decrease likely to raise inflation rates (Gherson, 1990).

Sectoral Shifts

In Canada, as in other industrialized countries, sectoral shifts in economic activity represent an especially dramatic illustration of economic change. Although the defining limits of economic sectors are becoming increasingly blurred as services play a larger role in the actual production of goods, it is perhaps still useful to track the shift in the roles played by the production of goods versus services in the economy of Canada (Economic Council of Canada, 1990, p. 4).[8]

The total proportionate contribution from the production of goods, which includes foodstuffs, raw materials, construction, as well as manufactured goods, to the total GDP expressed in constant 1981 dollars were, for the years 1960, 1970, 1981, and 1988, respectively, 38.2%, 37.8%, 34%, and 36.2% (computed from Charette, Henry, & Kaufmann, 1986, Table 2.3, p. 74, and Economic Council of Canada, 1990). Clearly, in terms of value created, the goods-producing sectors maintained their relative importance over this 28-year period. (The service sector, which includes utilities, transportation, finance, trade, and private and public services made up the remaining proportion of value created as measured by the Gross Domestic Product.) Manufacturing alone declined only slightly, the percentages being 21.1, 22.8, 21.7, and 19.7 for the four designated years (Charette, Henry, & Kaufmann, 1986, p. 74; Economic Council of Canada, 1990).

However, while the relative value of production by the goods-producing sectors has remained nearly constant, its share in total employment has declined. In 1960 this sector accounted for 46.5% of total employment. In 1970 and 1981 the proportions decreased to 37.4% and 32.5%, respectively. In 1988 the proportion of the labor force in the goods-producing sector was only 29.1% (computed from McKitrick, 1989, Table 16, p. 63), with 71% employed in the service sectors (Economic Council of Canada).[9] In manufacturing alone, employment declined from 24.6% of the employed labor force in 1960 to 22.3% and 19.3% in the years 1970 and 1981, respectively. In 1988, the percentage of the employed labor force in manufacturing was 17.2% (computed from McKitrick, 1989, Table 16, p. 63).

Like the trends previously experienced in the agricultural sector before, an increasing ratio of capital equipment to labor has maintained relatively steady proportions of value created as the content of labor has decreased. Meanwhile, gains in the service sector have occurred primarily in personal and business services, followed by public administration, trade, and finance, insurance, and real estate. These trends are similar to those that have occurred in the United States, Great Britain, West Germany, Sweden, and Japan, although in comparison Canada has the lowest proportion of her labor force engaged in manufacturing. (West Germany has the largest proportion of her labor force in manufacturing in particular and goods production in general.) (See Charette, Henry, & Kaufman, 1986, pp. 74-75.)[10]

Occupational Changes

There have been three interacting patterns of change among occupations in Canada: (a) shifts in the structure of occupations, (b) shifts in skill requirements, and (c) shifts in employment patterns. The most striking feature of change in the structure of occupations has been the job losses among middle-skilled but high-wage blue-collar occupations, accompanied by new jobs in the service sector in industries paying below average wages, such as retail trade, food-service operations, and banks.[11] One dramatic example of these shifts is the steel industry. In tracking the employment shifts of steelworkers between 1978 and 1983, Allen (1985) found that employment fell from 97,270 to 86,114, a result of 33,292 workers exiting the industry and 22,136 entering it. Of those who left and subsequently found other employment, 32% entered industries classified as "service, finance, government," 24% entered "primary industries, construction, utilities and other," 14% entered "trade," and 31% entered "other manufacturing" (reported in Baldwin & Gorecki, 1990, p. 103).

In terms of skill requirements, there is evidence that during the 1960s and 1970s demands for higher skill levels grew with the expansion of professional, technical, and managerial occupations. During the 1980s the market for skills became more complex. Three trends appear to have developed: (a) a growth in low-wage, low-skilled service jobs, (b) an increased demand for greater competencies in basic skills, and (c) continued demand for highly developed skills (Myles, n.d.; Myles, Picot, & Wannel, 1988). The Economic Council of Canada (1990, p. 14) estimates that highly skilled jobs accounted for one-third of employment growth from 1971 to 1981 and 77% of employment growth from 1981 to 1986.

In general, employers are demanding higher competencies in literacy, numeracy, and problem-solving abilities. In addition, they are seeking workers who can adapt easily to changing job requirements and who can communicate well. In large part these demands reflect an increased emphasis on "information-based" work. Jobs bearing this description probably accounted for two-thirds of the net employment growth from 1971 to 1986 (Economic Council of Canada, 1990, p. 3). But this represents a very broad category of skills ranging from routine handling of data to creating and interpreting information. Indeed, there is considerable evidence of a demand for both low- and high-skilled jobs. Such a bifurcation is supported by the growth in consumer-oriented jobs.

There are several reasons for growth among these low-wage, low-skilled jobs: a plentiful supply of youth, at least in the recent past,[12] demands for such services because of an increase in single-parent and single-person households, new management policies that emphasize the necessity for a "flexible" labor supply, and the effects of government restraints in providing public services (Myles, n.d., p. 20).

In addition to changes in occupational structure and skill requirements, there has been a growth in "nonstandard employment," the third change in the nature of occupations. "Nonstandard employment" deviates from the norm of a full-time, full-year job. It includes part-time work (jobs with fewer than 30 working hours per week), jobs lasting fewer than six months, jobs created by the self-employed, and jobs in temporary help agencies. This type of employment accounted for about 50% of all jobs created between 1981 and 1986. (Part-time employment alone accounted for 30% of total employment growth during the period 1975-88.) They made up about 30% of total employment in 1990 (Economic Council of Canada, 1990, p. 12).[13] That these employment arrangements are not necessarily desired by individuals in the labor market is indicated by the finding that nearly half of all part-time jobs created since 1981 were filled by people who preferred to work full-time (Economic Council of Canada, 1990, p. 11).

These occupation shifts have been accompanied by changes in the distribution of income among the Canadian population. Gini coefficients, which measure the degree of inequality, have been increasing since 1967 as the proportion of those earning "middle levels" of income (those earning between 75% and 125% of the median earnings) have decreased from 26.8% in 1967 to 21.5% in 1986. The accompanying shifts in the low-income-earning group (those earning up to 75% of the median earning level) and the high-earning group (those earning more than 125% of the median) during the same period moved from 36.4% to 39.4% for the low-income group and 36.9% to 39.1% for the high-income group. These disparities change only slightly when transfer payments and investment income are taken into account and when households rather than individuals are the primary referents. With these taken into consideration, the proportion of middle-income families (total pretax income) decreased from 26.1% in 1967 to 22.3% in 1986 (Economic Council of Canada, 1990, p. 15).

The increased income disparities are apparent in both goods-producing and service sectors, and it is only partly caused by the increased entry of women and youth into the labor force. There are some arguments that these trends are long-term, related to changes in technology and organizational structure. But there is evidence that the observed inequalities are "more related to wage distributions within industries and occupations" (Myles, Picot, & Wannell, 1988, abstract). It is possible that these are short-term trends, related to the ability of employers to initiate highly varied wage structures since the 1981-82 recession and encouraged further by a relatively large pool of youth and women. Demographic shifts in the labor force may make it more difficult for employers to continue these policies (Economic Council of Canada, 1990, pp. 14-16). (It may also increase the possibility of a revival of a lagging labor-union movement.)

Shifts in the Organization of Industrial Firms

Historically, Canada has been an active trading nation, with its resource sector playing a prominant role. But increased competition from foreign sources has increased the severity of Canada's already vulnerable position in world commodity markets. In addition, tariffs, originally designed to protect its manufacturing sector, have been reduced through changes brought about by the General Agreement on Tariffs and Trade (GATT) and, more recently, the Free Trade Agreement signed with the United States. The Free Trade Agreement has also increased the intensity of competition in a number of service industries, especially financial services.

The general response of Canadian firms to these competitive pressures has been to rationalize operations by changing the mix of product lines. Further, firms in Canada have tended to reduce their labor component relative to capital investments when faced with tariff reductions, although the use of labor per dollar of output differs by firm and industry. Part of this difference is due to technology and cost differences between labor and capital. But some of the difference is also due to degree of market control and ties with foreign sources of component goods or services. Firms in concentrated industries tend to be more capital intensive and use less labor, and they tend to restrict output in order to maintain profit margins. Foreign-owned subsidiaries in Canada tend to use less labor per dollar of shipments than domestic companies, in part because their sales are often based on products whose components may be manufactured at reduced cost by plants owned by the same firm outside Canada (Caves, 1990, p. 3).

There has been a general movement among firms toward designing organizational structures that are less dependent upon relatively fixed labor costs. In addition to reductions in the labor component in production, staff and administrative functions are being cut. Further, many firms are adopting a number of innovations that have changed the nature of employment. This has resulted in an increased use of "nonstandard" patterns of employment described above. Employers are experimenting with labor contracts that permit them to vary the number of employees on the job according to demand; reorganize jobs in order to permit more flexible deployment of employees; contract functions out to other firms, often in foreign countries where wages are lower, or to firms within Canada that have lower administrative costs; and initiate new policies designed to increase flexibility in wages (Pinfield & Atkinson, 1988, pp. 17-19; McAdams, 1988, pp. 17-19; Betcherman, Newton, & Godin, 1990).[14]

The current stress on "flexibility" and the focus on more efficient management of "human resources" has altered the work experience considerably. Employment security is less assured, even at management levels. Proprietary claims to specific job designations are being eroded, and employees are exhorted to become more adaptable. Accompanying these developments have been efforts to win increased employee loyalty, a paradoxical development given the heightened insecurity of employment in general (Johnson & Grey, 1988; Smucker, 1988).

Job Loss

Attempts have been made to isolate causes of job loss due to structural change from those due to general business cycles and to simple movement among jobs within a relatively stable structure, but the resulting estimates have been relatively crude. What is clear is that employment rates after the most recent recessions have not attained prerecession levels. Perhaps only two thirds of the 277,000 jobs lost in the manufacturing sector in the recession of 1990-91 will be regained.[15] Part of this loss will be made up, of course, by new jobs in other sectors, but it is likely that unemployment rates will remain relatively high after the recession. Further, government policy is based on the view that relatively high rates of unemployment (8%) must be tolerated in the interest of controlling inflationary rates, which ran at 6% in the first half of 1991. In the beginning months of 1992, the inflation rate was near zero, whereas the unemployment rate was 10.7% of the labor force.

Annual rates of unemployment steadily increased during the three decades under consideration. In the periods 1961-70, 1971-80, and 1981-88, the average annual unemployment rates were 3.8%, 7.9%, and 10.0% respectively (McKitrick, 1989, Table 125, p. 132). (After an unemployment rate of nearly 12% during 1982-83, the unemployment rate fell to 8.3% in 1988.)[16]

Currently, about one out of three workers experiences some unemployment or job change during a year. This includes searches for jobs by initiates into the labor market; those who voluntarily leave their jobs; and forced lay-offs, both temporary and permanent. What makes the experience of these people different from those experiencing lay-offs in the 1970s is that increasing numbers of those who voluntarily leave or who have been laid off from goods-producing jobs must look for new jobs in the service sector. Over 40% of those separated from goods-producing jobs who later were employed found their next job in services (Economic Council of Canada, 1990, p. 16).

Available statistics indicate a gradual increase in the proportion of the unemployed who have been without jobs for relatively long periods of time. In 1976, 33.5% of the unemployed were without jobs for 14 weeks or longer. This percentage steadily rose to 49% as of 1983 as a result of the effects of the 1981-82 recession but then declined to 39.7% in 1988, when the unemployment rate was an "acceptable" 8.3% (McKitrick, 1989, Table 32, p. 129).

In a study comparing long-term unemployment for the years 1981 and 1987, the proportion of unemployed workers aged 45 years and over who experienced 53 weeks or more of unemployment increased from 4.8% in 1981 to 16.9% in 1987. The corresponding figures for workers in the age group 25 to 44 were 5% and 10%; for those aged 15 to 24, 3% and 4% (Rahman, Gera, & Touchie, 1989).

In 1990 and 1991, overwhelming majorities of Canadians believed that unemployment would continue to increase. In 1990, 60% of Gallup poll respondents believed this to be true. In 1991, the figure was 81%. By contrast, 11% and 17% in the respective years believed the rates would remain the same (Gallup Canada, January 1, 1991).

The figures indicating whether individual Canadians believed that they were likely to experience unemployment are shown in Table 2. In the last year of the 1981-82 recession, 32% of Gallup poll respondents believed that they faced the likelihood of unemployment; 24% and 26% believed this to be true in 1985 and 1990, respectively, and 35% of the respondents in 1991 believed there was a chance of becoming unemployed. Interestingly, these perceptions match rather closely the estimate noted above that one out of three workers in Canada can expect to be unemployed during any single year.

The Besieged Union Movement

The economic and structural changes outlined above have taken a heavy toll on the Canadian labor union movement. Union membership in 1966 accounted for 31% of the nonagricultural paid workers and climbed to 40% in 1983. Membership then declined, reaching 36% in 1989 and about 34% in 1991 (Coates, Arrowsmith, & Courchene, 1989, Table 1, p. 18). There has been a slight decline of union membership in the goods-producing sector (e.g., in manufacturing, where union membership accounted for 43% of Canadian workers in 1966 but only 38% in 1986). Membership increased among workers in the private service sector from 25% in 1966 to 43% in 1986 and increased

Table 2. Job Security in the Future

Year	Response (in percentages)		
	Job as Secure	Chance of Becoming Unemployed	Don't Know
1982	64	32	5
1985	70	24	6
1990	70	26	6
1991	59	35	6

Note: N = approximately 1,000.
Source: Gallup Canada (Canadian Institute of Public Opinion). (Various years). *The Gallup Report* (February 10, 1991). Toronto: Canadian Institute of Public Opinion.

among workers in public administration from 12% in 1966 to 35% in 1986. The total service sector accounted for 59% of union membership growth from 1966 to 1986, while goods production accounted for the remainder. However, manufacturing accounted for 6% of the growth during this 20-year period (Coates et al.,1989, Table 12, p. 33).

Unions in Canada, though frequently militant and effective in achieving economic benefits, have seldom been able to present themselves as a united front wielding significant economic and political power. There are 917 unions, most of which are affiliated with central bodies, of which the Canadian Labor Congress (CLC) is the largest. Some unions are affiliated with both the CLC and the American central body, the AFL-CIO. Others are affiliated only with the AFL-CIO, and still others have no affiliation with a larger "central"[17]. Contributing further to this fragmentation is the variety of constituencies involved in the collective-bargaining process, which may take place at the plant or enterprise level and may involve one or more local unions. In the construction industry, bargaining may involve several local employers and one or more local unions.

The past decade was especially difficult for unions. They had to face the insecurities of two deep recessions and the increased competitive effects of the recently signed free-trade agreement with the United States while the Bank of Canada maintained relatively high interest rates. Unions also had to contend with a less than sympathetic government (Panitch & Swartz, 1985, pp. 30-57) and very aggressive antiunion tactics from managers. Whether Canadian unions will regain what strength they had in the coming years will depend on their organizing strategies in the service sector, where most jobs have been created, and on their ability to play a stronger role in job redesign and the incorporation of new technologies.

PERSONAL EXPERIENCES AND REACTIONS

While the state of the Canadian economy in gross terms has been relatively healthy (although in comparison to growth patterns in most OECD countries over the past 10 years its growth has been sluggish, not unlike that of the United States and Great Britain), structural shifts within the economy have created an economic and social world that is considerably more fluid and uncertain than that which existed after World War II until the mid-1970s. Both inflation and unemployment rates have become higher and less predictable at the same time that major shifts have taken place among industrial sectors and in the nature of employment demands and practices. In addition, there has been the constant presence of the overpowering American economy and the effects of the U.S. government's economic policies.

How have Canadians coped with these uncertainties? I can only venture a general answer based on aggregate trends. They reveal reactions in two spheres: as private individuals and as citizens involved in the political process.

Reactions as Private Individuals

Three issues appear to be especially salient for individual Canadians: Changing occupational trajectories and skill requirements, coping with the dual threats of inflation and unemployment, and confronting the effects of increased tax burdens. Indeed, when asked about the most "significant cause of stress in your life," "money" (25%) and "job" (22%) were the single most frequent answers given by respondents to a Gallup survey (15% indicated "nothing") (Gallup Canada, March 12, 1990).

Preparing oneself for the possibility of skill changes and changes in jobs has been a dominant theme in numerous accounts of the changing structure of employment (see, for example, Sharpe, 1990; Akyeampong, 1991; Duchesne, 1991). Most of these accounts are a lament on the failure of both the private and public sectors in upgrading basic skills.

On the other hand, there have been increased proportions of the population 15 years of age and older with "some" or completed postsecondary education, from 26% in 1977 (up from 12% in 1961) to projections of 38% in 2000 (Picot, 1980). There is also anecdotal evidence that increased proportions of older persons are entering universities.

The extent to which Canadians expect considerable movement among jobs is indicated by recent polls. A Gallup poll of full-and part-time workers conducted in April 1990 revealed that 45% of the respondents thought it "likely" that they would change employers in the next five years (Gallup Canada, April 12, 1990). Later that year, only 40% of the respondents employed outside the home "guessed" that they would be at the same type of job "you hold today" longer than 10 years, while 41% indicated they would be at the same job 5

years or less (Gallup Canada, November 19, 1990). In that same poll, 41%
of the respondents indicated that their job had "changed because of technology
in the last five years." In a study that surveyed students in two Canadian
universities, most respondents anticipated frequent moves among different jobs
in their occupational careers (Goldstein & Smucker, 1986).

The principal way in which Canadians are coping with the dual threats of
uncertain rates of inflation and the possibilities of unemployment appears to
be through increased participation rates in the labor force. From 1961 to 1989,
the rate of participation in the labor force increased from 55.1% to 67% (rates
based on the population 15 years of age and over) (see Table 3). The gradual
increase in participation rates can be traced back to 1901, when the rate was
53% of the population 14 years of age and over. (Of course, in a more
agriculturally based economy this low figure may be misleading.) Obviously,
this trend predates the period of change that is the focus of this chapter. Further,
it is one of gradual increase with no startling breaks in the pattern. However,
two features of this trend lead me to treat it, especially with regard to the years
since the mid-1970s, as one means of warding off the consequences of economic
uncertainties. These features are (a) differential rates of increase between males
and females and, controlling for gender, (b) differential rates of increase by
age group.

Clearly, the increased rates of participation for females account for the
increase in total participation as male rates decline and then hold steady. Four
explanations have been used to account for the increase in participation rates
for females: (a) industry has restructured its jobs in order to draw upon a pool
of low-wage female labor, (b) the feminist movement has encouraged women
to leave the household in search of independent means of livelihood, (c) women
are forced into the labor market in order to maintain a desired standard of

Table 3. Labor-Force Participation Rates[a]
15 Years and Over by Gender and Year

Year	Male	Female	Total
1961	80.8	29.1	55.1
1966	79.8	35.4	57.3
1971	76.4	39.9	58.0
1976	77.6	45.2	61.1
1981	78.3	51.6	64.7
1986	76.5	55.1	65.6
1989	76.7	57.9	67.0

Notes: [a] Rates are based on monthly seasonally unadjusted averages.
Source: *Historical Labor Force Statistics—Actual Data, Seasonal Factors, Seasonally Adjusted Data.* Ottawa: Statistics Canada (relevant years).

living for the household, and (d) women are forced into the labor market in order to provide security for themselves in the face of insecure marital relationships.

All of these explanations could be correct, but each one could be more relevant to a particular time period than another. The first explanation is usually documented by the growth of clerical occupations associated with organizational administration, a phenomenon that occurred before World War II and in the years after it. The second explanation usually accompanies accounts of the cultural revolution of the 1960s and early 1970s, and the last two explanations have been cited in accounting for participation rates from the 1970s to the present. When controlled for gender, the average annual percentage change in participation by age group indicates that the sequence of these explanations is indeed plausible (see Table 4).

The greatest average annual percentage change during 1961-71 occurred among the younger women, those 15 to 19 years of age and those 20 to 24. In 1971-81 the greatest growth rates occurred among females aged 25-44 years, and in 1981-88 the largest growth rate occurred in the age groups 24-44 and 45-65. These patterns may merely be due to the movement of a unique (baby "boomers") aging cohort of women through the labor force. The sequence of explanations may simply be following this movement. That more is at stake is indicated when these patterns of change are compared with those of males in similar age groups. They are decidedly different and provide comparative evidence that more older women entered the labor force than can be accounted for by an aging cohort. The aging cohort model does not explain the male pattern.

The hypothesis that the more recent increase in participation rates among women is a means of coping with uncertainty is given further credence by research on dual-income families and on participation rates of wives of high-income families.

Dual-earner families have increased from 34% of all family units in 1967 to 62% in 1986. Over the same period families in which the husband is the sole wage earner have declined from 61% to 27%. In 1986, dual-income families earned an average of $10,000 more than single-earner families, with the total averages being $50,000 versus $40,000. The average income level of wives was 29% of their husbands' incomes. Of the families in the upper fifth income quintile, 81% were dual earners, whereas in the lowest income quintile the share of dual-income families among husband-wife family units was only 35%. Four percent of dual income families were below the poverty line. Without the income of wives, the proportion of family units under the poverty line would have increased another 14% (Moore, 1989, pp. 24-26).

Finally, a recent finding that higher proportions of young adults are remaining with their families of origin indicates that households are becoming

Table 4. Average Annual Percentage Change:
Labor-Force Participation by Age and Gender

	Females			Males		
Age	1961-71	1971-81	1981-88	1961-71	1971-81	1981-88
15-19	4.2	3.4	-2.1	3.4	3.3	-2.6
20-24	7.3	3.7	-1.0	4.2	3.0	-1.7
25-44	1.2	7.6	4.8	1.2	2.6	2.2
45-64	2.7	3.5	2.9	2.1	0.6	0.3
65 +	3.0	2.0	-1.3	1.5	-0.9	-0.5

Source: McKitrick, R. (1989). *The current industrial relations scene in Canada, 1989: The economy and labor markets, reference tables.* Kingston, Ontario: Industrial Relations Centre, Queens University Press (Table 48, p. 159).

more important as economic units. This reverses a trend apparent during the period 1971-81 (Boyd & Pryor, 1988, cited in Myles et al., 1988, p. 98).

Participation in the underground economy is another form of coping with economic uncertainties and unacceptably high costs. Evidence of this activity has been presented in previous chapters. It is difficult to estimate the extent of this activity in Canada. Certainly, on an anecdotal basis everyone is familiar with unreported income payed for domestic services and home repair and renovation. Elsewhere, notably in Norway and Italy, there have been attempts to estimate the numbers of people involved in the underground economy, but such estimates are plagued by rather tenuous assumptions about the implications of changing rates of participation in the official labor force (Ethier, 1985, p. 82). There are a variety of other economic models that have been used, tax evasion estimates, cash transactions, and monetary methods (e.g., using the ratio between real per capital currency and demand deposits). Estimates of the extent of the underground economy in Canada, based on monetary models range between 5% and 8% of the GNP (Ethier, 1985, p. 101). But this result takes into account not only the transactions among individuals but corporations as well.[18] It is impossible to convert this figure into numbers of people.

Perhaps a more dramatic coping response, especially in circumventing increased taxation, an issue that is currently even more vexatious to Canadians than either inflation or unemployment, is illustrated by the huge increase in the numbers of Canadians making purchases in the United States. With about 80% of the Canadian population stretched along the United States border within a band 165 kilometres wide and some 3,000 kilometers long, the temptation to purchase clothing, groceries, gasoline, and other consumer goods at cheaper prices has proved irresistible. In a survey sponsored by the Ontario government, it was estimated that shopping in the United States "will drain $2.2 billion and at least 14,000 jobs from the Ontario economy this year [1991]" ("Shopping," 1991). Similar reports on other regions have been published.

The Reaction of Canadians as Citizens

While Canadians have been taking steps to protect their own individual economic interests, an additional question is whether they have changed their views regarding the effectiveness of governments and major institutions in society. Canadians are very much aware that the policies of their governments are highly influenced by foreign economies and the actions of foreign governments, particularly those of the United States. Nevertheless, like most electorates, they hold their own governments responsible for the well-being of the nation and, ultimately, the well-being of themselves.

Since 1964, and intermittently in the intervening years up to 1979 and then quarterly since 1983, when the Gallup organization asked its respondents about the major problems confronting their country, "the economy" (including "inflation") and "unemployment" have been the single most dominant responses (see Figure 2).

As Figure 2 indicates, the proportion of respondents who think the economy is the major problem tends to swing upward when there are rather sharp swings up in the consumer price index (CPI) for all products, but it decreases if the CPI maintains a steady, though modest, rate of increase. Worries about unemployment tend to follow variations in the unemployment rate. In recent years there have been smaller proportions of respondents defining the economy and unemployment as the major problems.

At the beginning of 1991, Canadian reactions to a list of issues "currently discussed in Canada" were registered by a Gallup poll. The issues eliciting the highest proportions of the response "very concerned" were "environment" (74%), "government tax levels" (73%), and "honesty in government" (72%). These issues were followed by "unemployment" (69%) and "inflation" (65%). Only 46% of the respondents indicated they were very concerned about "Canadian unity," and 26% were very concerned about "Quebec separation," although in Quebec itself 45% were very concerned (Gallup Canada, January 14, 1991).

The current government was elected in 1984 and re-elected in 1988 on a platform that characterized the previous government as having been engaged in profligate spending in support of programs that the country could ill afford. The central message of the Progressive-Conservative party was that less government intervention and greater freedom among economic actors would lead to a stronger economy. In general Canadians have supported the idea that government intervention is to be avoided. Trend data from Gallup polls reveal that a progressively larger proportion of Canadians believe that "big government" "will be the biggest threat to Canada for years to come."

It is somewhat difficult to ascertain whether the responses are reactions to the adjective "big" or to the referent itself. If the former, it suggests that

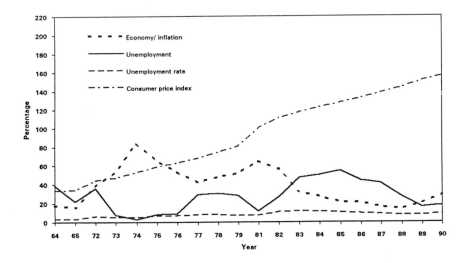

Note: Adapted from Gallup Canada (Canadian Institute of Public Opinion). (various years). *The Gallup Report* (January 1, 1991). Toronto: Canadian Institute of Public Opinion. For unemployment rates and the consumer price index: Statistics Canada (1990). *The Canadian Economic Observer: Historical Supplement 1989/90.* Ottawa: Minister of Supply and Services.

Figure 2. The Most Important Problem Facing Canada Today

Canadians support the neoclassical bent of the Mulroney government. If the latter, it suggests declining confidence in the government's policies. (The shifts have been largely from "big labor," whereas perceptions regarding "big business" have remained relatively constant.)

A first approximation to the answer is provided by trend data from Gallup polls on satisfaction regarding the "direction of the country" for comparable years from 1960 to 1990. These data show a relatively large percentage of respondents who were satisfied in 1960 (56%); a decline to 30% in 1980; a slight increase in 1985, the year following the election of the current government; and a fall to a low of 15% in 1990. There is evidence of a general lack of "respect [for] and confidence [in] governments." When poll respondents were asked to rank seven listed "institutions" according to these two criteria, only 17% indicated that they had a "great deal" or "quite a lot" of respect for the federal government; 28% gave the same response for their provincial governments. These percentages ranked below airlines (61%), banks (60%), and automobile companies (29%). The federal government ranked at the bottom, below steel companies (25%) and oil companies (19%) (Gallup Canada, September 17, 1990). In February 1991 the proportion of respondents having such confidence in the federal government fell to only 9%, marginally higher than "political parties" (7%) and well below banks, large corporations, provincial governments, and labor unions (Gallup Canada, February 20, 1991).

The evidence suggests a loss of support for government policies, not just the size of the government. Still, Canadians have not withdrawn from the political process. The proportion of Canadians who *disagree* with the statement that "the average Canadian can't really do very much to change the course of events in Canada" has *increased* from a low of 33% in 1980 to a high of 48% in 1983, dipping to 46% in 1990 (Decima Research, Spring 1990, p. 25).[19] Canadians may be disappointed in their government, but they have not given up on themselves.

A CHANGE IN VALUES?

Most observers tend to agree that the dominant political culture for the two founding groups of Canada, the English and the French, stems from a "Tory counterrevoutionary ethos," a reaction against the liberal revolutions of both the United States and France (Lipset, 1990b, p. 4; see also Lipset, 1990a). In this tradition the state is viewed as a key agent in protecting the rights of minority groups and in providing essential services for a widely dispersed population. The parliamentary system of government has provided the framework for institutionalized expressions of dissent. At the same time Canadians live with the constant presence of American expressions of classical liberalism and its emphasis upon individualism and basic distrust of statist solutions.

Canadians did not escape the effects of the American cultural revolution of the 1960s. Like the Americans, the unusually large cohort of youth who experienced the effects of that revolution appeared, by the 1980s, to have redefined the benign themes of "self-actualization," as defined by Inglehart, into economic-centered expressions of achieving affluence and security.[20] At least this is what public expressions of values seemed to portray. Expressions of the new form of individualism could be seen in images of "fast-track" achievers in advertisements; in the defensive postures of serious-looking clothing store maniquins; in popular American-made television programs whose central characters were tough business personalities or lawyers; and in increasingly brutal themes of individual prowess in films, also dominated largely by American producers. Those who became business leaders repeated the American motto of the need to become "mean and lean." Instead of the theme of the 1960s and early 1970s that one had to "drop out" of the system in order to achieve a desired quality of life, full participation in and the manipulation of the sytem came to be portrayed as the means to achieve that quality.

Whether these images were accurate indices of values that individual Canadians held or whether they were the expressions of a popular culture glorifying aggressive behavior in an ethos of economic insecurity is difficult to determine. Canadians altered their behavior and perceptions in the face of economic and political changes. It is not clear, however, that this has meant a fundamental change in values. As Merton (1957) pointed out long ago, individuals may employ very different means to attain commonly held cultural goals (or values) (pp. 273-320). Further, it is difficult to determine at what point "means" become entrenched as "values."

Inglehart believed, in the 1970s, that new values of self-actualization had replaced an earlier, largely instrumental orientation to economic survival. It is consistent with his thesis to argue that values would shift back toward an instrumental orientation if economic uncertainties return. Did these changes occur by the 1980s and, if so, is there evidence of further change at the end of that decade?

There is no good base-line data to assess this thesis, but if, during the 1980s, Canadians were more concerned with maximizing their economic standards of living than with achieving some level of "self-actualization," it would be reasonable on the basis of the general argument to expect that they would care less about the work that they do and more about merely gaining an adequate income.

Data gathered through Decima research from 1980 through 1983 indicate that the work people do was more important to them than the income they earned from it. This holds true for all levels of income, although the differences between importance of work and income decrease as the income level decreases. What is even more striking is that, as jobs became more insecure during the recession of 1982-83, the mean scores by which work was ranked as more important than income actually increased for all income quintile levels (*Decima Quarterly Report,* cited in Johnston, 1986, p. 151).[21] Of course, this may merely mean that the emphasis placed upon work indicates not a rejection of income as important but rather the concern for security—a steady job with an assured income.

This series of questions has not been continued, but in 1989 the Decima research organization found that 76% of its sample of Canadians agreed with the statement that "my job is a big part of how I see myself" and that only 39% agreed with the statement that "I only work to pay the bills" (Decima Research, Winter 1989, p. 170). Further, 48% of Decima respondents in 1990 indicated that they would continue to work at the same job, and 26% indicated they would work but at a different job even if they "didn't need the money" (Decima Research, Winter 1989, p. 171). This represents remarkably little change from a national survey conducted in 1974, in which 70% of males and 73% of females who were working indicated that they worked "more because I like to than because I have to" (Burstein, Tienhaara, Hewson, & Warrander, 1975, p. 19). In the same survey, only 16% of the respondents agreed with the statement that "work is a way to make money and I don't expect to get any special satisfaction or enjoyment from doing it" (Burstein, et al., 1975, p. 19). A survey conducted in Edmonton, Alberta, revealed similar responses. Only 11% of the respondents agreed with the statement, "I don't care what job I do as long as it pays well" (Krahn & Lowe, 1988, p. 158).

The intrinsic value placed upon work remained relatively constant from 1975 through 1990. But it is possible that this value takes on a different nuance as economic security changes. The importance placed on work in the 1970s may have meant that it should provide a context for self-actualization as described by Inglehart (1977, p. 55), whereas in the 1980s it may have meant a defense against economic and social insecurity. Accordingly, it is possible that, with the increased instability of the family unit, the work role has acquired increased importance not only as economic security but as a context for meaningful social support and identification.

In the survey by Decima in winter 1989, respondents were asked why they continued in their present jobs. Although 87% answered that salary was an "excellent" or "good" reason, 82% also answered that an employer's loyalty was also an "excellent" or "good" reason, as were co-workers (84%) and employers' sensitivity to personal needs (80%) (Decima Research, Winter 1989, p. 175).

These findings may encourage one to believe that, in the face of increased instability in marital relations and households, the work role is assuming expanded functions as an important locus for meaningful social relationships. However true this *may* have been in the recent past, current evidence indicates that it does not seem to be the case as the decade of the 1990s begins.

There is an abundance of material on the increase in insecurity and stress in individual lives created by dual career families, marital breakdown, and unstable household units. (For a recent review of the literature, see Burke & Greenglass, 1987). But, contrary to what one might expect, there is no evidence that Canadians care any less about family life.[22] In the Decima survey of 1989, 51% of all respondents who were working claimed that their families had become "much more important" to them as "a part of [their] lives," and 36% claimed that their families were becoming at least "somewhat more important." The responses varied by occupational level, with a slightly higher percentage of manual laborers or workers in semiskilled or skilled trades indicating that the family had grown in importance (91%) in contrast to those in clerical, sales, or service jobs (86%), those in technical or professional occupations (88%), and those in supervisory or managerial occupations (86%) (Decima Research, Winter 1989, p. 172).

Of course, no one knows the original reference point by which to assess "more important," but the data do provide evidence that the importance of the family is not to be dismissed. Despite the absence of base-line data for the early 1980s, it was argued in the *Decima Quarterly Report* (Winter, 1989, p. 163) that data gathered in 1989 indicated a shift in values from the 1980s, when "single-minded acquisition" seemed to characterize Canadians, back to broader values that include both the quality of the work role and the importance of family life. Work, according to Decima's interpretation of its surveys, has become a more important part of individuals' lives, but so too has the family. If this is indeed true, my interpretation would be slightly different from that of the Decima organization. There is reason to believe that Canadians in general never accepted the images presented by icons of popular culture in the 1980s even though they may have been forced to act as if they did.

The evidence seems to support the view that, at least since the mid-1970s, Canadians have never strayed from the idea that work should provide meaningful activity. They may have become more aggressive during the 1980s in making sure that they could obtain and hold on to jobs that they desired, and greater numbers of them may have had to seek employment in order to maintain a desired standard of living, but this apparently has not changed their basic values in the orientations they hold toward work and family.

If these interpretations are accurate, then it is not surprising that Canadians appear to be pessimistic about their lives in the near future. Both economic and political uncertainties have made it more difficult to act on the values they would like to associate with work and the family, the values of liberty, equality, and security. The economic and political mechanisms that once ensured a modicum of compatibility among these values seem to have failed. From the public's point of view, the solutions offered by the Canadian version of neoclassical liberalism, applied since 1984, have only made matters worse. Perhaps the 1980s showed the dark side of individual liberty and the prominence of security at the cost of equality. Whether these values can again be made compatible remains to be seen as the Mulroney era draws to a close.

ACKNOWLEDGMENTS

I wish to thank members of the research group for the effects of their stimulating discussions and insights in writing this chapter. The research was supported in part by funds from the Social Sciences and Humanities Research Council of Canada.

NOTES

1. The survey, conducted by the United Nations Development Program, based Canada's ranking on indicators such as life span, literacy, and purchasing power. Despite the country's ranking on these measures, the information officer of the program noted that Canada had one of the widest income disparities in the world—nearly "five times as bad as the best of the industrialized countries"—and exceeded only by the United States. The UN commission also noted the "weakening of social fabric among the wealthy industrial countries," including Canada.

2. Through the years, the more dramatic increases in pessimism appear to precede formal announcements from economists that a recession is in progress.

3. The other countries were the United States, Great Britain, West Germany, Switzerland, France, Austria, Greece, India, Uruguay, and The Netherlands.

4. One radio host of a weekly nation-wide phone-in show wrote in a national newspaper that politicians "ignore to their peril the depth of current Canadian wrath" (Conlon, 1991).

5. From 1945 through 1980, Canada experienced seven recessions: the fourth through the third quarters, 1948-49; the second through the fourth quarters in 1951; the third through the second quarters, 1953-54; the first through the fourth quarters in 1957; the fifth through the first quarters, 1960-61; the third through the first quarters, 1974-75; and the fourth through the second quarters, 1979-80.

Except for the recession after the Korean War in 1953, during which the real GNP declined by 2.6%, and the decline of 1.1% in 1960-61, the remaining recessions, including the one after the oil-price shocks of 1973, resulted in declines of less than 1%. This is in marked contrast to the recession of 1981-82, during which there was a 6.6% decline in real GNP. In the recession of 1981-82, 95% of all industries had declining output, 10 percentage points higher than the highest of all other recessions, 1979-80 (McKitrick, 1989, Table 10, pp. 39-41).

6. Having taken office after the 1981-82 recession, the new government had actually been more a beneficiary than an engineer of the reduction in unemployment at that time. The recession of 1990-91, during which Mulroney was still in office, again raised unemployment to nearly 11%, which nearly equaled the rates of the recession in 1981-82.

7. These rates varied considerably by industry. The most drastic declines were in mining, transportation, communication, transportation and storage, wholesale trade, and services. Other sectors, including manufacturing, maintained relatively constant real profits after taxes. Part of the variation, of course, must be attributed to taxation policies.

8. The increase in the production of specialized products rather than long production runs of standardized products, for example, requires increased input from engineers, production managers, and sales personnel, all of whom may be included in either the service sector or the manufacturing sector, depending upon the type of enterprise that hires them. Innovations in the organization of goods production such as "just-in-time" inventory control also increase the use of "services" (see Economic Council of Canada, 1990, p. 4; Reich, 1991, pp. 37-38). Still, the fact that many goods-producing enterprises increasingly rely on these services and contract many of them out to specialized agencies creates significant changes in the economic lives of many individuals.

9. The decline of employment in agriculture has been a major cause for the decline of the goods-producing sector. It should also be remembered that these are proportionate declines. Some sectors of goods production have actually increased, such as the manufacture of telecommunications equipment. Further, until 1990, the absolute size of the labor force had steadily increased from 7,493,000 in 1966 to 13,503,000 in 1989, with participation rates increasing from 57% in 1966 to 67% in 1989 (Statistics Canada, 1990, Table 2.1, p. 32; see also Baldwin & Gorecki, 1990, pp. 15-16). During 1990 the participation rate declined slightly to 66.7%.

10. The relatively small percentage of the labor force employed in services in West Germany may account, in part, for the low participation rates of women in the labor force there.

11. Some historical perspective should be added here. During the late 1950s and early 1960s goods-producing industries and manufacturing in particular underwent considerable structural and occupational change with the introduction of newly designed automated equipment. Baldwin and Gorecki (1990) point out that structural change was considerably less during the 1970s than in the two earlier decades.

12. As the number of young people has been declining, it remains to be seen how this will alter the nature and supply of these jobs (Kumar & Coats, 1989, p. 65). That this trend toward a bifurcated labor market is not merely a function of an "internal logic" of capitalism is indicated by its absence in Germany and Sweden. Esping-Anderson (1987) pointed out that wage policies and the comprehensive welfare state in Sweden crowds out the market for low-wage, unskilled service industries (cited in Myles, n.d.).

13. Part-time employment alone has increased from 6% of total employment in 1960 to 12% in 1970, 13% in 1980, and 15% in 1988. In 1988, 24% of those who were part-time employees preferred to work full-time, whereas in 1975 only 11% held to that preference (McKitrick, 1989, Tables 25 and 30, pp. 114, 120).

14. In addition to simple models of wage flexibility, many firms have adopted "nontraditional reward systems." They include gain-sharing, small-group incentives, pay for knowledge, lump-sum bonuses, profit-sharing, individual incentive schemes, all-salaried systems, earned time off, and two-tier wage systems. In a survey of some 1,600 firms in Canada and the United States, McAdams (1988) reported that over 75% of the sample had implemented at least one of these forms. Thirty to forty percent of the firms adopted "performance-based reward systems": gain-sharing, small-group incentives, pay for knowledge, or lump-sum bonuses, with the most prevalent being lump-sum bonuses (pp. 17-18).

15. What further complicates this prognosis are the simultaneous effects of (a) the recently signed free-trade agreement with the United States, (b) the high interest rate policy of the Bank of Canada, endorsed by the present federal government, (c) the resulting overvaluation of the Canadian dollar, and (d) the impending free-trade agreement between the United States and Mexico.

16. In 1989 the unemployment rate stood at 7.5% but then rose rapidly to 8.1% in 1990. At the end of 1990 the rate jumped to 10%, and by June of 1991 the unemployment rate surpassed 11%. (Part of this increase can be attributed to students seeking summer jobs.)

17. Until 1976 the movement had been dominated by American-based unions, with their Canadian counterparts often being treated as mere regional branches. This had not always served the best interests of Canadian workers. In 1989 the proportion of workers belonging to unions headquartered in the United States was 32.4%. (The highest proportion of Canadians belonging to American unions was in 1911, when these unions claimed 89.7% of Canadian members.) The proportionate decrease of Canadian membership in American unions has been partly due to the growth of union membership among workers in the public sector and a steady growth of smaller, Canadian-based unions in the private industrial sector. More recently, there have been withdrawals of a number of industrial unions from their American headquarters. Most notable in this regard has been the withdrawal of the Canadian subsidiary from the United Automobile Workers.

18. A major problem in making estimates of the underground economy is definitional. Clearly, cash transactions that are not reported for tax purposes are one form of activity in an underground economy. But exchange of services is more difficult to define in such a matter. When should household work be part of the official accounting of the GNP and when should it be part of the normal range of activities carried on outside the market?

19. In comparison to Americans, Canadians have a higher rate of participation in the political process (voting and party membership). This may be attributed to the party discipline of the parliamentary system and a greater number of political parties offering institutional expression of dissent.

20. Perhaps the archetype of this transformation is the person of Gerry Rubin, one of the "Chicago Seven" of 1986, who became a New York stockbroker in the mid-1980s.

21. The item was: "The amount of money I receive for the work I do is more important to me than the type of work I do." It was followed by a ten-point scale of agreement to disagreement (+5 to −5). An example of differences by income is the distribution of mean scores by income quintile in 1983. The scores favoring work, listed from the highest quintiles were: −.77, −1.32, 1.32, −1.58, −1.73.

22. Contrary to the current vogue within Canadian sociology to dismiss the family as a viable unit, the general population of Canadians appears to remain committed to at least the idea of it.

REFERENCES

Akyeampong, E. B. (1991, spring). Apprentices: Graduate and drop-out labor market performances. *Perspectives on Labor and Income, 3*(1), 7-15.

Allen, D. (1985, May). *Analysis of the steel industry labor market and the adjustments facing its work force.* Paper prepared for the United Steelworkers of America, Canadian Steel Trade Conference, Sault Ste. Marie, Ontario, Canada.

Baldwin, J. R., & Gorecki, P. K. (1990). *Structural change and the adjustment process.* Ottawa: Statistics Canada and the Economic Council of Canada, Minister of Supply and Services.

Bell, D. (1973). *The coming of post-industrial society.* New York: Basic Books.

Betcherman, G., Newton K., & Godin, J. (1990). *Two steps forward: Human resource management in a high-tech world.* Ottawa: Economic Council of Canada.

Boyd, M., & Prior, E. (1988, June). *The crowded nest: Living arrangements of young Canadian adults.* Paper presented at the annual meetings of the Canadian Population Society, Windsor, Ontario.

Burke, R. J., & Greenglass, E. (1987). Work and family. In C. L. Cooper & I. T. Robertson (Eds.), *International review of industrial and organizational psychology* (pp. 273-320). New York: John Wiley.

Burstein, M., Tienhaara, N., Hewson, P., & Warrander, B. (1975). *Canadian work values: Findings of a Wore ethic survey and job satisfaction survey.* Ottawa: Manpower and Immigration.

Canada second only to Japan in survey of best places to live. (1991, May 23). *The Globe and Mail,* A1, A2.

The Canadian Economic Observer. (1990). *Historical statistical supplement 1989/90.* Ottawa: Minister of Supply and Services.

Caves, R. E. (1990). *Adjustment to international competition.* Ottawa: Economic Council of Canada.

Charette, M. F., Robert P. H., & Kaufmann, B. (1986) The evolution of the Canadian industrial structure: An international perspective. In D.G. McFetridge (Research Coordinator), *Canadian industry in transition* (pp. 61-134). Toronto: University of Toronto Press.

Coates, M. L., Arrowsmith, D., & Courchene, M. (1989). *The labor movement and trade unionism reference tables.* Kingston: Industrial Relations Centre, Queens University.

Conlon, P. (1991, April 1). How angry are Canadians? Just listen to the phone calls. *The Globe and Mail,* A17.

Courchene, M. (1989). *The current industrial relations scene in Canada, 1989: Wages, productivity and labor costs, reference tables.* Kingston: Industrial Relations Centre, Queen's University.

Courchene, T. (1987). *Social policy in the 1990s: Agenda for reform.* Scarborough: Prentice-Hall Canada.

Decima Research (Various years). *Detailed analysis. The Decima quarterly report.* Toronto: Decima Research Ltd. and Public Affairs International Ltd.

Doern, G. B., Maslove, A. M., & Prince, M. J. (1988). *Budgeting in Canada: Politics, economics and management.* Ottawa: Carleton University Press.

Duchesne, D. (1991, spring). Gail Cook Johnson speaks out on human resource issues. *Perspectives on Labor and Income, 3*(1), 16-26.

Economic Council of Canada. (1990). *Good jobs, bad jobs: Employment in the servive sector.* Ottawa: Ministry of Supply and Services.

Esping-Andersen, G. (1987). *Post-industrial employment trajectories: Germany, Sweden and the United States.* Florence: Department of Politics, European University.

Ethier, M. (1985). The underground economy: A review of the economic literature and new estimates for Canada. In F. Vaillancourt (Research Coordinator), *Income distribution and economic security in Canada* (pp. 77-109). Toronto: University of Toronto Press.

Gallup Canada (The Canadian Institute of Public Opinion). (Various years). *The Gallup Report.* Toronto: The Canadian Institute of Public Opinion.

Gherson, G. (1990, April 30). Canada's economy shrugs off Crows's interest-rate burden. *Financial Times of Canada,* 4.

Goldstein, J., & Smucker, J. (1986, December). Multi-tracking: The success ethic in an era of diminishing opportunities. *Youth and Society, 18,* 127-149.

Inglehart, R. (1977). *The silent revolution: Changing values and political styles among western publics.* Princeton, NJ: Princeton University Press.

Johnson, G., & Grey, R. (1988, spring). Trends in employee attitudes: Signs of diminishing employee commitment. *Canadian Business Review,* 20-23.

Johnston, R. (1986). *Public opinion and public policy in Canada.* Toronto: University of Toronto Press.

Krahn, H., & Lowe, G. (1988). *Work and industry in Canadian society.* Scarborough: Nelson Canada.

Kumar, P., & Coates, M. L. (1989). *Industrial relations in 1989: Trends and emerging issues.* Kingston: Industrial Relations Centre, Queens University.

Lipset, S. M. (1990a). *Continental divide: The values and institutions of the United States and Canada.* New York: Routledge.

————. (1990b). Labor and socialism in Canada and the United States. *Larry Sefton Memorial Lecture,* Toronto, Woodsworth College, University of Toronto.

McAdams, J. L. (1988, spring). Performance-based reward systems. *Canadian Business Review,* 17-19.

McKitrick, R. (1989). *The current industrial relations scene in Canada, 1989: The economy and labor markets, reference tables.* Kingston: Industrial Relations Centre, Queens University Press.

Merton, R. (1957). *Social theory and social structure.* Glencoe, IL: Basic Books.

Moore, M. (1989). Dual earner families: The new norm. *Canadian Social Trends.* Statistics Canada, No. 12, 24-29.

Myles, J. (n.d.). *The expanding middle: Some Canadian evidence on the deskilling debate* (Research Paper Series, No. 9). Ottawa: Carleton University and Statistics Canada.

Myles, J., Picot, G., & Wannell, T. (1988). *Wages and jobs in the 1980s: Changing youth wages and the declining middle* (Analytical Studies, No. 17). Ottawa: Social and Economic Studies Division, Statistics Canada.

Panitch, L., & Schwartz, D. (1985). *From consent to coercion: The assault on trade union freedom* Toronto: Garamond Press.

Picot, G. (1980). *The changing educational profile of Canadians, 1961-2000.* Ottawa: Projections Section, Education, Science and Culture Division, Statistics Canada.

Pinfield, L., & Atkinson, J. S. (1988, winter). The flexible firm. *Canadian Business Review,* 17-19.

Rahman, S.S., Gera, S., & Touchie, J. (1989). *Long-term unemployment: The Canadian experience.* Paper prepared for the Economic Council of Canada, Ottawa, Minister of Supply and Services.

Reich, R. B. (1991, February). The real economy. *The Atlantic,* 35-52.

Riddell, W. C. (1986). *Dealing with inflation and unemployment in Canada.* Toronto: University of Toronto Press.

Sharpe, A. (1990, winter). Training the work force: A challenge facing Canada in the '90s. *Perspectives on Labor and Income, 2*(4), 21-31.

Shopping in U.S. hurting Ontario. (1991, June 7). *The Globe and Mail,* B3.

Smucker, J. (1988). La culture de l'organisation comme ideologie de gestion: une analyse critique. In G. Symons (Ed.), *La culture des organisations* (pp. 39-68). Quebec: Institute Quebecoise des Recherches sur la Culture.

Statistics Canada. (1990). *The Canadian economic observer: Historical statistical supplement 1989/90.* Ottawa: Minister of Supply and Services.

BRITISH ECONOMIC VALUES IN
MRS. THATCHER'S LABORATORY

Jonathan Gershuny

The various contributions to this collection of essays discuss the distinctive national experiences of economic changes in the 1980s. The changes in the Eastern European countries over that decade were as important as any in their histories. By contrast, changes in the West were, with one exception, relatively unexciting. The exception is Britain, which has also experienced a radical and quite unpredicted change of mood and style of economic management since the late 1970s.

The distinctive characteristic of economic change in 1980s Britain is that bundle of economic policies and moral prescriptions known as Thatcherism, named after the woman who served as British Prime Minister throughout the decade. Although the actual changes are of comparatively trivial importance to the lives of the majority of the population, the rhetoric (the counterrevolutionary slogans, the proclaimed determination to uproot the deeply buried mechanisms of state control and to banish socialism from British political life) is somewhat similar to the political language of the successful eastern European oppositions of the 1980s. Indeed, the widely expressed enthusiasm for Thatcherism, and for Mrs. Thatcher herself, from eastern European publics and politicians, as well as the new lines of economic policy adopted by many of the new governments in eastern Europe, certainly support this analogy.

Has the British economic counterrevolution been successful? If only because of the analogy with events in eastern Europe, the answer to this question is of more than merely local importance. Mrs. Thatcher's success would serve as an agreeably optimistic overture to the grand opera of Eastern European economic progress in the 1990s; but what if she has failed?

There are two components to the Thatcher program. The first has to do with the material facts of the structure and operation of the British economy. It involves the reduction of the discretionary role of the state in the management of the economy and the removal of organized labor from any position of influence on government; the ending of substantial state ownership of industry; the reduction of state expenditure on education, medical, and welfare services, to be replaced (in at least the latter two cases) by privately funded services for all but the poor and improvident; and the reduction of levels of taxation (and of unemployment support) to provide rewards for hard work (and sanctions against laziness). The second component is ideological. Accompanying the institutions of the welfare state is a political and economic culture that both supports and feeds on it. If Thatcherism is to be successful in demolishing the welfare state, it must also destroy what in its terms is the "welfare ideology." It must erode the public support for the old structures and modes of operation of the British economy. It much change the British economic culture.

The first component of the program has visibly had some considerable success. The recent changes in British economic structure and institutions are well known, and we shall not rehearse them here at any length. For the last decade the government has involved itself in the minimum of economic regulation, fixing tax and public expenditure levels and advising interest rate changes to the Bank of England, but has made no attempt to influence pay or price levels or the availability of credit, or to undertake any Keynesian countercyclical public works. It has rigorously excluded trades unions from any role in economic policy-making (and at the same time reduced many of the unions' previous legal rights and immunities). A large part of the previous state holdings of industries and public utilities have been placed in private ownership. State expenditure on the direct provision of services has been contained if not in real terms reduced. Levels of taxation on higher incomes have been very sharply reduced, while the real levels of unemployment pay, as well as the proportion of the unemployed who are permitted to claim it, have fallen.

But these changes will constitute a real and fundamental shift in economic direction only if they are sustained. And they can be only sustained if the underlying economic culture, the patterns of economic attitudes and behaviors, has also changed, and changed in the same direction. In what follows, I shall examine some of the evidence of change in British economic culture during the 1980s. But before we turn to the empirical material, I must first assert a particular view of the nature of economic culture in relation to what may or may not be underlying economic values.

ECONOMIC CULTURE AND ECONOMIC VALUES

"Culture" comprises phenomena that may be directly observed by social scientists. Where individuals' behavior is repeated with only trivial variation over time, we may infer that it is habitual; where it proceeds independently of calculations of personal advantage, and yet we find similarities in behavior across various individuals with broadly similar social locations, it may be presumed to be normal (i.e., informed by norms) or customary. Beliefs may be directly explicated by questioning. Some respondents, of course, may intentionally give misleading answers (and the beliefs themselves may be directly influenced by the questions asked and the way they are asked). Nevertheless, since the essence of the notion of a "belief" is that it is consciously believed, beliefs must be in principle ascertainable. Habits, customs, and beliefs may be quite straightforwardly and routinely measured.

These attributes of a culture change over time. Week by week, year by year, there emerge new habits, customs, and beliefs. The economic environment changes, new ecological consequences of behavioral patterns develop, or cultural attributes may spontaneously mutate. Thus, new technologies may lead to changes in labor demand and, hence, to novel work patterns such as job sharing. Thus, new patterns of women's paid work, or new beliefs about it, may lead to innovations in the leisure of men or in their patterns of involvement in childcare. Or, quite independent of any direct economic or social pressures, older women may seek paid employment, whereas previously women at a similar stage in their lifecourse might not have done so.

It is therefore quite meaningful for a politician to talk of the actions of the state as having the potential to bring about change in economic culture. Governments provide the framework within which economic activity takes place. If, for example, particular welfare services are desired, and continue to be desired even when the state ceases to provide them, then it is not implausible to think that people might wish to devote the extra disposable income that results from the lower taxes that come with lower levels of provision, to the purchase of similar services from some nonstate institution. And as such behavior becomes habitual and customary, so, since we all seek to make our beliefs consistent with our behavior, we might expect change in the nature of our expressed beliefs about the responsibility of the state for providing welfare services.

Obviously, beliefs do not change by fiat, and they do not change overnight. Some beliefs may be more difficult to change than others. But given time and the appropriate circumstances, some beliefs may change. The radical Thatcherite Tories could well have been acting on the basis of a quite sophisticated sociological notion, the management of cognitive dissonance. If we are made to do something, despite beliefs that would lead us to do otherwise, then, over time and providing that there are no pressing reasons to the contrary, we may well adjust our beliefs to bring them into consonance with their actions. *Ceteris paribus,* people take the line of least psychological resistance. Change what the state does, said the radical Tories, and over time we change peoples' beliefs about what the state ought to do.

But though politicians may *attempt* the manipulation of culture, the culture may not be readily manipulable in some particular directions. Below the surface of cultural attributes there are, or may be, deeper, much more difficult to observe phenomena, that may indeed only be seen directly under quite exceptional circumstances. There may be deeply held values, fundamental to the individual's personality and capable of acting as a constraint on changes in the individual's behavior and beliefs. People may be strongly encouraged to change their patterns of action or systems of belief in certain ways and indeed feel that it would be convenient to do so, but they may still find themselves incapable of changing them. The dramatic cases of religious and political martyrs are familiar. In a less dramatic way and among at least some members of some societies, there may be deeply held values in the economic sphere that concern such issues as distributive justice or the protection of the physical environment, values that will serve to constrain the direction of development of cultural norms and beliefs.

Such fundamental values, where they can be shown to exist, will have a complex relationship to the more superficial cultural attributes of the society. These deeply held values are essentially individual attributes; yet plainly they are learned, they are in some way inferred from the individual's own culture, or exceptionally from elsewhere. Culture produces the values. Yet most cultural beliefs may not represent deeply held values. The distinction as I have stated it so far is, of course, much too absolute. Even saints can be tempted. Values may be more or less deeply entrenched, and any individual might in principle hold a series of beliefs on various subjects, of which some change from day to day, others may be changed with difficulty over an extended period, and still others be completely immovable. We might, rather than a simple dichotomy, think of a continuum of ideological tenacity running from the superficial and malleable belief to the deeply held value.

The existence or potential existence of these more tenacious values poses a practical as well as a philosophical problem. We are accustomed to measuring beliefs through attitude surveys. People are able to tell us their current beliefs. But how do we set about empirically identifying which of these stated beliefs represent deeply held values that will not change in response to external pressures? Religious inquisitions and political police have access to experimental methods that are not available to social scientists. And if we cannot in general say which beliefs are held tenaciously, so the possibility of manipulating a culture in a particular direction will be difficult to predict.

We cannot identify deeply held values prospectively, but there are special circumstances in which we may be able to do so retrospectively. If, over an extended period of time, there are strong political and economic pressures of a sort that might encourage beliefs to change in a particular direction, and yet these beliefs do not change in this expected direction, then we may perhaps infer that the change is contrary to some more deeply held value. Of course, the influence of economic and political pressures on economic beliefs might be resisted because they cut across personal interests. But we can control them in our analysis. We must, of course, be cautious in drawing conclusions: There are other influences than just public policy (e.g., independent media, political oppositions) on the direction of public debate about economic issues, and they also must influence individuals' statement of economic belief. But the general principle stands: The more heavily the force of circumstances promotes the development of a particular belief, the more certain we may be that *resistance* to this belief indicates a strongly held underlying value.

BELIEFS ABOUT ECONOMIC POLICY

The practical study of change in economic beliefs requires suitable time series of attitudinal data. We are fortunate in the United Kingdom to have the British Social Attitudes Survey (BSAS). Six national samples have been taken since 1983 (yearly, except in 1988). There is an attempt to hold a high proportion of the questions as a core that recurs in each sample, so as to allow researchers to track change in beliefs. Quite a broad selection of these core questions relates to economic beliefs. There is, however, a problem. The survey started in 1983, well after Britain had swallowed the most bitter of the Thatcherite medicine, and at the point where the economic indicators were beginning to suggest that the course of treatment was successful. The evidence starts almost midway through the Thatcher period. It would have been nice to look at the whole process, but we will have to start in the middle. So, where did beliefs stand in relation to these two ideologies in 1983?

First, consider some of the relevant results from the first survey. One of the most revealing of the common core questions posits a "British economic problem" (BEP), without defining it, and asks respondents about their views on the solution to it. Some of the answers given relate to the general topic of government intervention in the conduct of economic policy. In 1983, 70% of the sample supported price controls, whereas 48% supported wage controls; there were substantial majorities in favor of import controls, job creation projects, and direct subsidies to private industry (see Table 1). These are hardly Thatcherite views. But 1983 was the early days. There is still time for these views to change to come into consonance with the changed economic reality. Other answers to this question relate indirectly to public spending and welfare issues. Fewer than half the 1983 sample supported reduction in defense

Table 1.   Partial Results of the British Social Attitudes Survey

Approach or Perspective	Percentage Agreement
Policies to Solve the British Economic Problem	
Intervention:	
Price control by law	70
Wage control by law	48
Import controls	72
Government subsidy for industry	64
Government construction projects for jobs	89
Welfare spending:	
Reduction of government spending on health and education	13
Reduction of government spending on defense	44
First/Second Spending Priority	
Intervention:	
Help for industry	15
Welfare spending:	
Education, health	57
Housing, public transport, social benefits	18
Roads, defense, police, etc.	11
Same or lower government tax and expenditure	63
Distribution:	
Tax on high incomes is too high or about right	65
Benefits to the unemployed are too low and cause hardship	46
Gaps between high and low incomes are about right or too small	25

spending for this purpose, and only 13% saw reducing spending on education and public health as the answer to the BEP.

A second general question in all the surveys concerns people's priorities for public spending. Reassuringly for the Thatcherite view on intervention, only very few saw spending on direct help for industry as a high priority (this is not inconsistent with the answers to the previously discussed question). But the views on welfare and other public spending were (at the time this chapter was written) less Thatcherite, 57% giving priority to spending on medicine or education, and only 11% giving priority to defense, police, or roads.

Note that these answers to the questions about "spending priorities" are in principle independent of respondents' views about the overall level of public expenditure, because increases of spending on these high priorities could be balanced by reductions in others. There is a more specific question that recurs in each survey: Should the government choose lower levels of tax and spend less on the provision of services; or keep tax and spending at their present level; or increase both? A comfortable majority (63% in 1983) thought current tax and spending either too high or about right.

A somewhat similar question concerns the distributive rather than the spending implication of tax: How do respondents view the level of taxation on people with high incomes? In 1983, 65% viewed the tax levels on the best-off part of the society as either too high or about right.

At the other end of the income scale, respondents were asked whether they thought benefits paid to unemployed people are too high and discourage people from finding jobs, or too low and cause hardship. Public opinion in 1983 was nearly evenly split, with 46% viewing benefits as too low. Finally, respondents were asked directly how they viewed gaps between the rich and the poor in Britain. According to 25% of the sample, the gap was too small.

Considered as a first-term report on the Thatcher experiment, these results can only be considered mixed. Indeed, that was the press response to the publication of these results in 1984.

CHANGE OVER TIME

The high levels of support for interventionist policy could be viewed as particularly disappointing. But from a more theoretically informed (and historically removed) perspective, the implications of this outcome are not so clear. Three or four years of Thatcherite policies are acting on a population whose consciousness of economic issues has been molded by three or four decades of quite contrary policies. Culture does not change overnight. The crucial question is not how beliefs stand at a particular point in time, but how they change over time as a consequence of the new influences.

In Tables 2 through 4 I have somewhat regrouped the questions so that they refer to the three general elements of economic ideologies: interventionism, public spending on welfare and other services, and distributional concerns.

First, I examine the indicators of views on interventionism. Before we look at the data themselves, let us consider how we would expect them to change if the Thatcher experiment is working—that is, how they would shift if dissonance between current lines of public policy and beliefs about economic processes and proprieties is progressively reduced over time.

On interventionism the cognitive dissonance expectations are, without exception, that support for all of these sorts of intervention should fall. The results, as exhibited in Table 2, are quite dramatic. Four of the six indicators of support for intervention, those relating to wage and price controls and subsidies to private industry, show that support has fallen considerably. Support for the other two policies—import controls and government job creation—has also fallen, though less significantly. Beliefs have changed, they have changed consistently, and they have changed in the direction the Thatcherites hoped and in the direction that the cognitive dissonance theory would predict.

Table 2.   Support in Britain for Economic Ideologies (in percentages)

Indicator	1983	1984	1985	1986	1987	1989
	Intervention					
Price control by law	70	66	64	61	58	56
Wage control by law	48	42	39	39	34	28
Import controls	72	67	67	67	68	67
Goverment subsidy for industry	64	60	61	61	60	53
Government construction projects for jobs	89	89	90	91	90	87
Priority: help industry	15	10	10	8	6	4
	Welfare and Other Spending					
Reduction of government spending on:						
Health and education	13	11	10	9	7	7
Defense	44	51	54	55	51	56
First/second spending priority:						
Education, health	57	63	62	66	68	69
Housing, transportation, social benefits	18	18	20	18	18	19
Roads, defense, police	11	8	9	8	9	9
Same or lower tax, spending	63	56	49	49	45	40
	Redistribution, Equality					
Tax on high incomes too high						
or about right	65	—	—	58	—	44
Unemployment benefits low, cause						
hardship	46	49	44	44	51	52
Income gaps about right						
or too small	25	23	20	19	19	18

Next, I examine the indicators on public spending. Through a decade of Thatcherite policies, we would expect an increase in the proportion of the sample wishing to reduce public spending on medical and educational services. We would expect an increase in the proportion of people saying that the government should hold down or reduce taxation. And (since Adam Smith identified "the fleets and the magistracy" as the sole legitimate area of public spending) we should expect a growing proportion of the respondents to give priority, in what public spending remains, to police, defense, and so on.

Evidence for this group of indicators shows equally dramatic changes (see Table 2). But this time, without exception, the changes in belief run counter to the Thatcher line, counter to expectations derived from the cognitive dissonance perspective. Most striking of all, the proportion of the sample saying that the government should choose the same or lower levels of public spending fell from 63% in 1983 to 40% in 1989. Beliefs about proper levels and destinations of public spending have shifted consistently, and in the main regularly from year to year, in a direction dramatically opposed to the trend of public policy.

As for distributional indicators, our dissonance-reduction expectations are that, as inequality rises in the society, concern about inequality in the society should diminish. So the three indicators of views on inequality (i.e., beliefs that tax is too high on high incomes, that benefits to the unemployed are too high, and that the income gap is too small) should all show increases. In fact, all three of the indicators showed substantial falls.

It might be objected that perhaps these views reflect expressions of direct material interests, that the increasing proportions of the sample supporting redistributive policies may reflect just the views of those worst-off in the society, who are the most directly damaged by the increasingly inegalitarian trend of British income distribution. We can test this by breaking down the sample by income levels. (I use a self-assessed relative income level, but the same results emerge from the alternative gross-income measure.) If the materialist objection is correct, then the shift in values should be concentrated among those with low incomes. And indeed, as shown in Table 3, in all the surveys, the richer the group of respondents, the lower the score in the three redistribution indicators.

Table 3. British Views of
Inequality in the United Kingdom

Income Group	Percentage of Agreement		
	1983	*1986*	*1989*
Tax and spending should be increased			
High	30.0	43.5	51.9
Medium	32.9	46.8	56.2
Low	32.9	45.2	56.1
Gap between high and low incomes is too large			
High	48.0	56.5	55.6
Medium	67.1	75.0	77.2
Low	79.1	82.0	84.2
Unemployment benefits are too low and cause hardship			
High	32.0	29.0	32.1
Medium	39.4	38.7	47.4
Low	52.9	50.6	57.5

But this difference in absolute levels is beside the point. We are concerned with changes. At least for the key question of the gap between high and low incomes, the high, medium, and low groups all showed the same trend. Indeed, support for the proposition that income gaps are too large increased in the high and medium income group more than in the low income group. Though the high income group (3% of the sample) showed no change in its view of taxation of the rich or of the appropriate levels of unemployment pay, the middle income group (50% of the sample) showed considerable support for distribution.

In Table 4, the cognitive dissonance-based expectations of change in beliefs are compared to the actual changes found in the BSAS. In the three different fields that constitute the opposing economic ideologies, Thatcherism has shown striking success in changing beliefs in one case (intervention) and an equally striking failure to change attitudes in the other two (attitudes to welfare and equality).

There are some important implications, both theoretical and practical, that emerge from these findings. But before we turn to them, let us first take the argument one stage further.

Table 4.   Cognitive-Dissonance-Based Expectations
of Change in British Beliefs Compared to Actual Changes
Reflected in the British Social Attitudes Survey

Measures	*Thatcherite change*	*Actual change*
Intervention		
Price control by law	—	—
Wage control by law	—	—
Import controls	—	(—)[a]
Government subsidy for industry	—	(—)
Government construction projects for jobs	—	—
Priority: help industry	—	—
Welfare, Other Spending		
Reduction of government spending on:		
Health and education	+	—
Defense	—	+
Spending priority:		
Education, health	—	+
Housing, transport, social benefits	—	(+)
Roads, defense, police	+	(—)
Same or lower tax, spending	+	—
Redistribution, Equality		
Tax on high incomes too high or about right	+	—
Unemployment benefits too low, cause hardship	—	+
Income gaps about right or too small	+	—

Note: [a] Parentheses indicate weak effects.

ECONOMIC IDEOLOGIES AND
THE NEW CENTER GROUND

One aim of Thatcherism was to replace what its advocates saw as an ideological consensus of the left, a set of "socialist" views on the role of the state in public policy, with an alternative consensus of the right, a set of "free-market" beliefs with an equivalent internal coherence and consistency.

There are several senses of the word consistent. Respondents' expressed beliefs may or may not be *logically consistent*. For example, respondents who believe that nuclear weapons make Britain safer are in a limited sense logically inconsistent if they also support unilateral disarmament. They are *technically consistent* if their beliefs make correct connections between policy means and policy ends. A belief that the gap between high and low incomes is too big is technically consistent with a view that high-income earners should pay a higher share of their earnings in tax than others.

Both of these cases rely on a relatively objective base of knowledge; a set of beliefs may be considered logically or technically inconsistent on the basis of a general agreement about the nature of things in the social world. We agree that sparks fly upwards, so the hungry person who puts firelighters on top of the fuel is acting inconsistently. A third concept relates not to intersubjectively agreed characteristics of the phenomenal world but to bundles of social and political beliefs that may be considered *ideologically consistent*. Certain views come in intellectual packages. Thatcherism provides an ideology in this sense: A Thatcherite believes that taxation and state spending should be reduced; that the duty of care for the individual's welfare lies with the family, not with the state; and that the state should not intervene directly in the management of the economy. Mrs. Thatcher came to power as a result of a clear challenge to another, almost precisely opposing ideological package ("welfare corporatism") whose advocates supported relatively high levels of tax and public expenditure, held the state ultimately responsible for individual welfare, and considered that the state should be actively engaged in managing the economy.

These opposing ideologies share the same elements. Ideological consistency would require that people hold either a completely Thatcherite bundle of economic beliefs or a welfare corporatist bundle. But, of course, there is no particular reason that people should hold ideologically consistent beliefs. Members of a reasonably well-informed society could be expected to show technical and logical coherence in their various views. We might even expect them to show what has been termed *normative consistency* (i.e., they organize their beliefs "according to more general principles or values"). Normative consistency does not require individuals to embrace an entire ideological bundle of beliefs. The ideology of welfare corporatism, for example, involves universal provision of welfare services, relatively high marginal levels of taxation on high incomes, and economic intervention. But an individual may find a normative congruence between, say, progressive taxation and universal welfare provision, without according the state a direct role in the management of the economy. Such a grouping of views could be said to show a normative, but not ideological, consistency.

The Thatcherite aim of transforming British economic culture was explicitly that of replacing one ideology with its inverse; the bundle of beliefs associated with welfare corporatism was to be replaced by the bundle of beliefs associated with market liberalism. We have so far seen that some individual beliefs have moved in a Thatcherite direction, whereas others have moved contrary to the flow of 1980s public policy. What we have not so far considered is how different beliefs fit together.

Let us take as indicators for the three central planks of the two opposing ideologies evidence contained in the first three tables in this chapter. For attitudes for or against intervention in the economy, we could construct an index based on the respondents' views of such options as price, wage, import, and exchange rate controls. For the sake of simplicity, however, the respondents' attitude to government subsidy for private industry is used in the following passages. In 1983, 67% of the respondents claimed they would support such subsidization, 33% opposed it. For attitudes to state welfare provision, we can take the first and second priorities for shifts in public spending. The 55% of the respondents for whom education, health, or housing were among the two top priorities in 1983 may be considered pro-welfare. For attitudes to the level of taxation, there is the direct question whose answers are summarized in Table 3; 33% were in favor of higher taxation in 1983. The evolution of these three views from 1983 to 1989 is summarized in Figure 1.

This evidence is not itself inconsistent with the existence of a strong and increasingly ideological organization of economic attitudes. On this evidence it could have been the case that, for instance in 1983, roughly one-third of the population supported higher tax, more public welfare provisions, and state interventionism, whereas another third of the population opposed these. This interpretation is consistent with the evidence in Figure 1. But this was not the reality. In fact, a very much smaller proportion of the population adopted these ideologically pure positions. In 1983, fewer than 16% of the sample held all three welfare corporatist views, and only about 10% held all three Thatcherite views. Through the Thatcher decade, to judge from the evidence of the BSAS sample, the proportion of the population holding to the welfare corporatist ideology grew to more than one quarter, whereas the proportion supporting a purely Thatcherite ideology declined to around 5% of the population.

The particular numbers involved here are, of course, a product of the particular indicators. Different indicators do certainly produce somewhat differing estimates of the proportions of the respondents claiming ideological purity. But the general message of Figure 2 emerges however the indicators

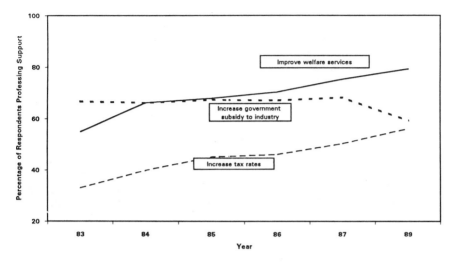

Figure 1. Three Components of Economic Ideology

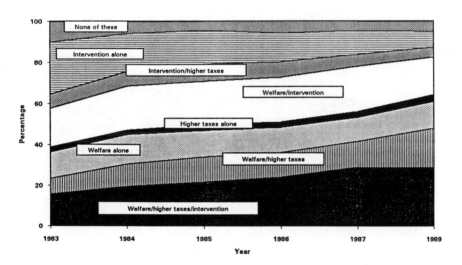

Figure 2. Economic Ideology: The Whole
British Social Attitudes Survey Sample

are constructed. Only a very small minority of the population held to the pure
Thatcherite faith, and the size of this minority declined over the 1980s. Support
for interventionism has declined overall, but those who still support it also tend
to support higher taxes and the traditional welfare state. The welfare

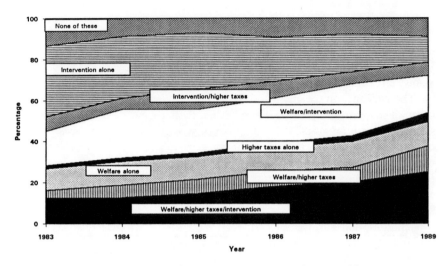

Figure 3.   Economic Ideology: Conservative Identifiers

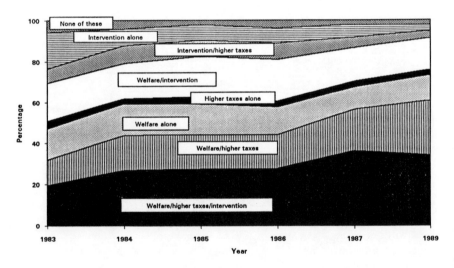

Figure 4.   Economic Ideology: Labor Identifiers

corporatist ideologists have increased from 16% to 29% of the sample. But the noninterventionists seem now to dominate, supporting higher tax rates and/or the traditional welfare state, but not direct involvement in economic management. The great majority of the population does not adhere to either of the opposing ideologies. Exclude those who hold to either ideology and what remains may be called the middle ground; the interventionist middle ground declined during the 1980s from 50% to 30% of the sample; the noninterventionist middle ground increased from 23% to 36% of the sample.

Throughout this chapter, readers may have noticed the use of some rather clumsy circumlocutions to describe economic ideologies: "Market liberalism" or "Thatcherism" on the one side, "interventionist welfare corporatism" on the other. The reason for using these rather than the more straightforward-sounding terminology of the political left and right is that the views I have been discussing, and in particular the patterns of change in these views over the period, are not very strongly associated with respondents' stated allegiances to the political institutions of the left and the right. Figures 3 and 4 plot the evolution of the various combinations of views for respondents with respectively Conservative and Labor party allegiances. There were a few Labor Thatcherites, and hardly more than one third of Labor voters held the pure welfare corporatist ideology. Only around 10% of Conservative voters were, by the time of the 1989 survey, Thatcher ideologists, and more than 20% of them held the full hand of interventionist welfare corporatist views. The same general pattern of change in views applies to both groups. In both cases the middle ground—noninterventionist, but concerned with improving welfare service and reducing gross inequalities in incomes—was the largest group.

THATCHERISM AS A MICROSOCIAL EXPERIMENT

There is a sort of international economists' cliché to the effect that the imposition of Thatcherite policies can be viewed as an experimental test of macroeconomic policy (along the lines of Chile in the 1970s: "Jolly interesting," our colleagues said, "glad we're not doing it"). Perhaps less obviously, Thatcherism can also be viewed as a microsociological experiment.

One reason that deeply held values are difficult to distinguish from more malleable and superficial beliefs is that we are often not conscious of exactly what our values are. Our knowledge about ourselves is generally restricted to what we need to know, and most of us can successfully conduct most of our lives without considering what it is that we really believe in. Values, as was suggested previously, are derived, or in an unconscious way inferred, from common cultural practices. For as long as practices remain stable, the values that are derived or inferred from them remain unchallenged. Survey respondents will, of course, always be willing to express beliefs when challenged to do so by an interviewer; that is the nature of respondents. But what do these expressions of belief mean while any underlying values remain dormant and unchallenged? Knowledge about the tenacity or rootedness of beliefs does not necessarily form part of everyday practical consciousness. We cannot straightforwardly tell whether any particular belief represents firmly held personal principles or merely a pious, but superficial, statement of the respondent's understanding of current conventions. (The observation of logical coherence in a series of beliefs expressed by one individual does not, of course, give us any purchase on this problem; the coherence may just as well derive from the terms of public debate as from the individual's own cogitation.)

We have considered an empirical procedure for testing the tenacity of beliefs. If expressed beliefs are challenged by new contrary conditions or practices, and yet do not change so as to become consistent with these new conditions or practices, we may perhaps infer the existence of an underlying value. The laboratory usefulness of Thatcherism for sociologists is that it provides just such a set of tests. By attempting to change British conventional economic practices, it tests for the substance of British economic values.

Some of the results reveal beliefs that turn out not to be backed by any strong values. There was certainly a 1970s consensus in favor of corporatist, interventionist, economic policy. Though Conservative policy in the late 1970s was strongly anticorporatist and antiinterventionist, the first BSAS (1983) showed that there was still majority support for statutory price control and for direct support for industry, and almost half the respondents supported wage controls. The balance of public rhetoric through the 1980s was predominantly against corporatism and interventionism, and public support for them has ebbed away through the decade. The inference must be that the expressed views on corporatism and interventionism did not represent deeply rooted political or economic values.

In matters of management of economic inequality and social welfare, there was also a reasonably clear 1970s consensus. Thatcherism runs directly contrary to this relatively egalitarian, welfarist agenda. But in this case, the development of antiegalitarian and antiwelfarist policies through the 1980s seems to have gone with growing public opposition. The inference we must draw is presumably that the new line of public policy challenged some more deeply held values concerning public responsibilities to care for the worst-off and to maintain the rights associated with economic citizenship. The Thatcher test shows that, although some beliefs may bend with the wind of politics, others strain against it. Corporatism may have disappeared: Welfarism is more with us than in the early 1980s.

SOME CONCLUSIONS

Britain's taste for postwar centrist welfare state orthodoxy was somewhat jaded by the economic failures of the 1960s and the 1970s. It was perhaps ripe for ideological adventurism. But the result seems to have been the emergence and confirmation of some rather centrist economic values.

The first sort of conclusion is rather theoretical, using 1980s Britain as a sort of macrosociological laboratory, testing for the strength of economic values. We started by saying that, all other things being equal, beliefs might be expected to adapt themselves to actual practices. When are things not equal? Under what circumstances might we expect that beliefs would not change so as to become consonant with actions? One possible answer is: when these beliefs are strongly or deeply held.

In most cases, most of the time, most of us do not really know what we believe. Our knowledge of ourselves is in general restricted to what we need to know, and most of the time we do not need to know what we really believe in. We express opinions when we are respondents in survey samples, we answer questions because that is the job of survey respondents. But we cannot really tell whether the opinions we express are deeply held or merely echoes of the last vigorously expressed arguments we participated in. Only when our beliefs are challenged do we discover what we believe.

One interpretation of the trends I have discussed is that the reversal of traditional patterns of economic policy has served to reveal or disclose what were previously latent, but tenaciously held, economic values. We did not know that we had strong views on the social rights implicit in the welfare state until the welfare state itself was challenged; we did not know that we strongly supported redistributive policies, until the society became less redistributive. We may have thought we supported corporatist state intervention in economic management, but when challenged, our beliefs evaporated.

We cannot really say anything definite about the evolution of individuals' values since (apart from a very small "panel" element in 1983-4) the BSAS has taken a fresh sample each year. But from the change in the yearly aggregates, we can nevertheless suspect that many of those who played with Thatcherite ideas in the earlier 1980s discovered that the practical application of these ideas offended against some more general values having to do with fairness or with the responsibilities of the state towards its citizens. Perhaps peoples' own underlying collectivist values have been revealed to themselves by their contact with the strongly anticollectivist trend of Thatcherite ideology.

This is all rather abstract speculation. A second sort of conclusion we can draw from this discussion relates to Mrs. Thatcher's loss of the leadership of the Conservative party. The evidence I have discussed suggests that the political excitement may have roots that go deeper than the current issues of Europe and the Poll Tax. What we have seen is a very steady movement, among Conservative and Labor supporters alike, through the 1980s, against important elements of the pure Thatcherite ideology. The results described above suggest that, in addition to the changes in style that have followed the leadership contest, many, even among the Tory government's own supporters, also want a change in the content of Conservative policies, moving them back into line with public opinion.

Finally, there may be a message for those most fanatical Thatcherites of all, who are to be found among the new political classes of eastern Europe. In eastern Europe, dissatisfaction with the outcomes of the application of collectivist-interventionist ideologies led to reform movements that propose a complete inversion of this ideology. But if, as appears to be the case in Britain, decades of collectivist policies leave latent, but strongly held, collectivist values deeply buried in the economic culture, then policies that have adverse consequences for income distribution and access to welfare services may have political consequences analogous to, but (in proportion to the relative severity of the economic circumstances in eastern Europe) more violent than, Mrs. Thatcher's own downfall.

VARIETIES OF "REAL CAPITALISM" AND THE DILEMMAS OF TRANSFORMATION IN EASTERN EUROPE

Avi Gottlieb and Marek Ziółkowski

It is not easy to take an analytical approach toward the recent developments in central and eastern Europe. The pace of events often tempts one to describe rather than to explain, to couch the narrative in journalistic rather than in scientific terms. Had we given in to this temptation, this book may never have been published. As it was, the swift and unexpected changes in this region frequently vitiated our sincere intentions to be punctual and obliged us to revise this chapter again and again. In an earlier age of inkwells and blotters, the expression "the ink did not have a chance to dry" would have been quite apt.

The former Soviet Union is perhaps the most extreme example of this rapidly changing political reality. When we first drafted this concluding chapter, the USSR was still very much in existence. Led by Michael Gorbachev, it was searching for a compromise between the precepts of socialism and the productive efficiency of a market economy. The Soviet leadership and its powerful and privileged corporate ruling class, or nomenclature, by and large appeared to be in support of reforms, and on the surface the political situation was quite stable.

Then came the preposterous, though dangerous, *coup d'état;* Gorbachev's overthrow and Jelzin's ascent to power; the banning of the CPSU; and ultimately, the disintegration of Soviet Union, followed by the founding of the Commonwealth of Independent States (CIS). These events comprised the

Soviet Union's *chant du cygne* as a nation and as the remaining stronghold of the communist order, and it launched Russia's—albeit somewhat irresolute—turn toward the policies of a market economy.

Recent events in the former satellites of the USSR, though perhaps less dramatic, hardly signify greater internal stability. Slovaks and Czechs have only recently opted to settle their national and economic animosities by partitioning the country.[1] The initial optimism regarding Poland's radical experiment with a market economy has reverted to a struggle with economic stagnation and poverty, a battle with which the frail administration can scarcely cope. Even the former German Democratic Republic, subsidized in 1991 alone to the tune of DM 180 billion, has so far failed to fulfill the promise of rapid recovery. Economic restructuring and privatization in eastern Germany have proceeded much more slowly than expected; the new federal states (*Bundesländer*) are reeling from an unprecedented rate of unemployment; alienation and social friction are growing, with a concomitant shift toward the extreme political right; and the recent, sometimes violent manifestations of racism and intolerance are reminiscent of the not-so-distant past.

There is little doubt that one may now pronounce the collapse of "real socialism" as a political, economic and social system—at least in Europe and at least for the time being. Beyond this indisputable assertion, however, the consequences of the recent developments in eastern Europe are anything but transparent. Considerable uncertainty surrounds primarily the endeavor to recover from the economic fallacies of the *ancien régime*, fallacies that only now, in the course of the transition, are being grasped in their entire scope and malevolence.

The theoretical concern, analytic emphases, and, hence, the structure and contents of this chapter are dictated by the conceptual issues raised by our colleagues' contributions to this volume. For self-evident reasons, we will devote most of our attention to the processes of change and adaptation in eastern Europe. Nonetheless, we also intend to examine more encompassing questions about the future prospects of market systems in both the East and the West. The substantive issues to be explored may be summarized as follows.

(a)   The collapse of "real socialism." We contend that "real socialism" ultimately destroyed itself from within, not as a result of the ramifications of the cold war or as the aftermath of its practice of political repression, but primarily because of the state's ubiquitous economic control and the consequent subordination of economic rationality to political interests.

(b)   Prototypes of advanced capitalism. In this section we survey the early sociopolitical discourse about alternatives to capitalism (the "third way") and examine the different variants of market policies and their origins.

(c)   Alternative paths of modernization and development. We argue that the prospects of eastern European countries to realize their objective of emulating the market economies of the West are rather dubious. The prototypes of "real capitalism" practiced by the West represent different attempts to resolve a series of fiscal and labor-market dilemmas shared by most advanced market economies. Yet the current employment and fiscal crises in eastern Europe, notwithstanding their gravity, differ fundamentally from the predicaments encountered by well-established market economies. Consequently, models of advanced capitalism are unlikely to meet the *bona fide* social and economic needs of former socialist countries. Moreover, the socioeconomic profiles of most eastern European countries predispose them to gravitate toward the periphery of international money and labor markets, and perhaps even to share the Third World's dependency on the West.

(d)   The transition from command to market. We delineate some of the alternative paths of development. While it is difficult to predict specific scenarios, we try to reflect upon the key dilemmas of the transition period and some of its more viable outcomes.

(e)   We conclude with an analysis of political legitimation. Eastern Europe's democracies continue to be volatile because they derive part of their legitimacy from the subjectively defined success of their market policies. We maintain that the currently evolving market-oriented policies must be supplemented by a series of social initiatives in order to secure continued political legitimation.

THE COLLAPSE OF REAL SOCIALISM

It would be futile even to speculate on the consequences of the unprecedented drama currently being staged in central and eastern Europe. Different countries may take divergent political and economic routes, and some may not even retain their national integrity. We should, however, be able to explain and conceptually account for the collapse of "real socialism," that is, socialism as it was actually practiced. In fact, and despite the relative paucity of western scientific analyses of socialist societies (Hollander, 1983),[2] many critics of the socialist order had cogently pointed to the deficiencies of the communist regime and of its economic policies long before its disintegration (e.g., Bottomore, 1990; Heilbroner, 1980; Ludwikowski, 1986; Miliband, 1977; Portes, 1981; Rostow, 1960), without, however, divining its quick, nonviolent and relatively painless disintegration.

From a sociopolitical perspective, the fundamental failure of real socialism was the inability of its politically unsanctioned and highly centralized regimes to guarantee those basic political rights and liberties that are taken for granted in any civil society. In neglecting to establish a society grounded in equality and social justice, socialist governments even inverted the most important precepts of Marxist ideology.

Although some communist policies, such as the Bolshevik predilection for dictatorship, may have evolved from historical antecedents (e.g., the heritage of totalitarianism in Czarist Russia), others were direct derivatives of traditional Marxist ideology—built-in flaws of Marx's socioeconomic conception, so to speak. Still others, branded as "real socialism," embodied fallacious translations of the Marxist creed into praxis. Real socialism consisted of a command economy based on centralized planning and decision-making; the abolishment of private property and the transfer of the ownership of the means of production to the state;[3] and the insistence on minimally differentiated wages, which, in effect, eradicated the incentive value of labor and production. It is factually correct, but practically immaterial, that Marx had viewed these strategies as transitory stages toward genuinely cooperative social production. In real socialism, they became ironclad facts of life.

The resulting maximization of the state's political and economic power constituted the total antithesis of democratic and market principles. Most significant was the violation of the premises of economic rationality: the maximization of productivity, the importance of individual achievement and merit, and the profit motive. These premises were subordinated to sociopolitical interests and objectives. Thus, the principal aim of production was defined not as economic growth and affluence, but as "the maximization of the volume of material means under the global disposition of the apparatus of power" (Feher, Heller, & Markus, 1983, p. 65). Full employment, which signified the conservation of human and material resources and which was considered the backbone of socialist superiority, could be achieved only at the price of direct state control of the labor market. Contrary to the capitalist economy, where employment is adjusted to the relation between profits and wages, socialist governments tried to adjust the relationship between profits and wages themselves, so as to provide full employment.

This economic system can prosper only if the allocation of means and ends is highly efficient, a task which was to be accomplished by central planning. But planning can guarantee efficient allocation only if it is impartial in defining needs and interests and in dealing with class conflicts. Needless to say, the socialist command economy did not meet these criteria. Thus, the very policies designed to guarantee social justice, equality, and full employment ultimately recreated the very conditions of social inequality that the socialist utopia was supposed to rectify.

The public did embrace egalitarian ideals, and socioeconomic differentiation did indeed diminish in the socialist systems of eastern Europe. Thus, differences in income and affluence were leveled, and conspicuous consumption was discouraged (Andorka, Jackson, Simkus, & Treiman, 1983; Charvat, Linhart & Vecernik, 1978; Dobson, 1977; Kolosi, 1988; Kolosi & Wnuk-Lipinski, 1983; Slomczinski & Krause, 1978; Zagorski, 1978). But even more remarkable was the mutation from a social structure stratified by individual merit to one stratified on the basis of political power. The productive sector soon found itself at the bottom of a socialist pyramid dominated by a nomenclature which had ensconced itself as the overlord of both state and economy.

As a result of this structural dichotomy, the relationship between these two groups was fundamentally based on exploitation and, therefore, by definition was characterized by antagonism and conflict. State power became associated with state ownership, and both were monopolized by the nomenclature, which, beyond political authority and economic privileges, also gained absolute control over economic planning and decision-making. Lacking even minimal economic expertise and entrepreneurship, it regulated the economy according to its own vested interests by appropriating and distributing surplus value, independent of productivity, according to plan and based on the extant organizational hierarchy (Wright, 1986). These inherent deficiencies of the centralized command economy constituted the root causes of real socialism's economic afflictions: the depletion of natural, capital and human resources, the neglect of industrial and technological infrastructures and capital investments, and the setting of misguided production goals.

The most visible outcome of this economic order was the emergence of a demand economy. Dominant suppliers created a permanent scarcity of consumer goods, an affliction that was, however, only one manifestation of the ubiquitous shortage economy. Less visible, at least initially, were the disincentives for entrepreneurs to find markets for their products, and the fact that money, which was more readily available than goods, had no real value. It is superfluous to add that no genuine market mechanisms could emerge under these circumstances.

The population, virtually enslaved by the state's encompassing economic control and regulation, adjusted in a predictable manner to the practices of real socialism. The absolute authority of the state engendered a dependency syndrome, and the undifferentiated wages actually discouraged productivity. Ideologically, the public supported political freedom and democratic rule, but it embraced, at least until recently, the prevailing economic system (Radaev, Ziółkowski, in this volume)[4]. These belief systems (Converse, 1965) were reproduced and solidified faithfully in the relation between the people and their government. Eastern Europe's socialist sovereigns and their subjects served as co-conspirators bonded by a peculiar contract of reciprocally low expectations. The government provided job security, passable social welfare benefits, and a minimal standard of living; in return, the labor force acquiesced to low wages and tolerated restrictions on its autonomy and liberty. The most astonishing feat was that these reciprocal concessions actually garnered the system a certain measure of stability.

Executives and managers in the production sector accommodated themselves quite well to the unique rationality of economic planning and control and to the perpetual material shortages. The performance strategies of the typical socialist manager primarily entailed the hoarding of resources and the understating of the enterprise's actual productive potential (Kornai, 1986; 1982). Central planning also made it impossible to enact or even articulate clear criteria of merit or to make anything but artificial assessments of productivity and economic vitality. In the absence of impartial evaluations, production had to be assessed exclusively by administrative decision. Consequently, the state became the only viable addressee for requisitions, claims, appeals, and bargaining activities.[5]

Here the vicious circle closes. The powerful and all-encompassing state not only exerted absolute control over all aspects of production but also gauged its own achievements, thus becoming inseparably intertwined with the administratively controlled redistribution of privileges. Centralized planning, the absence of production incentives, and deficient entrepreneurship, jointly precipitated an inevitable decline in the volume and quality of production, especially innovative, high-quality production with less intensive labor, fewer material and capital inputs, and a lower input/output ratio. Lacking any real impetus for change, the socialist bureaucracy also failed to convert industrial production from primary to consumer goods, from manufacturing to service industries, and from extensive to intensive patterns of growth.

This status quo was profoundly disrupted in the late 1970s, with the onset of the perhaps most acute economic crisis that the communist world had yet experienced. Struck by economic stagnation and diminishing productivity, socialist regimes were about to lose their ability to ensure adequate wages, protect the modest standard of living, and guarantee at least minimal social security. The populace came to define the socialist order as what it actually was: a hostile and antagonistic relation between "them" and "us," one based on power and domination (Ziółkowski, in this volume). The contract of mutually low expectations began to crumble at its edges. The absolute economic control that the state had exercised began to boomerang. Having overextended its power and capacities, the state was now held responsible for the failure of the very same policies it had unequivocally dominated before the crisis.

The public regarded itself as released from the obligation to take any personal initiative. Rather than help ameliorate these problems, the population treated the state as a psychological alibi for its chronic passivity. Although the government's authority was perceived as imposed and alien, its very omnipresence made it instrumentally necessary and indispensable, a clear manifestation of the learned-helplessness syndrome (Seligman, 1975) as part of the communist sociopolitical culture (Almond & Verba, 1963).

The dismal performance of command economies had been censured repeatedly by social scientists in both the West and the East (Brus & Laski, 1989; Drewnowski, 1982; Kornai, 1986; 1982; Winiecki, 1988), and even by leaders of the communist political establishment. Moreover, the communist leadership had ventured a series of economic reforms: in Poland in 1956-57 and again during the mid-1970s; in Hungary in 1956, when the incipient reform was suppressed brutally, and again since 1968 in the context of its "new economic mechanism"; in the CSSR in 1958, and later during the "Prague Spring" of 1968, which was again quelled by force; in the context of the German Democratic Republic's "new economic system" of 1963; as part of the economic renewal launched by Khrushchev and Kosygin in 1963; and, of course, as a regular feature of Yugoslavia's idiosyncratic policies.[6]

Since macroeconomic performance data from socialist countries are notoriously difficult to interpret, it is not always easy to judge the success of these ventures. Nonetheless, relevant indicators such as economic growth, industrial productivity, and the standard of living indicate that little more than a temporary economic recovery was usually accomplished (Brus & Laski, 1989).[7] Why did even those economic reforms that were not paralyzed by internal power struggles or suppressed by military force fail? Closer examination reveals that they, in fact, hardly took place at all. Because of the resistance by the ruling elites, bureaucratic vested interests, and managers' reluctance to give up security for efficiency, only those market mechanisms that were acceptable to the nomenclature were selectively adopted. The state refused adamantly to curtail its economic control to any meaningful extent, to permit the unrestricted accumulation of property, and to tolerate the evolution of a free market for capital, goods, and services[8]—all genuinely important elements of economic rationality and productivity.

Given the pervasive problems of real socialist economies, their unsuccessful attempts at reform, and the slowdown in growth and productivity since the late 1970s, one may well ask not why real socialism collapsed, but why it managed to survive so long. Western media reports and analyses tend to posit a surreptitious connection between the protracted survival of communist regimes and their sudden demise. The latter is attributed either to the ultimate eruption of public antagonism over the restriction of personal rights and liberties or to public defiance of the asinine economic system, which operated in complete disregard of the population's basic needs and desires and in complete neglect of its promise to provide greater affluence and an improved standard of living.

Both these explanations fall short. The populace, albeit politically alienated, did not initiate the events that led to the fall of real socialism; the transformation originated mostly from the top, with little grass-root involvement.[9] The second premise, the public's reluctance to bear the repercussions of the economic decline, does not hold much water either. After all, the malaise had lingered on for decades, while the nomenclature had remained dogmatic and unyielding and the public acquiescent.

All economic systems, be they capitalist or socialist, are political by their very nature (e.g., Buchanan, 1986; Hibbs, 1987; Mann, 1984). But real socialism evinced a particular propensity to intertwine politics and economics. Since the political elite completely dominated all aspects of economic life, it managed to create a practically self-sustaining system. So long as economic performance remained tolerable, the regime's political authority retained its stability, ensuring and even strengthening its economic dominance. But once the economic predicaments grew acute enough to circumscribe the government's own flexibility in selecting social and economic policy options, its authority diminished. Just as absolute control over a more or less functioning economy had guaranteed the regime its power, so it was its responsibility for the system's defeat which stripped the regime of its authority (Radaev, in this volume). In 1989, when the eyes of the world turned toward eastern Europe, only a hollow shell of the original power structure remained; little was needed to push it down.

PROTOTYPES OF ADVANCED CAPITALISM

Immediately after the dramatic events of 1989, the new governments and the liberated publics of central and eastern Europe embarked on an extended debate about "the third way"—a somewhat cryptic concept that presumably signified a compromise between control and market policies. The general inclination was to adopt most of the market principles of production but to sustain the socialist tenets of distributive justice and its traditional welfare policies. The "third way" is thus comparable to similar notions of economic reconstruction that had guided the earlier and more narrowly defined reforms of the 1960s and 1970s.

The repeated failure to conceptualize or implement a genuine alternative to the command economy and the market economy, and the demand for a more encompassing economic reorganization voiced by western governments, banking houses, and industry—on whose loans, credits, and investments the economic reconstruction largely depends—probably account for the fact that this approach abated rather quickly as a real policy option. Nonetheless, the notion of a "third way" does continue to linger in the public mind, perhaps because the unconditional espousal of capitalism has already bred harsh disappointments. The rapid economic liberalization did not, as expected, open the faucets of the thoroughly needed western aid and investments; and the public belief that capitalism would be a rapid cure-all for the afflictions of the socialist economic order stands in sharp contrast to recent experiences.[10]

Another dialogue, also concerned with the preservation of the remnants of the *ancien régime*, may be even more enduring. Here, the readiness to assimilate the more efficient practices of a market economy is accompanied by an aura of nostalgia, a tacit remorse about the loss of the endogenous heritage, ideals, customs, and ways of life. This outlook on modernization and development is reminiscent of periodic reactions to modernization in the Third World

(Harrison, 1988), which also reflect a desire to protect the indigenous cultural microcosm from the onslaught of economic development. This tendency appears to be gaining strength as the personal repercussions and risks of the current transition intensify (Radaev; Schlese, Pawlowsky, & Schramm; Ziółkowski, in this volume).

Once the "third way" had died its natural and, except in the former Soviet Union, relatively painless death, the discussion quickly shifted to the question how the market policies of the industrialized West might best be adopted and emulated. Yet, western market economies are rather variegated; as in socialism, capitalist ideology and praxis—"real capitalism"—often differ considerably and in intricate ways. The modern surrogates of "pure" capitalism range from Thatcher's minimal-government approach in Britain (Gershuny, in this volume) and the hands-off policies of recent Republican administrations in the United States to the social market economies practiced by most members of the European Community, and the advanced redistributive welfare state which has characterized Sweden until recently (van den Berg & Szulkin, in this volume).

This heterogeneity reflects different degrees of a unidimensional deviation from the original, conservative tenets of capitalist ideology (Adam Smith, 1776/1961). That is, underlying the diversity among modern market systems is a propensity to grant government more discretion in economic planning; the prerogative of owning and controlling economic resources and means of production; partial jurisdiction over investments and the flow of capital; the license to partially regulate the labor market (the "politization of accumulation"; Wright, 1985); and a leading role in reducing socioeconomic inequalities by means of income transfers, entitlement, and welfare benefits (Wright's "decommodification of labor")—in short, greater economic involvement and control. Many of these policies, especially those which tend to resemble traditional socialist principles, have been interpreted as an attempt to resolve the dilemmas of capitalism and to contribute to its continued vitality (Bell, 1976; Dahrendorf, 1988; Giddens, 1981; Schumpeter, 1975) or, if one is theoretically so inclined, to obscure its contradictions and to ensure its self-perpetuation (Braverman, 1974; Goldthorpe, 1984; Heilbroner, 1985; Mandel, 1975; Miliband, 1969; Offe, 1985; 1981; Przeworski, 1990).

Irrespective of the origins of these disparate policies, be it national traditions, cultural heritage, or prevailing power relations, they predominantly reflect different solutions to common fiscal and labor-market dilemmas that have afflicted the industrialized West since the 1970s. Most critical among them is a sizable and permanent rate of unemployment, which is due to the dissociation of economic growth and employment. In advanced capitalism, it is primarily rationalization, automation, and technology rather than labor that account for economic growth and productivity. Not even a booming economy can guarantee any longer that the labor market will expand[11] (Bolle & Greffe, 1989;

OECD, 1984). Moreover, because the modern welfare state assumes much of the responsibility for those excluded from the labor market, the original conflict between capital and labor is, in effect, transferred into the hands of the state, a shift that results in growing public expenditures and a permanent state budget deficit.

Of course, unemployment is not the only source of the fiscal crisis in advanced capitalism. Under the prevailing conditions, all public expenditures are prone to rise (O'Connor, 1987; 1973). Entrepreneurs' insistence on subsidies and on the provision of collective goods not available on the market increases investments in physical and human capital, growing public demands for an improved standard of living inflate allocations for collective services such as housing and medical care, and the contradictions of capitalism create growing entitlement claims and social welfare expenditures. The skyrocketing fiscal liabilities of the state are most likely to precipitate a fiscal crisis when economic growth reaches one of its periodic downward cycles (Rostow, 1978; Schumpeter, 1939).

Governments can circumvent the fiscal squeeze by expanding their share in the GNP (e.g., by increasing profits from state-owned enterprises, or by raising taxes), by borrowing (deficit financing), by capitalizing on external (e.g., environmental) resources, or by fundamentally reorganizing production, work, technology, and social services as part of the postindustrial transition (Block, 1981). However, this postindustrial revolution, which may already be in progress (Piore & Sabel, 1984; Bell, 1973), evidently produces new dilemmas. The public evinces new, nonmaterial interests—such as in the quality of life—which appear to exceed the capacities of the market system (Inglehart, 1990; 1977), and the labor force, which is satiated with income and consumption and which is growing restive about work conditions, is challenging employers with new demands regarding the work place and work time (Strümpel, 1989; Yankelovich, Zetterberg, Strümpel, & Shanks, 1985; see also Yuchtman-Yaar & Gottlieb, in this volume). The twin sins of depleting natural resources and polluting the environment, though hardly unique to capitalist societies, are also growing increasingly salient.

How have different western societies tried to cope with the dual crises of permanent unemployment and burgeoning fiscal liabilities? Let us try to illustrate the most common contemporary prototypes of "real capitalism" by referring to their distinct approaches to the labor-market dilemma. At the risk of oversimplification, we may distinguish between three ideal-type models, each involving distinct costs and benefits:

1. The labor force includes a high proportion of low-skilled, relatively unproductive workers in a labor market dominated by the private sector. This strategy curbs unemployment but handicaps productivity and growth (the "U.S. model").

2.   The labor market absorbs primarily highly skilled and productive workers, while the unskilled and unproductive are kept off. This approach facilitates economic growth but effects a relatively high rate of unemployment, which is usually balanced by generous unemployment benefits (the "German model").

3.   The marginal labor force is absorbed into an inflated public sector to keep unemployment at a minimum; in parallel, generous remedial measures (e.g., vocational training) are extended. These policies, which appear to result in a slow and even stagnating pace of economic growth, have been characteristic of the "Swedish model."

These paradigms are by no means fixed. Rather, relevant policy choices evolve dynamically as a function of changing pragmatic considerations. Thus, Sweden, driven by her concern about economic stagnation and budget deficits, is currently steering away from her redistributive policies. Germany, threatened by the collapse of the labor market in her eastern provinces, has been compelled to increase subsidies for state-supported employment and for vocational training. Even the still conservatively governed Britain is currently venturing a repeal of some of the more drastic measures introduced during Thatcher's regime.

ALTERNATIVE PATHS OF MODERNIZATION AND DEVELOPMENT

We will now try to establish that the problems confronting the new eastern European market economies differ from those in the West not only in magnitude but, even more importantly, in substance. The presumption that any western variant of "real capitalism" can serve as an appropriate model for the economic transformation in the East may therefore well be misguided. It is quite conceivable that some of these countries will evolve not toward highly advanced industrialism but rather toward one of the market systems typical of developing countries.

To substantiate these assertions, we wish to advance the following theoretical propositions:

1.   While the present rate of unemployment in some East European countries is critically high, it is likely to be transitory. More importantly, its root causes differ fundamentally from those in the West.

2.   It is not unemployment, but rather the scarcity of resources in these countries that constitute the most fundamental challenge to their economic transition and the most critical obstacle to the realization of their objectives. Here again, however, the causes of this fiscal crisis differ from those that have triggered the escalation of public expenditures in the West.

3. Former socialist nations are on the brink of modernization processes comparable to those experienced by many Third World countries, with all the risks and potentials involved.

The Transitory Nature of Unemployment

The crisis eventuated by the massive increase in unemployment in eastern Europe should not be underestimated. It is apt to breed discontent, may vent itself in social unrest and ethnic and national strife, and may even imperil the recently attained political and civil liberties. Even so, the diminishing volume of labor markets in the East cannot be attributed to the same causes as the contraction of the labor market in the West, nor can it be resolved by similar methods. In the West, the shift toward less labor-intensive production is the primary factor contributing to persistent and relatively high unemployment rates. Yet, as long as productive efficiency continues to rise, economic growth not only causes but also helps compensate for the contraction of the labor market, for it enables the state and the private sector to generate the revenues needed to extend retraining programs, provide generous unemployment benefits, reduce work hours, and so forth, and thus cope at least partially with the problem.

Unemployment in the East, not unlike the region's other economic predicaments, is a manifestation of the past, the hapless legacy of the *ancien régime*: its long practice of hidden unemployment, the protection of productive enterprises from exposure to competition and open markets, and the exercise of soft budget constraints. Free-market competition currently confronts entire industrial sectors with their own obsolescence; many are collapsing under their own weight, and their workers are buried under the rubble.

East European labor markets, then, are taking part in the sweeping disintegration of the socialist order and its industrial base, and the massive loss of jobs essentially reflects a phase of the transition rather than a permanent sociopolitical quandary. Once a modicum of economic growth is regained, unemployment is bound to abate. The prospects for such a development are quite sound because, contrary to the West, industrial production is likely to remain labor-intensive for quite some time. However, in order to regain economic growth and increase productivity, these economies must first rectify the damage perpetrated by real socialism: the ravaged industrial infrastructure; the absence of modern technology and investment capital; and the dearth of essential occupational sectors, an entrepreneurial middle class, and a highly skilled and motivated labor force. These, more than unemployment, are the pressing problems of the transition to a market economy.

The Fiscal Crisis in Eastern Europe

The new governments of eastern Europe continue to bear the burden of myriad entitlement claims propagated by their predecessors. Not only do welfare allocations and the privileges demanded by entrepreneurs exceed the standards common in the West, these nations, ravaged by decades of real socialism and burdened by the genuine financial needs of economic reconstruction, hardly have the resources to accommodate these claims.

And yet, these administrations entirely lack the West's flexibility in generating the supplementary sources of state revenue needed to fund their commitments. First, most state-owned enterprises are unproductive, unprofitable, and due for privatization. Second, the stringent conditions attached to loans from the World Bank, western governments, and private financial institutions severely curtail the options for deficit financing. Third, eastern European governments can hardly afford to impose higher taxes on their already impoverished populations.

Consequently, the central obstacle of eastern Europe's transition to a market economy is the state's inability to bear the tremendous cost of its most elementary responsibilities toward the productive process: the establishment of a broad infrastructure of technology, communication, transportation, capital, markets, and labor. This is the most fundamental complex of problems that should currently guide eastern Europe's economic policies, and prototypes of western market economies are hardly suited for realizing these objectives.

Alternatives to Advanced Capitalism

What are and what should be the long-range perspectives and objectives of the economic transformation in eastern Europe? Is it plausible to assume that one of the western prototypes of capitalism can be reconciled with domestic conditions in eastern Europe? That similar standards of economic growth, productivity, and affluence will be attained by emulating its principles and policies, even if only in the distant future?

To the best of our knowledge, political leaders in the East have yet to question the assumption that their countries will sooner or later join the small and privileged club of highly industrialized and affluent nations. Envisioning the models of advanced capitalism as the only viable options would be reminiscent of early and somewhat naive versions of modernization theory, which depicted societies as progressing through uniform stages of social, political, and economic development (Parsons, 1951; cf. Portes, 1976). Even the psychological make-up of their members, which some observers (e.g., McClelland, 1967) regard as a prerequisite for modernization, is similarly modified in all developing societies. It is presumably "upgraded" by contacts with modern institutions so as to evolve "individual modernity" (Inkeles &

Smith, 1974). In other words, modernization used to be conceptualized as an endogenous process and as a non-zero-sum game in which the entire international community stands to gain from the developmental progress of each of its members.[12]

This perspective, which is no longer considered credible (Griffin, 1989; Toye, 1987), has been replaced by an alternative conception of the international community as a single entity characterized by a universal division of labor and by cultural and perhaps even political convergence (Wallerstein, 1984; 1974). Most vital for our purposes, and for the dominion of capitalism, is the argument that this "world system" consists of a core and a periphery (Chirot & Hall, 1982; Hopkins & Wallerstein, 1980).[13] The core depends on the periphery for surplus resources, which, in turn, guarantee the core's growth and expansion. Thus, uneven development and the very existence of peripheries are not mere artifacts but inherent attributes of capitalism (Wallerstein, 1979). Advanced economies compete incessantly for core positions (Skocpol, 1979), and peripheral states continually struggle to escape their marginal status (Wallerstein, 1984).

The notion of uneven development is intimately related to the problem of dependency. Dependency theory (e.g., Apter, 1987) originated in South America, one of the developing regions Wallerstein denotes as peripheral, but is directly relevant to our current concerns. Since the core monopolizes international markets and technology, imposes protective trade barriers, extracts disproportional debt services, and withdraws profits in excess of its investments, peripheral nations become inevitably dependent on it (Furtado, 1970; Thomas & Meyer, 1984).[14] Economic dependence destabilizes the state (Thomas & Meyer, 1980), reduces the resources available for economic development (Meyer, Hannan, Rubinson, & Thomas, 1979), and increases social inequality (e.g., Portes, 1976). These traumata create a self-reinforcing cycle that locks weak economies into peripheral positions (Delacroix, 1977). In sum, the combined impact of marginality and dependency generates a zero-sum game in which only economies at the core of the world system can win.

In light of this analysis, eastern Europe's current economic objectives seem rather far-fetched. The West has gained substantial and perhaps irreversible advantages in controlling international money and labor markets and in regulating the price of raw materials and its own manufactured products and services. From the perspective of world-system theory, there are only negligible differences in the marginal status of eastern Europe and much of the Third World. The deficient technological infrastructure and the absence of a highly qualified and motivated labor force—problems that are hardly surmountable in any case, given the scarcity of available resources—will make it even more difficult to procure the essential prerequisites for growth, productivity, and efficiency.

Even the conventional argument that eastern Europe will benefit from its physical proximity to the West, its cultural similarity, and its overlapping traditions is not particularly convincing. Proximity is a trivial factor in this age of rapid transport and instantaneous communication (Walton, 1987), and the presumed cultural similarity apparently does not extend to workers' values, attitudes, work traditions, and productive behaviors, as recent comparative surveys suggest (Grootings, 1986; Šanderová & Kabátek; Schlese et al., in this volume).[15] The modernization of individuals may be impeded considerably if the modern institutions of which the individual is "to become a part" (Inkeles & Smith, 1974) are slow to evolve, or if the labor force perseveres in those attitudes and habits that have fostered adjustment to the old economic system but that have become detrimental now.

In any case, it is perfectly transparent that the most essential criteria of economic development and growth involve neither geographical nor cultural affinity, but technology, investments, the quality of educational institutions, and the qualifications of the labor force (Porter, 1990).[16] From this perspective the handicaps of East European countries, all propagated by the former command economies, are self-evident.

This reasoning suggests (the term "predict" would be too precarious in light of recent events) that the evolution from state-controlled to western-type market economies is infeasible in the short run and unlikely in the long run. Of course, these nations would hardly be alone in being relegated to the club of second-rank market economies; with the exception of the four Southeast Asian "tigers," which, incidentally, violate Berger's (1986) premise that an efficient market economy, democratic pluralism, and political emancipation must go hand-in-hand, this has been the fate of most South American, Asian and African nations that have opted for the capitalist course of development.

What are the viable alternative scenarios for the future if East European nations do indeed fail to make the quantum leap to one of the prototype western market economies? Space does not permit us to delineate these options in detail; a few representative illustrations must suffice.

1. The evolution of technologically less advanced modes of production. This course may be pragmatic and perhaps inevitable if the timely establishment of domestic infrastructures is obstructed, say, due to the government's inability to purchase western technology, insufficient foreign investment, or an inadequately qualified labor force. Industrial production may be oriented primarily toward internal markets and toward countries unable to purchase the more sophisticated, but also more expensive, western products.

2. In some countries and even in specific regions, lower-standard industrialization may be combined with an efficient, technology-based and export-oriented agricultural sector, or with the extraction of larger quantities of raw materials and energy resources. This pattern is common in much of the Third World, which also evinces some of its drawbacks. For example, such economies often neglect their industrial base and industrial production, and

they run the risk of exploitation by core nations, which use their market power to dictate the price structure of agricultural produce and raw materials.

3.   Other countries may embark on a course of regional development (see Vanhove & Klaasen, 1987, for a review). The experience accumulated in northern Italy (e.g., Cipolletta, Heimler, & Calcagnini, 1987; Masi, in this volume) and in other regions of Europe (Hatch, 1991; Sabel, Herrigel, Deeg, & Kazis, 1987; Pawlowsky, Schlese, & Schramm, in this volume) indicates that this arrangement primarily benefits traditional manufacturing industries and is less conducive to intensive technological development and innovation.

4.   Perhaps the most likely scenario is the emergence of an "extended workbench"—technology-based industrial sectors designed chiefly to provide services to the industrialized West. This is the potentially most precarious scenario because it puts the newly emerging market economies at risk of becoming overdependent on the core, to the point of economic colonialism.

5.   A final, though unlikely, possibility is the reinstatement, perhaps in modified form, of some of the policies of the centralized command economy, or even a "third way"—assuming it does exist.

THE TRANSITION FROM COMMAND
TO MARKET: RISKS AND OPTIONS

Even in light of these observations, the economic future of eastern Europe remains unfathomable. The current circumstances are still too enigmatic to permit sound inferences; and the historical, cultural, ethnic, and political heterogeneity of these countries hardly sustains sweeping generalizations. Rather than risk such tenuous projections, we draw now on the observations proffered above and on the other contributions in this volume to venture some conjectures on the hazards and opportunities arising from the current transition. Because these comments are extrapolated from the transition dilemmas of the region as a whole, they pertain by definition more to certain countries than to others.

Dilemmas of the Transition

The transition period involves a number of political, economic, and social dilemmas, all of paramount importance to its ultimate outcomes.

National and Ethnic Conflicts

The democratization of political, community, and social life is one of the more pronounced aspects of this new era. However, the revival of democracy is often accompanied by political extremism, and renewed manifestations of national, ethnic, and religious conflicts that had been ignored or suppressed by the former regimes. These confrontations divert national energies from the task of economic recuperation because they tend to overshadow economic difficulties and because parties representing the narrow interests of these groups frequently use the current economic hardship as a means to mobilize political support.

Physical and Human Capital

As a result of the policies of real socialism, East European countries lag considerably behind the industrialized West in mechanization, automation, and technology; the conversion from agricultural to industrial production; and the conversion from heavy, labor-intensive, and polluting industries to high-tech enterprises and an extended service sector. This protracted paralysis of innovation, production, and economic development directly affects the prospects of current reconstruction.

Eastern Europe's industries, which do not excel in technological sophistication, the quality of their products, or competitive prices, will undoubtedly find it difficult, if not impossible, to recover from their highly disadvantageous position on international markets. These industrial deficits must be redressed in the course of the economic reforms, but the impact of reconstruction is likely to reverberate throughout the social fabric. The labor force in particular will be required to make considerable adjustments, entailing not only a sweeping revitalization of its technological and managerial skills but also a reversal of its work ethic. These processes, in turn, are bound to cause additional economic and social hardship for large segments of the labor force, as those workers unable to acquire the necessary competencies (mostly older and less educated members of the labor force) are ousted from the labor market.

Scarcity of Capital

From the producer's as well as the consumer's point of view, the most conspicuous aspect of the current transition is the revolution in the nature of scarcity. Whereas the communist market place had been characterized by a scarcity of goods, capitalism is founded on the scarcity of capital. Though stringent fiscal restraints are obviously crucial to a well-functioning market place, the incipient market economies in the East are severely constrained by this stipulation, which further narrows their options for raising the funds for economic reconstruction. Thus, scarce fiscal resources paradoxically constitute both a remedy and an additional problem for the economic transition in eastern Europe.

Privatization

Needless to say, the prospective reduction of the government's economic control and involvement, especially the privatization of state-owned property, constitutes one of the fundamental aspects of the transition period. However, privatization is impeded by two prime obstacles: The limited availability of private capital and the legal intricacies of property ownership. The resulting slow pace of privatization throughout eastern Europe compels the state to resume its support and subsidies for a host of inefficient enterprises that it can neither revitalize nor sell. Consequently, industrial productivity and economic growth continue to decline.

Paternalism versus Welfare

East European governments have to contend with yet another legacy of real socialism, the entrenched paternalism that had controlled the entire system of entitlement claims in the command economy. The conversion of this presumably indulgent benevolence into a modern welfare state constitutes an additional obligation during the transition. Here, the difficulties caused by fiscal constraints are aggravated by the public's proclivity to sustain traditional notions of distributive justice, such as the right to employment and free education, and to resist new welfare legislation that might curtail these ensconced privileges (Ziółkowski, in this volume).

Strategies of Reform

It stands to reason that eastern Europe's new governments should give first priority to negating those aspects of the socialist legacy—be they economic, social, psychological, or political—that pose the most critical threats to the democratic order, societal harmony and peace, and rational economic performance. Let us briefly consider each of these dimensions.

Economic Considerations

There is no question that eastern Europe has launched its bid for sweeping economic reform under highly disadvantageous conditions and that its course and ultimate outcomes are anything but clear. Nonetheless, the region's new governments must now rapidly formulate and implement precisely those free-market agendas and policies that constitute minimal prerequisites for attaining the principal objectives of efficient industrial production and sound economic growth: the recruitment of resources (largely foreign) so as to revitalize the neglected infrastructure; the establishment of genuinely free markets, where prices are allowed to fluctuate according to the dynamics of supply and demand; the privatization of state property, preferably with the help of local investment such as the voucher system in the former Czechoslovakia (Šanderová & Kabátek, in this volume); the training and formation of a highly skilled, productive, and motivated labor force; and the predication of personal economic behavior and productive performance on the principles of individual interest and profit.

Social Costs

While the general decline in the quality of life and the prevailing economic insecurity in eastern Europe are inevitable consequences of the collapse of the *ancien régime*, the public's plight has at times been exacerbated by misguided policy decisions and by "big-bang" strategies that have enacted market strategies swiftly, but also painfully.

Some sectors have suffered considerably, even to the point of impoverishment; others have adjusted quickly. The transition has already generated its own "winners" and "losers" and has created a newly differentiated social structure based on achievement and merit rather than on political power. But the unaccustomed socioeconomic inequality is often severely criticized, and not only because it violates prevailing conceptions of social justice, equality, and meritocracy. Conspicuous consumption by the *nouveau riche* is a thorn in the eyes of those stricken by poverty; the new economic order often rewards illegitimate activities rather than merit and performance; and, worst of all, the old nomenclature repeatedly succeeds in joining the winners.

More importantly perhaps, the emergence of an impoverished underclass (Marks, 1991; Wilson, 1987) necessitates swift legislation of welfare programs to cushion the shock of the transformation and the loss of economic security. The already evident dilemmas of welfare and entitlement claims suggest that the reconciliation between economic rationality and socioeconomic justice is likely to become a key issue of the transition. Can a productive economy sustain the welfare expenditures needed to maintain a modicum of socioeconomic equality? Can economic growth and affluence be attained without leading to greater social inequality (Wnuk-Lipinski, 1991)? These apprehensions are not unknown in the West, but their urgency is even more compelling in eastern Europe, where public expectations are based on the traditionally comprehensive, albeit scanty, benefits dispensed by the former communist regimes and where scarce public resources must satisfy growing and competing social needs.

Psychological Ramifications

Public disillusionment may well constitute one of the more serious threats to the political stability of eastern Europe today. The prime reasons behind the prevailing dismay are to be found in the discrepancy between the public's initial—and usually excessive—expectations and its subsequent frustrating experiences: The growing impatience with the pace of economic progress, the threat of unemployment and impoverishment, rising prices, and the stagnating standard of living. These frustrations coincide with the plummeting of macroeconomic performance, and with the rapid decline in individual affluence.[17]

The most evident manifestation of spreading alienation and disaffection is migration. But perhaps more ominous is the growing nostalgia about those practices of the communist regime that had presumably guaranteed individual and social security (Radaev; Šanderová & Kabátek; Schlese et al.; Ziółkowski, in this volume). For the time being, this emotional response expresses itself only in the public's attitudes and not in its actions. Especially those economic reforms designed to enhance productive efficiency (e.g., rationalization, privatization) are increasingly viewed as the "dark side" of capitalism and support for them is steadily dwindling.

Disappointed expectations are probably also responsible for the relative lack of personal commitment and economic initiative. The tendency toward learned helplessness inculcated by the previous regime still predisposes many actors to retreat from any responsibility for political or economic reform; such change has always been the government's responsibility. This frame of mind has become so habitual that it is difficult to identify the measures that might restore individual motivation and initiative.

Perhaps less alienated, but no more energetic, are those occupational groups—the intelligentsia, industrial workers, peasants, and particularly members of the former nomenclature who have retained their economic prerogatives—that still have a vested interest in the socialist practices of centralized planning, control, protection, and distribution. The continued dominance of these interests is prompting many members of the industrial complex to engage in a variety of maladapted economic behaviors. They secure the savings dictated by hard budget constraints by cutting production and dismissing workers rather than by rationalizing and increasing the efficiency of production. By failing to adjust to the exigencies of the market, they continue to rely on the government to define production goals, allocate resources, and even identify demand and fix prices. The fact that the production sector summons the state to protect it from the bewildering dynamics of the market is truly paradoxical: It intimates that the government is expected to suspend the very economic policies it has just introduced.

Nonetheless, more encouraging attitudes and behavioral adaptations are also apparent. One is the unconditional public support for democratic due process, a shift that in some countries had already commenced prior to the events of 1989 (Hahn & Zierke; Ziółkowski, in this volume). Another is the growing acceptance of fundamental economic change and of economic policies based on free-market principles.[18] Last but not least, individual initiatives designed to cope with declining employment and income opportunities are one the rise. Along with the already-mentioned tendency of some groups to remain passive and dependent, many others are embarking or are engaged in a variety of activities such as secondary labor-market participation, self-provisioning, networking, or moonlighting—though many continue to evince little initiative, and to presume that they are helpless against their current ordeals (e.g., Hahn & Zierke; Ziółkowski, in this volume).

Political Aspects

There is some evidence that dissatisfaction with economic progress and the outcomes of market reforms manifests itself as disillusionment with the government, and more importantly, with democracy (Radaev; Šanderová & Kabátek, in this volume; see Ziółkowski for a dissenting view). It appears that public support for authoritarian rule and monopolized power has not quite dissipated yet. Such a proclivity would obviously constitute a serious threat sooner or later.

On a structural level, prevailing conditions have compelled the state to maintain considerable control of economic and market processes. Thus, the scarcity of private capital has prompted governments to retain large segments of industry and other means of production, despite intentions to the contrary. Welfare policies have also changed relatively little, for the process of impoverishment and persevering entitlement claims have obliged governments to yield to public demands. These extra expenditures place an additional burden on the already depleted state treasuries. The retrenchment of the state, which is likely to endure as long as these and similar policies are perpetuated, may be inevitable during the transition phase, but it involves profound risks for the future.

CONCLUDING REMARKS

Beyond the considerable variance among former socialist countries, we should emphasize one imponderable that, as a universal attribute of the democratic order, is shared by them all: the government's ability to cultivate and sustain its political legitimation (Habermas, 1975). In concluding this chapter, we turn to a closer examination of the political legitimacy and stability of the democratic governments of central and eastern Europe.

The elected governments in the East currently enjoy at least a modicum of popular support. This should hardly come as a surprise. The populations of these countries had supported political freedom and pluralism even before the former authoritarian regimes foundered (Ziółkowski, in this volume). But this endorsement does not necessarily guarantee political stability; indeed, the survival of eastern Europe's nascent democracies may still be at some risk.

Fluctuations in public support for political parties and leaders constitute an inherent and essential element of the democratic model. The very fact that governments cannot take their citizens' backing for granted serves to reinforce the democratic process. The political alternatives offered in a pluralistic system enable the electorate to express its disapproval of the government and even to replace it. Correspondingly, political parties are obliged to attend to and balance between the needs and demands of diverse interest groups. This inordinately romantic portrayal of democracy serves to make a point: It is the only political system that succeeds in both serving a multitude of social interests and maintaining societal consensus and solidarity.

But the very same attributes that constitute the mainstay of the established democratic societies in the West may imperil the emergent democracies in the East. Here, pluralism is still in its infancy; genuine political alternatives are scarce, and some elements, such as the old nomenclature and representatives of narrow ethnic and nationalist interests, can hardly be considered ardent adherents of democracy. Should the government fail to fulfill the public's expectations and lose support, it may well lead to a retreat to an earlier era, perhaps to the revocation of economic reforms and, more ominously, to the denouement of the brief democratic revival. These threats may persist as long as democratic and pluralistic precepts remain unassimilated, economic regression goes unchecked, and public yearning for the patronizing, yet comfortable, shelter of the *ancien régime* lingers.

Hollander's (1958) model of the ascent of leaders may help unravel the secrets of political legitimation. Individuals accumulate "idiosyncracy credits," and thereby rise to the position of leadership, by conforming to social norms and expectations. Having advanced to the top of the ladder, they may use (expend) the accrued credits to challenge and transform conventional practices, at the risk of becoming handicapped, or even of losing their status. The transliteration of this psychological abstraction into political terminology is obvious: Democratic governments derive their legitimation from their electorate, legitimation credits are accrued and maximized by accommodating the public's demands and expectations, and they are lost by violating these expectations.

Legitimation credits are available in three "currencies." Eastern Europe's governments have accrued *symbolic* credits because they are perceived as the constitutional, just, and moral replacement of the *ancien régime* and because their ascent to power coincided with the liberation from Soviet domination and with national independence. Symbolic legitimation in the former Soviet Union may be more problematic because the ousting of the communist dictatorship, rather than signifying national liberation, precipitated the end of the Soviet empire.

The basis for the accumulation of *political* credits is provided by the government's promotion and implementation of the precepts of democracy, pluralism, and human rights and liberties. *Economic* legitimation is directly related to the central task of the postcommunist governments: recovery from the economic afflictions caused by the policies of the former regime. This facet is contingent on the pace and the outcomes of the current reforms, or more accurately, on the correspondence between economic progress, especially regarding personal benefits such as a higher standard of living and greater affluence, and the public's initial expectations. At present, it appears that a majority of the population is still willing to accept the prevailing economic hardships as temporary and inevitable and to regard them as its contribution to a "package deal," which entails the public's willingness to tolerate the current sacrifices and to support the government's economic policies for the promise of a better future. In other words, the basis of economic legitimation is intangible. Since most promises of the reform cannot be realized immediately, legitimation must be grounded in long-term interests and expectations of future benefits, with the population's more immediate concerns often being violated.

For reasons we have already discussed at length, this implicit contract may be quite precarious. Eastern Europe's deficient infrastructure, its scarce capital, and its marginal position on international markets render the economic future of these countries highly uncertain. Moreover, the public, blinded by stereotypes and disinformation, had entertained unrealistic expectations of the market system from the outset. The policies of the industrialized, affluent West were viewed as a panacea for both macroeconomic and microeconomic prosperity, but the notions of how to achieve it were vague at best. Not unrelatedly, entrepreneurs and the labor force are still inclined to remain passive, and dependent on the government for economic recovery.

The public's misconceptions of what democracy and the dynamics of the market can and cannot accomplish may go well beyond inflated expectations and counterproductive behaviors. For example, there appears to be little awareness of the basic conflict—indigenous to western societies—between equal opportunity and the maximization of individual chances on the one hand, and the desire for equality and social security on the other. The former principle ("economic freedom" in the classification offered by Janda, Berry, & Goldman [1989]), envisions democracy primarily as support for individual entrepreneurship; for the latter principle ("economic equality"), democracy is the leading address for claims of entitlement. Both aspirations are difficult to realize simultaneously. Thus, it is a truism that "democracy is good in generating demands, but bad in satisfying them" (Burstein, 1981, p. 300). For much of the public in the East, this inherent contradiction does not appear to exist; the evident need to stimulate production has not produced a concomitant reduction in entitlement claims.

It would probably be illusory to assume that the political legitimacy of eastern Europe's governments will remain untouched by the volatile economic situation. Should these countries ultimately fail to achieve significant and opportune economic progress, or should the public's expectations not be realized, the symbolic and political legitimation of those governments may wane as well. Some of the available evidence, such as the tendency to blame the present governments for the failures of their predecessors and the nostalgic sentiments for the previous regime, appears to suggest that this process has already commenced.

Though it is difficult to imagine that the recently attained rights and liberties will be revoked or that these nations will actually revert to the false security of real socialism, the alternative of political instability, precipitated by an impoverished and disillusioned population, may be no less perilous. In any case, it would be practically impossible to complete the economic reforms in a vacuum of political legitimation, and in the absence of at least minimal social consensus.

In the long run, the current transformation cannot be carried by market mechanisms and changes alone. Modifications in individual circumstances, perspectives, and behavioral patterns are no less important. Several key points for future policy decisions come to mind:

- Current trends of unemployment and impoverishment and the standard of living must be stabilized before more severe alienation, the loss of political support, and even social unrest become a genuine risk.
- Principles of rational economic behavior rather than dependency and reliance on the government must be promoted and assimilated.
- Certain social and production problems must be transferred to the grass-root level so as to overcome the public's current passivity and dependency and to encourage greater initiative.
- Those societal sectors and groups that have a vested interest in the economic reconstruction—entrepreneurs, managers, and a highly skilled labor force—should be consolidated into a genuine social base that can support the government's reforms and policies.
- Ways must be found to diminish the tenacious estrangement between the state bureaucracy ("they") and the public ("we"), which stems from the legacy of distrust toward the former communist regime[19] but which is also grounded in the enduring propensity to charge the government with the total responsibility for achieving economic objectives.
- Most generally, measures should be taken to begin transforming eastern Europe's political culture from a society of "subjects" to a community of "participants," in other words, to initiate a conversion to a genuine civil society.

These initiatives are no less the government's responsibility than is the creation of other, more tangible conditions for economic reconstruction and change.

NOTES

1. This trend was already evident as early as 1990, when an impassioned political campaign nurtured support for the partition among both Czechs and Slovaks (Šanderová & Kabátek, in this volume).

2. The traditional reluctance of western, especially U.S., sociologists to study socialist societies is indeed puzzling, especially in light of the growing number defining themselves as Marxists (van den Berg, 1988).

3. For example, Marx (e.g., 1859/1973) had hoped to revolutionize the capitalist relations of production by replacing private ownership by social, not public, ownership of the means of production. The two are analogous only if the public proprietor is controlled by society. State ownership, on the other hand, is tantamount to the economic subjugation of the populace.

4. Janda, Berry, and Goldman (1989) illustrate patterns of public support for the political and economic order by juxtaposing political (freedom versus order) and economic (freedom versus equality) values. For example, the combined choice of political freedom and equality reflects the tenets of social democracy, which, although politically pluralistic, advocates government intervention in reducing socioeconomic disparities. The doctrines of real as well as "genuine" socialism are reproduced by the synthesis of political order and economic equality.

5. Although the interaction between the state and producers or managers was strictly regulated, relations between the state and the labor force or private households were presumably determined by the market. In practice, however, this freedom was severely curtailed by price controls, rationing, queuing, and the state's massive intervention in the labor market.

6. For more detailed descriptions and assessments of these reforms, see, for example, Deacon (1991), Jeffries (1990) and van Brabant (1989).

7. Even Hungary, which in the late 1970s experienced economic growth and an increase in productivity, later had to contend with a recurring slowdown, stagnating income, and inflationary pressures. Hungary did succeed in retaining several advantages, such as a convertible currency, wages and prices that reflected the dynamics of the market, and no consumer shortages.

8. Kornai (1986; 1982) illustrates this process with respect to Hungary's "new economic mechanism": Policies changed only in appearance, from direct (planning and allocation) to indirect (the use of credits to force the enterprises' compliance with government priorities) state control. The accumulation of resources at the expense of private consumption, the regulation of the labor market, soft budget constraints, and price-fixing were also continued informally. The reform thus cultivated neither a real capital market nor an authentic labor market.

9. This is epitomized by the example of the former Soviet Union. On the other hand, the former German Democratic Republic may constitute a partial exceptic.1. After all, the masses who congregated to chant *Wir sind das Volk!* [We are the people!] certainly hastened the collapse of this particular regime.

10. These beliefs illustrate how little the public knew about market economic processes. Obviously, capitalism does not guarantee affluence, certainly not in the absence of productivity. Note, however, that in Germany it was the federal government itself that induced such unrealistic expectations by underestimating the dimensions and overestimating the pace of social and economic recovery (Schlese et al., in this volume).

11. Although both stable and cyclical unemployment constitute inherent contradictions of the capitalist economy, they differ fundamentally. The former is due to the rationalization of production; the latter (Marx, 1867/1956) to the vicissitudes of supply and demand and to the

cycles of the capitalist market place. The West German economy exemplifies the former phenomenon at its peak. For the past 25 years, West Germany's GNP has grown at a respectable rate, while at the same time the country's labor market has stagnated and even contracted (e.g., Strümpel & Schramm, 1989; Schramm in this volume).

12. Some postsocialist reforms, such as the "big-bang" approach associated with the name of Poland's economic advisor Jeffrey Sachs, or the rapid market exposure pursued by the German government, may well be implicitly grounded in this linear theory of societal development.

13. As well as a semiperiphery, which, as pointed out below, may constitute one of the options for Eastern Europe.

14. Tellingly, these analyses ignore the possibility that developing nations may themselves wish to confine the social impact of modernization and development so as to protect national culture, heritage, and endogenous ways of life from external influence (e.g., Ners, 1990; Szcepanski, 1989).

15. Interestingly, workers appear to sustain traditional "protestant" values, although their work commitment and their identification with the work place are continuously declining. This certainly seems to be the case in the former German Democratic Republic (Schlese et al., in this volume).

16. These conditions have been spelled out quite clearly in the extensive empirical research on the "convergence hypothesis" (Moore, 1965), which originated from the premise that industrializing nations must respond to common technical and organizational imperatives and will therefore develop similar methods of production and distribution, social structures, and even cultural and national institutions. These prerequisites are the accumulation of capital; the mobility of money, property, and labor; a stable political order; and a committed industrial labor force (Form, 1979; Meyer, Boli-Bennett, & Chase-Dunn, 1975).

17. All East European contributions to this volume focus on this theme. Disenchantment with the economic reform is expressed both in personal frustrations and anxieties (regarding the standard of living, the threat of unemployment, and, in the former USSR, even the uncertainties of procuring basic necessities) and in the rejection of the reforms in principle. Radaev (in this volume) reports that the public regrets its initial support for *perestroika,* forecasts a major calamity (including famine and a civil war), and—more ominously—not only expects but would actually condone military or KGB intervention. This bleak picture is presumably brightened by more optimistic long-term perspectives, especially in the former German Democratic Republic (Hahn & Zierke; Schlese et al., in this volume); but given the sluggish pace of economic progress in Germany's new *Bundesländer,* the longevity of this sanguine outlook is, to say the least, questionable.

18. However, the endorsement of market policies is typically qualified. Certain groups (private sector employees, weaker social segments) are believed to be disadvantaged or exploited (Ziółkowski, in this volume), key socialist provisos (full employment, stable prices) are to be preserved in the transition to capitalism (Radaev; Schlese et al., in this volume), and privatization is to be circumscribed in various ways (Radaev; Ziółkowski; Šanderová & Kabátek, in this volume).

19. And, more specifically, from the unholy union between political authority and economic dominion practiced under real socialism (Ziółkowski, in this volume).

REFERENCES

Almond, A., & Verba, S. (1963). *The civic culture: Political attitudes and democracy in five nations.* Princeton, NJ: Princeton University Press.

Andorka, R., Jackson, J., Simkus, A., & Treiman. D. (1983). *Changes in social mobility in two semi-peripheral societies.* Amsterdam: Congress.

Apter, D. E. (1987). *Rethinking development: Modernization, dependency, and post-modern politics.* Newbury Park, CA: Sage.

Bell, D. (1976). *The cultural contradictions of capitalism*. London: Heineman.

———. (1973). *The coming of post-industrial society*. New York: Basic Books.

Berger, P. (1986). *The capitalist revolution*. New York: Basic Books.

Block, F. (1981). The fiscal crisis of the capitalist state. *Annual Review of Sociology, 7*, 1-27.

Bolle, M., & Greffe, X. A. (1989). Employment and productivity in Europe: What are the perspectives? In B. Strümpel (Ed.), *Industrial societies after the stagnation of the 1970s* (pp. 17-37). Berlin: de Gruyter.

Bottomore, T. (1990). *The socialist economy*. Brighton: Harvester Wheatsheaf.

Braverman, H. (1974). *Labor and monopoly capital: The degradation of work in the twentieth century*. New York: Monthly Review Press.

Brus, W., & Laski, K. (1989). *From Marx to the market: Socialism in search of an economic system*. London: Claredon Press.

Buchanan, J. M. (1986). *Liberty, market and the state: Political economy in the 80s*. Brighton: Harvester Wheatsheaf.

Burstein, P. (1981). The sociology of democratic politics and government. *Annual Review of Sociology, 7*, 291-319.

Charvat F., Linhart, J. & Vecernik, J. (1978). *Socialne tridni struktura Cekoslovenska* [Social structure in Czechoslovakia]. Prague: Horizont.

Chirot, D., & Hall, T. D. (1982). World-system theory. *Annual Review of Sociology, 8*, 81-106.

Cipolletta, I., Heimler, A., & Calcagnini, G. (1987, September-December). Restructuring and adjustment in Italian industry. *Review of Economic Conditions in Italy*, 341-381.

Converse, P. E. (1965). The nature of belief systems in mass publics, in D. Apter (Ed.), *Ideology and discontent* (pp. 206-261). Glencoe: Free Press.

Dahrendorf, R. (1988). *The modern social conflict*. London: Weidenfeld & Nicolson.

Deacon, B. (1991). *Eastern Europe in the 1990s: Past developments and future prospects for social policy*. Newbury Park, CA: Sage.

Delacroix, J. (1977). The export of raw materials and economic growth: A cross-national study. *American Sociological Review, 42*, 795-808.

Dobson, R. B. (1977). Mobility and stratification in the Soviet Union. *Annual Review of Sociology, 3*, 297-329.

Drewnowski, J. (Ed.). (1982). *Crisis in the East European economy*. London: Croom Helms.

Feher, F., Heller, A., & Markus, G. (1983). *Dictatorship over needs*. Oxford: Basil Blackwell.

Form, W. (1979). Comparative industrial sociology and the convergence hypothesis. *Annual Review of Sociology, 5*, 1-25.

Furtado, C. (1970). *Obstacles to development in Latin America*. New York: Anchor.

Giddens, A. (1981). *Capitalism and modern social theory*. Cambridge: Cambridge University Press.

Goldthorpe, J. H. (Ed.). (1984). *Order and conflict in contemporary capitalism: Studies in the political economy of Western European nations*. Oxford: Claredon Press.

Griffin, K. B. (1989). *Alternative strategies for economic development*. Basingstone: MacMillan.

Grootings, P. (Ed.). (1986). *Technology and work: East-West comparisons*. London: Croom Helms.

Habermas, J. (1975). *Legitimation crisis*. Boston: Beacon Press.

Harrison, D. (1988). *The sociology of modernization and development*. London: Unwin & Hyman.

Hatch, C. R. (1991). The power of manufacturing networks. *Transatlantic, 2*, 3-6.

Heilbroner, R. L. (1985). *The nature and logic of capitalism*. New York: W. W. Norton & Co.

———. (1980). *Marxism: For and against*. New York: W. W. Norton.

Hibbs, D. A., Jr. (1987). *The political economy of industrialized democracies*. Cambridge, MA: Harvard University Press.

Hollander, E. P. (1958). Conformity, status and idiosyncracy credit. *Psychological Review, 65*, 117-127.

Hollander, P. (1983). *The many faces of socialism*. Brunswick, MA: Transaction Books.

314 AVI GOTTLIEB and MAREK ZIÓŁKOWSKI

Hopkins, T. K., & Wallerstein, I. (Eds.). (1980). *Processes of the world system.* Beverly Hills, CA: Sage.
Inglehart, R. (1990). *Culture shift in advanced industrial society.* Princeton: Princeton University Press.
———. (1977). *The silent revolution: Changing political styles among western publics.* Princeton University Press.
Inkeles, A., & Smith, D. H. (1974). *Becoming modern: Individual change in six developing countries.* Cambridge, MA: Harvard University Press.
Janda, K., Berry, J., & Goldman, J. (1989). *The challenge to democracy: Government in America.* Boston: Houghton-Mifflin.
Jeffries, I. (1990). *A guide to socialist economies.* London: Routledge.
Kolosi, T. (1988). Stratification and social structure in Hungary. *Annual Review of Sociology, 14,* 408-419.
Kolosi, T., & Wnuk-Lipinski, E. (Eds.). (1983). *Equality and inequality under socialism: Poland and Hungary compared.* London: Sage Studies in International Sociology.
Kornai, J. (1986). *Contradictions and dilemmas: Studies on the socialist economy and society.* Cambridge, MA: MIT Press.
———. (1982). *Growth, shortage and efficiency: A macro-dynamic model of the socialist economy.* Oxford: Basil Blackwell.
Ludwikowski, R. R. (1986). *The crisis of communism: Its meanings, origins and phases.* Washington, DC: Pergamon Press.
Mandel, E. (1975). *Late capitalism.* London: NLB.
Mann, M. (1984). The autonomous power of the state. *Archives Europeennes de Sociologie, 25,* 185-213.
Marks, C. (1991). The urban underclass. *Annual Review of Sociology, 17,* 445-466.
Marx, K. (1859/1973). *Critique of political economy* (edited by M. Nicolaus). Harmondsworth, England: Penguin Books.
———. (1867/1956). Capital. In T. B. Bottomore, & M. Rubel, (Eds.). *Karl Marx: Selected writings in sociology and social philosophy.* London: Watts & Co.
McClelland, D.C. (1967). *The achieving society.* New York: Free Press.
Meyer, J. W., Boli-Bennett, J., & Chase-Dunn, C. (1975). Convergence and divergence in development. *Annual Review of Sociology, 1,* 223-246.
Meyer, J. W., Hannan, M. T., Rubinson, R., & Thomas, G. M. (1979). National economic development, 1950-1970: Social and political factors. In J. W. Meyer & M. T. Hannan (Eds.). *National development and the world system* (pp. 85-116). Chicago: University of Chicago Press.
Miliband, R. (1977). *Marxism and politics.* Oxford: Oxford University Press.
———. (1969). *The state in capitalist society.* New York: Basic Books.
Moore, W. E. (1965). *The impact of industry.* Englewood Cliffs, NJ: Prentice-Hall.
Ners, K. J. (1990). *Trzeci Swiat: Dylematy rozwoju.* [The Third World: Development dilemmas]. Warsaw: Panstwowe Wydawnictwo Naukowe [Polish State Scientific Publishers].
O'Connor, J. (1987). *The meaning of crisis: A theoretical contribution.* Oxford: Basil Blackwell.
———. (1973). *The fiscal crisis of the state.* New York: St. Martin's Press.
OECD. (1984). *Employment outlook.* Paris: Organization for Economic Cooperation and Development.
Offe, C. (1985). *Disorganized capitalism.* Cambridge, MA: MIT Press.
———. (1981). *Contradictions of the welfare state.* Cambridge, MA: MIT Press.
Parsons, T. (1951). *The social system.* Glencoe, IL: Free Press.
Piore, M. J., & Sabel, C. F. (1984). *The second industrial divide: Possibilities for prosperity.* New York: Basic Books.
Porter, M. E. (1990). *The competitive advantage of nations.* New York: Free Press.

Portes, A. (1976). On the sociology of national development: Theories and issues. *American Journal of Sociology, 82,* 55-85.

Portes, R. (1981). Macroeconomic equilibrium and disequilibrium in centrally planned economies. *Economic Inquiry, 19,* 559-578.

Przeworski, A. (1990). *The state and the economy under capitalism.* Chur: Harwood Academic Publishers.

Rostow, W. W. (1978). *The world economy: History and prospect.* Austin, TX: University of Texas Press.

_____. (1960). *The stages of economic growth: A non-communist manifesto.* Cambridge: Cambridge University Press.

Sabel, C. F., Herrigel, C. B., Deeg, R., & Kazis, R. (1987). *Regional prosperities compared: Massachusetts and Baden-Württemberg in the 80s.* (WZB Discussion Paper IIM LMP 87-10b). Berlin: Wissenschaftszentrum Berlin für Sozialforschung.

Schumpeter, J. A. (1975). *Capitalism, socialism and democracy.* New York: Harper.

_____. (1939). *Business cycles.* New York: McGraw Hill.

Seligman, M. E. P. (1975). *Helplessness: On depression, development and death.* San Francisco: Freeman.

Skocpol, T. (1979). *States and social revolutions.* Cambridge: Cambridge University Press.

Slomczinski, K., & Krause, J. (1978). *Class structure and social mobility in Poland.* New York: Sharpe.

Smith, A. (1776/1961). *The wealth of nations.* Edited by E. Cannan. London: Methuen.

Strümpel, B. (1989). Popular bases of conflict and solidarity: A review of the evidence from a decade of *économie problématique.* In B. Strümpel (Ed.), *Industrial Societies After the Stagnation of the 1970s* (pp. 185-208). Berlin: de Gruyter.

Strümpel, B., & Schramm, F. (1989). *Arbeitslosigkeit und Arbeitsumverteilung in der Bundesrepublik Deutschland: Betroffenheit, Konflikt, Reformpotential* [Unemployment and redistribution of work in the Federal Republic of Germany: Impact, conflict, and reform potential]. Advisory paper prepared for the Office of the Federal Chancellor. Berlin: Free University of Berlin.

Szcepanski, M. (1989). *Modernizacja, rozwoj zalezny, rozwoj endogenny: socjologizne studium rozwoju spolecznego* [Modernization, dependent development, endogenous development: A sociological study of social development]. Katowice: Uniwersytet Slaski.

Thomas, G. M., & Meyer, J. W. (1984). The expansion of the state. *Annual Review of Sociology, 10,E 461-482.*

_____. (1980). Regime changes and state power in an intensifying world state system. In A. Bergesen (Ed.), *Studies of modern world-systems* (pp. 139-158). New York: Academic Press.

Toye, J. F., Jr. (1987). *Dilemmas of development: Reflections on the counter-revolution in development theory.* Oxford: Basil Blackwell.

van Brabant, J. M. (1989). *Economic integration in eastern Europe: A handbook.* New York: Harvester Wheatsheaf.

Van Den Berg, A. (1988). *The immanent utopia: From Marxism on the state to the state of Marxism.* Princeton: Princeton University Press.

Vanhove, N., & Klaasen, L. H. (1987). *Regional policy: A European approach.* Aldershot: Asebury.

Wallerstein, I. (1984). *The politics of the world economy.* Cambridge: Cambridge University Press.

_____. (1979). *The capitalist world economy.* Cambridge: Cambridge University Press.

_____. (1974). *The modern world system: Capitalist agriculture and the origins of the European world economy in the sixteenth century.* New York: Academic Press.

Walton, J. (1987). Theory and research on industrialization. *Annual Review of Sociology, 13,* 89-108.

Wilson, W. (1987). *The truly disadvantaged: The inner city, the underclass and public policy.* Chicago: University of Chicago Press.

Winiecki, J. (1988). *The distorted world of Soviet-type economies.* Pittsburgh: University of Pittsburgh Press.

Wnuk-Lipinski, E. (1991). Wolnosc czy Rownosc: Stray dylemat w nowym kontekscie [Partial disintegration: Essays on the sociology of system transformation]. In E. Wnuk-Lipinski (Ed.), *Rozpad polowiczny: Szkice z socjologii transformacji ustrojowej* [Freedom or inequality: An old dilemma in the new context]. Warsaw: Instytut Studiow Politycznych.

Wright, A. (1986). *Socialism: Theories and practices.* Oxford: Oxford University Press.

Wright, E. O. (1985). *Class, crisis and the state.* London: Verso.

Yankelovich, D., Zetterberg, H., Strümpel, B., & Shanks, M. (1985). *The world at work: An international report on jobs, productivity and human values.* New York: Octagon Press.

Zagorski, K. (1978). *Razvitie selskih naselenii* [Development, structure, and social mobility]. Moscow: Statistika.

ABOUT THE AUTHORS

AVI GOTTLIEB is Senior Lecturer of Sociology at the Tel Aviv University, and Director of its graduate program in Society and Ecology. He is also Visiting Professor at the Research Institute for the Socio-Economics of Labor at the Free University of Berlin. His research interests include social change, post-industrial society, social values, and environmental sociology. He is currently working on an extension of the research project summarized in this book, and on a comparative study of environmentally sustainable growth.

EPHRAIM YUCHTMAN-YAAR is Professor of Sociology and former Dean of the Faculty of Social Sciences at the Tel Aviv University. His major interests lie in the areas of complex organizations, industrial society, social inequality, and political sociology. He is currently engaged in a comparative analysis of work culture in advanced industrial societies. His most recent publication (with Y. Peres) is *Trends in Israeli democracy: The public view.*

BURKHARD STRÜMPEL was, until his untimely death in 1990, Professor of Economics the Free University of Berlin. He also founded and served as Director of its Research Institute for the Socio-Economics of Labor. This book reflects one of the more prevalent among his myriad academic interests: the individual experience of and responses to economic and work-related processes.

GEORGE MUSKENS is presently Research Fellow at the European Centre for Research and Documentation in the Social Sciences (Vienna Centre), and at the Netherlands Institute for Coordination of Research in the Social Sciences. His responsibilities include the initiation and coordination of projects, seminars and publications on the social and cultural reconstruction in central and eastern Europe.

317

ABOUT THE AUTHORS

PETER PAWLOWSKY is Acting Director of the Research Institute for the Socio-Economics of Labor, Free University of Berlin. His interests include labor-market policy, industrial relations, personnel development and management, and organizational learning. His recent publications include "Betriebliche Qualifikationsstrategien und organisationelles Lernen" [Internal qualification strategies and organizational learning], in W. Staehle and P. Conrad (eds.), *Managementforschung 2* [Management Research 2]; and (with J. Bäumer) "Funktionen und Wirkungen beruflicher Weiterbildung" [Functions and consequences of continued vocational training], in B. Strümpel and M. Dierkes (eds.), *Innovation und Beharrung in der Arbeitspolitik* [Innovation and perseverance in labor policy].

MAREK ZIÓŁKWSKI is Professor of Sociology and Director of the Institute of Sociology at the Adam Mickiewicz University, Poznań. He also serves as Professor at the Institute of Political Studies of the Polish Academy of Sciences and as President of its Sociology Committee, and is Director of UNESCO's Polish Committee (Social Sciences Section). His interests include sociological theory, the sociology of culture and of knowledge, political sociology, and social structure. He is the author and co-author of numerous books and journal articles, including the recent *Knowledge, individual and society; Workers, 1984; and The mentality of Poles.*

VADIM RADAEV is Director of the Research Section on Economic Sociology at the Institute of Economics of The Russian Academy of Sciences. His interests include social stratification and economic sociology. Among his most recent publications is a chapter entitled "Power stratification in the Soviet-type system," in J. Eades and C. Schwaller (eds.), *Transitional agenda*; and "Work alienation: history and contemporaneity," in *Ekonomika* (in Russian).

JADWIGA ŠANDEROVÁ is Senior Researcher at the Institute of Social and Political Sciences, Charles University, Prague.

ALES KABÁTEC holds the Chair of Sociology of the Faculty of Philosophy at the Charles University, Prague.

TONI HAHN currently directs the KAI-Adw Research Project on the social transition in the former German Democratic Republic. Until 1989, she was Director of the Institute of Sociology and Social Policy at the Academy of Sciences of the former German Democratic Republic. Her research interests include occupational careers, unemployment, social stratification, and social justice. Her most recent publications include articles about the social transition and unemployment in eastern Germany, and (with R. Welskopf) *Innovation* *und Motivation in Forschung, Entwicklung und Überleitung* [Innovation and motivation in research, development and transition].

IRENE ZIERKE is currently Co-Director of the research project *Sozialstruktur- und Milieuforschung* [The study of social structure and milieu]. She was previously Senior Researcher at the Institute of Sociology and Social Policy of the Academy of Sciences of the former German Democratic Republic. Her areas of interests include social stratification, social inequality, leisure, and social values. She has authored articles and chapters on the recent transition in eastern Germany, including "Sozialpolitik in der ehemaligen DDR—ein Modernisierungsfaktor?" ["Social policy in the former GDR—a modernizing factor?"], in W. Glatzer (ed.), *Die Modernisierung moderner Gesellschaften* [The modernization of modern societies].

MICHAEL SCHLESE is a Ph.D. candidate at the Department of Sociology, Halle University. In recent years, he has also worked at the Wissenschafts-zentrum Berlin für Sozialforschung [Berlin Center for Social Research], at the Institute of Sociology at the Heidelberg University, and at the Institute of Sociology at the Free University of Berlin.

FLORIAN SCHRAMM is Lecturer of Economics and a member of the Institut für Allgemeine Betriebwirtschaftslehre at the Free University of Berlin. His interests include the labor market, work attitudes and personnel policies, and organizations in decline. His most recent publication is entitled *Beschäftigungsunsicherheit: Wie sich die Risiken des Arbeitsmarkts auf die Beschäftigten auswirken–Empirische Analysen in Ost und West* [Occupational uncertainty: How labor market risks affect employees—Empirical analyses in East and West].

AXEL VAN DEN BERG is Associate Professor of Sociology at McGill University, and Visiting Research Fellow at the Swedish Institute for Social Research. He is currently engaged in a comparative study of the effects of labor-market policies on workers' acceptance of industrial change, and in an analysis of the impact of socio-economic characteristics on political attitudes and values in Sweden (with Ryszard Szulkin). His other interests include the critique of Marxism and neo-Marxism, and the comparison of economic and sociological explanatory models. He is the author of *The immanent utopia: From Marxism on the state to the state of Marxism*.

RYSZARD SZULKIN is Research Fellow of Sociology at the University of Stockholm. Together with several other Swedish sociologists, he is currently analyzing both the Swedish Establishment Survey, and the Swedish Level of Living Survey. He is also collaborating with Axel van den Berg in an analysis of the impact of socio-economic characteristics on political attitudes and values in Sweden.

ANTHONY C. MASI is Associate Professor of Sociology at McGill University, and Director of its Faculty of Arts computer laboratory. He is also a member of the Canadian Labor Market Research Group. His interests include deindustrialization, industrial government policies, and the steel industry.

JOSEPH SMUCKER is Professor of Sociology and Anthropology at the Concordia University, Montreal. His major interests include organizations, industrialization, the sociology of labor markets, and the sociology of work and occupations.

JONATHAN GERSHUNY is Fellow of the Nuffield College, Oxford University, and Visiting Professor at the School of Social Studies, University of Bath. His research interests include time budgets, work histories, and social and economic change. He is the author of numerous books and articles, including *After industrial society?,* and *Social innovation and the division of labor.*

AUTHOR INDEX

SUBJECT INDEX